HANDBOOK OF SIMULATOR-BASED TRAINING

MASTER

Handbook of Simulator-Based Training

ERIC FARMER
DERA, UK

JOHN VAN ROOIJ
TNO, The Netherlands

JOHAN RIEMERSMA
TNO, The Netherlands

PETER JORNA
NLR, The Netherlands

JAN MORAAL
TNO, The Netherlands

Routledge
Taylor & Francis Group

LONDON AND NEW YORK

First published in paperback 2024

First published 1999 by Ashgate Publishing

Published 2016
by Routledge
4 Park Square, Milton Park, Abingdon, Oxon OX14 4RN

and by Routledge
605 Third Avenue, New York, NY 10158

Routledge is an imprint of the Taylor & Francis Group, an informa business

Publisher's Note
The publisher has gone to great lengths to ensure the quality of this
reprint but points out that some imperfections in the original copies
may be apparent.

British Library Cataloguing in Publication Data
Handbook of simulator-based training
   1. Flight simulators - Handbooks, manuals, etc. 2. Air
   warfare - Computer simulation - Handbooks, manuals, etc.
   I. Farmer, Eric II. Simulator-based training
   629.1'3252'078

Library of Congress Cataloging-in-Publication Data
Handbook of simulator-based training / Eric Farmer ... [et al.].
      p.   cm.
      Includes bibliographical references (p.   ) and index.

   1. Computer simulation Handbooks, manuals, etc. 2. Computer
simulation--Military aspects Handbooks, manuals, etc. I. Farmer,
Eric.
   QA76.9.C65H347   1999
   371.39'7--dc21   99-43343
                                                        CIP

ISBN: 978-0-754-61187-5 (hbk)
ISBN: 978-1-032-83876-2 (pbk)
ISBN: 978-1-315-25367-1 (ebk)

DOI: 10.4324/9781315253671

Contents

SECTION III: TRAINING MEDIA SPECIFICATION

SECTION IV: TRAINING EVALUATION

EPILOGUE

Preface

Nowadays, practically no military training programmes exist without some form of simulation or use of a simulator. Although simulation technology has made tremendous progress, there are still limitations to what can be simulated. In addition, the costs of training simulators may vary substantially, presenting the challenge of improving effectiveness and efficiency and optimising the benefits/costs ratio.

For a long time, simulator procurement for military training purposes has been mainly a technology-pushed process driven by what is offered on the market. In short, the more sophisticated the simulator's capabilities, the more attractive it is to procure. Training programmes are later developed based upon the device procured, sometimes only for the training developers to conclude that the simulator 'did not meet the requirements' or, even worse, that it was unusable because of a complete mismatch between the capabilities and limitations of the device on the one hand and the basic characteristics and needs of the trainees on the other.

The MASTER project adopted the opposite approach: *analysing and defining* the basic needs of the trainees to enable them to comply with military missions and tasks, *formulating* principles and guidelines for training programme design, and *specifying* the required characteristics of the training media, i.e., the simulation devices. The fundamental objectives were therefore defined as follows.

- to formulate standard protocols for the description of missions and tasks;
- to develop generic methods for the analysis of training needs;
- to formulate guidelines for effective training programme design;
- to develop means of matching device fidelity to training needs;
- to develop measures for training performance and training transfer;
- to create a general body of concepts and guidelines, as generic as possible, and a common philosophy and terminology that are accessible by the participating countries and other countries within the WEAG.

After more than three years of preparation, MASTER started on 29 January 1994 as EUCLID RTP 11.1 on 'Training System Concepts for Simulator-based Military Training'. The original project plan included two phases. The first phase was aimed at developing and harmonising the training- and skill-based approach to simulation.

The second aimed at the application of the methods, procedures and tools to a weapon platform common to most nations: the attack helicopter. Planning and budgetary constraints within the EUCLID programme at that time led to the exclusion of this phase from the final contract. Later, the project title 'Military Applications of Simulator and Training concepts based on Empirical Research' (MASTER) was adopted for this theoretical and experimental work. In this 10m Euro project, the knowledge and experience of 23 research and industrial organisations from five countries — France, Germany, the Netherlands, Spain, and the UK — were combined in an integrated effort to develop generic concepts and common guidelines for the procurement, planning and integration of simulators in training. Any simulator for ground-, sea-, or air-based mobile weapon systems was within the remit of the project.

MASTER also provides a unique framework for future co-operation among industry and defence organisations, both between and within countries. Co-operation might range from development and exchange of military mission and task analysis, through investigations into existing knowledge gaps, to training system development or even full specification of training simulators, all starting from the generic guidelines of MASTER.

To say that MASTER was a rather complex project may seem an understatement to those who were involved. The large number of participants, the division of work packages over two or more countries, and the backgrounds of the individual participants — varying from human factors and informatics experts to system designers and engineers — were a tremendous challenge for communications within the consortium.

MASTER is unique in the history of simulator-based training: in bringing together a large number of people from various organisations on a European scale, in advancing understanding of the basic problems of simulator-based training, and in learning to develop common concepts and methods to deal with these problems. The advantages of this first step, however, will be lost unless it is followed by the implementation and further development of the results. In this respect, each participating country has, of course, its own responsibility. National efforts are useful, but the complexity of and efforts involved in creating state of the art training are not to be underestimated, as the MASTER experience clearly revealed. A combined effort between nations would again distribute the workload and the costs by sharing the burdens of the implementation of the results of the project. The envisaged phase two of the project would provide an excellent opportunity not only to use the training design tools but also to produce the real training systems. Such a project would greatly enhance the exploitation of MASTER results, at the same time enhancing the capabilities and interoperability of training systems and their products: highly skilled and specialised military personnel.

As the project manager of MASTER, I should like to render my thanks to all contributors for their efforts in working towards the final results. I hope that all will pursue any possibility of stimulating further developments in this area.

Professor Jan Moraal, Project Manager
TNO 1998

General Introduction

The MASTER project, of which this Handbook is one product, was inspired by the changing and increasing needs of simulator-based training. One of the key factors is a changing world with evolving conditions and constraints. Environmental pressures are leading to insufficient availability of training grounds, training sorties and military budgets for training; there is also a trend towards sub-contracting of military training to the armed forces of other countries or third parties. Secondly, the rapid development of advanced weapon systems is complicating the assessment of associated training needs and the timely development of training programmes and means. The enhanced flexibility of new technologies often implies changes in human tasks from direct control to supervision/decision making, and hence makes these tasks and the required training more complex, demanding and diverse. The third, and possibly most important, change is the increase in types of mission undertaken by the Armed Forces. Training for peace-keeping operations, and joint (multi-national) missions at lower levels of integration, requires a large variety of training scenarios and considerable flexibility in tuning scenarios to actual missions and specific joint force configurations. This all leads to an urgent need for an integrated framework for training and simulation research and development, to meet the increasing training demands of the next 10-15 years.

Current experiences are that simulators often do not meet the expectations and/or are very expensive. The main reason is not so much a *lack* of knowledge (although certainly gaps can be identified) but a failure to use knowledge gained elsewhere. To be able to design and implement efficient and effective simulator-based military training environments, one must understand thoroughly the nature of the military training needs and the possible ways of meeting them. Simulation by itself cannot teach. This understanding has to be shared by the prospective readers and users of this Handbook:

- members of military staffs involved in specifying requirements for simulator-based training systems;
- designers, manufacturers, and suppliers of training devices/material;
- the scientific community involved in research on military training and simulation.

This Handbook aims to enhance the effectiveness and efficiency of military training for mobile land, sea and air weapon systems operators and crews. It provides the background knowledge on how to improve training simulator design methodology by integrating this methodology with the development of effective training programmes. It is based on a programme of research that included conceptual as well as device-oriented studies. This programme was conducted under the auspices of a large European programme: EUropean Co-operation for the Long term In Defence (EUCLID). The EUCLID goal is to: 'Develop, establish, and maintain an advanced technology base for simulation for military training purposes, enabling the European Industry to develop and produce in a cost-effective way the systems that can fulfil future European military needs, thereby ensuring European independence in the subject areas.'

In this spirit, the Handbook is the result of a research endeavour by a consortium of 23 partners from five European countries, under a prevailing attitude of co-operation between the industries and research laboratories involved. This co-operation is based on a shared belief in the mutual benefits to be gained. Sharing of knowledge and resources in this major research effort is a step towards the realisation of a truly European simulation and training technology community. Such a community is in our view the only platform able to develop well investigated and tested solutions for the major training problems our defence organisations face in the years to come. This requires that, parallel to the development of guiding principles, the knowledge gained be effectively communicated to the key military personnel and decision agencies involved in the specification and procurement of training systems, to the industries, and to the researchers in the field of simulator-based military training. This Handbook of Simulator-Based Training is intended to do just that: communicating to all involved in simulator procurement and use the relevant considerations in buying and using simulators, and how to avoid the many pitfalls in this procurement process. In the long term, also, the simulator industries themselves can only gain from becoming 'smart buyers'. Quality considerations and tailoring of simulators to well-defined training trajectories can provide a competitive edge for the European simulator industry over more technology-driven developments elsewhere.

The Handbook aims also to be instrumental in overcoming the continuing large differences between nations with regard to, for instance, underlying training philosophies and educational theories and practices. Existing conceptual barriers, accentuated by subtle discrepancies in the meaning of terms in different languages, had to be overcome by adopting a common terminology. There also remain differences in outlook between navies, air forces and armies, and, last but not least, differences in outlook and values between different people involved in training system design: military personnel, engineers, psychologists, training designers, training managers, and so on. The research programme upon which this Handbook is based involved people from five participating nations with a variety of backgrounds. It is our hope that the Handbook will set a new standard for a common terminology and for harmonising the existing perspectives on training programme design and the procurement process of training simulators.

The Handbook addresses the key issues for the development of simulator-based military training: transfer of training to actual military operations, retention and continuation training requirements, mission rehearsal, resistance to stressful circumstances, and systematic development of training trajectories with feedback based on adequate performance measures. It contains discussions of guidelines and requirements for training programme design and training media specification, and reports experimental demonstrations of their applicability. The results have also been implemented in a set of tools and techniques facilitating the adequate specification of simulator-based training programmes and the training media needed for the implementation of these programmes.

The development of training programmes is often hampered by lack of knowledge, guidelines and tools for the effective analysis of missions and tasks, for training programme design and for the evaluation of training, and therefore is too often adapted to the limitations of the particular simulator procured. Evaluation of a training system is hardly ever conducted, although awareness of the importance of such endeavours has increased. Paramount prerequisites are carefully stated training objectives and valid, comprehensive performance measurement. In their absence, it remains unclear what should be evaluated in the first place, resulting in a waste of effort and time. Incorporating expertise on human factors, learning theory and system operation early in the training programme development process and in the specification of training media can greatly improve the validity and cost-effectiveness of training. There is still a gap between human factors research on the one hand and the training research and development community on the other. The need for a firmer connection between these two fields is emerging, although it is not yet recognised by everyone. New training concepts and technologies such as networked simulation almost inevitably necessitate multi-disciplinary collaboration between experts in the fields of team performance, social psychology, learning and instruction, information and communication technology, and ergonomics.

Issues treated in this Handbook are how to conduct mission and task analyses, how to choose and specify appropriate training simulations, and how to use them in training programmes to obtain effective transfer to missions and operations, taking into account logistic, budgetary and technical constraints. Retention of military knowledge and skills is an important aspect to be considered. Training programmes must optimise the skill acquisition process with respect to the robustness of acquired capabilities during periods of non-practice.

The scope of training considered is primarily skill acquisition at the level of the individual operator or the crew. However, the individual operator is always part of a larger unit, in a real sense (for instance, as a crew member) or in a virtual sense (e.g., the communication requirements of a forward air controller). These aspects must be incorporated since they have an impact on skill acquisition at the level of the individual operator and the way in which individual tasks can be organised. Although the focus is at the level of interaction/simulation required for the acquisition of individual skills, acquisition processes always have to be studied in the broader task environment. Mission-essential skills can be acquired only in unit and collective training. Much of the methodology developed in MASTER is also relevant to the design and implementation of such training.

In the first section, on Training Needs Analysis (TNA), an inventory of existing methods of mission and task analysis is presented. These methods are discussed in the framework of the requirements of training programme design, thereby elucidating their strengths and weaknesses in this respect. This formed the basis for a comprehensive field orientation examining methods in use by training institutions and during the specification of training simulators. In reality, use is seldom made of these analytic techniques. Reasons include poor communication between different players in the simulator specification and procurement process, resulting in a highly technology-driven rather than learning outcome-driven procurement process. Poor communication stems from the lack of a common framework harmonising different perspectives, together with a less than optimal way of designing and implementing procurement procedures. The clearest symptom is the almost universal lack of re-usable documentation during the process of procurement and implementation.

In the second section, on Training Programme Design (TPD), the available knowledge, both theoretical and practical, with respect to the use of simulators for training has been organised. The focus is clearly on training programme design itself as a precursor to the specification of the means to be used: a training simulator. It is argued that many gaps between theory and practice still exist, and that the methodology developed for TPD is the only starting point that can close these gaps. The central role of training programme design, as the link between training needs analysis and training media specification, is recognised. One of the basic tenets, therefore, is that simulator requirements should be based on training programme requirements. This implies that training programmes should be designed as a basis for deriving the specification of simulator requirements or for assessing the implications for training of several alternative solutions proposed by industry. After the training system is procured, the results of the TPD analysis and specification can be used in the further detailing of the actual training programmes and scenarios. Quite obvious in current practice is the failure to specify in advance the facilities needed to support the instructional process, e.g. a well designed Instructor Operating System (IOS) that is geared to the specific role of the training staff and supports the accurate measurement of performance and the delivery of feedback. Since high-quality feedback, based on accurate measures of performance and diagnosing real shortcomings in skill or knowledge, is central to effective learning processes, this frequent omission can be repaired only by focusing on the training programmes and systematic ways of implementing them.

In Section III, a methodology for deriving simulator requirements (Training Media Specification: TMS) is described. Starting point are the training scenario descriptions and associated instructional specifications, which are the outcome of the Training Programme Design phase. The methodology should replace the frequently adopted strategy of striving for realism. This strategy not only often leads to very high cost, but from a more didactic point of view cannot be the basis for answering questions about which skills can or cannot be acquired by training on a simulator. To answer this question, and the related question of how to avoid unintended acquisition of non-transferable, simulator-specific skills, one has to analyse more thoroughly the *cueing requirements*. Cueing is the information from the environment and/or the system as sensed by the operator and used in controlling the process of task execution. A thorough discussion of these sensory cues and their implications for simulation is presented in separate chapters. It provides the basis for the specification of sufficiently detailed *functional* simulator requirements.

Skill development can be greatly enhanced by providing auxiliary cueing and feedback. This may be generated either by the system or by the instructor. Hence, much attention is also devoted to the specification of instructional facilities.

Section IV, on training evaluation, gives an extensive overview of the ways to measure performance and workload. As already discussed, the accurate measurement of performance is a prerequisite for effective feedback to trainees to induce the correct learning processes. But much more is at stake here. Accurate measurement of performance also serves in evaluating the way training is delivered and thereby furthers the learning of the training organisation. It enables, too, estimation of the contribution of learned skills to operational readiness and fighting power and the need for continuation training once skills have been acquired. The current reliance on often subjective and unreliable judgements of poorly supported instructors or training staff can only be counter-productive in this respect. Measurement of workload serves mainly in testing the validity of the simulator in presenting real-world pressures and stress and in assessing progress in skill acquisition during periods of overlearning. The contribution of Section IV is mainly the presentation of well-considered and standardised methodologies for supporting training evaluations. This is illustrated by empirical research demonstrating the usefulness of enhancing the quality of assessment by using validated batteries of performance measures. Main areas for further development identified are measures of decision-making quality and team skills. A brief discussion of simulator-based trainability tests is included.

Organisations that contributed to the MASTER project

Germany
IABG-ORA
IABG-TVO
STN-ATLAS Elektronik
CAE Electronics
Daimler Benz Aerospace
Daimler Benz Aerospace/Dornier
Eurocopter
ESG, Elektoniksystem und Logistik
TZN

France
Thomson Training and Simulation
Dassault Aviation
Prodec
Imassa-Cerma
DGA/Celar

The Netherlands
TNO Human Factors Research Institute
National Aerospace Laboratory (NLR)

Spain
SAINSEL

United Kingdom
Defence Evaluation and Research Agency
British Aerospace Sowerby Research Centre
Thomson Training and Simulation
Roke Manor Research Ltd
Marconi Simulation
Logica

Section I
Training Needs Analysis

1 Introduction

The importance of starting the specification and procurement of training programmes and equipment with a Training Needs Analysis (TNA) derives from dissatisfaction with current procurement practices and methods of meeting the related training needs. Deficiencies often noted are the failure to reach the required level of performance after training, the time lag between procurement of systems and the delivery of (adapted) training packages or devices, the failure to consider the implications of new equipment for the role of training personnel, and, last but not least, the often unsatisfactory quality of training material and training devices. Low or even negative transfer of training on a training simulator is an example of the high risks of inadequate specification of training needs, training programmes and training media such as simulators. To these considerations can be added the increasing need for more efficient training programmes due to decreasing budgets and training time, and the requirement for highly effective training programmes, enabling high-level operational performance in the very first missions assigned to a military unit ('first shot' performance). The public accepts neither high military losses nor failures in peace-keeping or peace-enforcing operations.

The gradually increasing awareness of current deficiencies and risks were the major impetus for starting a research and technology project under the EUCLID programme (EUropean Co-operation for the Long term In Defence) on training systems concepts for simulator-based training, with a focus on training for mobile weapon systems. To emphasise the role of empirical research in building a common understanding of the requirements for effective and efficient training concepts and media, the project was called MASTER: Military Applications of Simulation and Training concepts based on Empirical Research.

Operators have to acquire knowledge and skills that are transferable from the simulator into the real world. The tasks that operators have to learn with the aid of simulators are not only procedural ones, but also psychomotor tasks such as driving and gunnery and more cognitive, higher-level, tasks that increasingly require reasoning and planning skills.

For a long time, improving simulators meant improving the physical representation. Although this may be fairly appropriate for the acquisition of psychomotor and procedural skills, more is needed to achieve the objectives of optimising training in terms of efficiency and effectiveness and of acquiring and improving cognitive skills. Specifically, it is important to address the *functional* representation, and the design of the instructional strategies and the training scenarios. The emphasis on functional representation calls for analysis methods that take functional aspects into account. In the literature, one often finds a distinction between goal-oriented and technology-driven methods. A goal-oriented approach seems much more suitable, the more so when focusing on cognitive aspects. The important issues in Training Needs Analysis are:

- goal-oriented approach;
- functional task breakdown;
- cognitive skills of the operator;
- transfer between the simulated task and real world task;
- focus on effective training of the task;
- results that are usable for the design of training programmes and simulators.

TNA is the first step of the MASTER methodology and is related to the other main steps: Training programme design (TPD), discussed in Section II, and training media specification (TMS), described in Section III. Training evaluation concepts, guidelines and facilities are incorporated in many of the steps comprising TNA, TPD and TMS; this theoretical and essential topic is addressed separately in Section IV of the handbook.

During TNA the training need is determined and described in terms of a set of related training objectives. During TPD, training objectives are translated into training programme requirements. Finally, during TMS, training programme requirements are translated into simulator requirements. Each of these main steps is subdivided into a number of more elementary sub-steps that are joined together by means of input/output relations to guarantee consistency.

Global Steps in Training Needs Analysis

The purpose of TNA is to define the training need in terms of a set of related training objectives. This is accomplished in a number of consecutive iterative steps: mission analysis, task analysis, trainee analysis and training analysis. The first two steps, mission and task analysis, are required to describe the operational behaviour of the system and its operator(s), respectively. In the context of the description of the behaviour of man-machine systems, behaviour is considered to be the result of the goal-directed co-ordinated deployment of environmentally constrained system (or operator) functions. This implies that any description of behaviour should comprise a description of the goal, the required/available functionalities, the environment, and the strategy used to achieve the goal.

This approach can be contrasted with the more common approach of restricting training needs analysis to a hierarchical functional decomposition of systems and associated tasks. Such a one-sided approach neglects, for instance, the strategic aspects underlying behaviour and its dependence on environmental contingencies. It is assumed that, by extending this approach to include strategic, temporal and environmental aspects, more valid and more comprehensive descriptions can be obtained.

The assumption that behaviour is organised in terms of goals implies that it can be broken down similarly. Therefore, the starting point of both mission analysis and task analysis is the identification of goals and their inter-relations. In describing the behaviour of any particular system or operator, a large number of different goals can be distinguished. Exactly how many need to be covered in the analysis depends on its scope and the level of detail required. The scope, the comprehensiveness of the analysis and the level of detail needed are determined by the purpose for which the analysis is conducted. Mission and task analysis can play an important role in the development of doctrine and the design of weapon systems, and as the basis for the design of training programmes and media. In the context of TNA, the purpose of mission and task analysis is to provide a sufficiently comprehensive and accurate description of operational behaviour, i.e., a description that can be used as a basis for identifying and defining training objectives. Training objectives should be specified in such detail that they indicate the skills that operators should acquire to perform their tasks adequately.

Once the goals have been identified, the behaviour associated with the accomplishment of each of the selected goals is elaborated and described. Of course, any given goal may be accomplished in different ways. However, for the purpose of training needs analysis, one is not interested in all the variations that might occur. What is aimed for is a more or less abstract, idealised description of behaviour that can be assumed (by subject-matter experts) to be representative of operational requirements. Hence for each goal only a limited number of prescribed behaviours need be distinguished. Thus, missions and tasks constitute the units of description in analysing the behaviour of systems and operators. The result of conducting consecutive mission and task analyses is a comprehensive list of reference missions and associated sets of tasks. Later, these terms will be further defined. It should be noted, however, that the MASTER usage of the terms 'mission' and 'task' differs from the common military usage of these terms. For instance, the term 'mission' is usually used to denote a particular mission assignment or accomplishment. Similarly, the term 'task' is usually used to denote a particular responsibility (task assignment).

The process of mission and task analysis should result essentially in the specification of the required functionality of the operator, i.e., his skill profile. The links established with mission aspects and task specifications in the process are useful products that can be re-used during the specification of training tasks and training scenarios.

Before the results of TNA can be defined in terms of a set of related training objectives, two further steps have to be taken: trainee analysis and training analysis. One of the main purposes of trainee analysis is to assess the extent to which the required skills are already available in the (potential) candidate group. This information is necessary to determine whether or not a training need exists, and the trainee recruitment and selection strategy to be used. The purpose of training analysis, the final step of TNA, is the identification and definition of training needs in terms of a set of related training objectives that may be used as the completion criteria for training. Training objectives are defined in terms of performance objectives, conditions and norms (Mager, 1962).

2   Mission Analysis

Introduction and Main Concepts

Mission analysis is aimed at the description of behaviour in terms of missions and the analysis of specific missions in terms of goals, system requirements, environmental dependencies, and processes. The terms 'mission' and 'mission analysis' have several connotations. In military usage, the mission is 'a clear, concise statement of the task of the command and its purpose' (Webster's New World Dictionary), or a 'specific combat operation assigned to an individual or unit; more specifically for the air domain: a single combat flight by an airplane or group of airplanes' (DoD Dictionary). Mission analysis is 'the process to determine the operational capabilities of military forces that are required to carry out assigned missions, roles and tasks in the face of the existing or postulated threat, with an acceptable degree of risk'. This refers clearly to an actual combat situation in which missions have to be completed. To be *prepared* for these missions, however, one has to design weapon systems, train the troops, develop plans and doctrines, and organise a force unit for a particular mission. Guidance for these activities is provided by operational analysis and analysis of possible future, *more generic* mission types. It is in the latter sense that the terms mission and mission analysis in this overview are envisaged.

A more abstract conception is thus needed of ways of reaching a particular goal. An example may clarify this notion: a mission in abstract terms might be to take control of a town; a concrete instance of this mission might be the assignment to take control of Sarajevo in February 1993. The definition of 'mission' in the MASTER glossary (Riemersma *et al*, 1994) is consistent with the military description: 'the designated, goal-oriented activity that a system is intended to accomplish'. A 'system' is in the context of System Theory not meant to be a technical system but rather a generic system in the sense of a set of items (technical, human, organisational) so related or connected as to form a unity or organic whole. Mission analysis then defines what the system (e.g., a task force) must do (the operational requirements), the circumstances and the environment in which it must be done, and how it can be done.

In human engineering, the combination of mission and scenario analysis appears. The term 'scenario' can be used with different meanings; in the MASTER glossary it is 'a script describing a possible sequence of events and circumstances'. This is consistent with its more general definition as 'sketch or plot of a play, giving particulars of the scenes, situations etc' (Webster's dictionary). Given a mission, already described in terms of phases and mission profiles, a scenario has to describe the events implied by the profile and the circumstances. A mission profile shows the relevant system activities and significant mission events plotted against time and/or space, and is usually graphically depicted (Beevis, 1992).

Mission analysis results in a systematic description of all the missions in which a system performs or should be able to perform (van Rooij *et al*, 1996). The analysis should lead to a valid description of the goals of the overall system, how these goals should be achieved, the required functionalities of the system components and the relevant circumstances or environmental conditions.

Importance of Mission Analysis

Several methodologies for training development have been reported in the literature (van Berlo, 1996). Most extensive methodologies follow a systems approach. In the European literature, the systems approach is known as 'Systems Approach to Training' (SAT). A well-known example of a SAT methodology is the 'Inter-service Procedures for Instructional Systems Development' (IPISD; Branson *et al*, 1975a, b). In every SAT methodology, an analytic phase can be distinguished that infers the training goals to be pursued, although methodologies vary in the way this phase is structured. The analytic phase has four successive steps: mission analysis, task analysis, trainee analysis and training analysis. As a result of the systematic construction of the analytic process, the training goals can be defined and operationalised.

A valid, complete and consistent representation of missions is a necessary basis for task analysis and training analysis, the specification of training scenarios, and ultimately the specification of the functionalities of a specific simulator to be used for training. An important starting point in the development of training is a clear description of the (future) trainee tasks. The evolution of these descriptions is the objective of mission and task analysis.

What are the risks of not performing mission analysis prior to task analysis? The first risk is an excessively narrow focus on individual tasks and disregard for team tasks, such as co-ordination and communication, that are intertwined with the individual tasks. The second risk is that not all personnel affected by system changes are identified and that consequently their education and training are not modified in response to these changes. The third risk is inadequate specification of all critical conditions in which a task is performed, leading to inadequate training for such conditions. A fourth risk is over-emphasis on training only partial tasks that seem superficially to be the primary task content; for example, a tank gunner may be well trained for gunnery performance on a shooting range, but may learn only in a rudimentary way how to search for and identify threats and targets in unknown terrains. A fifth risk is inadequate specification of performance and process measures, with consequent less effective feedback and hence ineffective training.

Requirements for Mission Analysis

Several data sources can be tapped for the purpose of mission analysis. They may differ in costs and in the validity, comprehensiveness, reliability and consistency of the information. Therefore, a combination of methods is typically used.

Existing descriptions of operational situations (research reports, management reports, simulation models, and so on) often differ in perspective and level of abstraction, and are rarely used as a basis for the analysis of training goals. An attendant complication in the military field is that what is considered relevant is usually built on certain assumptions and estimations of future operations that may turn out to be too restricted or no longer valid.

Differences in descriptions of 'the operational situation' are rather difficult to reconcile with attempts to reach a common starting point in the development of training, especially when training also comprises the co-ordination of interacting weapon systems on different levels of command. Generally, further data are required.

Several sources of information can be distinguished: documents, subject-matter experts, and direct observation. Examples of documents are manuals and research reports. 'Lessons learned' reports can also be valuable. Such documents are not usually produced with the objectives of mission and task analysis for training programme design. This necessitates a process of 'translating', augmenting and filtering relevant information, which can be very difficult and time-consuming and does not guarantee completeness.

The information that can be gathered from subject-matter experts is usually more up-to-date than that in available documents, and, if the interview is well structured, also more focused. A drawback of using experts is that their information may be biased. For the military, expert knowledge is further often based on possibly limited training experience. To overcome these limitations, the use of more than one expert is recommended, with the additional risk, however, that one has to choose between possibly contradictory information. Comparison with information from other sources may be a solution.

Direct observation is usually much more expensive and time-consuming, and in some instances may even be impossible. To provide initial orientation for the analyst, it is usually very useful. Later, after document study and interviews, observations can also be useful to complete the information or to resolve contradictions in the material gathered.

Procedures for Mission Analysis

The examples reported in the the literature review (Riemersma *et al*, 1997a) presented a variety of approaches to mission analysis, classification and description. This illustrates the need for a more generic approach. The various approaches shared enough common underlying elements to be further elaborated in a generic protocol comprising four main components: global system description, environment description, process description, and weapon system description.

Before a mission analysis begins, the training need has to be identified and described in global terms. This provides the starting point as a list of reference missions, a training needs description, and a preliminary specification of the system as matched to the mission.

Usually the system will be identified by analysing the organisational context, reflecting the goal structure of the larger unit. Mobile weapon systems are typically embedded as autonomous systems in a hierarchy of physically discriminable systems; they may have relationships with higher-order super-systems and co-level systems of the same or different type.

An example illustrating the need to consider the next higher level is for the weapon system Tornado, in the role of fighter bomber. This aircraft can operate solo or in a tactical formation of a particular number of aircraft. Supporting facilities include:

- Aircraft (e.g., AWACS, friendly EW-aircraft, Laser designator aircraft);
- Personnel (e.g., Forward Air Controllers);
- NATO plans and procedures such as:
  — communication plans;
  — electronic warfare procedures.

In the case of Close Air Support with the presence of a Forward Air Controller (FAC), one can argue that the 'system' is the combination of the weapon platform Tornado and the FAC officer. Even then, the wider context, e.g., intelligence information gathered by an AWACS and close co-ordination with ground forces, has to be considered in the analyses. After further analyses, it may become necessary to reconsider the system definition for the TNA.

A further important question concerns the relevant aspects that should be included in the description of a mission. Earlier, it was stated that the mission model comprises four components: global system description, environment description, process description and weapon system description. However, a system does not usually operate in isolation. Thus a description of the larger tactical/organisational context in which the system operates comprises the first part of the system description. A second part consists of a description of the system in structural terms. A third part is a description in functional terms. A generic functional system description depends on the identification of common system functions. System functions describe a broad category of goal-directed activities performed by a system regardless of the specific ways in which they are implemented. But global system functions are not always required; this depends on the type of mission.

A system description thus also contains a description in terms of system functions. A functional description excludes all system-specific details that are irrelevant to the goal of the mission analysis. System functions reflect the internal functionality of the system. Each system embodies several system functions; the amount and content depend on the type of system. A first attempt to distinguish between those system functions is by means of a *functional analysis* of the system. A function is a logical unit of system behaviour. Functional analysis is an essential step in the systems engineering process and analyses the system in terms of the functions that have to be performed, rather than the set of specific, structurally differentiated sub-systems by which the functionality is implemented. Function analysis is hierarchical in nature and proceeds in a top-down direction (Beevis,

1992). In car driving, for example, the transport function can be broken down into speed control and direction control; direction control can be further broken down into lateral control and heading control.

A further element is a description of the tactical/threat and geographical/climatic environments. Elements and aspects from the environment influence the (sub-)functions and may limit the possible mission outcome. Reactions to contingent changes in the environment typically belong to the mission description. An example of a contingency is unexpected enemy fire during movement of the task force.

Mission phasing and mission profiles are used to introduce the time factor into mission descriptions. They give guidance on the decomposition of the goal of the mission and on detailing the system functions further. A mission phasing is a time-dependent list of sub-goals, system actions, and system and environmental conditions. It allows a description of threat-imposed constraints, tactical decisions to be made, resource employment, and so on. A generic mission phasing may have the form of an event tree.

Process description forms the third main ingredient of a mission description. It specifies the most effective way of succeeding in a mission, given the circumstances. The specificity of the process descriptions is related to the specificity of the goal descriptions. Systems behaviour is described in terms of series of actions that connect the initial situation to the goal situation defined in the goal description. The process description is a discrete description in terms of a sequence of actions. The possible actions result from the possible connections/interactions between system and environment. These in turn are determined and limited by the system functionality. An example is the rate of movement as constrained by the soil conditions and wheel/track interactions with the soil.

Two methods are used as tools for mission analysis: the narrative description and the graphic mission profile. A narrative description represents the events of a mission in detail. It includes the characteristics, sequences and timing of mission phases and events, mission constraints, the 'external' events that dictate the activities of the system, and environmental conditions. Such a description may be in a highly structured, point-by-point form or a free-flowing narrative. It may describe several missions, or mission segments, or one composite or reference mission entailing all the unique mission activities. The output should be sufficiently detailed to identify the upper-level functions performed by the system (Beevis, 1992).

A series of actions can result from a mission plan or from a specific contingency. They are then called 'reactions'. Reactions, like actions, are marked by starting points and ends. They are described in the event-reaction list. The definition and classification of actions and reactions need to correspond closely to the 'natural' elements of behaviour (Newell *et al*, 1989). Although it will not be easy, an unequivocal definition of actions and reactions in the process description will benefit the mission analysis results.

Mission analysis can also be carried out on the basis of graphic mission profiles. Based on the mission objectives and operational requirements, they show the relevant system activities and significant mission events plotted against time and/or space. System variables that are represented include system state, geographical position, tracks, altitude or depth, and speed. The profiles can be complemented with text to show the sequence of operational events or situations that will determine the system functions and performance requirements of the system. Implicit in the requirements is the overall performance of the operators.

Narrative descriptions and graphic mission profiles are tools for mission process descriptions. The mission plan describes all alternative sequences of actions between the starting point and the goal. In practice, the composition of the mission plan depends to a large extent on the amount of preparation. The more preparation, the more detailed the planning and the fewer unexpected situations arise during the mission. With less preparation, more replanning and improvising will be needed to make the mission a success.

Outline of a Generic Mission Analysis Approach

During mission analysis, one tries to describe the missions of a specified system as economically as possible (van Rooij *et al*, 1996). The analysis should cover the complete range of the system activities with a minimum amount of (reference) missions and relations between missions. The description of a mission should always contain the specification of its goal and the environmental conditions in which the system must operate. The missions can be analysed at different aggregation levels. This hierarchical analysis leads to the description of missions as tree structures. A given system may be able to perform several missions. The collection of missions of a system is the list of reference missions.

The purpose of mission analysis is thus to describe the operational behaviour of a weapon system in terms of units of behaviour. This is accomplished in a number of sub-steps: global system description, environment description, process description and weapon system description.

As a starting point, there are usually documents describing the training need at the organisational level, the system and the system requirements; and operational manuals describing tasks, which have to be re-used as much as possible. From these, it is necessary to distil a list of reference missions, a training needs description and an initial specification of the system.

Global System Description

During global system description, the system in question is identified and demarcated in terms of its relations with other systems with which it interacts. The systems and the relations identified are depicted in a *system diagram*.

The example of Close Air Support in the presence of a Forward Air Controller has already been described. One can argue that the 'system' in this case is the combination of the weapon platform Tornado and the FAC officer, since their activities are tightly coupled and inter-dependent in reaching the mission goal.

The system diagram is used as starting point for a goal inventory in which the operational objectives of the system (with or without the collaboration of related systems) are identified and defined. Operational objectives are stated in terms of observable performance, and specify the goals the system has to achieve and the conditions under which it has to achieve them. The goals of a particular system are usually set by one or more superordinate system. Therefore, the goal inventory starts with the identification of relevant superordinate goals. As an example, the goals of a team of tank and infantry platoons determine those of the individual platoons, and these in turn set the goals of the individual weapon platforms.

Next, each of these superordinate goals is decomposed in terms of goals of the system in question and co-ordinate goals (the operational goals of a co-ordinate system, which may impose extra requirements on the system of concern in terms, for example, of position and timing). Again, only those co-ordinate goals are distinguished that are relevant to the system of concern.

The levels of these different types of goals reflect the chains of command and the span of control of the respective systems. As such, these relations also reflect the organisation and doctrine of the respective systems. For many domains and weapon systems, goal hierarchies can readily be derived from operational doctrine and associated regulations. The result of a goal inventory is a set of goal clusters, each describing the lower-level goals associated with a particular superordinate goal. Each goal cluster consists of a number of associated goals (of the system of concern and co-ordinate goals) that are related by means of vertical and horizontal relations. Each goal in the goal cluster may be broken down further into sub-goals.

The global objectives of tactical air operations in support of land and sea operations include:

- attaining and maintaining a desired degree of air superiority for the superordinate goal of protecting own land operations and friendly air capability against air attacks;
- air attacks against enemy's ground potential not yet engaged in close combat with friendly troops, as indirect support of own land operations by preventing strengthening of the enemy forces in the theatre of operations;
- direct support of own land operations by air attacks against enemy ground targets that are in close combat with friendly troops (or are already in the battle area but not yet engaged by the friendly land forces);
- support of friendly maritime forces;
- gathering intelligence information for identification of targets to be attacked and of the tactical situation at large.

From these descriptions, it is clear that goals are always embedded in a larger context of higher-order goals, and that sub-goals, such as elimination of enemy weapon systems, have to be seen in the context of strategical and tactical objectives.

Environment Description

Besides a description of the system, the mission description also includes a description of the environment. The environment of the system is described such that limiting conditions under which the system should function properly are specified. Therefore, the description of the environment will focus initially on relevance to the functionality of the system. This means that aspects of the environment will be viewed from a system perspective: which aspects influence the system and how does the system influence the environment?

Physical Environment

The aspects that describe the global characteristics of the environment are spatial- or medium-related. 'Spatial' aspects describe the spatial dimensions of the geographical environment in which the system of concern and other relevant entities operate. This description is limited to that part of the environment that is of direct concern to the system. The position of the other entities is relative to the position of the system. A 'medium' is the atmosphere or the water in which aircraft, ground vehicles and sea platforms operate. Climatic variations may have effects on control behaviour as well as on signal propagation. A medium such as the atmosphere also modifies the illumination.

Threat and Non-threat Tactical Environment

An entity can be viewed as a whole and independent from the physical environment. There are two types of entities in the environment: agents and objects. An 'agent' is an autonomous system that forms part of the environment: it can move freely and is able to influence the environment. Examples include other (friendly or enemy) weapon systems, other vehicles (military or civil), humans and animals. 'Objects' are entities that do not interact in a relevant manner with other entities in the environment. Examples are bridges, rivers, buildings, and trees. They are part of the tactical environment. An example of a target and threat description for air force missions is:

Airborne targets
• type of target (e.g., fighter, fighter bomber, transport, helicopter);
• number;
• target location.

Surface targets
• type of target (e.g., tank, armed personnel carrier, bridge, bunker);
• number;
• target location (co-ordinates, penetration range into hostile territory).

Tactical environment: threats
• airborne threat;
• ground threat (e.g., surface-to-air missile [SAM] sites);
• hostile EW (influence on communication, navigation).

Tactical environment: objects
• landmarks.

The connections between a system and the environment account for the external functionality of a system. Initially, the description of connections results from abstraction of geo-specific situations. In practice, performance depends on the specific properties of the environment, for example the characteristics of the terrain (relief, overgrowth, nature of the soil) in the theatre of operation. The attainable rate of movement is dependent on such characteristics. The distinguishable connections can be classified later, according to system function (e.g., co-ordination, mobility, target acquisition or weapon delivery). The different connections of system and environment determine the sequence of interactions that can be realised. The selection of combinations that are actually used depends on the goal that is pursued. These combinations are described later in the process model.

Process Description

Given the goal hierarchies and the results of the functional decomposition, the behaviour that is required to achieve each goal can be specified. This behaviour is described in terms of sequences of actions known as 'mission plans'. The determination of such sequences requires a specification of the initial state and the mission strategy adopted to proceed from the initial state to the goal state. Usually one or a limited number of initial states is distinguished, e.g., degrees of readiness. Given the initial state and the goal state, the required actions are identified by specifying intermediate action goals and their inter-relations and by taking into account the system functions that will be identified at a later step.

In addition to the planned, idealised, mission scenarios, events may occur that necessitate deviation from the planned sequence of actions. The latter type of occurrences are specified in terms of so-called event-reaction lists. Such lists may be general (applicable to the scenario as a whole) or specific (applicable to an action or set of actions). Taken together, mission scenarios and the associated event-reaction lists constitute the mission repertoire, i.e., the end result of mission analysis.

Weapon System Description

Structural decomposition A system usually consists of sub-systems, operators or crew by which the required functionalities are implemented. At a certain stage of the analysis, the system has to be analysed to identify the prescribed allocation of (sub-) functions to human components. The identified system has to be further described in terms of the man-machine interface. What are the parts or subsystems and the crew composition and what are the relations between these elements?

Functional decomposition The capacities that the system of concern requires to achieve its operational goals are described in terms of system functions. These are identified by means of a hierarchical functional decomposition of the system of concern (usually already performed in the design phase of the system). But often this information is not available in a form suitable for training needs analysis. One should be aware that functionalities change less than missions, and so the analysis should be valid for all missions identified for a particular system. In this approach, the system of concern is treated initially as a 'black box'. The internal workings of this black box are left unspecified for the time being. The capacities of a black box are described entirely in terms of relations between specified inputs and specified outputs, without considering how these relations are physically realised. Such a functional approach enables abstraction from details of implementation. Such details can be added at later steps.

To differentiate inputs and outputs in more detail, the black box can thus be hierarchically split into constituent system functions. This process is called system reticulation or 'box cutting'. Box cutting ensures that lower-level system functions are explicitly linked as much as possible to a higher-level system function. In this way the consistency and the transparency of the decomposition are retained. The result is a description of the functionality of the system of concern.

For weapon systems, a general taxonomy of system functions is given as a starting point. In applying the MASTER methodology, the terminology and distinctions have to be further adapted to the domain under analysis. With respect to functionality, a further useful distinction is between internal and external functionality. The description of the external functionality of a system consists of a description of all those system functions whose inputs originate from the environment and whose outputs are directed to the environment. The description of the internal functionality of a system consists of a description of all those relations between system functions whose inputs and outputs originate from or are directed to other system functions.

The specification of the external functionality describes the possibilities for interaction between the system and its environment, and thus also describes in an implicit way the environment. By describing the environment strictly from the point of view of the system, redundancies are prevented and the descriptions of system and system environment remain consistent.

Common to all mobile weapon systems seem to be the following system functions:

Co-ordination Sequencing and tuning of inter-dependent behaviours: the division of tasks over system components (team members, machines) necessitates co-ordination of the individual task executions when they are inter-dependent. Usually this co-ordination function is subsumed under the command and control activities within the system. For the larger system of which the present system is a subsystem, the same applies. One should discriminate between internal and external co-ordination. Co-ordination is the central function needed for the tuning of functions to each other. By means of input-output relations, this function is typically coupled to all other system functions. It can be subdivided into communication and mission management or control. Communication enables the exchange of information. Mission management is a more intelligent function entailing information processing, decision making and command and control. Further subdivision of communication is possible with respect to information content and to information channels. Likewise, mission management can be further subdivided into information storage, information processing and evaluation, decision making, and command and control.

Mobility Mobility consists of:
- navigation: planning and control of movements between (map) positions; includes the use of navigational aids (GPS, maps, compasses, charts, dead reckoning) to determine position, rate of movement, direction, orientation, and so on;
- propulsion: the capability of movement relative to the environment;
- steering: control of speed and change of position during actual displacements, obstacle avoidance.

Mobility is a function of environmental properties and system capabilities. It is the system's contribution to the manoeuvre capabilities of the larger unit.

Target acquisition Search, detection and identification of targets by means of the weapon system sensor systems and/or human perceptual capabilities, directed by knowledge about the tactical picture: scan for targets, and after detection identify them. This leads to an updated tactical picture. This is a critical system function that in general has output relations with all other system functions, primarily weapon delivery.

Weapon delivery Selection of target, choice of position, aiming, and delivery. Evaluation of the tactical picture within the mission framework determines which target to attack with what means. This may include pre-attack manoeuvres and post-attack assessment of effect.

System preservation Self defence: detection and assessment of threats to system integrity and adoption of countermeasures; intentional threats to the system have to be detected and countermeasures taken. The measures can be of a preventive nature (camouflage, protective fighting positions, protective equipment, security, detection enhancement by electronic means) or reactive (smoke and obscurants, attack of opposing force, withdrawal). Preservation/maintenance of operational readiness: internal threats to the system integrity are malfunctioning of subsystems, disorderly behaviour. Measures can again be preventive (maintenance, teambuilding, leadership) or reactive (repair, reconfigure, disciplinary actions).

These system functions are described at the highest level. They provide a useful starting point for detailing the commonalities and special features of mobile weapon systems. (Sub-)functions can be equated with tasks if allocated to humans. During function analysis and allocation, system functions are analysed in terms of sub-functions and assigned to specific agents. A task is a part of a system function allocated to one or more persons. The total set of tasks assigned to an individual constitutes his/her job content or assignment/job.

In completing the steps of mission analysis, a description of the idealised or hypothesised operational behaviour of a particular system is obtained. The required comprehensiveness and the level of detail of this description cannot be specified *a priori*, but depend on the requirements of subsequent steps, which are not all known in advance. Rather, the purpose of the methodology is to make explicit and elaborate these requirements. Essentially, this requires an iterative process and a number of rules for maintaining consistency and transparency between inputs and outputs of consecutive steps. At each step the user has to make decisions. To a large extent, user decisions will determine the results of applying the methodology. In essence, the methodology only systematises the process and, through this systematisation, facilitates it and renders it traceable by the user and other interested parties. The strength of the methodology lies in its support of global as well as very detailed analyses in the same overall framework.

The results of the mission analysis thus depend on the domain that is analysed, the goal of the analysis and the chosen methods. These factors are not independent.

The system and its borders are defined by the analyst. A given system might be able to perform very many missions, which can make mission analysis very broad, requiring more time and money than available. In a practical situation, however, one is probably interested in the achievement of a relatively specific goal. This might help in choosing suitable methods for analysis and description of the relevant system missions. The development of an entirely new training curriculum for personnel will necessitate a broader analysis, for instance, whereas the evaluation and improvement of one specific training component will necessitate very detailed in-depth analysis with a much more restricted scope.

Likewise, for the size of the chosen domain, it is also important whether one is analysing an existing system or a future system. The analysis is often an iterative process whereby analysts look for the best representation. They might make use of the results of earlier analyses or analyses of other systems. On the surface, these might seem very different, even if their deep, functional structure is still very similar.

The mission strategy is specified in terms of a number of decision points with 'if ... then ...' rules. These decision points are inserted between the actions. As a guideline, each action should be associated with only one system function. Thus, decomposing functions implies decomposing actions and vice versa. In this way a one-to-one correspondence between system functions and actions can be maintained.

Taxonomies of Missions

One may wish to create or identify an absolute inventory of missions. However, such a list cannot be exhaustive; lists evolve with new tactical frameworks. Taxonomies may further be different from one system to another. Use of the same model to gather information on sea, ground and air systems using the same taxonomies risks generation of a model usable only with great difficulty in each domain.

As a starting point, several domain-specific lists of distinctions/classifications/ taxonomies are given below for distinguishing, ordering, and describing missions. They can serve as an initial orientation, but were not produced with the design of training in mind.

For airborne systems, the RAFTS Report (1986) gives mission categories, mission types and forms. NATO Tactical Air Force operations and missions have to be seen in close connection with the overall warfare, especially when supporting land and sea operations. The categories of basic Tactical Air Force Operations are:

- Counter Air.
- Air Interdiction.
- Tactical Air Reconnaissance.
- Offensive Air Support.
- Tactical Air Support of Maritime Operations.
  Mission categories are given as:
- Fighter missions.
- Air Attack.

- Reconnaissance.
- Observation.
- Electronic Warfare.
- Command/Control.

In NATO terms these are 'aircraft assigned roles'. Mission categories can be further broken down into a list of mission types. Types of Air Attack are:

- Close Air Support (CAS).
- Battlefield Interdiction (BI).
- Deep Strike (Tactical).
- Deep Strike (Strategic).

Each of these mission types can be broken down further into mission forms or variants by various parameters:

- Targets.
- Weapons to be delivered.
- Flight compositions.
- Operating doctrine.

An empirical question is how such a system of classification is useful in mission analysis, geared to training design.

For helicopters a different taxonomy for missions is used (Table 2.1). Civil missions are outside the scope of MASTER.

Table 2.1. Helicopter missions (examples)

Civil Missions	Military Missions	
	Assistance	Battlefield Engagement
Personnel Transport	Search and Rescue (SAR)	Reconnaissance
Material Transport	Material Transport	Anti-Tank Warfare
Support Operations for	Troop Transport	Air-to-Air Warfare
agricultural,	Logistic tasks	Air-to-Ground Support
environmental,	Combat Rescue	etc.
organisational tasks,	Casualty Evacuation	
etc.	(CASEVAC)	

Types of mission as distinguished in the naval domain are:
- Anti-Air Warfare (AAW).
- Amphibious Warfare (AMW).
- Anti-Surface Ship Warfare (ASW).
- Anti-Submarine Warfare (ASUW).
- Command, Control and Communications (CCC).
- Constriction (CON).
- Electronic Warfare (ELW).

- Fleet Support Operations (FSO).
- Intelligence (INT).
- Logistics (LOG).
- Mine warfare (MIW).
- Mobility (MOB).
- Non Combat Operations (NCO).
- Special Warfare (SPW).
- Strike Warfare (STW).

In the German Navy, the following, more global, types of mission are distinguished:

- Coastal protection.
- Sea control (of defined areas).
- Sea Lines of Communication (SLOC) protection.
- Sea denial (by use of mine warfare).

For ground-based systems, the joint essential mission types provide an example. In the Universal Joint Task List, a distinction is made between four levels of war:

- Strategic level: national.
- Strategic level: theatre.
- Operational level.
- Tactical level.

Level of war has to be understood in this context as corresponding globally to the three inter-related hierarchical tiers: (individual) crew and squad level; unit and lower formation level (up to brigade, air wing and naval task group/force); and battle staffs and higher headquarters.

The tactical level is the level of mobile weapon systems. It is described as the level of war at which battles and engagements are planned and executed to accomplish military objectives assigned to tactical units or task forces. Activities at this level focus on the ordered arrangement and manoeuvre of combat elements in relation to each other and to the enemy to achieve combat objectives. The main global tasks are:

- conduct manoeuvre;
- develop intelligence;
- employ firepower;
- perform combat service support;
- exercise command and control;
- provide mobility and survivability.

Since co-ordination is restricted either to co-ordination of one combat function along the dimension of level of war or to co-ordination at one level of war over combat functions, this gives a relatively simple global overview of operational requirements and thus of mission categories (Table 2.2).

Command & Control are depicted as either horizontal or vertical arrows in this scheme to express mainly the external co-ordination provided. Of course, within each cell internal co-ordination must also be effected. A horizontal linkage is defined in the context of a military operation. Different tasks (functions) have to be performed in careful co-ordination with one another to achieve the desired effects.

The co-ordination among such tasks may be in terms of timing, space, etc. Vertical linkages connect tasks at one level of war to related tasks at other levels, e.g., intelligence, movement and manoeuvre, firepower, sustainment, protection, and command and control.

Table 2.2. Operational requirements

Level of war	Combat functions	Combat support functions	
Strategic (theatre)	Deployment, concentration & manoeuvre Employ strategic firepower	Strategic intelligence Sustain forces Provide protection	▲
Operational	Conduct operational movement Employ operational firepower	Operational intelligence Operational support Operational protection	
Tactical	Conduct manoeuvre Employ firepower	Develop intelligence Combat service support Mobility and survivability	▼
Horizontal C^2	◄──────────────►		Vertical C^2

Combat functions can be further subdivided into:
direct combat
- conduct manoeuvre: navigation; position, reposition; negotiate, control tactical area.
- employ fire-power: target acquisition; weapon delivery.

support functions
- develop intelligence: develop requirements; collect information; process information; disseminate information.
- combat service support: military police; supplies and transport; repair/maintain equipment.
- mobility and survivability: engineering; protection; security.
- command & control: assess situation.
- planning: plan generation; plan selection; plan implementation.
- co-ordination: external; internal.
- communication.

Current Applications of Mission Analysis

Mission analysis is seldom conducted in the context of the design of training devices; even when it is attempted, it is usually unstructured, incomplete and unsystematic (Riemersma *et al*, 1997a, b), and the results are not used rigorously in designing the training programme. Much is left to the practical experience of instructors and their implicit knowledge about systems, missions and tasks. Factors hampering progress are lack of guidelines, of systematic approaches and often also of time. The situation is further complicated by the often inadequate maintenance of existing training programmes and devices. Upgrades to the training programmes and media tend to lag far behind system upgrades. Maintainability is thus an issue that deserves much more attention, and this can be guaranteed only by a systems approach to training.

The tools for mission analysis (narrative descriptions and graphic mission profiles) allow only a partial and, in a sense, biased approach to mission analysis as conceived in the MASTER project. Mission analysis of the Tank Platoon (van Rooij *et al*, 1996) is perhaps an exception.

In Beevis (1992), a number of existing techniques for function analysis are described. A *function flow diagram* identifies the sequential relationships of the functions required to perform the mission and operations. *Sequence and timing (SAT) diagrams* show the sequence of activation of the sub-systems as necessary system functions are performed. The *structured analysis and design technique* (SADT) describes complex systems that may include any combination of hardware, software and people, and consists of diagrams, text and a glossary, all cross-referenced. A hierarchy of inter-connected diagrams is the resultant organised description of the system. *Information flow and processing analysis* (or the 'decision-action diagram') describes the information flow and processing required to accomplish the system objective, and includes the decisions and actions (operations) involved. *State transition diagrams, Petri nets* and *behaviour graphs* are further techniques. State transition diagrams show the relationships between 'states' and 'events'. A Petri net is a graphical and mathematical modelling tool to describe and study information processing systems in which concurrent, asynchronous, distributed stochastic processes can occur. Behaviour graphs show system behaviour as a function of time, and combine control and information flow graphs.

Conclusions

The examples of mission analyses examined for air, naval and ground-based systems present a large variety of approaches to mission analysis, classification and/or description. This illustrates the need for a more generic approach. There are common underlying elements in the approaches, enabling a 'generic' protocol and format to describe missions of mobile weapon systems. This format comprises at least four main generic components: global system description, environment description, process description and weapon system description. These descriptions vary in emphasis and scope. Within the MASTER framework, mission analysis results are used as input for task analysis, and the task analysis results in turn form input for training programme design and training media specification. For the design of training systems, therefore, the results of a mission analysis specify, among other things, the criticality, frequency, duration, conditions, required performance levels and task dependencies. The output of task analysis, on the other hand, should be skill requirements and task descriptions, specific enough for the design of effective training programmes and the specification of training media.

A goal description should be part of the mission description, but in practice goals are often not made explicit at the level of detail needed for the derivation of performance standards. The goal description is also important because it shows the relationship of the mission goal to other goals/missions in the mission repertoire and hence helps in planning tasks and priority assessments.

The mission description includes a description of the environment, with emphasis on limiting conditions under which the system should function properly. Therefore, in the first instance the description of the environment should focus on those aspects that interact with the functionality of the system. This means that aspects of the environment have to be viewed from a system perspective: which aspects influence the system and how does the system influence the environment? A broad distinction between geographical/atmospheric and tactical/threat environments has been identified.

Mission phasing and mission profiles are used in many approaches to introduce the time factor into mission descriptions. They can give guidance on the decomposition of the goal of the mission, and assist in later more detailed analysis of the system functions. A mission phasing is a time-dependent list of subgoals, system actions, and system and environmental conditions. It allows a description of threat-imposed constraints, tactical decisions to be made, resource employment, and so on.

A weapon system description contains a structural description in terms of system elements and a functional description in terms of system functions. A functional description excludes all system-specific details that are irrelevant to the goal of the mission analysis. System functions reflect the internal functionality of the system.

It is still open to question whether the identified generic system functions are sufficient for mission analysis at the most global level, and whether mobile weapon systems of all three forces can be covered by them, but preliminary findings are encouraging in this respect.

Mission analysis as reported in the literature is mostly related to the design of systems rather than the design of training programmes and devices. However, it appears to be an essential first step in the systems approach to training, to specify the wider contexts of a task and to derive conditions and standards. The comprehensive and generic approach attempted by MASTER should be further elaborated. Work in the field of mission analysis remains to be evaluated and incorporated into the approach. Major remaining obstacles are discrepancies in terminology and emphasis between the military services, and differences in the objectives of mission analyses reported in the past.

3   Task Analysis

Introduction and Major Concepts

The next main step of TNA is task analysis. There is a certain degree of possible commonality between the approaches used for mission and task analysis, since both are concerned with the description of behaviour. The difference between these approaches is that, during mission analysis, the behaviour of the system is the focus of analysis, whereas during task analysis the focus of analysis is narrowed to the behaviour of the operator or crew manning the system. The operator or crew is embedded within the system, and so it is important also to describe the man-machine interface (MMI) in a task-related manner.

The output of mission analysis consists of the mission descriptions, a specification of the (intended) operational behaviour of the system in terms of a representative set of reference missions. Each individual mission description contains a description of the goal, the operational conditions, the system functions, and the sequence(s) of actions (mission plans) to be performed. The output of task analysis consists of the task descriptions, which describe the operational behaviour of the operator or crew. Analogous to the mission descriptions, each task description contains a description of the task goal, the operational task conditions, the operator functions (skills), and the sequences of activities (task procedures) to be performed. In this context 'skill' is defined as a learned capacity to perform a certain type of activity.

The term 'task' is used in the literature with different meanings, and different dimensions of tasks are studied. The MASTER glossary (Riemersma, 1994) describes a task as a 'goal-directed composite of related operator or maintainer activities, performed for an immediate purpose, i.e., in response to a specified input and yielding a specified output'. Essentially, a task is a system function that has been allocated to a human operator or a team. Task analysis is described as 'a systematic, typically time-oriented, description of a task performed by an operator, controller or maintainer, and showing the sequential and simultaneous cognitive and motor activities'.

A given task can be performed in different ways, sometimes leading to the same results and sometimes to different results. There is not always a single optimal way to perform a task, leading to the best results or the greatest efficiency. The concept of task can have different connotations (Normand, 1992):

- the task as prescribed task, where the task is seen as an assignment to be completed (e.g., according to a task manual);
- the actual task; the way in which the task is performed by an operator in reality;
- the task representation as it is perceived by the operator, which is not necessarily identical either to the prescribed task or to the way in which the task is actually performed.

Training usually focuses on the first meaning, although a large discrepancy between the prescribed and the actual task is indicative of less than optimal design of system and tasks, and thus should lead to reconsideration of the prescribed task. A task is thus any piece of work assigned to an operator or team of operators that has identifiable start and end points. The set of tasks assigned to an operator or team of operators is called a function or job.

Not all tasks are specific to a particular job. The notion of 'generic task' (Schaafstal & Schraagen, 1992) can be used for classes of tasks that share knowledge and strategies needed for performance. Examples are planning, diagnosing and designing. If the knowledge and strategies needed to perform generic tasks can be identified, one has a good starting point for the design of training, ensuring that general applicable strategies are taught, and not only those that are specific to one task.

Importance of Task Analysis

Task analysis is useful for training systems development because its results are used in formulating training objectives (Patrick, 1992), by:

- identification of final behaviour;
- describing important conditions under which behaviour will be expected to occur;
- specification of criteria for acceptable performance.

During task analysis, information is collected that is used in later steps to decide:

- what to train;
- how to train;
- how well to train;
- how much to spend on training.

Task analysis results should thus directly support the subsequent process of training design, in which is specified:

- the course content;
- the output or criterion performance;
- the method(s) of training.

In the context of training on simulators, the purpose of task analysis is more specifically given in the *Handbook of Human Factors* (Salvendy, 1986): 'The task analysis identifies the information needed to support the operator's task practice in the simulator and also defines the training and learning functions to be supported in the simulator'.

A problem with some of the stated purposes of task analysis may be that it is primarily concerned with the description of operational task behaviour. This should not be confused with the analysis of training tasks or methods. Training tasks can be quite different from operational tasks as analysed in task analysis, as long as the acquired skills transfer to the operational task. A clear example is part-task and even part-function training (Blessing *et al*, 1996).

Requirements for Task Analysis

Task analysis leads to the description of the operational behaviour of operators within the context of a mission. A task can be defined analogously to a mission by specifying goals, task processes, operator functions (skills) and a task environment, and three sources of information can again be differentiated: documents, subject-matter experts, and direct observation or registration.

Tasks may be distinguished with respect to the goal, the nature of the skills they require, and conditions. Much confusion arises from the fact that frequently a task is equated with a task goal. Exactly how tasks are diffentiated, and the level of detail, depend on the purpose. Allocating work to different members of a team will result in a different set of tasks from those resulting from task description for equipment design. In the context of MASTER, the main purpose of the differentiation of tasks is as a preliminary to training programme design and, ultimately, the specification of training media. This means that tasks assigned to two or more persons should be broken down in such a way that each sub-task can be assigned unambiguously to one and only one person, thus resolving crew tasks into tasks of individual crew members. Working as a team or crew generates, of course, new parallel tasks of co-ordination and communication.

Procedures for Task Analysis

For task analysis a large number of approaches have been proposed, mainly in the context of system design. An overview is given in Kirwan and Ainsworth (1992). The contents and methods of task analyses vary according to the information requirements for training design. For example, training may focus on the task behaviour alone or may include the cognitive elements underlying the task behaviour. With the increasing emphasis on cognitive tasks, there is a growing need for techniques to analyse such tasks. Aspects of cognition include perceiving, imagining, remembering, conceiving, reasoning, judging and decision making. These basic functions are used in higher-level tasks generically expressed as goal setting, considering alternatives, deciding, planning, organising and controlling.

Gagné and Briggs (1974) identified five components that have to be specified to determine training objectives: the situation, the object, the action, the tools, and the skill to be learned. An appropriate task analysis could then be used to identify and structure the information relevant to the formulation of training objectives. Patrick (1992) argued that it is difficult to determine these objectives systematically, although he suggested that techniques such as Hierarchical Task Analysis (HTA) might provide the answer.

HTA is a popular method. There are, however, problems with the use of HTA in the context of training system design, due to its failure to consider relations between concurrent tasks, and the fact that it is not embedded in a larger analysis framework. Further, the failure of HTA to indicate the type of cues used to perform the task represents omission of the 'input' as described in the MASTER Reference Framework (Riemersma *et al*, 1994). HTA is useful for representing overt activity such as manipulation of controls, but less so for covert cognitive activity. Without knowledge of the cognitive activity required, it is impossible to specify the 'operation' as required in HTA. For training programme design, a number of characteristics of a task must be specified that are not included in the HTA framework. Task descriptions (Riemersma, 1997) should include:

- task content, task type, input, and output;
- contextual and environmental conditions;
- frequency and duration;
- criticality (consequences of wrong decisions/actions);
- difficulty indications, including workload and stress;
- relevant cue indications;
- identification of the initial entry state that defines the conditions for the initiation of the task and of the end state;
- the goal condition that the task must achieve, and performance measures;
- constraints/aids provided by environmental and technological factors.

Tasks may be performed in different ways, all of which may lead to an acceptable output. This may cause a problem for the description of a task as well as for the design of a training programme, because it is not always feasible to design a system that allows for this kind of flexibility. If there are several possible ways to perform a task, they may not be equally easy to learn.

Task decomposition is a method of subdividing task descriptions into more detailed information of particular interest to the analyst. For each task element, information is then gathered concerning important aspects of the task and the context in which it occurs. Possible categories suggested by Patrick (1992) include the following:

- task element;
- purpose;
- cue for element;
- decision;
- action;
- displays;
- controls;
- likely errors.

Most of these elements are consistent with the MASTER framework, since they correspond to input, operation and output factors. Although some inconsistencies are apparent, these elements have been integrated within the MASTER approach.

Cognitive Task Analysis

A distinction can be made between different types of cognitive task analysis relevant to training:

- task modelling: focusing on decomposition of tasks into goals and subgoals;

- knowledge modelling: focusing on the task requirements, in terms of the strategies and knowledge that the operator must possess;
- cognitive modelling: focusing on the task performer.

Although both knowledge and cognitive modelling take into account the performer of the task, knowledge modelling is geared to optimal or expert task performance. Cognitive modelling takes into account the different and sub-optimal ways of task performance and also models the behaviour of inexperienced operators.

For the purposes of designing training systems, all three types of modelling seem necessary: one has to have detailed information about the tasks to be trained, about the optimal way of performing the task and the knowledge needed to do so, and about the beginner's performance. An integrated approach is needed in which all these approaches are present. Such an integrated approach can be called a cognitive task analysis. In this specialised type of task analysis, three levels of knowledge about the task that is to be trained can be distinguished (Schaafstal & Schraagen, 1992):

- task structure: goals to be fulfilled during task execution, global strategy;
- local strategies (procedures), by means of which values are obtained for goals;
- description of underlying domain knowledge.

Another method of performing cognitive task analysis (Seamster *et al*, 1993) uses modelling techniques to build up a mental model of the task. The advantage of mental models is that they can be used directly for the design process of training. The mental models represent the models that learners should acquire. The process by which such models are constructed is:

- task decomposition;
- development of a detailed task model;
- development of a mental model.

Another method of analysis leading to mental models is given by Patrick (1992):

- describing tasks by taking an information processing approach in which tasks are represented in terms of input, process and output;
- gathering ability requirements;
- representing the knowledge needed for task performance:
  — identify types of knowledge involved;
  — make alternative representations of knowledge;
  — assemble the representations into an expert model.

To summarise, although there are many different methods in the domain of cognitive task analysis, the process often consists of the following steps:

- identification of relevant tasks;
- decomposition of all selected tasks;
- acquisition of knowledge about the (decomposed) tasks and performance;
- representation of the results in a framework or model.

These steps are iterative, and do not necessarily have to be performed sequentially.

Outline of a Generic Approach to Task Analysis

In the following, the main steps are briefly described.

Operator Identification

This is a seemingly trivial step, yet in practice it is easy to identify cases in which it has been omitted, with an adverse effect on training. After a system upgrade, for example, there is sometimes a failure to identify all the operators whose tasks are affected; their training is therefore not adapted accordingly.

Task Goal Inventory and Decomposition of Tasks

Task goals are identified in the context of actions. From the mission analysis, a list of tasks equated with assigned (sub-)functions serves as primary input for a further decomposition of tasks. This is related to the goal hierarchy as described in the mission analysis phase. In this step, the gross tasks are further decomposed into intermediate sub-tasks. The level aimed at is purposeful activities that can be equated with skill requirements. This decomposition is guided by the further decomposition of mission goals, such that each sub-task relates to a sub-goal and vice versa.

Task Specification and Description

A large number of alternative models and techniques have been used in modelling task performance (Kirwan & Ainsworth, 1992; RSG-14, 1992). A common idea in modelling tasks is that they should be analysed in terms of a hierarchy of operations or processes (Looren de Jong & Sanders, 1990; Carroll, 1993) that have a distributed memory representation (McClelland & Rumelhart, 1985). A description of the task includes a further refinement of the description of the system interfaces. MMI elements from the structural system description are specified for each task in the description of the input/output relations with internal and external elements. In addition, a description of job aids or other equipment used for the tasks (e.g., magnifying glasses, radio equipment) is added. This represents a task-oriented extension of the structural system description. The ways of communicating between crew members must also be further specified. A structural description of the human component is usually taken for granted: the senses, the cognitive faculties and the motor apparatus are essentially given. But in the functional description a *skill* description is necessary.

Task analysis is supported by a number of specific techniques to collect and organise information and subsequently make judgements or design decisions. The method of task analysis provides the user with a 'blueprint' of human involvement in a system, creating a detailed picture of the system from a human perspective. This structured information can then be used to ensure (by design or training) that the system goals and human capabilities and organisation are compatible, so that the system goals will be achieved.

Techniques for task description are time-line analysis, flow process charts, critical task analysis, operational sequence diagrams, and decision tables (Beevis, 1992):

- Time lines show the sequence of operator tasks and provide a basis for analysis of workload and resource estimation.
- Flow process charts depict the sequence of operator and machine activities along a vertical dimension. Each of five types of activity (operation, transportation, inspection, delay, and storage) is graphically depicted by a symbol.
- Critical task analysis is a standard technique for detailed analysis of operator tasks that impose high workload or are critical to system safety or the success of the mission.
- Operational sequence diagrams are extensions of flow process charts that provide a graphical representation of the flow of information, decisions and activities in a system.
- Decision tables are tables of conditions and their combinations, and the allowed or optimal actions for each combination of conditions.

Skill Decomposition

Skill decomposition is generally conducted to learn more about the knowledge and skill requirements of a task or set of tasks. This type of information is important for selection and for training analysis and design. Once the task analysis is complete, required skill profiles can be derived from the individual tasks identified. This will distinguish the physical and mental activities required to perform the tasks. A reasonable first-level grouping would be at two levels: general requirements and mission-specific requirements. These would require further breakdown until a full understanding of each individual task was obtained. Once the required skills have been identified for all tasks, a criterion for acceptable level of performance for the most demanding tasks requiring the skill can be identified, from which training objectives can be set. This is the level of performance that must be reached by the trainee at the end of training.

Taxonomies of Tasks

Tasks and associated goals must be categorised. In the literature, a number of task taxonomies have been proposed (see Fleishman & Quaintance, 1984). An example of a simple taxonomy is:

- perception (search/monitoring, detection, identification);
- diagnosis/classification/assessment;
- decision making;
- communication;
- tracking;
- steering;
- aiming.

A problem is the domain-specificity of tasks, which makes the usual taxonomies either too global or not fully applicable to the specific domain under study. Task taxonomies must be developed according to their objectives, e.g., defining requirements for the design of a simulator device or training aircraft, training syllabus/curriculum development, or training programme design. Fleishman and Quaintance (1984) present alternative taxonomic systems, based on different assumptions about the underlying common factors in task performance and geared to different applications. In the *criterion measures* approach, the classification is guided by the dependent measures available, such as probability of detection, reaction time, percent correctly coded responses, and time-on-target or integrated tracking error. The *information-theoretic* approach is based on a general model derived from information processing theory. A task is described only as the transfer of information between components, and classified according to the nature and locus of constraints for transfer and the information content of the input and output. The *task strategies* approach is founded in task-analytic work and focuses on task functions. The most generic are input reception, memory, processing and output effectors. To these functions are added strategies. Behavioural strategies are techniques to maximise the operator as a processing resource. An example is adaptation of scanning strategies to external probabilities of change in information. Task strategies are thus techniques for coping more effectively with uncertainties. In the *ability requirements* approach, tasks are described in terms of the human abilities required to perform them effectively. A problem of using this classification in a training domain is the shift in underlying abilities during training. In the *task characteristics* approach, no relation to human performers is strived at. Only characteristics of the tasks *per se* are used for classificaton. Using this approach, task complexity can be more easily varied for training purposes and training methods selected.

For the purpose of this review, only a global distinction between perceptual-motor, procedural, and cognitive tasks is used. A perceptual-motor task is a task in which the primary activity to be performed involves co-ordination between perceptual inputs and motor outputs. A procedural task is a task in which the primary activity involves the execution of an algorithmic sequence of discrete actions. In a cognitive task, the primary activity involves the heuristic analysis and synthesis of different types of information. The adjective 'primary' serves to indicate that most realistic tasks involve a mixture of these types of activities. The topics of time-sharing of tasks and team tasks will also be discussed briefly.

Perceptual-motor Tasks

Perceptual-motor tasks can be sub-divided into genuine perceptual-motor tasks, perceptual tasks and motor tasks, the latter involving primarily perceptual or motor activities, respectively. For instance, many monitoring/inspection and target acquisition tasks, such as sonar and radar tasks, can be classified as perceptual tasks, whereas many task components associated with driving and weapon delivery would be classified as motor tasks. However, the distinction between perceptual and motor tasks is usually a matter of degree. Most tasks involve a mixture of perceptual and motor components. Perceptual skills may be very task-specific. They denote the ability to search, detect and interpret task-relevant information.

Perception can be subdivided into attention and interpretation. Attention is goal-directed and is directly related to proficiency in detecting possible relevant information. The interpretation skill underlies the ability to discriminate between task-relevant and task-irrelevant information, and to evaluate the information for correct task execution.

A further distinction can be made between discrete and continuous tasks. An example of a discrete perceptual task is checking a symbol on a display; an example of a continuous perceptual task is searching a sector. Corresponding examples for motor tasks would be shooting at a target and tracking a moving target, respectively. Many continuous tasks are subject to vigilance problems (perceptual) and fatigue (motor).

Perceptual tasks can be further subdivided according to the type of activity involved, e.g., search, detection, discrimination, identification, and perceptual modality.

Discrete motor tasks are reaction time tasks that may be 'simple' (responding to a particular stimulus) or may involve a choice between two or more alternatives. These types of tasks have been and are widely used within research paradigms aimed at uncovering basic human information processing characteristics and strategies.

For continuous perceptual-motor tasks the processing by an expert is so fast that it is no longer under conscious control, and thus it is often difficult to specify which cues are relevant for the task at hand.

Other important types of motor tasks distinguished in the research literature are serial or sequential reaction time tasks and discrete movement tasks. Research on these types of task is easily confused with research on procedural tasks. The main distinguishing feature is timing, which is usually a more critical factor for motor tasks than for procedural tasks.

Procedural Tasks

Procedural tasks involve the execution of an algorithmic sequence of discrete actions. They require few decisions and are generally performed in the same way each time. Such tasks vary in (1) the amount of required planning, (2) the number of steps, (3) the amount of inherent cueing, (4) the number of decision points or branches, and (5) the number of permissible sequences (Konoske & Ellis, 1986). Examples of types of procedural tasks are assembly tasks, maintenance tasks, system management tasks (e.g., standard monitoring and control tasks and tasks during powering up or shutting down a system) and simple diagnosis and troubleshooting tasks. Procedural tasks are usually routine, and are very prevalent in the military domain. Unfortunately, the procedural skills associated with these tasks are generally not well retained.

The introduction of advanced technology has substantially altered the nature of professional jobs. Procedural aspects are becoming increasingly more important. The operational power of civil and military organisations is, to a large extent, determined by the competence of their personnel in acquiring and retaining skill in procedural tasks. The question of how acquisition and retention of competence in these tasks can be improved through instructional techniques is therefore considered of great importance.

Procedural tasks can thus be described as tasks comprising a necessary sequence of discrete responses. Procedures are 'paths' that the user must follow to achieve a task goal. The path is defined by an expert or a specialist (for example, a test pilot or an engineer for an engine procedure) who validates this path and determines it as a valid rule, or by the user himself, who in real operations has to find a solution to reach the stated objectives, this solution becoming a procedure only when standardised. The objective of education and training is to allow the future user to learn all the required procedures to achieve the task goal.

It is clear that, in performing a task, one uses not only perceptual-motor skills but also reasoning. Task knowledge also comprises knowledge about the conditions of application for the task execution.

With the growing importance of technology, the role of the human operator in modern military systems is increasingly that of a monitor, decision-maker and process controller. As a result, there is a gradual shift in emphasis from skilled perceptual-motor control to the performance of procedural tasks, such as troubleshooting a defective piece of equipment or following normal and emergency procedures. Examples of the types of procedural task most often required from trainees are those associated with starting up an aircraft, preparing a navigation or weapon system, in-flight monitoring, interceptions of targets, and weapons delivery. The lower the level of the task (perceptual-motor, with a prescribed series of actions), the more 'locked' (rigid and difficult to override) the procedure. Conversely, the more a procedure calls for reasoning, for multiple, complex information monitoring, the more it will be 'open-ended'. The procedure is then more cognitive, governed by general rules and adaptable to the situation.

In the literature it has been found that procedural tasks are most vulnerable to deterioration, falling back to operationally unacceptable levels after periods of months or even weeks of non-utilisation. The more complex a procedure, the less the separate steps are intrinsically cued; when the skill has only recently been acquired or updated, it will easily be forgotten, and the user may erroneously revert to an older procedure. Mengelknoch *et al* (1971) found, for instance, that the discrete and procedural components of complex tasks were more susceptible to forgetting than tracking skills.

Cognitive Tasks

In cognitive tasks, the goal cannot be attained by a pre-determined or straightforward course of action, largely because of the complexity or the uncertainty of the task. These properties necessitate the use of heuristics, i.e., problem-solving and decision-making strategies, instead of algorithms for successful performance. Examples of cognitive tasks are complex monitoring and control, diagnosis, problem solving, and, more generally, all tasks involving decision making in a complex and/or dynamic situation. Colley and Beech (1989b) used a classification system based on dimensions relevant to learning methods. One such dimension was 'simple-complex'. For simple tasks, practice may be sufficient to enable mastery; for complex tasks, however, merely practising may not improve performance if the task is not structured appropriately. Air traffic control is an example of a complex task requiring integration of a large amount of information and application of a complex set of rules.

Other dimensions are:

- divergent-convergent: applying well-defined rules to find a single solution is convergent in nature. When the rules are less well defined or more individually interpreted, a novel product may result from more divergent processes. Many complex tasks have both convergent and divergent elements;
- algorithmic-heuristic: the difference between following a recipe and working from knowledge of underlying principles;
- inductive-deductive: logical deduction works from evidence to solutions whereas induction generates on the basis of instances a general framework to solve a new problem;
- open-closed: refers to the predictability of the environment;
- universal-specialised: skills such as reading are almost universal; others are possessed by only a few experts.

Time Sharing

Time sharing refers to the ability to execute different tasks or task components simultaneously, and is one of the defining characteristic of high-performance tasks (Schneider, 1985). Findings from research on dual-task performance (see Barber, 1989) are extremely relevant to part-task training strategies and curriculum design (see Section II). Of particular importance are studies showing limited transfer of single-task training to dual-task performance (Schneider & Fisk, 1983) and experiments pointing to the unique character of time-sharing skills. These results suggest that dual tasks have characteristics that do not exist in single tasks, and further that dual-task performance requires subjects to adapt to the peculiarities of the combination of tasks (Korteling, 1994). Much effort has been devoted to establishing whether individuals possess or can acquire a specific time-sharing skill (Damos & Wickens, 1980; Ackerman *et al*, 1984; Wickens, 1989).

Team Tasks

Traditionally, selection, training, and human factors engineering efforts have focused rather exclusively on individual task performance. However, it is increasingly recognised that many modern, complex systems require effective team performance. Precise co-ordination of performance in time and space is becoming ever more decisive for total system performance. One further impetus for the study of this topic is the fact that many aircraft, nuclear power plant, and industrial incidents and accidents can be attributed to inadequate team or crew co-ordination. Another impetus is the empirical finding that a group of experts, proficient in the individual tasks, may not be an expert team (Salas *et al*, 1995b). Development of the co-ordinated behaviour so characteristic of an expert team usually requires considerable experience of working together. In the area of military training and simulation, the emergence of technologies such as networked simulation has also stimulated growing interest in aspects of team performance. For the purpose of this review, a team is defined as a group of people who have a common goal and act inter-dependently and adaptively to achieve this goal. They also have distinct tasks and roles.

Team tasks are tasks that are in a way superordinate to the tasks assigned to individuals. Depending on task requirements, the organisational structure of the team relies on sharing of task information between the individuals who constitute the team, and on co-ordinating their behaviour. Communication, co-ordination and co-operation are crucial for optimal team performance. Although several factors have been identified, the question of what determines successful team performance largely remains to be answered (Rouse *et al*, 1992).

There are essentially two directions for training. Soft skills such as communication, assertiveness, and leadership are trained in Crew Resource Management courses and focus on the more social side of team interactions. A growing body of research now distinguishes the prerequisite knowledge and skills for effective team performance by focusing on the team tasks of communication and co-ordination in a task-related sense. The concept of shared mental models characterises this approach. Models of the situation, the team tasks and the task structure, the capabilities and limitations of other team members, and a shared communication model have to be developed. Ways of speeding this process as compared to merely gathering experience are available only in a rudimentary form. Cross-training and its variants, for example, have been studied by Schaafstal and Bots (1997). Cross-training is a form of training in which team members are trained in the tasks of the other team members, with the objective of making communication and co-ordination easier and more effective.

Domain-specific Taxonomies

Several possible other types of task taxonomy have been identified, all based on the task description table in the MASTER Reference Framework. An example of a task description table appears in Table 3.1.

The task descriptions identify the major tasks within each function and the input, operations and output factors for each task (note that 'output' does not necessarily imply an overt action by the operator). It is suggested that there are several different ways of representing this information to achieve a more comprehensive taxonomy of tasks.

In terms of training system design, the method of classifying tasks described in the MASTER Reference Framework is useful, since it denotes the environment in which the task occurs, the sources of information used by the operator, the equipment with which the operator interacts, and the required operator/system behaviour.

Skills

A task has to be considered a requirement of behaviour. A skill, on the other hand, is a characteristic of an individual person that enables the person to perform particular tasks. This characteristic is latent and becomes manifest only in the performance of a particular task or test. Tests are the traditional means of assessing skills in individuals. A large number of tests have been designed, mostly for the purpose of selection.

One could describe training needs simply in terms of decomposition of tasks. This would guarantee that all tasks and related skills were covered in the training programme. A drawback is that one would neglect the existing overlap in skill requirements across tasks, perhaps resulting in acquisition of narrow, task-specific skills that could hamper transfer to tasks with slightly varied characteristics. Also, the distribution of training time would then be determined by the structure of the tasks and not by the requirements of skill acquisition. This might give rise to very inefficient training programmes.

Table 3.1. Example of a task description table

Task	Input	Operation	Output
Position mapping	Instruments Environment	Matching	Updated position information
Route planning	Waypoints Outside view Tactical environment Goals (co-ordinates)	Decision making	Plan of route

The opposite approach is to describe training needs only in terms of skills. This has the risk that the acquired skills are too specifically aligned with the chosen training tasks and do not apply to the range of task variations in an operational setting.

Clearly some compromise between the opposing approaches is needed, which enables the abstraction of commonalities in skill requirements while still retaining the link with task contexts. This requires an analysis of task-skill relations given task-specific skill profiles. On this basis, a choice can be made of crucial skills to be trained with the highest priority. Consequences for later stages in the training process (in on-the-job training, for instance) can be sketched. Skill analysis in some form or another thus has to be part of the methodology for training needs analysis.

Most tasks can be viewed as drawing upon the co-ordinated deployment of multiple skills. A crucial question is to what extent tasks impose the same functional requirements and on which level of analysis the link between tasks and skills must be made, as economically as possible. To a certain extent this remains a matter of choice: the lower the level of detail of the decomposition of tasks, the smaller the number of tasks that are distinguished and the larger the number of skills that are needed to describe performance on any given task. However, in the case of a high level of decomposition, the number of skills may none the less be large, simply by breaking skills down into more detail.

Because each skill profile is described in terms of the same set of skills, skill profiles can be compared and distinguished across tasks. Thus, tasks can be compared, selected, and sorted on the basis of their skill requirements. However, as the interest is in elaborating the training need, the primary emphasis will be on skills. It should be noted that, for a particular application, the number of tasks, and consequently the number of skill profiles, may be very large. However, there will usually be considerable overlap in skill profiles across tasks. At this stage an important consideration is whether skill requirements should be aggregated across tasks or remain disaggregated. This depends on the type of skill, or more specifically on the applicability of the same skill in a class of related tasks. Transfer of training studies on skill level should provide the guidance needed at this stage of analysis.

Skill profiles have been composed on the basis of a pre-established skill taxonomy that is not likely to fit all tasks. Skill specifications may have to be adapted and differentiated in terms of the task-specific context by using context-sensitive lists. In all cases, attention has to be given to differential weights (criticality, difficulty), hierarchical skill relations (strategic, tactical, and operational) and meta-skills (knowing how to deploy skills in the context of different tasks, time-sharing, crew skills).

Almost every practical task requires a set of skills related to input processes (acquisition of information from displays and other sources), central processes (operations such as memorisation or calculation performed upon the input), and output processes (a response such as a control adjustment). However, in most instances one of these sub-skills is predominant. For example, radar monitoring draws heavily upon input (perceptual) skills, with relatively trivial central processing and output requirements; tactical decision making is essentially a central task; and steering is mainly an output task. It is therefore essential that the mapping of tasks onto skills include an indication of the importance of each sub-skill.

The 'operations' category of the task taxonomy in the MASTER Reference Framework shows high-level cognitive and psychomotor functions such as 'matching' or 'decision making'. However, effective training programme design may require identification of specific types of skill. A taxonomy of abilities/skills, consistent with the MASTER task taxonomy, was developed (Farmer *et al*, 1995).

Skills can be classified in terms of the system with which the operator must interact (e.g., 'keyboard skills'), the task that the operator must perform (e.g., 'watchkeeping') or the central nervous system (CNS) processes underlying the operator's activity (e.g., 'motor control'). The first two methods of classification are often appropriate for studies of a specific domain, such as fast jet training; however, for generic research such as that represented by MASTER, the most efficient approach is that based upon CNS processes, independent of particular systems or tasks. Such an analysis of skills (Farmer *et al*, 1995) enables a large number of military tasks to be mapped onto a set of core skills for which training must be provided. Where necessary, environmental factors associated with particular tasks should be considered: for example, a task that must be performed in an environment rich in distracting stimuli may require skills of selective attention in addition to those skills inherently related to the task.

Several methodologies have been used to analyse skill requirements of tasks. For a recent overview of existing approaches, see Ackerman and Kyllonen (1991). With respect to the study of individual differences in task performance, Pellegrino and Glaser (1979) distinguished between the cognitive correlates and the cognitive components approach.

The *cognitive correlates* approach (Hunt *et al*, 1973; Hunt & Lansman, 1975) consists of correlating task or test performance with a set of measures that presumably represents more basic information processing abilities. The resulting pattern of correlation thus provides an indication of the relative importance of these basic abilities in determining performance of the target task, and constitutes a task decomposition. The cognitive correlates approach is similar to the test-battery approach used in research on issues of selection. Of course, the method presupposes the availability of a set of 'basic' measures and capitalises on the existence of individual differences.

The *cognitive components* approach (Sternberg, 1977) consists of (1) decomposing a test or task *a priori* into more basic components or processing stages; (2) defining separate performance measures for these components or stages; and (3) correlating these performance measures with performance on the whole task or test. The cognitive component approach resembles the analysis of task performance by means of the additive factors technique (Mané *et al*, 1983); it assumes a more or less complete model of the task and, like the cognitive correlates approach, capitalises on the existence of individual differences. Thus far, both methods have been applied mainly to analyse conventional aptitude constructs, notably verbal ability (e.g., Hunt, 1978) and analogical reasoning tasks (Sternberg, 1977).

A more laborious approach is the *cognitive training* approach (Sternberg, 1984), which consists of training an experimental group on a particular component or test that is hypothesised to affect performance on a more complex task or test, and comparing the performance of this group with performance of a control group who received no training. Again, the efficiency and success of using this approach rely on the availability of a more or less complete model of the task. Also, in this case the presence and size of the effect are determined by amount of training.

All three approaches discussed above rely on a relatively complete hypothetical model of the task. Establishing such a model will be easier for tasks that are fairly simple and well researched. For more complex tasks, the formulation of a model seems less straightforward. Most realistic tasks comprise multiple components that may interact in complex ways; interactions that will not always be apparent from correlation patterns. Of course, the latter may be amended by the application of more advanced analysis techniques such as confirmatory factor analysis. However, in the skill analysis of more complex cognitive tasks, task-analytic techniques are favoured over the aforementioned experimental approaches. Generally, task-analytic techniques are based on establishing a model of task performance. For instance, such an initial model may be based on existing research findings on similar tasks, existing expertise with respect to the task, and the assumptions and intuitions of the analyst. Subsequently, records of performance of the task (e.g., verbal protocols, video-recordings, data-logs) are analysed in terms of the model; based on the extent to which it is able to provide a satisfactory account of the performance records, the model is accepted, rejected, or amended. Since the model is derived from skill assumptions underlying task performance, evaluation of the model may be construed as a skills analysis similar to the analyses provided by the approaches discussed previously.

Current Applications of Task Analysis

Descriptions of task analyses as reported in Riemersma *et al* (1997a, b) vary in emphasis and scope. Within the MASTER framework, there must be a relation of mission analysis results as input for task analysis, and the task analysis results as input for training system design. Descriptions in the literature review only implicitly refer to the wider context in which tasks have to be performed. For the design of training systems, however, task analysis has ideally explicit input in the form of the results of a mission analysis specifying the criticality, frequency, duration, conditions and required performance level. The output should be task descriptions, specific enough for the design of effective training programmes.

The underlying implicit reasoning may be that training analysis leads directly to a description of *training* tasks, which may not be the case. This depends on the identified skill requirements or capabilities and the most efficient way of acquiring these skills.

Common elements in most descriptions are the identification of goals (objectives), task behaviour, information needed for starting, executing and stopping the task, the environment or conditions, and performance standards. Crew aspects (team tasks) were addressed only in the RAFTS report (1986).

Mission and task analysis are thus in practice seldom used in a systematic way. The general impression is that they are complex and time-consuming and can be performed only by specialised personnel. Further, software tools are not yet available to overcome some of these obstacles. Yet in practice simulators are specified, training programmes developed, assessments made, feedback given and so on. How is this achieved? From the field orientations, the picture emerges that much is left to the instructors to find out the possibilities and limitations of the training devices, which were usually specified by other personnel. This decoupling of the acquisition and use of training simulators is the most obvious obstacle to the acquisition of effective training programmes and devices. The emphasis on system fidelity and the neglect of other important elements of the training environment, such as other intelligent actors, performance measurement and feedback support, networking capabilities, and instructor support, is a logical consequence of this decoupling of system and training expertise. A second profound disadvantage is the resulting lack of shared documentation.

Conclusions

Common elements of most task analysis methods and descriptions are the identification of goals (objectives), task behaviour descriptions, descriptions of information needed for starting, executing and stopping the task, descriptions of the environment or conditions, and descriptions of performance standards. Crew or team aspects have scarcely been addressed in an explicit way.

The starting point for a task analysis geared to training programme design should be the task as prescribed. This may differ from the actual task or from the task representation as it is perceived by an operator. It is clear, however, that large discrepancies between these instances have to be resolved before an effective and efficient training programme can be specified.

Task analysis usually involves some kind of decomposition. Most methods decompose relevant tasks into smaller sub-tasks, constructing hierarchies in the form of a tree or using a graph as a representational form. Although more elaborate knowledge modelling techniques can be used, in many cases some form of hierarchical task analysis may form a good starting point. For each sub-task the name and definition, the objectives, the procedures, the prerequisites and the structure of the components have to be represented.

With respect to the use of task analysis to determine training objectives, the following questions play a role: 'what level of analysis is necessary?' and 'can operator 'plans' be determined to find the relation between tasks and their sequencing?'.

The appropriate level of detail in a task analysis seems to depend upon the training objectives, the context in which the task takes place, and the discrete/continuous nature of the task. Moreover, many system functions may have to be performed continuously, producing difficulty in specifying a 'plan' describing the relationships between tasks; the timing and sequencing is likely to depend upon the situation. It may be impossible to elaborate a plan specifying the relationships between task elements and the sequencing and timing of the tasks/sub-tasks. Another problem in decomposing tasks is that, if the decomposition is to a high level of detail, the sub-tasks may be too specifically described in relation to a particular configuration of equipment in a particular system.

A popular task analysis method such as HTA does not satisfy all the task description requirements outlined in the MASTER Reference Framework. It specifies task content, but not criticality, difficulty, frequency, duration or cue indications; and the goal conditions to be achieved are not specified further, for example, than the requirement to achieve climb. Task decomposition methods may be better able to account for these variables, if sufficient categories for decomposition are created.

Failure to make explicit the exact performance goal may make it difficult later for the instructor to determine whether this goal has been reached. The failure of both types of task analysis method to focus on human abilities has also been highlighted. A special problem area is task analysis for heavily cognitive tasks, usually comprising general or specific strategies. Strategies that are used by operators to perform their tasks should be identified at different levels, general and local, because these strategies have to be taught during training. The notion of generic tasks is important if the training is focused at more general skills and not only on the performance of a specific task.

Although there are many different methods of cognitive task analysis, it often follows the same steps:

- identification of relevant tasks;
- decomposition of all selected tasks;
- acquisition of knowledge about the (decomposed) tasks and performance;
- representation of the results in a framework or model.

These steps are iterative, and do not necessarily have to be performed in a sequential order. Methodologies differ both in style and in content for the following reasons:

- the lack of standardised training needs analysis methods within both the organisation and the training profession as a whole;
- the different personalities carrying out the analyses: each analyst brings unique experience that will be reflected in the analyses performed;
- the different tasks to be analysed: training analyses for different roles within civilian and military applications have led to different methodologies being used and adapted.

In this light, it seems appropriate that, whilst it is useful to have a single methodology, it is important that some flexibility remains.

Aspects of task analysis methods important for the purposes of training programme design are:

- transfer between simulated task and real world task;
- focus on training of the task;
- results that are usable for the design of training simulators;
- functional task breakdown;
- goal oriented approach;
- cognitive skills of the operator.

Analysing errors and variations in tasks can give further valuable information that can be used in developing training linked closely to job performance in real life.

Extending task analysis methods to make them more suited to the analysis of tasks that are performed collaboratively is recommended; and more attention to tasks with a critical time element is needed. A further useful approach would be to integrate information from the literature on ability and skills (particularly taxonomies of abilities) with the task taxonomies indicated above. Carroll (1993) factor analysed most of the human cognitive ability literature and produced a definitive taxonomy of great relevance to MASTER. He placed abilities into a three-stratum hierarchy from specific to highly general, and categorised each ability into one of ten domains.

The following questions remain for further investigation:

- Is there an advantage in training at the level of psychological abilities? For example, should trainees be taught to reason deductively?
- Can taxonomies of abilities guide task analysis of cognitive skills?
- What tools can be used to tap the skills required during task performance?

4   Trainee Analysis

The output of a mission analysis consists of mission descriptions that specify the intended operational behaviour of the target system for a representative set of operational missions. Each individual mission description contains a description of, *inter alia*, the goal, the operational conditions, the mission-specific configuration of the system, the system functions, and the sequences of actions to be performed. From these descriptions is derived a list of tasks for each crew member. The output of task analysis consists of the task descriptions and skill requirements, which describe the operational behaviour of the operator or crew. Task descriptions consist of a description of the task goal, the operational task conditions, the required operator skills, and the sequences of activities (task procedures) to be performed. 'Skill' is defined as a learned capacity to perform a certain type of activity, and is thus considered to be a characteristic that enables an operator to execute a particular set of tasks.

Importance of Trainee Analysis

The skills identified during task analysis are required to perform the tasks adequately. One of the main purposes of the next step, trainee analysis, is to assess the extent to which these skills are already available in the potential candidate groups. This information is necessary to determine whether or not a training need exists, or the trainee recruitment and selection strategy to be used. The information acquired during trainee analysis is also useful during the subsequent design of the training programme (see Section II), to determine the training strategy.

Requirements for Trainee Analysis

Given the results of task analysis, the question for the organisation is: 'Do we already have the right people to perform these tasks, i.e., people who possess all the required skills?'. This question can be answered by comparing the skills of available candidates within the organisation against the skills that have been identified during task analysis. If the available skills match precisely the required skills, no *immediate* training will be required. If the prospective life cycle of the system exceeds the prospective career path of its operators, if retention of skills is problematic, or if system updates occur, then initial, refresher, continuation or conversion training will sooner or later have to be provided.

If the available skills of candidates do not match the required skills, personnel will have to be recruited and selected from within or outside the organisation. However, the required personnel may not be available in sufficient numbers either because they simply do not exist or because the organisation is not sufficiently attractive to them. If, for whatever reason, people with the required skills are not available, then there will be a training reqirement. The next issue to be resolved is then how to recruit and select people such that training costs are minimised, given the current organisational, budgetary, and technological constraints. Training costs are the costs of the training time of the trainees and the cost of all resources required for training, including instructors and their training, maintenance personnel, training materiel (procurement and maintenance costs, operational costs) and the training organisation (accommodation, management).

Training time is dependent on:

- The number of trainees: This factor interacts with the maximal trainee throughput of the training system. Mismatch between resources and number of trainees results either in idle time for the resources or idle time for the trainees.
- The learning difficulty of the skills to be acquired: Some skills take more time to learn than others. Much depends, however, on how the end-of-training criterion is defined, e.g., whether training emphasises the acquisition of 'narrow' (task-specific) skills, more generic skills, or retention of skills already acquired. It should be noted that, since learning progress follows the 'power law of practice', a law of diminishing returns, aspiring to a slightly higher level may result in a disproportionate increase in the amount of training time required to achieve that level.
- Variability in the initial skill level of trainees: Usually, the trainees with the lowest initial skill level determine total training time. However, the contribution of this factor will depend also on learning potential: if the initial skill level is low but learning potential is high, the total training time may still be relatively short.
- Variability in learning potential: Usually, the trainees with the lowest learning potential determine total training time. As noted before, the contribution of this factor will depend on skill level: if learning potential is low but initial skill level is high the required training time may still be short.

The last two factors are the major characteristics that have to be taken into account during trainee analysis.

Procedures for Trainee Analysis

With respect to procedures for trainee analysis, a distinction must be made between the purposes of selective recruitment and selection.

Selective Recruitment

The first step during trainee analysis is to identify potential groups of trainees. This can be done on the basis of analyses of people holding similar jobs or having relevant educational backgrounds. These trainees can then be compared to the required skill profiles. Because the number of tasks and, consequently, the number of skill profiles can be very large, an option is to limit the comparison to a reduced set of skill profiles, for instance by excluding skills or skill profiles that are very likely to be present or absent in the groups considered. Such a comparison may be conducted in terms of subjective assessments of the extent to which representatives of the identified trainees possess the skills that appear in the required skill profiles; e.g., in terms of percentage ratings. In rating skills it may be of interest not only to assess the average skill but also to take into account the variability of skills by estimating minima and maxima (skill range). Assessments like these may be conducted by people who are relatively familiar with these groups (e.g., school instructors, job supervisors). To check against biases in these assessments, they should preferably be made by different people so that inter-rater reliabilities can be determined.

A more objective way to proceed is to compose a set of tests that tap the skills that appear in the skill profile or specific skills of special interest. Such a set of tests can be administered to representative samples of potential applicants. It goes without saying that, although the results obtained may be more informative, this approach will be more time-consuming and more expensive. The benefits and costs of the approach that is adopted should be weighed against the benefits and costs of the alternatives to selective recruitment: selection and training.

Another option is to combine the two approaches. For instance, a global subjective assessment may be followed by a more specific and objective assessment that focuses on specific blind spots or on specific skills that have shown low inter-rater reliability. In assessing discrepancies between required and available skills, it is important to realise that skills may have to be differentiated, e.g., by applying weights according to learning difficulty, generality, or criticality.

During trainee analysis, it is also advantageous to assess other general trainee characteristics such as motivation. Such characteristics may substantially affect trainee drop-out rate and therefore total trainee throughput. Other trainee characteristics of potential relevance are intelligence, educational level, sex, age and learning experience/style. These characteristics may be used later in the selection of the training strategy, and taking them into account may substantially improve training effectiveness and reduce training costs, thereby increasing training efficiency.

During the identification and skill assessment of potential groups of trainees, it should be checked whether the groups identified can be recruited in sufficient numbers; the recruitment strategy can then be determined. On the basis of the expected results of recruitment, i.e., the expected number or trainees and their qualifications, a further selection strategy can be devised.

Selection

The purpose of selection is to select, from among the group of people who apply for training, those who possess specific critical skills identified as predictors of training success. Various selection procedures can be adopted. Their effectiveness can be compared in terms of psychometric criteria such as reliability and validity. Of course, the cost of these procedures is also an important consideration.

For the purpose of selection, a broad distinction can be made between general standardised tests and work sample tests. General standardised tests are tests that have been developed to test specific fundamental abilities or skills that are assumed to underlie performance on a variety of tasks. The best known example is the intelligence test. Examples of more specific tests are tests of divided attention, tracking, memory and reaction time. Test batteries comprise a wider range of (skill-specific) tests and thus are assumed to measure a broader range of skills. These tests are usually designed on the basis of psychological theories of human information processing and of factors underlying individual differences in performance. Originally, these were 'paper and pencil' tests; in the last few decades many have been replaced by PC-based versions.

If less is known about the skills underlying successful task performance, or if no tests are available to tap the skills assumed to determine task performance, the use of work sample tests may be considered. Work sample tests assess job-specific skills by letting subjects perform characteristic job tasks. Essentially, these tests can be regarded as measures of the amount of transfer from previous education and experience to job performance. Work sample tests have a high degree of face validity for both the subjects and the tester, but assessment is usually subjective and therefore may be less reliable. However, assessment may become more objective if work sample tests are conducted on a simulator and if the performance measurement capabilities of simulators are exploited. None the less, work sample tests are likely to remain more time-consuming and more resource-intensive than other types of tests. A frequently used option is to use standardised psychometric tests for the initial phases of selection and to use the more time-consuming and resource-intensive selection procedures during subsequent phases of the selection process, with the fewer remaining applicants.

The aforementioned types of test all yield an estimate of skill level, but do not provide information about the learning potential of trainees. As noted earlier, learning potential may be an important determinant of training time and, hence, of training costs. Learning potential can be assessed by means of trainability tests.

Selection procedures can be evaluated in terms of their predictive validity. The predictive validity of a selection procedure is the extent in which test scores correlate with the criterion to be predicted. The size of this correlation is determined by the reliability of the selection procedure and the criterion, the choice of the criterion and the characteristics of the sample (notably the amount of variance in the selection and criterion scores). It should be noted that, even when the correlation between selection and criterion scores is low, the cost savings in using the selection procedure may be so high that its use will be warranted.

The determination of an optimal selection strategy may be very time-consuming and costly. Whether or not these costs are warranted depends on the availability of applicants, the distribution of skills within the pool of applicants, and the cost of training. If there are just enough applicants, there is no point in investing much time and money in developing a selection procedure. If there are many applicants or if skill levels vary considerably, it may be more efficient to invest in the development of an efficient selection procedure, notably if training is very costly. It is not surprising that the majority of the literature on selection deals with selection in the context of military aviation.

The intended outcome of the selection procedure is a group of trainees whose skills are within the range that is assumed at the beginning of training. Selection and training serve the same goal: improving the fit of individuals to task requirements at the lowest possible costs. Ultimately, the training need is determined by the discrepancies between the required skills and the skills already available within the pool of selected applicants.

Current Applications of Trainee Analysis

Although the importance of trainee analysis is widely recognised, this topic is systematically addressed neither in research nor in practice. Most of the research effort has been devoted to selection issues; to a much lesser extent, the interaction between trainee characteristics and training and instruction strategies has been studied. An exception is the body of literature on Aptitude Treatment Interaction (ATI) and learning styles. Trainees who participate in military simulator-based training programmes may vary widely in skill profile, ranging from novices to experts and with educational levels ranging from lower vocational training to university level. Only some training programmes employ admission criteria. For flight simulators, trainees usually have some experience of flying, albeit with a simple aircraft. Most courses require general, basic military training. Few start with formal testing of baseline performance.

In most training programmes, trainee drop-out is reported anecdotally to occur fairly infrequently. However, drop-out is not systematically recorded. Often a drop-out percentage of 5% or less is reported. This percentage is very low in comparison to civil training programmes; there are several possible explanations:

- During the selection of trainees, very strict selection criteria were used so that all the trainees selected were able to succeed. For pilots, for example, only a small percentage of applicants are admitted to the training programme. As already noted, however, most training programmes do not use such strict selection criteria.
- Trainees have the opportunity to train, as long as they require, to perform up to standard. However, this situation was not encountered often in the MASTER field orientation; usually the available training time was fixed.
- The training programme is so easy, or so good, that nearly all trainees are able to succeed. This is unlikely to hold for most training programmes, which often address rather complex skills and which are usually designed and delivered by personnel who are temporarily assigned to the duty of instruction.
- In some cases, drop-out may be low because, if required, extra training time is allotted or remedial training is provided. However, these options are seldom incorporated into the training programme.
- Trainees who do not achieve mastery of the skills at the end of the training programme pass undetected. As assessment at the end of the course is often at best informal, this certainly might occur (but is difficult to substantiate).

Conclusions

The MASTER methodology provides general guidelines with respect to recruitment and selection and makes explicit the implications of selection decisions for training need identification. Such guidelines are provided in the form of a recommended procedure for conducting trainee analysis. Among other things, such a procedure provides user support (1) in composing a skill profile on the basis of the output of task analysis and selecting relevant trainee characteristics (for instance, using pre-specified checklists), (2) in using this skill profile to identify potential groups of applicants and to assess their skills, (3) in determining relevant recruitment criteria and efficient recruitment strategies, and (4) in determining relevant selection criteria and efficient selection procedures.

5   Training Analysis

Training analysis constitutes the final step of TNA. Its purpose is the definition of training needs in terms of a set of related training objectives used as the ultimate criteria for training success. As with trainee analysis, training analysis is distinguished as a separate step neither in theory nor in practice. This is not meant to imply that training objectives are not considered, but rather that the way in which they are derived is not systematically addressed and generally left obscure.

The starting point ·for the definition of a training need is the discrepancies between required and available skills. The required skills will already have been identified during task analyis, and the available skills during trainee analysis. What remains to be done is the explicit definition of what exactly has to be trained, given the discrepancies between available and required skills.

In the sense in which it is used within MASTER, a task is a requirement of behaviour. A skill is a characteristic of an individual person, a characteristic that indicates to what extent the person is able to perform a particular activity. The concepts of task and skill are related in the sense that a skill is a latent characteristic that can become manifest only in the performance of a particular task or test. The latter is the traditional means of assessing individual differences with respect to skills. Essentially, a test is a standardised task that is designed in such a way that individual differences in skill can be considered to be the primary source of differences in performance. A large number of such tests have been designed, mostly for the purpose of selection.

A skill is a learned capacity to perform a particular activity at a specified level of proficiency. The same skills can be deployed in the context of different tasks. In this sense, skill-task relations are one-to-many relations.

Training analysis is thus concerned with the specification of the training need in terms of a set of related training objectives. In essence, this specification consists of a translation of the discrepancies between required and available skills into a set of objective skill tests that, when successfully passed, provide guarantees that trainees will be able to meet operational performance requirements (as specified by the task repertoire).

Importance of Training Analysis

An accurate description of training objectives is very important because it specifies the final criterion of training and because it is the primary starting point for training programme development. Potential risks of incomplete, inaccurate, or vague training objectives are: (1) acquired skills that do not match the task requirements, (2) allocation of too much (or too little) training time, i.e., inefficient training, (3) inefficient training programme design, and (4) an inefficient training programme.

Transfer of Training

No matter how good or efficient the training programme is in achieving its training objectives, if these objectives do not match job requirements the training programme will be of no value. This is what is usually understood by 'external validity'. If the training objectives have been achieved, i.e., if training has been adequate (internal validity), their external validity can be assessed by measuring transfer (see Section IV). Considering only the effects of the definition of training objectives on transfer, the following results may be obtained: zero transfer indicates that skills have not been learned (for instance, because they were not defined as a training objective); negative transfer may indicate that the wrong skills have been learned (for instance, the wrong skills were defined as training objectives or the skills were defined in the wrong way); less than perfect positive transfer may imply that too low a standard of performance was defined by the training objectives or that training was insufficient. By maintaining the link with actual missions and tasks, the external validity of the training objectives can be kept high.

Training Time

By definition, training objectives specify the standard of performance to be achieved by training. If this standard exceeds job requirements, too much training time will be incurred. In this respect it is important to realise that the relationship between skill level (i.e. the effect of training) and training time is generally described by a power curve: as training progresses each increment in skill level requires an increasing amount of training time (the law of diminishing returns). Thus, even relatively minor over-estimation of the required standard of performance may result in a considerable increase in the amount of training time required, and hence in the cost of training. On the other hand, as already noted, setting the standard of performance too low may reduce transfer. As a consequence, operational readiness will be proportionally lower and more on-the-job training will be required before trainees become fully deployable. Of course, if there is ample opportunity to compensate for this, there is no problem. This may even allow us to 'save' on training time. It should be obvious, however, that this 'saving' is more apparent than real: training has to be continued but usually in a more inefficient way that ultimately requires more training time (the reason for training in the context of a specifically designed training programme is precisely that training can proceed more efficiently).

Training Programme Design

Too often, training objectives are formulated too vaguely. The risk of vague or ambiguous training objectives is that they may be interpreted differently by staff, instructors, and trainees. In addition, they provide insufficient guidance and constraints in focusing training programme development. The consequence may be a more time-consuming development process due to the extra iterations required to resolve ambiguities or inadequate results.

In many cases, lack of specificity is also associated with a neglect of the relations between training objectives. The deployment of skills usually occurs in relation to other skills, and always in the context of particular tasks. The set of tasks under consideration determines the nature of the skills and their relations. Different types of relation can be distinguished. These relations and contexts constrain the specification of training objectives and may also have implications for the subsequent training programme design (e.g., for sequencing of training objectives and for specifying training tasks and scenarios, as discussed in Section II).

Training objectives need to be specified such that all required skills are covered and their relations are accounted for. Thus, a training objective describes behaviour showing that the required skills have been acquired, and can be used in specified conditions leading to performance up to standards derived from the most demanding mission context.

Training Programme

The focus on required skills is essential. The alternative is to train all identified tasks under all possible operational and environmental conditions, which is usually not efficient and may be impossible. The analysis at skill level is aimed at focusing on the minimal set of tasks, and the task conditions that encompass all relevant skills at the highest level required in the task repertoire under the most demanding conditions. The assumption is that transfer to all other tasks requiring the same skills, but at a lower level and in less demanding conditions, will be almost perfect.

Requirements for Training Analysis

The starting point for the specification of training objectives is the output of task analysis and trainee analysis. The output of task analysis consists of the ordered sets of mission-related task descriptions. These task descriptions include a specification of operator functions and skills required to perform the tasks (skill profiles). The output of trainee analysis consists of skill profiles of the potential groups of applicants who may apply for training.

Procedures for Training Analysis

The first step is to delete from the skill profiles obtained from task analysis the skills that are already sufficiently mastered by the trainee groups (and not used in new ways with skills still to be gained). The result is a specification of training needs in terms of a reduced set of task-specific skill profiles.

The second step is re-ordering the task/skill profiles to select a minimal set for reworking to training objectives. Tasks that require the same types of skill can be clustered. The number of skills indicates the complexity of the task or task cluster. For each skill, relevant tasks are listed. The number of tasks indicates the generality of the skill for the domain. Tasks are then ordered in terms of the level of skill that they require. It can be assumed that ability to perform a skill at the highest level implies that all lower-level skill requirements will be met. The highest level specifies the level to be achieved by training. The associated task can be used to define the training objective for that skill.

To prevent the development of narrow skills, some level of abstraction from the specific task context is required to assure variety of practice in acquiring the skill. This can be done by considering the overlap in skills across tasks, and tasks requiring multiple skills. Training objectives should be described in such a way that they can be used as final criteria for training and should be defined in a testable form.

A training objective, according to this conception, is an operationalisation of a test item or test intended to tap a particular skill. The specification of training objectives can be viewed as the design of a domain-specific test battery. Essentially the latter is also what happens in education: educational objectives are specified in terms of tests or test items (Bloom, 1956). The foregoing implies that many of the guidelines with respect to the design of tests and test items can be used as guidelines for defining training objectives.

On the basis of analyses of links between tasks and skills, an inventory of commonalities and discrepancies in skill requirements across tasks can be compiled. These commonalities and discrepancies may be used to aggregate or disaggregate original skill distinctions. Thus, at this stage, the skill taxonomy, as developed during task analysis on the basis of the MASTER skill taxonomy, can be given a more trainee-specific interpretation, tailored to the trainees identified during trainee analysis. The way in which this should be accomplished is still the subject of study. There is a dilemma between, on the one hand, the operational relevance of training objectives and, on the other, the instructional relevance of training objectives (it could be argued that training objectives should be distinguished only if they have different implications for training and instruction).

One solution is to keep analysis and design issues separate. This may be accomplished by a) initially limiting training analysis to identifying tasks clustered according to their skill requirements, thus yielding provisional skill clusters that can be used to specify provisional training objectives, and b) introducing additional instructionally-relevant distinctions (training objectives) by returning to this step when the need arises during subsequent design steps (see Section II). Such an iterative approach may enable one to retain the links between training objectives and operational tasks and skills and, at the same time, may enable one to introduce instructionally-relevant distinctions.

Training objectives, once defined, can be evaluated and validated by testing qualified operators; for new systems, more elaborate validation test designs may be required. If such validation is too laborious or time-consuming, it can be restricted only to training objectives that affect training time or are critical for operational performance.

Frequent iterations between task, trainee, and training analysis will be required to maintain the required consistency between tasks, skills, and training objectives.

Taxonomies of Training Objectives

Several taxonomies of objectives have been developed (e.g., Bloom, 1956; Harrow, 1972). Since these taxonomies were specifically developed for educational settings, they are relatively broad and general. Given the more restricted domain of MASTER, it seems feasible to develop domain-specific taxonomies of training objectives using the skill taxonomy as a starting point. An important consideration during this development is finding a compromise between objectives that make sense from the perspective of the domain and those that have specific implications for instructional design, in the sense that they are associated with different instructional treatments (van Berlo & Verstegen, 1995). Although the MASTER methodology provides the concepts and methodology for developing these taxonomies, their development was not possible within the time and resource constraints of the project.

Current Applications of Training Analysis

Training programmes must be based on a TNA. Training objectives must be based on analysis of the tasks that the operator has to perform and on a subsequent didactic analysis. In practice, however, training objectives have often taken the form of long lists of procedures to be mastered. In other cases, training objectives were derived directly from the performance of the simulator, merely listing the procedures that could be trained with it. Elaborate task and didactic analyses and complex training schemes are seldom encountered in practice. The most widely used training principle, and often the only one applied, is sequencing training objectives from easy to complex.

In most cases, training programmes are specified directly in terms of scenarios (given the possibilities of the training simulators) rather than in terms of training objectives. These scenarios are mostly modelled as closely as possible to operational tasks and conditions. Training objectives are usually defined *post hoc* or at best in parallel with training programme development. Training objectives are often used to arrange responsibilities between training establishments and operational units or to specify training assignments for trainees, rather than as input for training programme design and the specification of training media.

Conclusions

Much has been written about the way in which training objectives should be specified and classified. However, the way in which they should be derived from the results of mission and task analyses has barely been touched upon in the literature. Clearly, this aspect deserves more attention in the future. In this chapter some suggestions have been provided with respect to how this may be accomplished. It is still an open issue whether the suggested approach is feasible and will yield useful results.

6 Discussion and Conclusions

In this section an inventory of existing methods of mission and task analysis, reported in the literature or in use by research institutes or industry, has been presented, together with findings on how these methods are used by military training institutions. The starting point was an outline of the MASTER methodology, providing a baseline for describing existing methods from the perspective of the comprehensive outline developed. In this way, discrepancies could be identified that indicated areas in which existing methods fail to elicit sufficient information for the design of training programmes.

The purpose of the field orientation in the MASTER project was to provide an inventory of current practices in mission and task analyses, which could assist the specification of the training content and the requirements for training devices. The information made available suggested that in many cases the specification of the training device and the development of the training programme were rather system-driven, i.e., guided by the technical capabilities of training systems rather than by training requirements. This may have been the reason why relatively few facilities were available to support the instructor in monitoring trainees, giving feedback and assessing their performance, and why a certain neglect of other important entities in the training environment was apparent.

In general, it was found that training device specification and procurement and training programme design were not based on explicit, systematic mission and task analyses. Rather, the training device itself was procured without much involvement of the future users, and the training programme was designed by individual instructors or a committee.

An integrated approach was lacking in almost all the training facilities visited during the field orientation of the MASTER project. Lack of co-ordination and re-use of information gathered earlier was most obvious in the lack of proper documentation for the users of the facilities. This situation can be remedied only by supporting mission and task analyses with a validated methodology and guidelines, by organisational changes in the procurement of new systems and accompanying training devices and training programmes, and by documentation geared to a succession of users of relevant information.

The effectiveness of training in terms of training time requirements and transfer to operational tasks cannot be optimised without the results of mission and task analyses. One of the main themes that emerged from the UK part of the survey was the wide variety of methodologies employed. Although most analyses had as their goal the elaboration of training objectives with respect to performance, conditions, and standards criteria, each practitioner took a slightly different approach based on the type of weapon system and user role. Despite this lack of standardisation within the training profession, there are strong generic elements present in most analyses. In most cases, the training needs analysis is derived by subtracting the current performance capability from the performance requirements (usually for a new weapon or training system). A training baseline analysis is usually the first step, conducted by means of interviews, questionnaires, or review of existing training documentation. To develop the performance requirements, a task analysis is carried out, identifying the critical training tasks, along with a trainee description. In addition, a separate analysis is often carried out to determine the training device suitability and to identify alternative or future devices. A rating of fidelity requirements is often assigned at this stage. Within the analyses, there are often differences in the level of detail focused on. For example, some analyses concentrate on the specific skills and knowledge required to fulfil a task; others take a more global approach and focus instead on an analysis of the whole job and its surrounding conditions.

Several issues were identified that may need to be considered in the development of future TNAs. Most of the current approaches appear to be non-iterative, in that training designers are often given the recommendations resulting from the analysis stage without any input to the analysis itself. This may lead to a lack of understanding by the designers of the importance of some recommendations, and may influence whether the recommendations appear in the training programme. The following are needed:

- Systematic approaches to mission and task analysis: For training programme design (including the training course syllabus), mission and task analyses as they are often performed in the design phase of a system may not be sufficiently complete or detailed. Yet re-use of the results of the design process analysis should be made possible. This information is currently usually lost, or does not become available to training device procurers and training programme designers. Ideally, in the design phase of a system the consequences of decisions for the resulting training needs and effort for the total life-cycle cost should be a design parameter; the same applies to the information gathered in the procurement phase of the training device. This information is usually not available to the instructors, and hence a mismatch between training device capabilities and requirements from the training and instruction point of view easily occurs.

- Software tools to support the analyses: The burden of performing mission and task analysis can partly be alleviated by software support tools. The need for specialised personnel depends on the amount of guidance they deliver. The users of training devices should be able to work with the support tools, thereby ensuring a closer connection between the results of mission and task analyses and the resulting training programme.

- Organisational changes in the procurement methodology: It has already been stated that system design, training device specification and training programme design should be more closely integrated. A supporting argument is that for most systems the human component rather than the technology is the limiting factor. System performance can no longer be predicted on the basis of hardware and software alone; and the amount and way of training the human component are decisive for overall performance.
- Enhanced flexibility, enabling adaptation to changing needs: A finding of the field orientation was low flexibility to adapt training devices and training programmes. The result was often a mismatch between operational system and training device and programme, leading to low transfer of training. This problem could be alleviated by a transparent design methodology, modular approach, standardisation, and consideration of foreseen future developments.

Even if these suggestions are pursued, the required effort in performing mission and task analyses remains substantial. This has to be weighed against the benefits to be gained in several areas:

- Specification of training simulators: Although most interviewees in the field orientation wanted full-fidelity simulators as training devices, such fidelity can never be reached. For example, there are limitations in the way system dynamics or the behaviour of intelligent simulated opposing forces can be simulated. Trainees may thus gain a false impression of the system behaviour and capabilities (cf. the unrealistically high hit rate using the Talissi-Dragon simulator) or acquire skills that do not transfer to the real system (e.g., gunnery tracking in the first Leopard 2 simulator, as described by Jorna, 1988). Without a thorough mission and task analysis, such problems are not easily detected in the specification phase; even worse, possible approximations of reality that could reduce training device costs considerably cannot be traded off against expected loss of training effectiveness.
- Valid assessment during training: The method most often encountered is an unstructured assessment by the instructor. The assessment is very subjective, and the trainee depends on the instructor not only for a fair judgement but also for informative evaluation of the training session to allow improved performance in the future. The simulator can support a much more structured and standardised approach: when measurable criteria are derived from the results of mission and task analysis, the performance of trainees might be measured, evaluated and logged by the system. In some cases assessment might be fully automated; in others the instructor might be further supported by checklists and easily available performance measures. Such evaluation is also useful for allocating total training time to tasks and skills that have been specified and prioritised in the mission and task analysis.
- Effective feedback during training: Performance monitoring and measurement might be automated to some extent. It might be possible to provide some feedback automatically, e.g., on frequent and easily detectable procedural errors. In other cases, the instructor might be supported by information about students and their performance on certain tasks. Appropriate performance measures and methods of feedback will be partly dependent on detailed accounts of the tasks and even the

missions from which they were extracted. Either way, the trainee can be monitored more closely and receive informative feedback more quickly.

- Define crew training: Training programme design still focuses excessively on the individual operator to be trained, at the expense of the team context in which most military tasks are executed in a co-ordinated and inter-dependent way. Only by performing a thorough mission analysis can this wider context be described and the training needs formulated. For team or crew training, the interaction between team members could be monitored and feedback given addressing team performance.

- Provide the basis for the design of training programmes and scenarios: Results of mission and task analyses are useful in defining representative scenarios and the design of training programmes. The use of standard training programmes and scenarios will lighten the task of the instructor during training, allowing him to focus on monitoring and feedback. Facilities should allow quick and easy change of scenarios and development of new scenarios, e.g., adapted to certain missions and encompassing the naturally occurring variability in circumstances and conditions.

One of the issues for future work and discussion may be how to determine the level of mission and task analysis required. This depends in turn on whether more detailed information is necessary for training, and also whether such information can be effectively used, given present training tools and taking into consideration the cost/benefit trade-off of such training. Particular attention should be given to developing effective methods of specifying a 'plan' within task-analytic techniques.

Section II
Training Programme Design

7   Introduction

In this introductory chapter, a preliminary characterisation of simulator-based training is provided, and the main issues with respect to such training are outlined. Against this background, several reasons for the importance of Training Programme Design are discussed. The relation between Training Needs Analysis and Training Programme Design is elaborated. The chapter concludes with an overview of the contents of this section.

Simulator-Based Training and Instruction

With advances in simulation technology, an increasing amount of training and instruction is delivered on training simulators rather than the real system. The most important practical reasons for using training simulators are that many skills required during the execution of operational tasks cannot be trained on the real system, because:

- it is too dangerous (e.g., training of emergency procedures);
- the necessary conditions are not available (e.g., for training desert operations in The Netherlands);
- there are insufficient opportunities to train on the real system:
    a. it is too expensive (e.g., due to the expenditure of fuel or ammunition or due to the increased wear and tear incurred during training);
    b. there is insufficient time available on the real system (e.g., due to maintenance duties and/or because of operational deployment);
    c. the circumstances required for training do not occur frequently enough;
    d. the possibilities for training are restricted by environmental regulations related to noise, pollution, and so on;
    e. safety regulations preclude the execution of particular tasks or manoeuvres, such as high-speed car pursuit.

Unfortunately, there are limitations to what can be simulated. These limitations may reduce the perceived realism (face validity) of a training simulator, and hence its acceptance as a training device by trainees and instructors. Also, apart from user acceptance, these limitations may reduce or impede the transfer of skills from the training simulator to the real system. In addition, the cost of training simulators may be very substantial. Procurement costs of training simulators may exceed the procurement costs of the real system (for a driving simulator this is almost certainly true, but in general the costs depend mainly on the functionality that the simulator provides); the same applies to the costs of operating and maintaining training simulators. For this reason, much effort is being invested in investigating ways of optimising the benefit/cost ratio of training simulators (Orlansky, 1989; Boldovici, 1987). However, it should be noted that empirical benefit/cost studies are relatively rare. Most of the studies that are reported in the literature focus on issues of fidelity, i.e., the extent to which the behaviour of the simulator mimics the behaviour of the operational system.

The comparison and assessment of the results of these studies are complicated by several factors, the lack of consistency in the definition of fidelity being the most prominent. In particular, older studies and engineering-based approaches (e.g., Allen *et al*, 1986; Thomson, 1989) apparently fail to appreciate the fact that it is not the fidelity of the simulator that is the goal of simulation but the efficient transfer of training. Although these goals are certainly related, they are by no means identical (Lintern *et al*, 1989). After reviewing the available literature, Korteling *et al* (1997) proposed the following subdivision of the term fidelity: *physical fidelity* (simulator behaviour as specified by the mathematical model, including face validity), and *psychological* or *functional fidelity* (pertaining to the similarity of trainee behaviour on the simulator and on the real system). In some cases, then, it is clearly suboptimal to strive for high physical fidelity in simulation (Lintern *et al*, 1989; Patrick, 1992). The level of physical fidelity needed to achieve functional fidelity is related to the type of task to be trained, proficiency level, the difference between criterion performance and maximum performance (Boer, 1991a, b), and, last but not least, didactic factors.

Didactic Aspects of Simulator Training

Apart from the aforementioned practical reasons for using training simulators, there are also specific didactic reasons for using training simulators instead of the real system:

- control of the type and timing of training events that are presented and, hence, the learning experiences that are offered to the trainee(s). This enables the provision of more learning experiences per unit of time and the planned distribution of learning experiences;
- adapting the training task to the performance of the trainee(s);
- providing augmented cueing and feedback, i.e., cues and feedback extrinsic to the (training) task;
- registering and diagnosing trainee performance, e.g., for debriefing and/or administrative purposes;
- automating the process of training and instruction and consequently improving efficiency.

Compared to research on simulator fidelity, much less research effort is being invested in investigating the possibilities for exploiting the didactic possibilities that training simulators may offer. As noted earlier, the design and interpretation of simulator studies is usually construed in terms of the effect of different levels of fidelity on transfer. In most of these transfer studies, an experimental group of subjects that is trained on a simulator is compared with a control group that is trained by conventional means (on the real system). Many transfer studies confound the effect of fidelity with the effect of training programme. Not only is the experimental group trained on a different system, but also the way in which trainees are trained differs qualitatively from the way in which trainees are conventionally trained. This potential confounding means that the results of such studies are difficult to interpret and permit only relatively crude assessments (e.g., are the results obtained with simulator-based training similar to those associated with conventional training, or does simulator-based training result in cost savings?). One might argue that knowledge about training and instruction factors that determine training effectiveness is a prerequisite for progress in research on the relation between simulator fidelity and transfer.

Another, and perhaps even more important, reason for being interested in the relation between training effectiveness and training and instruction factors is that, to a large extent, these latter factors determine training effectiveness and efficiency independently of the medium that is used for training. Given the same training simulator, training results may differ widely depending on the way in which the training programme has been designed and delivered. In this respect, the way in which instructional support is implemented (Polzella, 1983) is also an important determinant of training effectiveness and efficiency. Currently, the instructional support that is provided ranges from no support to instructor-controlled monitoring and control facilities; semi-automated facilities are still relatively rare.

A major problem in designing effective training programmes is that the knowledge base with respect to training and instruction is not well organised and suffers from a lack of theoretical cohesion (van Rooij *et al*, 1995, 1997a). Most of the guidelines that are encountered in the literature are formulated rather generally, although they have been developed in the context of specific tasks. This renders it difficult to apply them. Another major problem is that most of the research focuses on individual performance and skill acquisition in the context of relatively simple, well-structured tasks. In particular, there is a paucity of research on the integration of skills, e.g., part-task training of time-sharing skills or the acquisition of team skills.

High-performance Skills

The most critical skills trained with the aid of training simulators are skills required for the performance of so-called high-performance tasks. These tasks are defined as complex, time-critical tasks where the operator is in the primary control loop of the system (cf. Schneider, 1985). Most vehicle control tasks conform to this definition. An example is piloting a combat helicopter. The time-critical aspect derives from the fact that the system to be controlled is dynamic and operates in a dynamic and often dangerous or hostile environment. The complexity of these tasks resides in the number of, and interactions between, multiple requisite skills that typically require time-sharing with subsidiary procedural and cognitive skills in addition to perceptual-motor skills.

One of the training characteristics of these skills is that many people fail to develop proficiency, so that selection is often required. Even after selection, the training duration required to reach an operational level of performance may be considerable. Typically, there are large differences between novice, advanced, and expert operators, both quantitatively (speed and accuracy of performance) and qualitatively (use of different strategies).

In practice, simulator-based training of high-performance skills usually proceeds in interaction with a training scenario and under the close supervision of an instructor. This approach to instruction is frequently referred to as 'apprenticeship instruction' (Schank & Jona, 1991). Training scenarios are usually composed by the instructors on the basis of more or less typical real-life conditions and events, and are presented from simple/elementary to more complex/demanding. Most instructors are experienced operators who are assigned to the duty of instruction.

The Importance of Training Programme Design

Usually operational requirements are translated rather directly into simulator requirements. There are several reasons why it may be advantageous to insert the specification of training programme requirements as an intermediate step:

- There is usually a relatively large gap between the global level at which operational requirements have been specified and the high level of detail of technical simulator requirements. This may render it difficult to provide sufficient underpinning of simulator requirements. Where budgets are under pressure, this may be a significant drawback.
- For the training of many skills, only particular types of cue and/or a limited level of cueing fidelity is (minimally) required. To be able to assess which skills can, and which cannot, be trained given particular types of cue and cueing fidelity, the nature of the skills that are to be trained must be specified in sufficient detail.
- For training purposes it may be more effective or efficient to provide extra cues and feedback, i.e., information unavailable under operational conditions. The need for or possibility of providing such information can be identified only on the basis of a specification of appropriate training and instruction strategies.
- A specification of training and instruction strategies is also required to be able to specify instructional facilities that are required to author, deliver, and evaluate training.
- An accurate specification of what and how to train is also required to be able to choose between alternative training media and to assess whether the projected training and training media meet existing logistic and organisational criteria, resources, and constraints.

Training Needs Analysis and Training Programme Design

During Training Needs Analysis, the training need is specified in terms of a set of related training objectives that specifies the desired outcomes of the training programme; in other words, the criteria against which the training programme will be evaluated. The effectiveness and efficiency of training are determined to a large extent by the results of Training Needs Analysis. For instance, if particular tasks have been overlooked during TNA, the prerequisite knowledge and skills for those tasks will not be acquired. Also, if the performance standards have been set too high or too low, the amount of training will in turn be too high or too low, and hence training will be less efficient. The results of TNA also comprise a specification of the entry level of prospective trainees. Again, much of the effectiveness and efficiency of training depends on the comprehensiveness and specificity of this information. Desirable properties of a training programme are that learning processes proceed smoothly and quickly; that the acquired knowledge and skills transfer readily from training to operational conditions; and that the knowledge and skills are retained well, even over long periods of non-use. Unfortunately, trying to design a training programme that meets all three criteria may lead to conflicts. For instance, varied practice is conducive to better transfer of acquired knowledge and skills to operational conditions, but this inevitably requires more training time. Similarly, overlearning (continuing training after training criteria have been achieved) furthers retention of skills but again requires more training time.

The outcome of Training Needs Analysis does not specify *how* the criterion levels of performance must be achieved given the entry levels of prospective trainees. In principle, there may be many ways that ultimately lead to a satisfactory result, but they may not be equally desirable or feasible. In practice, many factors constrain the feasibility of particular training options. Often the time available is limited and training periods have to fit within particular schedules determined by the number of people to be trained and the time they have available. Also, the means available for training may limit training options. For instance, there may be only a fixed number of instructors and a fixed set of training facilities and no budget for procuring additional training media. In cases where there is a budget, there will always be limits to what can be procured.

In short, compromises have to be made, and two extreme strategies can be distinguished. One is first to specify what one would consider optimal and only afterwards look at what is feasible. The risk of such a need-driven strategy is that much time may be spent on a design that is simply not feasible. Another approach is first to determine the constraints that are applicable and then try to fit the design to these constraints. The risk of this constraint-driven strategy is that much time may be spent on designing a training programme that is feasible but not effective.

Of course, both strategies represent extremes on a continuum that ranges from exclusively need-driven to exclusively constraint-driven. As already noted, there may be more than one way to meet a particular training need. For each alternative, different constraints or trade-offs may apply. Also, the constraints that are applicable may become apparent only during the design process. In practice, training programme design is a process during which training programme requirements are gradually elaborated in a top-down fashion. During this process, earlier design decisions will often be revised to accommodate or consider new or alternative design options or constraints.

Section Overview

In the remainder of this section the state of the art with respect to training and instruction will be reviewed. This review is selective in the sense that it addresses only those topics relevant to issues involved in the design of simulator-based training and instruction.

Chapter 8 (Current Practices) gives a review of current practices with respect to the development and procurement of training simulators, and the design, implementation, and delivery of simulator-based training programmes.

In Chapter 9 (Principles of Training and Instruction), it is argued that current practices partly reflect ideas about how training should be conducted and organised and partly result from lack of knowledge with respect to principles of training and instruction. In this chapter, some of these ideas are critically reviewed. Subsequently, an overview is given of current theory and research with respect to training and instruction. This overview sets the stage for more in-depth coverage of some of the main issues that are considered particularly relevant for the design of simulator-based training and instruction, viz. the sequencing of training objectives, the specification of training activities and scenarios, and the design of instruction.

In Chapters 10 through 12, ideas and findings with respect to each of these issues are examined in more detail. Chapter 10 (Sequencing of Training Objectives) contains a description of current ideas and findings with respect to the issue of how training objectives may be sequenced and elaborated into a comprehensive training trajectory. Chapter 11 (Specification of Training Activities and Scenarios) contains a description of ideas and findings concerning methods of designing training activities and scenarios, given a particular training trajectory and given particular types of training objectives. In Chapter 12 (Design of Instruction), options for the design of instruction are reviewed.

In Chapter 13 (Methodology for Training Programme Design), an attempt is made to integrate the results and conclusions of previous chapters into a common framework, viz. a methodology for training programme design. The chapter concludes with a summary of the development efforts that took place within the context of the MASTER project.

In Chapter 14 (Optimisation of Training Programmes), the role of evaluation in the context of training programme development is discussed. It is argued that the design of any training programme is (or at least should be) only the first phase of a more comprehensive iterative process of evaluation and modification.

Chapter 15 (Discussion and Conclusions) concludes this section on Training Programme Design by considering relevant future developments. The main issues for further research and development are also identified in the context of the proposed methodology.

8 Current Practices

Field Orientation

In the literature there is a paucity of data on the development and procurement of training simulators and on the design and implementation of simulator-based training programmes. Therefore, in the MASTER project a field orientation was performed to provide an inventory of current practices in developing simulator-based training programmes and in the delivery of instruction. To this end, MASTER contributors visited a number of training establishments and administered questionnaires to personnel involved in simulator-based training, in most cases instructors. The main issues addressed by the questionnaires were: the role of simulators in overall training; the selection and characteristics of trainees; the selection and responsibilities of the instructors; the composition of training sessions; the role of feedback and assessment; the transfer and retention of knowledge and skills; the facilities available to support the instructors; the development and/or procurement of the simulator; the limitations of the simulator; and expected future developments.

In addition to the results of the field orientation, the contents of this chapter draw heavily upon the authors' consultancy and research experience in many simulator projects.

Training Programme Requirements and Simulator Requirements

Human factors issues are increasingly recognised as important during system design. However, in practice training requirements are typically not considered a major focus during system design, despite the fact that training costs constitute a substantial proportion of the total life-cycle costs of most man-machine systems. In cases where training requirements are taken into account, assessments are relatively crude and non-specific. One major reason for this neglect of training issues is the lack of methodologies for systematically listing the training (and cost) implications of design alternatives. Consequently, when a system becomes operational, operators may have to learn knowledge and skills that are more difficult to acquire and to retain, and hence require more and/or more costly training than would be necessary for another, operationally equivalent, design.

Similarly, during system procurement, training requirements are not a major focus. The specification of system requirements is typically driven by the operational goals that the system is to accomplish. These goals are determined by operational personnel, not those involved in training. Operational staff are often unaware of the importance of taking training requirements into account, their main concern being to acquire the best *operational* system the available budget allows for. Thus, for people involved in system procurement, training is not a major issue, and may not be an issue at all. Moreover, the responsibility for training usually rests with a separate department with its own budget. There may sometimes even be biases against the procurement of simulators, for instance, because of fear of reduction of flight hours. This lack of concern with the requirements of training may have considerable financial, logistic, and *operational* consequences. For instance, once the contract for procuring a particular system has been signed, the manufacturer of the system may have a monopoly on much of the information and material required to develop the necessary training facilities (e.g., the simulator model required to develop a simulator).

Even when the need for a training simulator is indisputable, there may be a neglect of training programme requirements during simulator development and procurement. Frequently, operational requirements are translated rather directly into simulator requirements, the main consideration being how to achieve the highest possible level of simulation fidelity given the available budget.

One reason for this neglect is that the personnel involved in designing the simulator are those who built the operational system. For them, the most straightforward way to build a simulator is to stay close to the system requirements. Where simulator developers have not been involved in building the operational system, they tend to be technologically oriented and, more specifically, oriented towards the technology that they know best or to which they have access. Another reason is that customers are usually either operational staff who are strongly biased towards operational fidelity, or those with a technical background. Strange though it may seem, instructors are often not involved in the development and/or procurement of the simulator. This may account for the general lack of instructional facilities. Parenthetically, it should be noted that for new systems there is generally a lack of operational and training experience. Even if such experience is available and instructors are involved in the procurement process, this does not guarantee that all pertinent training programme requirements are taken into account. Instructors are mostly experienced operators assigned to the duty of instruction. Even if they have simulator experience they may be biased towards 'their' training programme and they may have learned to 'work around' the limitations of the simulator to which they are accustomed. In other words, even if expertise in simulator training is available, this expertise may be limited, highly specific, and/or biased. Thus, in many cases, even the involvement of instructors in simulator development and procurement provides few guarantees. Instructors frequently have little or no didactic background, and are often unaware of the possibilities offered by state-of-the-art simulation and instructional technology.

In cases where fidelity is the main consideration, the issue to be resolved during procurement becomes how to achieve the highest level of fidelity given the available budget, and attention focuses on the main cost drivers. Another reason for the emphasis on cost drivers is that procurement costs are much easier to specify than benefits. As a result, issues easily become misconstrued and overly simplified, e.g. 'do we need a motion platform?' or 'do we need a simple or an advanced image system?'.

As noted in the Introduction, there are several reasons for considering training programme requirements prior to the specification of simulator requirements. However, it is not unusual for the decision to procure a simulator to be made prior to the analysis and specification of training needs and the design of training programmes, and without consideration of other available options for training. Such decisions may simply be based on the fact that simulators exist or that other system users also use a simulator for their training.

The Design of Simulator-Based Training Programmes

System procurement usually precedes simulator procurement. Thus, systems may be introduced into the organisation before the simulator is available. This implies that emergency measures are required to ensure that people are trained. In such cases, one option is to contract out training to other training establishments or to use the training facilities of other organisations. Even if possible, these options are likely to be quite expensive. A problem is that the system that is procured is often leading edge, and appropriate training programmes or training facilities are unavailable. Sometimes training facilities may have to be used that do not correspond to one's own system, for instance, because they represent an older or a different version. It is obvious that this may create transfer problems.

Simulator procurement may be a lengthy process if only because the amount of money involved necessitates adherence to formal and time-consuming procurement procedures. In addition, the specification of simulator requirements may take much time. One frequently adopted shortcut is the use of existing simulator specifications, e.g., previous specifications or specifications from other training establishments. Another option is simply to buy 'off-the-shelf' or to buy what others use.

All too frequently, the design of the training programmes starts only after the simulator is delivered. Hence, the training programme is fitted to the simulator instead of vice versa. Only after the training programme has been developed may it become apparent that some skills cannot be trained adequately and ways have to be devised to work around these limitations. Naturally, in these cases it may take a considerable additional amount of time before the simulator can be used.

The design of the training programme is usually the responsibility of subject matter experts. For new systems, there is often little or no training expertise available. In such cases, recourse to experts from other organisations is necessary, or a 'train-the-trainer' approach may be used to bootstrap the requisite expertise within one's own organisation. There is frequently considerable time pressure to start training and hence to complete the design of the training programme; sometimes parts of the training programme become operational as soon as they are available. In many cases, there is no systematic approach to training programme design, and instructors use whatever information is at hand. This information is frequently limited to technical documentation of the system and the simulator. Instructors have to learn to operate the simulator; typically, they undergo an industry course that familiarises them with the simulator but is too limited to allow them to become proficient users. Thus, designing training programmes and learning to operate the simulator may occur in parallel. Once the training programme has been finalised, modifications are common. Often these changes are made on an *ad hoc* basis and remain undocumented.

Despite the aforementioned complications and obstacles, most instructors consider their simulator an effective training medium. However, it should be noted that, due to a general lack of systematic and explicit evaluation, they have little evidence to substantiate these claims.

Some instructors are dissatisfied with the level of fidelity offered by the system, and the available facilities to create or modify scenarios, provide an overview during training sessions, record and replay the trainees' performance, or simulate other actors in the scenarios. The documentation for the training programme is sometimes also considered unsatisfactory. Many of the simulators that were visited during the MASTER project are quite old and are scheduled to be replaced within five years. With respect to replacement, there seem to be two opposing trends: the acquisition of technologically more advanced and more comprehensive high fidelity systems, on the one hand, and the acquisition of simple, low-fidelity, and mobile simulators on the other.

Characteristics of Simulator-Based Training Programmes

Training Goal and Simulator Fidelity

The required fidelity of the simulator depends on the goal of training. Typically, a high level of fidelity is demanded when the goal of simulator training is to practise tasks that cannot be practised in the field because they are too dangerous, too expensive, or threatening to the environment. Flight simulators, for example, provide the opportunity to practise emergency procedures. In tactical training, trainees learn to apply command procedures and combat techniques that are used only in times of war. Some forms of target acquisition, e.g., launching ground-to-air missiles, provide another example: the real weapon can only rarely be fired in field exercises because missiles and the associated targets are too expensive. Here, simulator training takes the place of practice in the real task environment, i.e., training with the simulator is the only opportunity to practise certain parts of tasks. Thus, it is of the utmost importance that training be adequate and complete, that the simulator provide an environment that caters for all situations, and that it conform as closely as possible to the envisaged operational reality.

A moderate level of fidelity is deemed sufficient when simulator training is meant to replace only a part of the field exercises. A helicopter simulator, for example, can be used by pilots to maintain their skills when they cannot complete enough flight hours in the helicopter. In this case, no great difficulty is experienced if some aspects cannot be trained adequately with the simulator, because they can be trained in the real task environment. In a helicopter simulator without an image system, for example, one can practise only IFR flight; VFR flight can be practised in the real helicopter.

A relatively low level of fidelity will suffice if the simulator is used merely as a training opportunity to prepare for training in the real task environment. In the simulator of a frigate command centre, for example, trainees learn the basic aspects of the command & control system and the procedures to be applied. They continue their training in the real task environment, applying the acquired skills on board. In these cases, initial training is conducted with the simulator for reasons of efficiency: often, initial training with a simulator is far more efficient than training on the job. Because the trainees will train in the real task environment in the later stages of training, it is acceptable that the simulator cannot fully simulate the real systems. A low-fidelity or part-task simulator may suffice for this purpose.

Some trainers are generic, which means that they do not simulate a particular weapon system. For example, tactical trainers are not limited to a specific vehicle type. Flight simulators and driving simulators, on the other hand, are used for only one type of system. In generic trainers, a balance has to be found between generality and fidelity. For example, a tank commander who trains in a tactical trainer has to learn the general procedures for all tank units, but must be able to recognise enough of the situation in the real tank that he or she commands.

The Place of Simulators in the Training Curriculum

Simulators are used to train a wide variety of tasks, ranging from tank driving to command & control, and they also differ widely in complexity and fidelity. Training simulators are used to train at initial, intermediate, and advanced levels, including refresher training. Depending on the tasks to be trained, the trainees may be individuals or crews, varying in experience and prior education. Often there are some admission requirements; formal testing of entry levels, however, rarely occurs. This, of course, renders it difficult or impossible to assess training gains. In most cases dropout rates are not officially recorded, but they are anecdotally reported to be about 5%. This seems extremely low, even if one takes into account the effect of selection. Due to problems in recruiting sufficient personnel, especially in the military, these low dropout rates may be due to some extent to pressures to retain personnel.

Initial training (i.e., acquiring basic knowledge or learning simple procedures) is usually provided by instructors in a classroom or a briefing, or by the study of textbooks. For example, trainees may go to the simulator cockpit with a book indicating the function of the different buttons. In other training programmes, cardboard replicas and flight cards are used to teach operational procedures and the location of the instruments. Initial instruction is rarely supported by a full-task simulator or an associated form of computer-assisted learning. Part-task simulators are sometimes used for initial training in training programmes, in which many different (sub)tasks have to be trained.

Simulators are sometimes used in the initial phases of training a new task or for refresher training. In initial courses, the simulator-based training can be combined with other teaching methods. Often, the course starts with theory taught in the classroom followed by practice with the simulator. After the course the trainees sometimes go to a military range or take part in a field exercise to consolidate the new skills in a more realistic setting. They may simply go to an operational unit to perform their job (or continue with other courses). They often, but not always, come back regularly for refresher training with the simulator to keep the acquired skills up to criterion level.

Many simulators are used for training at all levels. Sometimes the training programme is the same for beginners and experienced operators; sometimes scenarios of different levels of difficulty are available. In the early stages of learning, the trainees have to learn how to perform the components of the task and to learn a sequence of actions. Especially when the task is complex, the most desirable way would be to train the parts of the task step by step until they have been mastered, raising the complexity gradually during training. Practising a certain task in a large variety of situations (i.e., different scenarios) is a suitable training method for more experienced trainees and for refresher training of already acquired skills.

Individual and Crew and Unit Training

Depending on the task, simulators provide training for individuals and crews. Sometimes simulators are used for both: for example, a helicopter simulator can be used to train an individual pilot or a pilot and co-pilot. Some simulators, such as tactical trainers, require a crew. Just as with simulators for individual training, crew trainers provide an opportunity to practise in different circumstances (scenarios), but they often do not support the instructional process itself, i.e., many unit trainers lack the necessary facilities for training teams. Usually one or more instructors have to coach all the team members without additional system support. In many cases, the instructors are standing or seated next to or behind the trainees. However, if the crew is located in a cabin it is often not possible to monitor crew interaction directly.

Training and Instruction Strategies

Responsibility for simulator-based training rests with the instructor (the most common situation), the unit commander, or the trainees themselves. Where the unit commander is responsible, the instructors take the role of system manager, providing training facilities and support for the commander. This is most often the case in tactical trainers. Where trainees themselves are responsible (for example, fighter pilots engaged in recurrence training) the instructor also assumes the role of system manager and training administrator, providing the opportunity to train, to receive feedback and to keep track of training results and training hours.

In practice, the design of training scenarios is the responsibility of instructors. In some cases, scenarios are based on training objectives derived from a task analysis. Usually, the design of training scenarios is determined by the technical possibilities of the simulator, and the scenarios are simplified/adapted versions of operational scenarios. Typically, a limited set of basic scenario variants is employed. These variants may be modified during scenario execution to adapt training to the performance of the trainees.

Training scenarios are scheduled in terms of training sessions, which often have a fixed duration. To give some rough indications:

- flight simulators: 1-2 hours;
- gunnery simulators: 20-30 minutes;
- tactical trainers: sessions lasting up to a day.

Most simulator sessions require a high level of concentration; scenarios often have many events that call for timely and accurate responses. This means that training sessions cannot last for many hours. Most simulators do not induce high stress conditions directly. However, high workload may occur, and this may cause stress for the trainees.

Training scenarios may be more or less complex, and for difficult scenarios the design process is a specialised job. Also, depending upon the complexity and the difficulty of managing the scenario, during scenario execution instructors may be assigned exclusively to the duty of managing or participating in the scenario.

Instruction, feedback and assessment are usually the responsibility of the instructors. In many cases, the training procedures to be used are not explicitly specified. Therefore, the quality of training is difficult to assess and depends heavily on the capabilities of the instructor. Another drawback is that expertise is lost when the instructor receives another job assignment. Due to the job rotation system used in most military services, this occurs relatively frequently and often so abruptly that there is little or no opportunity to transfer expertise to successors.

Scenarios are presented in a fixed order, usually from easy to difficult. A more complex scenario is presented when the instructor thinks that the trainees have mastered the procedures taught in the simpler ones. Further adaptation to the individual performance of trainees is generally not possible. Sometimes trainees have some freedom in choosing what to train. For example, experienced pilots can ask to train some specific scenarios or procedures during a session. Sometimes scenarios are written or adapted to prepare for a particular field exercise or for a mission (mission rehearsal). This entails, for example, training with specific maps or weather conditions. Providing for such just-in-time training opportunities requires a number of flexible design facilities that most simulators do not yet possess.

Trainee Assessment and Evaluation of Training Programmes

Assessment is the term used for the procedures applied to determine whether individual trainees have achieved their learning goals. Obviously, a prerequisite for assessment is the availability of criteria. During the field orientation, however, situations were encountered in which the criteria were not related to the task to be taught or were even completely absent. In other cases, the criteria were not measurable, or unclear or intractable weighting rules were applied to determine the trainee's final grade from several performance measures. Four different types of assessment methods were encountered:

Self-assessment In some cases the instructors do not assess the performance of the trainees: the latter have to judge whether their performance is up to standard from the feedback provided by the system. No training programme was encountered in which trainees explicitly and systematically discussed their own experiences. Sometimes no assessment at all took place.

Unstructured instructor assessment In this approach no checklists or formal, measurable criteria are available. The instructor merely offers his or her impression of the trainee's performance. For example, flight simulators often do not provide a formal assessment; the instructor tells the trainee what could have been done better. If the commander of a unit is responsible for a training session, assessment takes the form of debriefing after the session. The commander gives his or her opinion about the exercise. Unstructured assessment by the instructor is a very common method, used for example with tactical trainers. Even when facilities for assessment are available, they are sometimes ignored and substituted by or combined with the subjective judgement of the instructor(s).

Structured instructor assessment   Using this method, the instructor keeps the scores, for example by using a checklist or a rating scale. Special test scenarios can be run on the simulator. The instructor might base his judgement on measurements or information that the system provides, such as the output of the Instructor Operator Station (IOS).

Simulator assessment Here, the simulator provides scores for the different sub-tasks and/or an overall score for the performance of the trainee. For example, some simulators systematically score and record several aspects of task performance. The scoring system is usually rather simple, such as gunnery trainers giving a hit rate. None of the simulators that were visited had a more advanced assessment system. There is a requirement for more possibilities for assessment of processes and not only of outcomes, and for assistance in the assessment of soft skills and not only of hard skills such as hit rates. For the assessment of team/unit skills, no system assistance has yet been developed.

Training Programme Evaluation

Typically, the final assessment of the trainees' performance is the subjective opinion of the instructor, and no systematic procedures are available for evaluating the effectiveness of training programmes. At best, instructors receive some incidental feedback from operational units.

The skills acquired by the trainee have to be retained for a longer period of time and should transfer to the real task. In most cases, no formal evaluation studies have been conducted with regard to the transfer of the learned skills to the job environment or with regard to retention of skills. Consequently, few or no data are available on the retention of the learned skills and on the transfer of skills to the real task environment, and so it is difficult to determine how effective training programmes actually are. One of the findings of the field orientation is that it is difficult formally to establish the effectiveness of the training programmes. The learning gains of the simulator cannot be measured because there are often no tests upon entering and exiting the training programme. Instructors claim that almost all trainees reach a criterion level of performance, but the assessment at the end of training is often lacking or rather subjective.

Instructor Tasks and Qualifications

In many instances, the instructors are responsible for all tasks regarding the simulator, viz. developing or revising the training programme, delivering training and instruction, and conducting management, administrative, and maintenance duties. Instructors are selected for their experience and/or didactic qualities. They usually undergo basic didactic training but learn to teach with the specific simulator 'on the job', coached by fellow instructors. Instructors build up a lot of expertise, but this is not always documented or recorded. Even when there is an instructor syllabus, much knowledge is left implicit and is not documented.

9   Principles of Training and Instruction

Introduction

To a large extent, many of the problems identified in the previous chapter require organisational solutions. Clearly, many problems also originate in a lack of knowledge concerning effective specification of training requirements. And the way in which training is organised reflects the military training philosophy. The term 'training philosophy' refers to a related set of assumptions, conceptions, and guidelines used implicitly or explicitly in organising and designing training. In what follows, the main emphasis will be on the military training philosophy, elements of which can also be encountered in other domains of professional training.

The 'Train Like you Fight' Doctrine

The dominant military training philosophy can be succinctly summarised in the adage 'train like you fight': the way in which people are trained and the way in which training is organised should correspond as closely as possible to operational practices. This notion is reflected in a number of related ideas frequently encountered in practice. Some of these ideas and their consequences are briefly reviewed below:

The way in which training is organised should be modelled on the way in which operational units are organised Training constitutes a part of system development. System development and system deployment have different objectives and require different types of organisation and procedure. For example, system development requires continuity, whereas system deployment requires operational flexibility. By requiring the training organisation to be as flexible as the operational organisation, continuity may be compromised; e.g., job rotation may be a good principle for operational units but is often highly wasteful of training resources.

The commander is operationally responsible and therefore should also be responsible for the content of, the amount of, and the approach to training This idea confuses operational responsibility with the responsibility for training. The commander is responsible for the performance of the members of his unit. Given this responsibility, he should provide them with sufficient opportunities for training. This does not imply that he should also dictate the content of, the amount of, and the approach to training. This idea also confuses responsibility with expertise: being responsible for training does not imply that one is, or should be, a training expert.

The Subject Matter Expert (SME) is the best training expert This idea confuses operational expertise with training expertise. Although a good instructor will generally also be an expert, an expert is not necessarily a good instructor. Quite the contrary: experts may have become so detached from their training history and learning experiences that they find it very difficult to appreciate the problems and misconceptions trainees may have. Apart from 'naturals', it usually takes specific didactic knowledge and training for SMEs to be able to function as an instructor.

In practice, however, the responsibility for designing, delivering, and evaluating training is assigned rather indiscriminately to SMEs who are generally not well prepared by sufficient training. As a consequence, with respect to the issue of how training should be conducted, many fallacies are still encountered (for a more extensive discussion, cf. Schneider, 1985):

- 'if individuals continue to perform a task their performance will improve, reaching near optimal levels';
- 'it is best to train a skill in a form similar to the final execution of the skill';
- 'once trainees have a conceptual understanding of the system, proficiency will develop in the operational setting';
- 'skill training is intrinsically motivating and, thus, adding extrinsic motivators is inappropriate'.

The operational environment is the best training environment This conviction seems to be particularly deeply ingrained. It is manifested in a preference for using the real system and the real environment for training and a concomitant opposition to the use of simulation. Apparently, advocates of this approach do not realise that, in one way or another, all training is simulation. This idea capitalises on the assumption that the operational environment is well known. However, ideas about the operational environment are abstractions and extrapolations from past experiences. This particularly applies to the military case. In this respect, it should also be noted that generally there is a substantial lack of consensus with respect to what constitutes the operational environment. Also, history has shown that many firmly held beliefs and expectations have been proven to be quite wrong.

The idea that '*The operational environment is the best training environment*' has implications not only for the way in which the similarity between operational environment and training environment is conceived, but also for how training should be conducted and evaluated.

The approach to training associated with this conviction is that it is best to train in an operational context, e.g., by executing operational tasks with integral crews or teams. Training sessions are planned and executed like operational missions. Clearly, operational missions are planned in such a way that the chances of mission failure are minimised. A mission fails if the mission goal is not achieved. However, for training, the goal is to acquire or improve knowledge and skills, i.e., to achieve particular training objectives, and the mission goal is at best a means to this end. The ultimate goal of training, of course, is to be better able to achieve mission goals, but only *after* training has been completed.

A drawback to training in the context of operational tasks and with integral teams is that the training process becomes intractable. However, proponents of this approach argue that operational events and conditions are unpredictable and that training therefore may, or even should, also be unpredictable. Not surprisingly, they resist the use of standardised pre-defined training scenarios by arguing that the use of such scenarios would reduce the capability to learn how to handle unfamiliar or unexpected situations. A number of comments are in order here. First, most training scenarios cannot be strictly pre-defined. In this respect, opposition to the use of standardised training scenarios is groundless. Secondly, the idea that standardised scenarios reduce the capability to learn how to handle unfamiliar or unexpected situations confuses standardisation with homogeneity. By composing a heterogeneous set of standardised scenarios that contains a representative sample of unfamiliar or unexpected situations, handling such situations can be learned in a way that is controllable and transparent *to those who deliver the training*. The latter part of the previous sentence has been italicised to draw attention to the fact that predictability to those who deliver the training is frequently confused with predictability to those who are trained. Even if a training scenario proceeds exactly as planned, it may be entirely unpredictable for the trainees. Being able to predict training scenarios is highly desirable for those who deliver the training, because it enables them to generate expectations about the behaviour of trainees and, hence, to provide adequate and timely guidance and feedback.

Proponents of the idea that '*the operational environment is the best training environment*' typically also subscribe to the notion that training should be evaluated in the same way as operational missions. Operational missions are usually evaluated by means of a debriefing session. During debriefing the focus is on determining the extent to which the mission goal has been achieved; determining how a particular result is accomplished is often not possible or considered less or not at all relevant.

As noted earlier, the goal of training is to achieve particular training objectives. To assess whether this goal has been achieved, the training process should be assessed and evaluated in terms of the associated training objectives. This requires an altogether different perspective and approach than an operational analysis would need or assume. For instance, an operational analysis would perhaps de-emphasise particular errors, particularly if they were corrected or compensated for and did not compromise the final result. From the point of view of training, errors are opportunities for improvement. To exploit these opportunities, they should be detected and responded to, irrespective of their impact on or consequences for subsequent events and the overall operational outcome. Perhaps the major reason for the aforementioned confusion between operational and training perspectives is a potential confounding between training and testing. It seems that often training is also viewed as an opportunity for testing. However, these are distinct activities that may have quite divergent implications for the design of the environment and the procedures adopted for their execution and evaluation.

Whatever the reason may be, it is believed that many of the aforementioned fallacies and pitfalls can be avoided by taking into consideration results from research on learning and instruction. In the remainder of this chapter, the main theories and findings from research on learning processes are reviewed. This review is followed by a synopsis of research findings on training and instruction. It should be noted that research on learning processes is often difficult to dissociate from research on training and instruction. The reason is that learning processes have to be studied in a particular context of training and instruction. Conversely, training and instruction cannot be studied without making assumptions about learning processes. The reason for reviewing these topics separately is mostly a matter of expository convenience.

One purpose of both reviews is to provide some counterweight against 'professional' training doctrines. It should be noted that these reviews are intended merely to provide a broad overview. For a more in-depth treatment of topics, the reader may wish to consult applicable key references that are mentioned in the text. In addition to providing an overview, both reviews serve as a background and introduction to subsequent chapters.

Learning Theory

Learning can be defined as the acquisition of a relatively permanent change (improvement) in task performance as a result of training and instruction (intentional learning) or experience (incidental learning). Learning has an emergent property in that it cannot be directly observed but has to be inferred by comparing performance records at different trials or instances of time.

Research on learning constitutes one of the major topics in psychology and has a long history. Much of the earlier research on learning has been summarised by Hilgard and Bower (1975). For a more recent overview, see Patrick (1992, chapter 2). In subsequent sections, the learning process is treated as a more or less general phenomenon, i.e., one that is relatively invariant across different types of skill. Another contention is that learning is skill-specific and that learning effects can be differentiated accordingly. This viewpoint will be taken up subsequently.

Models of the Learning Process

Learning-curve models and stage models of skill acquisition can be distinguished. Both types of model will be briefly reviewed below; for more extensive reviews and discussions, see Lane (1987) and Patrick (1992, chapter 2).

Learning Curves

There is a long-standing tradition within psychology of describing and summarising learning effects by means of learning curves, and a large number of alternative mathematical functions (e.g., hyperbolic and exponential) have been proposed as models of the learning process (Mazur & Hastie, 1978; Newell & Rosenbloom, 1981).

Since Newell and Rosenbloom (1981), the so-called 'power law of practice' has gained widespread acceptance as a general learning-curve model. This law represents a quantitative empirical relationship between the time to perform a task (e.g., reaction time) and the number of practice trials. Newell and Rosenbloom (1981) argue that this relationship is best described by a power function.

This general learning equation was apparently first noted by Snoddy (1926), in an experiment on mirror-tracing of visual mazes (Fitts, 1965; Newell & Rosenbloom, 1981). Snoddy proposed the log-log law of practice, the equation of which as proposed by Newell and Rosenbloom (1981) is as follows:

$$\text{Log } (T) = \text{Log } (B) - a \text{ Log } (N)$$

Where:

    T is the time required to perform the task
    B is the performance time on the first trial
    a is the slope of the line, i.e., the learning rate
    N is the trial number

The equation of the power law of practice (Newell & Rosenbloom, 1981) has the form:

$$T = BN^{-a}$$

It has also been termed 'the ubiquitous law of practice' since it applies to a wide variety of tasks and performance measures. Tasks include perceptual-motor tasks such as cigar manufacturing, perceptual tasks such as learning to read inverted text, memory tasks, and problem solving tasks (cf. Newell & Rosenbloom, 1981).

In their review of the literature, Newell and Rosenbloom concluded that the power law of practice holds not only for speed measures of performance, but also for other measures such as accuracy. However, they also stated that the power law effect is not as strong for accuracy measures as it is for speed measures of performance. It should be noted that, although the overall (power-law) trend is the same, there are large differences in the parameters of the power law across tasks, individuals, and learning conditions.

Several theories have been developed to explain the power law. Crossman (1959) proposed a theory of skill acquisition in which subjects sample from a pool of available methods/strategies for task performance until they find the fastest one. This theory applies to situations where there are several methods/strategies for performing a task and trainees have available all the different strategies when they start training. There is no provision for learning new methods or improving existing ones. Newell and Rosenbloom (1981) proposed a theory based on the concept of chunking (cf. Miller, 1956), whereby trainees learn increasingly larger chunks as learning progresses. This mechanism seems to apply best to tasks where the stimuli are highly hierarchically patterned. MacKay (1982) proposed a mechanism in which learning occurs by strengthening connections between nodes in a hierarchical network.

These approaches are all attempts to integrate performance models with models of learning. The fact that the theories have been derived from different backgrounds may be one of the reasons for the relatively large number of different accounts. It is also possible that different tasks require different learning mechanisms or different combinations of learning mechanisms.

In contrast to the aforementioned performance-oriented theories, there have also been theories that have approached the phenomena of learning from a more formal mathematical perspective. These approaches are generally subsumed under the heading of the general term mathematical or stochastic learning theory. Most of the models developed within this context deal with animal and simple human learning. The assumptions underlying these models concern statistical properties of hypothesised 'mental' elements or entities such as response tendencies, habits, expectancies, and hypotheses. Based on these assumptions, the process of learning is modelled in its quantitative aspects by changes in the number and distribution of elements.

Two general classes of model that have received much attention and are of more general theoretical interest are *accumulation* and *replacement* models (Restle & Greeno, 1970). In accumulation learning, elements are added to elements already present. In replacement learning, some elements are replaced by others. One of the interesting aspects of these models is that they yield different transfer predictions. An accumulation process becomes 'stiffer' (more resistant to change) as elements accumulate, whereas a replacement process does not. A recent approach that can be considered an accumulation model is that proposed by Logan (1988a) where 'instances' assume the role of mental entities. Approaches that view the process of learning as an adjustment or modification of an internal mental model, e.g., the schema theory of motor learning (Schmidt, 1975) and connectionist models of learning (Hanson & Burr, 1990), are more consistent with predictions from replacement models. These conceptions are closely associated with research on the specificity of practice, an issue with important implications for the relation between training and simulation fidelity (Boer, 1991a, b).

Stage Accounts

In learning-curve models, learning is considered as a continuous process (Newell & Rosenbloom, 1981). But many theorists (Fitts, 1965; Fitts & Posner, 1967; Adams, 1971; Shiffrin & Schneider, 1977; Schneider & Shiffrin, 1977; Anderson, 1980, 1982, 1992; Logan, 1988a) have offered a description of the learning process in terms of phases or stages of skill acquisition, i.e., a consecutive set of learning mechanisms. These accounts can be subdivided into those that postulate two and those that postulate three stages.

Two-stage accounts of the learning process have been provided by Adams (1971), Schneider and Shiffrin (1977), Shiffrin and Schneider (1977), and Logan (1988a). Schneider and Shiffrin developed a two-process theory of visual detection, search, and attention. The theory posits two qualitatively different modes of processing: automatic and controlled. Automatic processing is characterised by fast (parallel) information processing that can be executed virtually independently of other concurrent tasks, i.e., it demands little or no attention. Automatic processing develops under so-called consistent mapping conditions, i.e., conditions where the mapping between stimuli and responses remains the same. Controlled processing is a slow, serial, but flexible mode of processing that is under conscious control, i.e., it is highly demanding of attention. Controlled processing develops under so-called varied mapping conditions, when no consistent rules or consistent sequences of information processing components are present in a task, or when a task is novel and consistencies have not yet been learned/automated.

This theory has generated a great deal of research (see Logan, 1988a, b, 1991, 1992 for reviews) and many of its concepts have been generalised and adapted to other task domains (notably by Fisk, 1987, 1988). Several mechanisms have been proposed to explain the development and the conditions for developing automaticity. Schneider (1985; Schneider & Detweiler, 1987) has developed a theory of how automatic processing develops, involving two kinds of learning processes: priority learning and association learning. This theory has been developed to account for learning of skills involved in simple visual and memory search tasks. Logan (1988b, 1992) has proposed an 'instance theory of automatisation', a two-process learning mechanism that accounts for the power-law of learning and thus establishes an explicit link between a learning-curve model and a stage model of skill acquisition.

Three-stage accounts of the learning process have been given by Fitts (1965), Fitts and Posner (1967), Anderson (1980, 1982, 1992) and Neves and Anderson (1981). As will be noted, these accounts are highly similar.

The first phase starts when the trainee faces the task for the first time. It has been termed the *cognitive* phase by Fitts (1965) and Fitts and Posner (1967), and the *encoding* phase by Neves and Anderson (1981). After instructions about the task are given to the trainee, he/she begins to understand the basic task requirements. The trainee then formulates a general idea about the task requirements. At this stage, *declarative knowledge* is used by the trainee to recall the instructions and the rules applying to the task to be performed (Anderson, 1980). Declarative knowledge is represented in a way that generally allows conscious retrieval (Shiffrin & Schneider, 1977). Thus performance at this phase is slow, attentionally effortful, and error prone (Fisk *et al*, 1987; Schneider & Fisk, 1983).

The second phase of skill acquisition has been called the *fixation* phase by Fitts (1965), the *associative* stage by Fitts and Posner (1967), and *proceduralisation* by Neves and Anderson (1981). The mechanism that leads the acquisition of skills from the cognitive or declarative stage to the *procedural* one is called the *knowledge compilation* process (Anderson, 1982). Knowledge compilation occurs during the *associative* stage. The main element of performance improvements during this phase is an increase in the strength and efficiency of associations between stimulus conditions and response patterns (Fitts & Posner, 1967). Knowledge compilation at this stage is associated with converting declarative knowledge into *production rules* (Anderson 1992). Knowledge compilation does not eliminate declarative knowledge, rather it remains available as an alternative means for performing the task (Anderson, 1992). At this stage, accuracy and speed of performance are increased (Anderson, 1982; Colley & Beech, 1989a; Fitts & Posner, 1967).

The third phase is known as the *autonomous* phase (Fitts, 1965), *composition* (Neves & Anderson, 1981), or *proceduralised knowledge* (Anderson, 1982). In Anderson (1982), the *proceduralisation* and *composition* phases are assimilated into one (*proceduralisation*). When the trainee has reached a skill level such that performance requires minimal attentional effort, and at the same time is fast and accurate, then the knowledge to perform the task has been automated (Shiffrin & Schneider, 1977). Fitts (1965) also called this stage *automation of performance*. In contrast to declarative knowledge, procedural knowledge does not require conscious mediation. If performance on the task has been sufficiently proceduralised that declarative knowledge is no longer involved in accomplishing the task goal, declarative knowledge about how to perform the task may become unavailable to consciousness with no decrease in task performance (Anderson, 1982).

Individual Differences

Skill development has also been studied from an individual differences perspective, i.e., by means of correlational and factor-analytic techniques. From this perspective, a number of approaches have been used to analyse changes in skill with training: analyses of changes in the variability of performance, in the pattern of inter-trial correlation patterns or factorial structure, and in ability-performance correlations, with practice. Most of the relevant literature has been critically reviewed by Ackerman (1987, 1988). Based on this review and a number of additional experiments, Ackerman (1987, 1988; see also Ackerman & Kyllonen, 1991) developed an integrative theory of skill development that links the three-stage account of skill acquisition described earlier with three cognitive-intellectual ability factors: general intelligence, perceptual speed, and psychomotor ability. General intelligence or ability is a broad factor that underlies non-specific information-processing efficacy, and is associated with phase 1 performance. Perceptual speed is the speed of consistent encoding and comparing of symbols and is primarily associated with phase 2 performance. Psychomotor ability is the speed and accuracy of motor responding, i.e., responding that involves little or no cognitive processing and is determined primarily by psychophysical limitations. Psychomotor ability is the primary source of individual differences during phase 3 performance. However, an interesting aspect of the theory is that the exact relation between the ability factors and phases of skill acquisition is hypothesised to be moderated in specific ways by factors such as task complexity, consistency, motivation, initial performance, and efficiency.

The Learning of Specific Skills

The learning curve and stage models of skill acquisition described earlier are quite general and do not always differentiate explicitly between different types of tasks, although many of these models originated in research on highly specific experimental tasks. In this section some lines of research are described that address learning in the context of particular types of skill.

A perceptual-motor skill is one in which the primary activity involves co-ordination between perceptual inputs and motor outputs. In a procedural skill, the primary activity involves the execution of an algorithmic sequence of discrete actions. The primary activity in a cognitive skill is the heuristic analysis and synthesis of different types of information. Team skills involve sharing information and communicating with other team members. In a time-sharing skill, a number of qualitatively different tasks are co-ordinated.

Most real-life tasks involve a mixture of these types of activity. It should be noted that the literature is inconsistent in the use of these categories, but the definitions given are adequate for present purposes. Where necessary, in subsequent chapters these distinctions will be elaborated further.

Perceptual-motor Skills

For earlier, behaviourist, positions concerning the learning of perceptual-motor skills, see Hilgard and Bower (1975); Adams (1987) provides a historical review, and a recent overview of motor skill learning is provided by Salmoni (1989). The domain of Ackerman's theory is that of complex perceptual-motor skills in general. More specific theories are the closed-loop theory of motor learning (Adams, 1971) and the schema theory of motor skill learning (Schmidt, 1975).

Although the theory is assumed to have wider implications, Adams's closed-loop theory primarily deals with a rather narrow class of motor tasks: linear positioning (e.g., drawing a line). Schema theory extends the notions of the closed-loop theory to other, discrete movement, tasks.

Hammerton (1981) reviewed research on tracking performance. Most of this research has been aimed at developing control models of steady-state tracking performance and has been less concerned with learning. Most of the research dealing with learning of tracking tasks has focused on the use of adaptive training strategies (Kelley, 1969; for a review see Lintern & Gopher, 1978). As part of a programme of research on the feasibility and utility of automated training devices for perceptual-motor skills, Gaines (1972a, b, 1974) developed a state-space account of the learning of perceptual-motor skills based on concepts from adaptive control and systems theory. Although applied initially to tracking skills, this account probably has wider applicability.

Procedural Skills

There are no theories of learning specifically geared towards the learning of procedural skills. Considering the fine distinction between procedural and cognitive tasks, it is not surprising that with respect to learning most accounts are derived from cognitive theories of learning; notably the ACT theory of Anderson.

Research on the learning, transfer, and retention of procedural tasks has been reviewed by Konoske and Ellis (1986), Farr (1987), Christina and Bjork (1991) and van den Bosch (1994). Most of the research has focused on training and instruction strategies that optimise transfer and retention. In particular, factors that affect retention of procedural skills have received great attention because procedural skills appear to be particularly prone to decay.

A central theme in current approaches is that trainees have to acquire a mental model of the task, i.e., an integrated representation of the knowledge, structure, and principles underlying task performance. An important issue is the determination of the kind of information incorporated within the mental model, how this information can be acquired most efficiently, and how it affects transfer and retention.

Studies of these issues generally distinguish between conceptual and operational knowledge (van den Bosch, 1994). Conceptual knowledge relates to the functional principles underlying the operation of the system and its components. Operational knowledge relates to the internal task structure and the connections between system components. Rouse and Morris (1986) summarise some of the findings: conceptual knowledge does not necessarily enhance task performance, and measures of such knowledge are not good predictors of performance. The utility of conceptual knowledge depends on the form in which it is presented and the guidance for its use. Guidance can be explicit, using procedures and cueing, or implicit, providing a range of instructional experiences that foster or require the use of knowledge. *A priori* knowledge can be a powerful basis for gaining new knowledge or, if incorrect, an impediment to gaining correct knowledge; both cases argue for consideration of *a priori* knowledge in devising instructional strategies (briefing).

Several studies (e.g., Dixon & Gabrys, 1991; Carlson & Lundy, 1992) indicate that operational knowledge is important for transfer but conceptual knowledge is not. Studies by Kieras and Bovair (1984) and Konoske and Ellis (1986) suggest that both the acquisition and the retention of procedural skills are furthered by the provision of conceptual knowledge. However, there are arguments for supposing that these types of knowledge affect acquisition and retention differently. A hypothesis advanced by van den Bosch (1994) is that operational knowledge is primarily important for acquisition whereas conceptual knowledge is primarily important for retention.

Cognitive Skills

Traditionally, cognitive psychology has been concerned more with the long-term memory representation of knowledge and its use than with learning mechanisms (Bourne *et al*, 1979; Wessels, 1982). A large number of different memory systems have been proposed to account for human performance across an equally large number of tasks and domains. The major memory systems are sensory, short-term, and long-term memory, but these are often sub-divided. For example, semantic memory and episodic memory are different long-term memory systems.

Learning phenomena have been primarily conceived in terms of transfer from short-term to long-term memory, a process assumed to be mediated by elaborative rehearsal based on integration with existing knowledge (as opposed to rote 'maintenance' rehearsal). Loss of knowledge from memory, i.e., forgetting, has been interpreted primarily in terms of interference theory, at least for simple material. Remembering more complex information, e.g., stories and eye-witness reports, is generally conceived of as a re-constructive process. An interesting phenomenon associated with remembering information is encoding specificity, whereby contextual cues that are present during acquisition, whether processed intentionally or incidentally, act as effective retrieval cues.

The most well-known computational learning theories proposed to account for the acquisition of cognitive skills are ACT, ACT* and PUPS (Anderson, 1987; Anderson *et al*, 1990) and the chunking mechanism proposed by Newell and Rosenbloom (1981) and incorporated in SOAR (Laird *et al*, 1986, 1987). Although these theories have focused primarily on the acquisition of cognitive skills, they have also been claimed (and used) to account for the acquisition of perceptual-motor and procedural skills.

Within cognitive psychology, much of the research on learning is associated with research on Intelligent Tutoring Systems (ITSs). Because this research focuses on instruction strategies and technological issues rather than learning processes and mechanisms *per se*, it is reviewed in the next chapter.

For team skills and time-sharing skills, no specific learning concepts have been developed. However, some recommendations have been proposed for training these types of skill (see Chapters 10 and 11).

Summary

The improvement of performance with increasing practice that is typically observed across a wide range of different tasks can be summarised relatively well by a power function. Several theories have been proposed to account for this phenomenon; they can be differentiated according to the number of learning mechanisms or stages that they assume. These theories have been developed within the context of particular tasks. Therefore, in many cases, the extent to which theories can be generalised to other tasks remains unclear.

Generally, the more complex a task, the larger the number of mechanisms that may be hypothesised. Also, the interactions between different learning mechanisms in theories that assume more than one learning mechanism remain largely obscure.

Training and Instruction Strategies

Most of the research reported in the open literature addresses the acquisition of scholastic knowledge and skills. Many of the theories developed in this context have recently been summarised by Kearsley, and can be found on the World Wide Web (http://www.gwu.edu/~tip). A number of instructional design models have been developed as an aid in the specification of strategies and tactics for training and instruction (Reigeluth, 1983). These are mostly based on concepts and generalisations derived from, or inspired by, hypotheses and findings from experimental research. In a review of research on learning, Glaser (1990) lamented that the hypothesised learning processes and their implication for training and instruction show very few commonalities across task domains. He suggested that an integrated theory prescribing a mix of instructional approaches for specific training purposes should be developed.

In more recent years, several developments, such as the increased concern for maintaining the motivation of students and the increased availability and capability of educational software and hardware, have resulted in greater interest in learning as it occurs in practice. This has stimulated interest in the context in which learning occurs (*situated cognition/action*), for the conditions of learning, such as on the job (*computer-coached or embedded instruction*), and for the learning strategies people use in real life, including collaborative (*collaborative learning*), exploratory (*microworlds*) and supervision by an expert (*apprenticeship instruction*).

Situated action/cognition Cognitive psychology has long been dominated by the view that behaviour is the result of strategies executed on internal knowledge (cognitive) representations. Accordingly, studies of how knowledge is represented mentally and how such representations are acquired should provide the key to understanding learning and behaviour. A major objection to this view is that it disregards the influence of the environment (the external representations) in which the knowledge is acquired or applied. Recognition of this shortcoming has led to a new movement in cognitive psychology: situated action theory (e.g. Brown *et al*, 1989). Situated action theorists emphasise that task performance is largely regulated by cues associated with the specific context in which the behaviour takes place. Consequently, understanding task performance and knowledge acquisition processes should involve the important role of the environment in the acquisition, representation, and application of prerequisite task knowledge.

Computer-coached instruction The assumption underlying this type of instruction (Lajoie & Lesgold, 1989) is that knowledge and skills should be taught in the context of their use, trainees being given the ability to request support ('coaching') that is gradually withdrawn ('fading').

Collaborative learning Much real-life learning occurs in a social context, i.e., with other people. From a psychological viewpoint, we have only a very modest insight into the phenomena that play a role in collaborative learning. The literature on this topic has only recently begun to accumulate. Issues to be addressed are: in what situations does collaborative problem solving enhance (or degrade) performance, and, more importantly, what are the *mechanisms* involved? Is it reduction of working memory load, acceptance of another person as a role model, or sharing of knowledge, or are there factors of a more social nature involved? Presumably, many factors exert an influence, but, as yet, the mechanisms are still poorly understood and worth researching. The goal of this research should be a model of collaborative learning constructed in the same way as models of individual learning. Such models may be of particular interest for crew and team training.

Microworlds Brehmer and Dorner (1993) discuss experimental work with computer-simulated microworlds as a means of overcoming the tension between laboratory research and field research in psychology. Microworlds are simulations of processes, systems or organisations with which the trainee may interact. Usually these interactions take the form of discovery or exploratory learning: the trainee is supposed to learn by interacting more or less freely with the micro-world, sometimes with the support of a coach.

Research on microworlds involves the study of how subjects interact with complex computer simulations of real systems, such as a small town or a forest fire.

This kind of research has adopted three different approaches: individual differences, case studies, and experimental. In the first approach, large groups of subjects interact with a given system, and the difference in their behaviour is noted and related to various measures of abilities and personality. In the second, the behaviour of individual subjects is analysed in great detail to find typical and atypical examples and hence to generate hypotheses. In the third approach, the effects of various system characteristics on behaviour are studied at the group level. A problem with using microworlds and other 'situated' approaches is that research results are difficult or impossible to compare (Buchner & Funke, 1993).

Apprenticeship instruction   Apprenticeship instruction is the traditional method used in teaching vocational skills on the job. The trainee watches an expert perform a task 'on the job' and subsequently attempts to master this task under the supervision of the expert. Collins *et al* (1989) identify modelling, coaching, scaffolding and fading as the primary activities involved in apprenticeship instruction. Apprenticeship instruction is the typical setting upon which the development of most Intelligent Tutoring Systems is built (Burger & DeSoi, 1992).

Schank and Jona (1991) conducted a strength/weakness analysis of traditional teaching strategies, and suggested a number of alternative teaching strategies that in their view better exploited the possibilities of the computer as a teaching medium. A central theme in their framework was that the student/trainee should be given more control over the instruction.

   Probably also inspired by his earlier work on *scripts* (Schank & Abelson, 1977), this framework has been elaborated subsequently by Schank (1994) in the concept of Goal-Based Scenarios (GBSs). GBSs are learn-by-doing tasks in a particular domain that present definable goals and encourage learning that achieves these goals. A GBS comprises a specific set of inter-related components (e.g., a mission structure and scenario operations) that impose specific constraints on the selection of material to be learned, the goals that the trainee will pursue, the environment in which the student will work, the tasks that the student will perform, and the resources made available to the student. Although developed in the context of computer-based education, these concepts and the associated guidelines may also have applicability to simulator-based training, notably to the design of training scenarios.

   It should be noted that all the approaches described above focus primarily on acquisition of scholastic knowledge and skills, i.e., they are primarily knowledge-oriented rather than task-oriented. Also, the primary emphasis is on the computer as a medium for training.

Complex Skills

Relatively little research has been conducted that explicitly addresses the acquisition of complex skills typically required in the performance of more realistic tasks, presumably since research in this area is methodologically much more complex. The fact that the learning of many relatively simple tasks is still a poorly understood phenomenon also discourages the tackling of more complex issues.

Intelligent Tutoring Systems Most research on the acquisition of more complex skills has been conducted in the context of the development of Intelligent Tutoring Systems (ITSs). The purpose of these developments is to design computer programs that teach in a more intelligent way. Researchers have tried to achieve this by applying tutoring concepts derived from the research literature and Artificial Intelligence techniques. The idea is to provide individualised and flexible tutoring in a way similar to human tutors. The main goal of ITS research is to implement, test and evaluate tutoring principles and implementation methods.

ITSs are supposed to be more flexible than traditional Computer-Based Training (CBT) programmes because they adapt training and instruction to the particular student. To realise this adaptability, designers have typically followed a modular design approach, segregating as far as possible the different types of knowledge that are supposed to be involved. It is generally assumed (e.g., Wenger, 1987) that an ITS should include knowledge of the following:

- what is being taught (contained in the domain model);
- the level, the strengths and the weaknesses of the particular student working with the system at a particular moment (contained in the student model);
- instructional strategies and tactics (contained in the pedagogical model);
- ways of transmitting information to and from the student (contained in the interface model).

To be truly intelligent, all four components should be fully developed and integrated. Most ITS studies concentrate on one of the models, the other models being designed in a very rudimentary way or even not at all. Therefore, many well-known ITS systems have never been fully developed or used in practice, and only a few have been evaluated with students.

Most ITS developments are based on assumptions and concepts about tutoring derived from the literature, rather than from an analysis of the way in which human tutors work. There is evidence that the tutoring provided by human tutors differs from that provided by ITSs (Merrill *et al*, 1992). However, the implications of these differences remain unclear. Is the goal to develop an optimal tutor or a tutor that accurately mimics the behaviour of human tutors? If the latter, one should try to minimise these differences. There are some difficulties here: human tutors differ from each other, and commit errors. If the goal is to develop an optimal tutor, one has to specify criteria. However, it is not possible to define absolute criteria. One can conclude only that one tutor produces better results than another. In short, this issue is an empirical one.

Another characteristic of research on ITSs is that it has been conducted predominantly in the context of relatively homogeneous and well-structured tasks (e.g., problem solving tasks) that do not possess the dynamic, time-critical, and time-sharing aspects of high-performance tasks. Given the complexity and dynamics of high-performance tasks, it is questionable whether current analytical approaches are appropriate for these types of task. Nevertheless, a few research programmes have been undertaken to fill this gap, notably the *Learning Strategies Program* and a research project initiated by the US Air Force Armstrong Laboratory.

The Learning Strategies Program (LSP) The LSP (Donchin, 1989; Lintern, 1989) constituted a systematic examination of the effects of practice on skill acquisition to improve the design of training and instruction strategies for complex flight tasks. More specifically, its purpose was to examine the extent to which it is possible to improve on unsupervised practice (Foss *et al*, 1989) when subjects must master a rather complex task. This was accomplished by a comparative assessment of several alternative strategies, such as adaptive training and part-task training, in a number of experiments (Foss *et al*, 1989; Frederiksen & White, 1989; Gopher *et al*, 1989; Mané *et al*, 1989; Newell *et al*, 1989; Fabiani *et al*, 1989) using the complex Space-Fortress Game (Mané & Donchin, 1989). The LSP is the first relatively large-scale study of the training of complex tasks conducted in a laboratory setting.

A related effort currently in progress and wider in scope than the LSP is the research project by the Armstrong Laboratory at Brooks Air Force Base (Regian & Shute, 1993). This project seeks to contribute to knowledge of automated instruction by (1) adopting a standardised taxonomic characterisation of human performance to guide research and support generalisation of principles; (2) designing and developing a set of criterion tasks that serve as benchmarks for instructional research (including high-performance tasks such as Space Fortress); (3) developing theory-based, automated instructional systems for these criterion tasks; and (4) empirically comparing performance on the criterion tasks after various instructional interventions.

Simulator-Based Training and Instruction

Most of the concepts and findings reported in the open literature focus on scholastic knowledge and skills and relatively simple and well-structured tasks. This makes it difficult to assess their relevance for training high-performance skills, i.e., the type of skills typically trained with the aid of simulators. Although a considerable amount of research has been conducted, little is specifically devoted to simulator-based training. Most work on simulator-based training has been concerned with issues of fidelity and transfer of training. Nevertheless, many principles and strategies may be relevant to simulator-based training. What is needed is a framework that enables mapping of these concepts and findings onto issues relevant to simulator-based training.

Most training programmes conform to essentially the same template: a particular sequence of training scenarios. Depending on the complexity and scope of the training programme, such sequences may or may not consist of several phases. Frequently, assessment takes place between these phases to determine the course of subsequent training. Typically, scenarios are preceded by a briefing and followed by a debriefing. During the course of the scenario, specific guidance and feedback may be provided by the instructor and/or automatically by the simulator.

This structure may provide a starting point for attempts to organise concepts and findings into a common frame of reference. However, first this idea will be elaborated and an attempt will be made to clarify the terminology.

Training and instruction In the human factors literature, these terms are used interchangeably. Both refer to the problems of what kind of information should be provided to the learner/trainee, when it should be administered, how learning/practice should be arranged, and by what means instruction/training should be supported (instructor, computer-based, simulator, or on-the-job).

The differences between instruction and training are subtle and are not always made explicit in the literature (see, for example, Lintern, 1991). Both share the final goals of the learning/acquisition of knowledge and skills and their transfer to an external setting: the society outside the school classroom, or the job a professional must execute. The term instruction is used more for the organised learning process in educational environments, whereas training is widely used in the field of human-machine systems.

A more constrained position about the differences between instruction and training is that adopted by Annett (1991) and Holding (1987). These authors distinguish instruction and training with recourse to the paradigms used in the processes of skill acquisition research. Thus, there are two main research paradigms, practice and instruction, each with its own characteristics. In practice experiments (corresponding to training in applied settings), the trainee makes repeated attempts to perform the task (Annett, 1991). Within instruction, the experimenter (or trainer) supplies the learner with verbal instruction, advice, and correction (Annett, 1991; Fitts, 1965; Holding, 1987). Within the MASTER project, training and instruction are defined similarly. Training is defined as trainee activities that are executed in interaction with a scenario, and that are intended to induce or promote learning. Instruction is defined as those activities executed in interaction with a training process that are intended to enhance training efficiency. Thus, instruction is regarded as a means of supporting training, and hence is subsumed under training.

Generally, the better the training is designed the less instructional support is required during training. In other words, the better the sequencing of training and the better the design of the training scenario, the less instructional support will be required. Thus, there will generally be a trade-off between training and instruction.

The main issues that have to be resolved in designing a typical training programme (as described earlier) can be distinguished as training issues and issues associated with instruction.

Training Issues

With respect to training, the major considerations are: (1) sequencing of training objectives and (2) specification of training activities and scenarios. The way in which these issues are resolved determines what, how, when, and how long trainees are supposed to train.

Sequencing, clustering and decomposition The ordering of a given set of training objectives is by no means a trivial problem. Theoretically, given n training objectives, the total number of possible permutations is $n!$ (n factorial). For 10 training objectives there are 3,628,800 possible orderings. Of course, in practice many constraints limit the number of alternatives. Even so, the number of alternatives may cover a wide range of options differing considerably in terms of training effectiveness and efficiency.

During sequencing, it may become apparent that training objectives are missing or have been specified too vaguely. Hence, the process of training needs analysis may have to be partly re-iterated. Another possibility is that, after training objectives have been put in order, particular steps or transitions may be found to be too large and have to be broken down further. It may also turn out that particular training objectives have to be clustered for resource or logistical reasons, for example, because they all require the same training device. Apart from allocation of training media and resources, other relevant considerations are the options for spacing training activities in time and, of course, the time available for training. The options for assessing performance during training differ considerably depending upon whether training duration is fixed or variable.

Training activities and scenarios Another major issue to be resolved is the specification of training activities and scenarios. Training activities are the activities that trainees must perform to achieve their training objectives. It is generally assumed that different training objectives require different training activities. Training activities may be derived from or modelled on operational activities. However, for various reasons it may be desirable to specify training activities solely and specifically for the purpose of training. Such activities may bear little resemblance to operational activities. With the possible exception of mental rehearsal, training activities are not performed in a vacuum but require an appropriate training environment (inputs, feedback, and so on) for their proper execution. This training environment is specified in terms of a training scenario. An important requirement for any training scenario is that it is functionally valid. For each training activity, more than one training scenario may be required, for instance, to prevent scenario recognition with repeated execution or because the conditions in which skills have to be exercised are intrinsically variable.

Issues of Instruction

The role of instruction, as defined in the context of MASTER, is primarily as a catalyst in the training process: instruction should facilitate the training process without the trainee coming to rely on it. Instructional activities can be distinguished in terms of whether they occur prior to, during, or after scenario execution ('briefing', 'tutoring', and 'debriefing', respectively). Ultimately, the timing, form, and content of these activities will depend to a large extent on the nature of the training activities and the composition of the associated training scenarios, which provide the goals and context of instruction, respectively. Of course, learner characteristics also play an important role. Briefing, tutoring, and debriefing are closely related and an important issue in the design of instruction is how to combine them in an optimal way.

In resolving the issues associated with the design of training and instruction, many trade-offs have to be made. For instance, the way in which training objectives are sequenced determines the content and the nature of the training activities and the training scenarios. In turn, the training activities and the composition of the training scenarios determine the kind of instruction that may be required. In addition to constraints such as available time, the resolution of these trade-offs depends on the overall training strategies and instruction tactics adopted:

- skill-oriented or task-oriented;
- mastery- or duration-driven;
- learner-controlled or instructor-controlled;
- adaptive or invariant;
- explicit or implicit guidance and feedback;
- focused on error prevention or error correction;
- strict or liberal monitoring and control.

Obviously, strategies may be applied in combination (e.g., in an extended training programme where trainees pass through several distinguishable levels of expertise from novice to advanced to expert). The choice of strategies and tactics may depend on the training philosophy of the organisation, the nature of the task and skills, learner characteristics, the didactic expertise and preferences of designers and instructors, and so on. It is important that the choices are made explicit at an early stage, since this may considerably enhance the consistency of the design process and ultimately the consistency and acceptance of the training programme.

In the following three chapters (10-12), the issues discussed above will be elaborated further. In the process, an attempt will be made to draw together concepts, findings and experiences relevant to simulator-based training. Issues of design and evaluation of simulator-based training programmes will be taken up in Chapters 13 and 14, respectively.

10 Sequencing of Training Objectives

Introduction

The number of training objectives that comes out of a Training Needs Analysis may be large because the domain is large (many tasks, many different operators) or because the range of knowledge and skills is very diverse. The level of analysis adopted during Training Needs Analysis also determines the number of tasks that is distinguished. Typically, the minimum level of detail will be such that tasks can be assigned unambiguously to individual operators; thus team tasks are broken down in terms of tasks that can be assigned to a particular team member.

There is frequently much confusion between the concepts of 'task' and 'skill' and their relationships with the concept of 'training objective'. In Section I, the MASTER approach to these concepts was described. Because the distinction between them is also of fundamental importance for training programme design, these concepts will be elaborated somewhat further here.

Definition of Task

The concept of 'task' can be viewed from different perspectives. For instance, a task can be viewed as a *responsibility* assigned to a person. The term 'task' can also be interpreted as referring to the operational *goal* that is to be accomplished as part of a particular responsibility. In addition, it may be used to denote the *procedure* that is to be executed to achieve an operational goal. These alternative interpretations are used rather loosely. As a consequence, the danger of confusion looms large: different procedures may be used to accomplish the same goal; also, the same responsibility may be served by the accomplishment of different goals.

Another source of confusion arises from the fact that the same task can be described in different terms, such as input-output mappings (perceptual-motor characteristics), sequences of steps to be executed (procedural), or goals, principles, rules, and heuristics (cognitive). In essence, these differences in terminology represent different levels of description. Again, at each level of description different frames of reference may be adopted. For example, tasks described in cognitive terms can be phrased in terms of scripts, production rules or semantic networks. Essentially, the choice of a particular level of description and a frame of reference depends on the goal of the description and is to some extent a matter of convenience and parsimony.

Definition of Skill

A 'skill' is the learned capability of a person to perform particular acts; it is thus a characteristic of a person. A person is considered to be 'skilled' if his capability has reached a specific level of proficiency. Usually a particular level of proficiency is implied in the definition of skill. Skill proficiency can be assessed by means of a test, which can be viewed as a standardised task designed to measure a particular skill. Typically, skills are assessed relative to the way in which a person performs on the test. Thus, the concept of 'skill' is used in a more restrictive sense than the concept of 'task', but like tasks it can be used at different levels of aggregation. For instance, flying an aircraft may be referred to as a skill and implies mastery of all the relevant flying skills.

Mappings between Tasks and Skills

The same skill, such as driving skill, can be used for different tasks. The same task, such as transporting a cargo from A to B, can similarly be accomplished by different skills. Among other things, the way in which a task is accomplished depends on available expertise, i.e., the set of skills available to a person. Different people, even experts, may perform the same task by using different skills. A task can be restructured or redesigned to require different skills (or, in the case of automation, no skills at all). For instance, a sonar task, which requires auditory skills, can be turned into a task that relies more heavily on visual skills. Similarly, a skill can be made more or less specific as a result of different amounts of training or by using different training strategies. The foregoing implies that the nature of the tasks and the skills within a domain may be subject to change. Hence in most cases a taxonomic approach to the specification of tasks and skills can be only a first approximation (though a very useful one).

A task can be specified more or less rigidly. This constrains the number of possible acts that may be used to accomplish the task, i.e., the number of degrees of freedom available to the operator and, hence, the types of skill he may use for task execution. In principle, a task specification can be made so specific that it can be performed only in one particular way. Such tasks are sometimes referred to as closed tasks. Performance on closed tasks can be highly automated and the resulting skills are referred to as closed skills (as opposed to 'open' skills). Notably, in this context the distinction between 'task' and 'skill' is often obscure.

The close correspondence between task and skill raises the question of what distinguishes the two. To re-iterate: the concept of 'task' refers to a performance requirement and is usually stated in terms of a goal and a procedure to be used to achieve the goal. In essence, a task definition represents a performance standard that is defined independently of the person who executes the task. The concept of 'skill' refers to the potential to perform a particular act. In essence, a skill definition refers to a property of a person. A skill cannot be directly observed but has to be inferred from performance on a test. For many skills, no tests are available and these skills remain hypotheses about individual differences in task performance. Thus, it is not always possible to define exactly the nature of the skills that are required to perform a task, although there may be some ideas. Experts in particular may find it difficult to verbalise their knowledge and skills, which, due to their extensive training and experience, may have largely become implicit.

Not surprisingly, in practice the distinction between task and skill easily becomes blurred. In any particular case the distinctions made will, to some extent, remain a matter of definition and a matter of choice. It is important that the definitions adopted be made as explicit as possible. It is advisable not to rely on the opinion of only one expert. Experts may use different skills (and cues) to perform the same tasks. It may be very important to take these differences into account.

Definition of the Training Objective

A training objective is the specification of a level of skill proficiency given a particular initial level; i.e. a training objective specifies a skill gap. The set of training objectives constitutes a specification of the expertise that is to be developed by the trainees. However, in practice, there is a strong tendency to define training objectives in terms of a list of tasks. By doing so, individual differences in initial level are left unspecified. These differences may be quite large; so large that they require adapted, or even separate, training programmes.

By defining training objectives in terms of tasks, important commonalities in skill requirements may not be taken into account. As a result, much training effort may be wasted due to redundancy, and sequencing may be less than optimal. By simply listing tasks, dependencies between tasks may be overlooked. However, these dependencies may have important implications for the way in which training objectives are sequenced and, hence, for the efficiency and effectiveness of the training programme.

The set of training objectives constitutes a specification of the expertise that is to be developed by the trainees. The first problem to be addressed during training programme design is to 'unfold' this expertise along the training axis. This unfolding implies assumptions about the learning curves or stages of learning through which trainees have to pass on their way from novice to expert. The extent of this unfolding depends on the initial level of expertise, the learning potential of the trainees, and the criterion level of the expertise to be acquired. The nature of this unfolding depends on the relations between the different skills, the nature of the skills, the training and instruction strategies that are adopted, and the applicable constraints.

Unfolding comprises sequencing, clustering, and decomposition of training objectives. One purpose of unfolding is to keep the cognitive load imposed on trainees within bounds. Another purpose is to programme training in such a way that the time required to achieve the training objectives, and hence to complete the training programme, is minimised. In the process, a large number of constraints must be taken into account.

Unfolding is a highly iterative process that requires designers repeatedly to go through the sequence of training objectives and consider alternative ways to sequence, cluster, or decompose training objectives. During this process, gaps, inconsistencies or obscurities may well appear within the set of training objectives. It seems most prudent to return to the previous needs analysis phase to ensure consistency between operational requirements and training programme requirements. During subsequent elaboration of the training programme, the original sequence of training objectives may also have to be revised.

Sequencing and Clustering of Training Objectives

In this section, approaches and considerations with respect to the sequencing of training objectives are reviewed. This is followed by a review of considerations with respect to clustering training objectives. Finally, some notes will be made about the amount and spacing of training.

Sequencing Principles

One of the major principles in sequencing training objectives is that the task load of trainees should be kept within bounds. What constitutes a minor load or no load for experienced operators may constitute a significant or insurmountable load for trainees.

Use of high task-loads and stressors during training A task load may be defined as a demand imposed on the operator. A stressor is defined as a task-irrelevant and task-interfering distractor. We can distinguish between endogenous stressors (e.g., fatigue) and exogenous stressors (e.g., noise or heat). Workload results from the demands imposed on the operator (by task loads and stressors). These demands may originate from input demands (information acquisition), central demands (cognitive load), output demands (motor requirements), and time pressure.

A general recommendation from research is to train without high task loads and stressors until performance has reached an asymptote (since skill acquisition rate will be highest in the absence of high task loads or stressors). At asymptote, high task loads or stressors can be introduced. The result will be a drop in performance followed by a return to an asymptote. When performance has returned to asymptotic level, training can continue (when overtraining is desired), can be terminated, or another stressor may be introduced.

Sequencing principles can be sub-divided into team-based principles (related to the dependencies between the tasks of different team members), task-based principles (related to dependencies between the tasks assigned to an individual operator), part-task principles (related to dependencies between task components), and part-skill principles (related to dependencies between constituent skills).

Team-based Sequencing

In principle, team training should commence only after other (individual) skills are mastered to a sufficient degree. Team-based sequencing involves intertwining training programmes of different team members into one composite team training programme. The first step in designing a training programme may consist of mapping team-training objectives onto the training axis/time-line. This requires taking into account dependencies between task contributions of individual team members. During this process it may be beneficial and efficient to combine team members in such a way that some lead the training of others, thus enabling forms of peer tutoring. Another consideration is whether team members are to be trained in the same team composition throughout training or will rotate across different team roles. Partly this depends on how teams will be operationally deployed.

Team-based sequencing of training objectives requires information about dependencies between the task execution of individual team members in relation to the overall team task. As an intermediate step towards training skills in a whole team context, training may proceed in a part-team context.

The main problem in team training is the 'degrees-of-freedom' or complexity problem, i.e., the issue of how to maintain a sufficient overview of and control over the training process without compromising its validity. To increase the effectiveness of team training and to exploit the full potential of training technology, this issue must be addressed.

The key to keeping the complexity within bounds is to break it down into more manageable parts. Crudely speaking, three main sources of complexity can be identified:

- the complexity of the team;
- the complexity of the environment;
- the skill level of team members.

The complexity of the team The larger the team that is to be trained and the more complex the organisation of the team, the more difficult it will be to maintain an overview of what is going on during training. However, it is not always realised that, for most team members, interactions are limited to only a small number of significant team members. This implies that a considerable part of training may be conducted independently of other team members. Obviously, apart from rendering the training process more transparent, this also greatly simplifies the sequencing problem.

In many modern military weapon systems, interactions are becoming increasingly proceduralised and/or automated. These cases, particularly those in which interactions do not require face-to-face contact, facilitate the simulation of team members; thus further reducing the number of team members who have to be physically present to support training. Finally, it is expected that advances in technology will enable more naturalistic simulation of team members, thus enabling agent-based team training, i.e., training with simulated team members.

The complexity of the environment For most military teams the environment can be characterised as complex, dynamic, uncertain, and hostile. The complexity of the military environment arises from the complexity of the physical environment (the number of objects and the level of detail) and the number and behaviour of enemy forces. The complexity of the environment may be reduced by limiting the training environment to the part that has significance for the team members who are to be trained, and by reducing the number of objects, the level of detail, and the number and sophistication of enemy forces. By taking these factors into account, several increasing levels of environmental complexity may be distinguished and used as a basis for sequencing.

The skill level of team members One important principle is that the sequencing of training objectives should match the developing skills of trainees. At the initial stages of training, the behaviour of trainees will be more erratic and error-prone, that is, more complex. This implies that:

- the training scenario should be kept simple and brief;
- the scenario should be closely monitored and controlled;
- the guidance and feedback should be more detailed.

As skills develop, behaviour changes into smoother and more regular patterns, which means that complexity is reduced. Consequently, the complexity along the team and/or environment axis may be allowed to increase. This will result in more complex scenarios of longer duration, more liberal monitoring and control, and changes in the content and timing of guidance and feedback.

Task-based Sequencing

As noted in the Introduction, it is assumed that the training objectives that result from Training Needs Analysis are specified up to such a level of detail that they can be uniquely identified with one individual operator or team member. Some of these training objectives will have relations with training objectives of other team members. The sequencing of these training objectives has been reviewed in previous paragraphs. Here the focus is on those training objectives that are associated with only one particular operator or team member, i.e., training objectives that do not involve relations with the training objectives of other team members. Each trainee has a set of such 'individual' training objectives.

Usually, these individual training objectives will have been derived more or less directly from operational tasks. Most straightforwardly, these training objectives are sequenced according to the order in which they are executed under operational circumstances. This perhaps renders the sequencing least problematic. However, a caveat must be recognised. Using solely mission-related chronology as a basis for sequencing may be highly inefficient because, for instance, it may neglect many important differences between training objectives such as:

- differences in initial skill level;
- differences in training difficulty;
- differences in frequency of occurrence;
- differences in operational importance.

Also, commonalities between training objectives may be overlooked. For instance, training effort can usually be used more efficiently by taking differences and commonalities between training objectives into account.

Rules that may be used are to sequence from high frequency to low frequency, from typical/standard/normal to atypical/non-standard/abnormal (e.g., standard operating procedures before emergency procedures). Other rules are to sequence from simple/easy/low task load to complex/difficult/high task load, or the other way around. Another option is to sequence or group together on the basis of commonalities between training objectives. Evidently, rules may conflict and priorities may have to be set. Whatever the rules used in any particular case, usually several iterations will be required to arrive at a more or less satisfactory sequence.

The training objectives that come out of a Training Needs Analysis specify operational skill requirements. The learning 'chunks' as defined by these training objectives may be too large, i.e., they may exceed the cognitive capacity of trainees. This is particularly likely to be the case for the phase of skill acquisition. In such cases, a further breakdown of training objectives into intermediate objectives may be in order. This breakdown may be based on a decomposition of operational tasks in terms of constituent part tasks. Another possibility is to decompose training objectives in terms of hypothesised constituent skills.

Part-task Sequencing

Many tasks can only be trained or are better trained by decomposing the task into smaller, more manageable, components (part-tasks) and by gradually synthesising these components into the whole task during training. This analysis and synthesis strategy underlies most approaches to training. Although it is not always realised, most training approaches involve some kind of part-task training in that most instructors and/or trainees implicitly follow some kind of step-wise strategy in teaching/mastering a new complex task. The way in which this strategy is implemented may vary from training task components separately to emphasising different task components during whole-task training (while neglecting other task components). Part-task training is training whereby two or more components of a task, the part-tasks, are trained according to different training schemes. For instance, in learning to drive, trainees first learn how to steer and subsequently learn additional driving skills. Part-task training is quite common. Not quite so common are attempts to systematise and optimise part-task training.

There are several ideas about why part-task training may be more advantageous than whole-task training. One is that trainees may become overwhelmed and frustrated by being confronted with the whole task. Another is that training a complex task by first letting trainees gain experience with its constituent parts may give them a better insight into the critical aspects of the whole task. Finally, it can be argued that part-task training is more efficient because it enables more training trials per task component than when it is embedded in the whole task.

Typically, relations between task components are distinguished in temporal terms (e.g., sequential, parallel, and overlapping part-task relationships). A number of part-task training schemes are distinguished in the literature. A few of these and their relation with task structure have been described by Wightman and Lintern (1985), such as forward and backward chaining, simple part training, progressive part, and cumulative training. Depending on the set of training objectives, several or all of these sequencing strategies may be combined into a single training programme.

Drawbacks of part-task training Two drawbacks of part-task training have been identified. First, there is the issue of identifying those parts of a task that can be trained consistently with the development of skill. Closely related to this is the issue of determining where in the task problems exist. Secondly, once the trainees have experienced part-task training, they may have difficulty in reassembling the parts.

Part-task trainers also show the limitation of failing to provide an opportunity for practice in time-sharing attention in tasks (Williges *et al*, 1973). The issue is an important one, since many operators such as pilots need to perform several tasks concurrently. Part-task training, however, often involves training individual tasks that are later practised in series with different tasks, rather than in parallel with other parts of the same task. Thus, time-sharing is not typically simulated.

Although many alternative part-task training strategies have been described (Wightman & Lintern, 1985; Ash & Holding, 1990), the literature provides little guidance in choosing a particular method given a particular task. Most research has focused on the broader issue of whole-task versus part-task training (Bilodeau & Bilodeau, 1954; Briggs & Fitts, 1958; Briggs & Waters, 1958; Briggs & Naylor, 1962; Naylor & Briggs, 1963). Earlier research results do not always favour whole-task training (see Wightman & Lintern, 1985, for a review).

The effect of part-task training appears to be mediated by a large number of factors: the type of task and the type of part-task training scheme, the distribution of training effort across different part-tasks, and individual differences in ability (Wightman & Lintern, 1985; Schneider, 1985; Frederiksen & White, 1989; Newell *et al*, 1989; Mané *et al*, 1989). For instance, it has been hypothesised that part-task training is most beneficial for low-ability subjects (Wightman & Lintern, 1985).

Two characteristics have been identified as important in determining the use of part- versus whole-task training methods (Naylor & Briggs, 1963; Blum & Naylor, 1968): task organisation and task complexity. Task organisation relates to the demands imposed on the trainee by the inter-relationship between the task dimensions. Information flow between task dimensions may be simple or complex, as in the case where time-sharing is required. There is also the demand placed on the trainee's information processing capacities by each of the task dimensions separately. Task complexity refers to the difficulty of each of the separate task components. These two task dimensions are believed to act multiplicatively to determine task difficulty. Naylor and Briggs suggested two principles to determine the selection of training methods based on the task dimensions:

- For tasks of relatively high organisation, as the task complexity is increased, whole-task training should become relatively more efficient than part-task methods.
- For tasks of relatively low organisation (all task dimensions being independent), an increase in the task complexity should result in a part-task method becoming superior to the whole task method.

Based on the above principles, the following recommendations have been identified within the literature:

- Where extremely complex tasks need to be trained, part-task training may be necessary. Most of the experiments reported use fairly simple tasks, which often results in non-significant results when compared to whole-task training.
- Many complex tasks fall into a series of unrelated sub-tasks, related only in order of occurrence. Where the activities are performed together or in close temporal order, Stammers (1982) suggests that whole-task training should be used.
- Where poor performance on a later sub-task is likely to disrupt performance, then part-task methods should be used.
- The time taken to train whole tasks can be reduced if only those parts that show an improvement during training are practised in parts, to be integrated into the whole task using the isolated-part method (Seymour, 1956).

Annett and Kay (1956) argue that skill acquisition is mediated by the change in informational value of the signals given to the trainee during the course of learning. Learning can be viewed in the context of two different types of tasks: those in which the subject's responses do not influence the nature of subsequent signals and those where responses change the signals displayed. In tasks where responses do not influence the signals displayed, the subject's task is to learn the sequence and characteristics of the display and respond. Here, Stammers (1982) argues, whole-task training is appropriate. In the second type of task, however, where the trainee's responses alter the signals of subsequent responses, the trainee can learn the sequence of actions necessary only when the sequence of signals remains stable. In this instance, part-task training of sub-tasks would be more appropriate. The principle then proposed by Annett and Kay to take account of this is as follows: 'if elements of a task are highly independent, the task is best learned as a whole, but where the elements are highly interdependent, they should be split up and the task learned in parts'. This at first appears to be a contradiction of the Naylor principles, but Stammers offers a reconciliation between the two. He argues that the organisational demands of the task should be first viewed from the context of Annett and Kay's high interdependence, which indicates whether part-task training is appropriate. If high organisation is present, but not of the Annett and Kay type, then organisational demands in the sense of Naylor suggest the use of whole task training.

In designing training programmes based on the practice of part tasks, the central issue is the determination of the optimal size of learning unit. Stammers (1982) points out that there are no clear-cut answers in this respect. Experiments in the 1960s by Sheffield and colleagues (Margolius & Sheffield, 1961; Weiss *et al*, 1961) suggest that lengthy chains within a task should be broken into shorter units; yet no definitive advice is given concerning the size of the units or rules for their separation, only that they should be easily learned by themselves and amenable to integration with the other units. Sheffield describes as a 'Natural Unit' a segment of several elements of a sequential task that are fairly readily integrated into a superordinate unit of the total task (see also Newell *et al*, 1989).

Evidence is mixed on the value of natural units. In a study of training procedures on a moulding machine, Blankenbaker (1971), for example, found that a part demonstration and practice procedure with a preview of the whole task showed better results than whole practice with a preview. Miller (1971), however, found no advantage of step-by-step demonstration and practice over a whole demonstration and practice. To test these principles experimentally, Stammers (1982) conducted a series of experiments to evaluate part- versus whole-learning for a procedural task and list learning. Whole-task training was compared to three different types of part-task training: pure part-training, linked part-training, and transition method training. Measurement of transfer was on the basis of change to whole-task performance by the whole group. The results showed no overall differences between the various training methods. The pure part group did not receive practice of the transition between the units and this was reflected in longer pauses between parts. The linkage between parts in a serial task was therefore found to have an influence on learning of the task. In addition, it was found that part methods suffer from recency effects, those parts practised earlier being recalled less well on testing. Stammers argued that, given the problems of part-task training (including the problem of not knowing when to change to whole practice), the best approach is one of cautious whole-training, with a series of successive approximations of the whole task (cf. recommendations by Gopher *et al*, 1989).

Whole training (full-task training) Stammers (1982) evaluated part-task training in comparison to whole-task training. The results failed to exhibit significant differences between the various methods of training. None the less, some disadvantages of part-task training have been reported, such as the fact that it seems to lead to less effective transfer. The author suggested that the decision to use part/ whole-task training should be carried out within an adaptive systems model of training. The model should include a feedback loop as a way of evaluating the quality of the training received. Stammers gave guidelines for where part- and whole-task training may be applied, the more important points being:

- Whole training will first be attempted if activities are performed together or in close temporal contiguity.
- Part-training is called for when there is an important inter-dependency between performance of a later part task and performance of an earlier one.
- The task-analysis stage of training is seen as crucial, as this allows the identification of task inter-dependencies.
- Practising as part tasks only those tasks that show improvement during training can prevent time being wasted and allow for their later integration in the whole task.

    Billman (1987) proposed three cases in which whole training is advantageous:

- when the 'intelligence' of the learner is high;
- on distributed rather than massed training;
- when the training tasks have high organisation and low complexity.

Part- and whole-training combined A combination of whole- and part-training has been suggested by Gopher *et al* (1989). In their combination, subjects were trained on the whole task but different parts were emphasised sequentially during training. The benefit of this programme of training was that there was no longer a need to reintegrate the parts at the end of training. Emphasis of the parts was manipulated by providing a display that gave additional feedback in the form of knowledge of results for the relevant task aspect. Subjects who received emphasised training of more parts were found to perform better than those subjects who experienced part-task emphasis on only one part. Performance was also superior to that of the whole-task training group. It is unclear, however, whether this advantage was the result of the emphasis or of the additional feedback, i.e., whether the result was a training- or an instruction-based effect.

Despite its potential benefits and the ubiquity of this topic in texts on training research and practice (e.g., Morrison, 1991; Patrick, 1992), there has been relatively little research on part-task training (Wightman & Lintern, 1985). The main reason is the complexity of the topic and the fact that it is very time-consuming and costly to conduct experiments. Thus far, the major focus of research has been on the issue of whether part-task training is better than whole-task training. For several reasons, this question may be rather pointless. From a practical point of view, even if a part-task training schedule is just as, or even less, effective than whole-task training, it may still be preferable because it is cheaper or offers other logistic advantages. The reason why this question is also scientifically pointless is because specifying a scheme for part-task training is an inherently multi-factorial problem: the answer to the question of whether part-task training is better or worse than whole-task training depends on a large number of factors and hence cannot be answered in a general way.

Part-skill Sequencing

It has been suggested that part tasks should be constructed such that they have meaning for the operator, rather than on the basis of task characteristics (Patrick, 1992; Frederiksen & White, 1989). Frederiksen and White argued that part training could be effective in a task with high organisation (high inter-relatedness of parts), which would call for whole training according to Naylor and Briggs (1963).

The key to the use of part-task training in this context was to decompose the task in terms of the trainee's goals and to construct strategies necessary to achieve the goals. Frederiksen and White examined performance on the PC-based Space-Fortress Game, identifying three major goals and necessary strategies. Twenty-eight games were devised to develop these strategies. Games involving the full strategy were placed last in the sequence of instruction because learning the 'optimal' strategy was felt to require a knowledge of ship control and game characteristics, and basic motor skills. The ordering of learning was given as motor skills followed by ship control heuristics and strategy development. Superior game performance was found for the group that was trained according to the part-skill training, compared to those subjects trained on a whole task.

Retention

Most approaches with respect to the evaluation of part training strategies have focused on transfer to the whole task as the effectiveness criterion. Another perspective is to look at retention as a criterion.

Studies that have addressed the retention of complex tasks have consistently found that it is the procedural elements of the task that are most vulnerable to decay, sometimes falling to operationally unacceptable levels over periods of months or even weeks of non-use. In contrast, continuous motor elements of complex tasks appear to be relatively resilient to decay (e.g., Mengelknoch *et al*, 1971). Such findings strongly suggest that re-training programmes should focus on procedural tasks rather than continuous motor tasks.

To promote the retention of complex, procedural skills, the following points should be noted:

- skill loss increases with the number of task steps;
- task steps that are not cued, either explicitly or implicitly by the previous step in the sequence, are particularly likely to be forgotten.

Finally, research in the field of skill retention has occasionally been criticised for being too focused on very simplified tasks performed in the laboratory, whilst failing to address the characteristic complexity of tasks performed in typical military operations (e.g., Schendel *et al*, 1978). Although task complexity relates to the number of sub-task elements, task organisation refers to the logical arrangement of these elements. As complexity increases, so does the need for good internal organisation. Organisation influences the operator's understanding of the task, which in turn influences how the operator co-ordinates his or her multiple activities to complete the task.

Through training and practice, operators actively develop their own understanding of a task's structure — a 'mental model' of task organisation — that may or may not be consistent with the structure of the task itself. In general, tasks that are mentally well organised are retained better than tasks that are not (Schendel & Hagman, 1991). For example, a task that has internal cues, such that one element leads onto or triggers the next element, is well organised and is likely to be amenable to mental organisation and hence to be easier to retain. Another possibility is that these tasks require less memorisation.

Clustering Principles

Apart from sequencing training objectives and breaking them down into more manageable intermediate training objectives, it may also be necessary to cluster them into separate groups or training phases. Thus, clustering may be motivated by training considerations. Some of these considerations have already been mentioned. Clustering may also be motivated by resource considerations (logistic and organisational constraints) and by the possibilities and limitations of available training media.

Training considerations Training objectives that share common features may be clustered. Particular sequences or dependencies between training objectives may require more coherence than others. This may be a reason for distinguishing different phases separated by break points. The break points may be used as a basis for planning assessment or for scheduling training sessions. With respect to the latter aspect, logistic considerations also enter the picture (availability of sufficient trainees and instructors, frequency of training, organisational issues, and so on). Logistic considerations are usually also tightly linked to factors such as availability of buildings, and training media.

Media considerations   There are several reasons for preferring to use one training medium over another. A particular medium may be inherently more suited to training particular skills than others, for instance, because it offers a training environment that is more valid or because the type of instructional control that may be exercised is more suitable. The considerations that are relevant and the way in which they are weighted will vary substantially from case to case. As the current emphasis is on simulator-based training, in the remainder of this paragraph the issue of when to choose a training simulator will be the main focus.

In selecting media for training, the main choices, in increasing level of realism, are Classroom and Computer-Based Training (CBT), Simulator-Based Training (SBT), and Real-system-Based Training (RBT).

CBT in combination with multimedia can be used for *familiarising* trainees with basic operating concepts and interface principles and characteristics. In addition, multimedia CBT may offer good opportunities for training many individual perceptual and cognitive skills (cf. Chapter 11).

For actually *training* skills by means of executing tasks under more or less realistic circumstances, a Procedure Trainer (PT), i.e., some form of SBT, is minimally required. Part-task training may be cheaper not only because it is more training-effective but also because it allows training to be implemented on part-task trainers. Generally, part-task trainers may be more cost-effective not only in terms of procurement but also because they offer logistic advantages, e.g., higher trainee throughputs and more flexibility.

A simulator consists of a more or less realistic replication of the behaviour of an operational system and its environment, including the displays and controls that are available to the operator(s). In addition, a training simulator is equipped with specific facilities to support training and instruction; typically implemented in the Instructor Operator Station (IOS). A wide variety of different training simulators can be subsumed under the heading of SBT. Simulator configurations are usually distinguished on the basis of the type (comprehensiveness) and realism of the training options/credits that they offer. A diagrammatic representation of the components of a full-blown simulator is shown in Figure 10.1 (adapted from van Rooij *et al*, 1997a).

In a specific implementation, not all of the parts need to be present. In Figure 10.1, only one processor, the central computer, is shown. In reality, all processing may be done with a configuration of dedicated processors or with one integrated system.

The main guideline for assigning training objectives to a simulator is to train those topics that cannot be trained on the real system, because:
- it is too dangerous;
- the appropriate conditions are not available;
- topics cannot be trained sufficiently on the real system:
  — it is too costly (for instance, due to wear and tear to the real system);
  — there is insufficient time on the real system (e.g., during periods when the real system is operationally deployed);
  — the conditions for using the skill in practice occur too infrequently;

— training opportunities are constrained by environmental or safety regulations (noise, pollution, too dangerous).

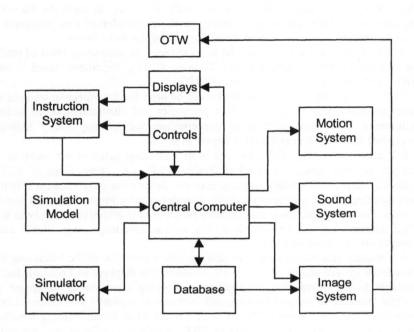

Figure 10.1. Schematic overview of a comprehensive training simulator

Apart from these considerations, it is important to note that technological limitations may preclude the simulation of particular cues, such as sustained vestibular motion cues. Training the skills that rely on these cues may leave only the real system itself as the training 'medium of choice'. The same applies to training of many of the skills that are involved in assembly, maintenance and inspection tasks.

Networked simulators primarily extend the scope of training along the dimension that represents team complexity, e.g., multi-crew training. Networked simulators also enable one to extend the complexity of the environment but mainly along the dimension of tactical realism/complexity. The limitations with respect to the realism of the physical environment are the same as in the stand-alone case.

Networked simulators lack the *physical* realism of field exercises but the range of training scenarios that can be implemented may be much more comprehensive. A problem with using networked training simulators for training is the difficulty of keeping training scenarios 'on track' and retaining an overview of what happens and why, so that timely guidance and feedback can be provided. If this problem is not solved the main uses of networked simulators are likely to remain restricted to the areas of mission rehearsal, testing of operational readiness of crews or units, and testing of operational doctrine or new technologies. Solving this problem requires much more insight into team performance, team performance measurement, and team training strategies than is currently available.

Amount and Distribution of Training

The ordered and elaborated sequence of training objectives that results from the 'unfolding' of training objectives is sometimes denoted by the term 'training scheme'. A training scheme specifies the order in which training objectives are covered in the training programme. The term 'training schedule' refers to the temporal organisation of training sessions, i.e., their duration, frequency, and variation (within a training phase; for an overview cf. Schendel & Hagman, 1991; Patrick, 1992, Chapter 9; Schmidt & Bjork, 1992). In this section a number of relevant issues are covered: the variability of practice hypothesis, the contextual interference effect, the issue of massed vs. distributed practice/training, mastery learning, overlearning, and refresher training.

The Variability of Practice Hypothesis

The variability of practice hypothesis was advanced by Schmidt (1975) in the context of his schema theory of motor skill acquisition (for a critical review, see Rossum, 1991). The variability of practice hypothesis states that performance of a novel task variant, i.e., transfer, will be better following training on a number of other, randomly ordered, task variants (variable training), than following training on a single task variant (constant training).

The Contextual Interference Effect

Contextual interference occurs when several variations of a task are learned during training which involves high levels of interference, e.g., training task variations in random order. Such a condition has generally been shown to result in poorer performance during acquisition but to lead to better transfer and retention (for a general review, see Lane, 1987). The effect was first demonstrated by Battig (1966) for verbal material. The following discussion focuses on motor skill learning. For a review within the domain of motor skill acquisition, the reader is referred to Magill and Hall (1991).

In laboratory research, the effect has been found across a range of different motor tasks. Non-laboratory tasks have been studied in less detail, but in the available studies the effect has also been demonstrated. However, the contextual interference effect is not global. Magill and Hall (1991) hypothesised that the occurrence of this effect depended on whether the skill variations in different contexts were associated with the same motor programme. Motor programmes are understood as generalised motor programmes in the sense of Schmidt's schema theory mentioned earlier. Where skills are controlled by different motor programmes, the contextual interference (training schedule) effect is obtained;

where the same motor programme is involved, no contextual interference effect will be observed.

The contextual interference effect has been found to interact with type of task and level of expertise. A general finding is that, for closed skills, interference early in practice produces the contextual interference effect. However, for open skills, high interference early in practice has not been proven to be beneficial. It seems that for the latter type of skills it is important first to 'get the idea' of the action/movement that is required before progressing to training conditions with high levels of interference.

An interaction with learning style (the reflexivity-impulsivity dimension) has also been found. A reflexive learning style favours accuracy whereas an impulsive learning style favours speed. Only the data of reflexive trainees have been found to display the contextual interference effect.

Several explanations have been put forward to explain the contextual interference effect. Approaches include the elaboration and the action plan reconstruction theory (cf. Magill & Hall, 1991). According to the elaboration theory, increased multiple and variable encoding processes lead to a more distinctive and elaborate memory representation. According to the action plan reconstruction theory, on the other hand, the contextual interference effect is due to similarity in the processing demands between training and subsequent transfer and retention tasks. Proponents of this view argue that contextual interference during skill acquisition results in the learning of a specific ability in establishing a control structure for processing task-relevant information.

Variability of practice and contextual interference   There are possible links between the variability of practice hypothesis of Schmidt's schema theory and the contextual interference effect. For a discussion of these relations, see Magill and Hall (1991). In essence, the variability of practice hypothesis applies to variations of motor programme parameters that belong to the same motor programme whereas the contextual interference effect applies to interference between different motor programmes.

Massed Versus Distributed Practice

In massed training, the interval between successive training trials is minimised; in distributed training, the intervals between training trials are wider. Obviously, then, the distinction between 'massed' and 'distributed' is a relative one. Generally, compared with distributed training, massed training results in worse performance during training and in approximately the same performance after training. The depression of performance during acquisition is generally hypothesised to be the result of fatigue or reduced motivation.

The effects of massed and distributed training on skill acquisition and retention depend on the type of task. For verbal tasks, performance during acquisition is better with massed training. However, retention is better following distributed training. For motor tasks, performance during acquisition is better under distributed training schedules, but is approximately the same for retention.

The fact that, for motor tasks, massed and distributed training schedules produce comparable learning effects (as indicated by retention tests) does not necessarily imply that in particular instances a distributed training schedule will be advantageous (for instance, in dangerous training situations where the fatigue that may ensue in a massed training schedule may put trainees at risk and in cases where trainees are suspected to be poorly motivated).

Mastery Learning

Mastery learning is an approach in which the amount of training is not fixed but is made dependent on the mastery of training objectives (Block, 1971). Usually the amount of training is fixed and expressed in terms of training hours. From an organisational/logistic viewpoint, such a scheduling approach is much more convenient. A major drawback is that individual differences in learning speed are not taken into account, and hence trainee motivation may be reduced and training resources may not be used optimally.

Mastery learning may obviate these drawbacks. The cost of implementing a training schedule based on mastery learning is that it may require a considerable rescheduling and re-organisation of training and a more differentiated approach to the assessment of the process and results of training. With respect to the latter aspect, for instance, it will require more frequent and more explicit assessment of trainee progress.

Overlearning

The long-term retention of task competence can be enhanced by providing additional practice after initial mastery is achieved. This is known as 'overlearning'. Overlearning is effective for perceptual-motor, procedural and cognitive skills, although the effects are stronger for cognitive tasks (Driskell *et al*, 1992). The greater the amount of overlearning, the greater the beneficial effect on skill retention, although diminishing returns can be expected (e.g., McGeoch & Irion, 1952). For cognitive tasks, the longer the delay between overlearning and retention performance, the weaker the beneficial effect of overlearning will be. This may also be true for other types of tasks, but there is a lack of supporting experimental evidence. To maintain optimum performance in a cognitive task, the interval between overlearning and performance of the task should be no longer than a few weeks (Driskell *et al*, 1992).

Refresher Training

Refresher training is often given following long periods of non-use of the skills acquired during initial training. The purpose of refresher training is to re-attain task proficiency in these skills. Refresher training should not be confused with continuation training or conversion training, both of which aim to train new skills and/or tasks or develop existing skills/tasks to new levels of competency. The nature, timing, amount and frequency of refresher training required to re-attain task proficiency depend on various factors, such as the type of task to be learned, the conditions and strategies of training, the level of original learning, and the individual's learning capacity. Unfortunately, there is no clear theoretical framework that describes the impact of these factors and their interactions. Therefore, the following recommendations should be considered with care.

It should be decided whether refresher training should concentrate on maintaining a criterion level of task performance (as is required for task execution in sudden emergency situations), or on bringing deteriorated skills back to initial mastery. In the latter case, it may be worthwhile to consider whether refresher training is really necessary at all. Job conditions may permit the student to regain the former competence level independently by making use of other information (e.g., manual) and by 'learning on the job'.

Initial task acquisition and subsequent task re-learning involve different learning processes. This implies that the nature of refresher training need not be identical to the original training. More cost-effective methods may be equally or more appropriate, such as using low-cost training devices, mental rehearsal and learning through testing.

There is some evidence that the interval between successive refresher training sessions should equal the expected non-use retention interval separating successive occasions of task performance in the real task environment. In addition, competence in complex tasks has been found to start deteriorating rapidly after six months, suggesting that refresher training should be delivered within that period of time (O'Hara, 1990).

The amount of refresher training should be sufficient to bring students back to criterion level, possibly followed by some overtraining. This requires in general less than 50% of the time required for initial training (e.g., Mengelknoch *et al*, 1971). Providing refresher training at expanding intervals is less costly than at constant intervals, and certainly as effective (Bjork, 1988).

The amount of skill loss will be reduced if there is some opportunity to rehearse or practise the skill (or parts of the skill) during the retention interval, such as in a simulator. The more the rehearsed activities resemble the actual task, the more benefit will be derived from the rehearsal.

11   Specification of Training Activities and Scenarios

Introduction

The Specification of Training Activities

The specification of training activities is aimed at those activities that should be performed by the trainee to achieve the training objectives in the most efficient manner. Thus, training activities specify what *trainees* actually have to do in order to learn. The specification of training activities depends greatly on the composition of the training scheme. This is why the training scheme has to be specified first.

Training activities should be distinguished from operational activities. Operational activities are intended to achieve operational objectives; training activities are intended to realise training objectives. Because operational objectives may differ substantially from training objectives, operational activities may differ from training activities. For instance, many training activities are aimed at achieving intermediate skills or skill levels and may never occur under operational conditions (part-skill training).

In current practices, the specification of training activities is not distinguished as a separate step and, consequently, there is no differentiation between different types of training activity. Generally, training activities are simplifications, adaptations or variations of operational tasks. However, there are several good reasons for explicitly separating the specification of training objectives from the specification of training activities. Training objectives specify standards of performance that are to be acquired, but do not specify *how* these standards of performance are to be achieved. By explicitly separating performance goals from the way in which those goals have to be achieved, room is created for considering alternative methods. There may be more effective or efficient ways than simply replicating operational activities that, from a *training* point of view, may contain much slack activity. Also, the type of training activity depends not solely on the nature of the training objective and its operational referents but also on the relative position of the associated training objectives within the training scheme. Moreover, depending on the entry level of trainees and the composition of the training scheme, intermediate training objectives may have to be inserted; for example, to bridge differences between consecutive skills that may be too large. Generally, the larger the gap between criterion level and entry level, the larger the difference between training activity and operational activity. Being temporary and to some extent artificial, these intermediate objectives may require the execution of training activities that bear little or no resemblance to operational activities. The explicit linkage of performance goals with activities also provides better guarantees that all goals are covered during training. Another advantage of keeping the specification of training activities separate is that assessment of trainee performance may be made more transparent. Finally, this approach may provide the possibility of applying adaptation of training activities to trainee performance.

The Specification of Training Scenarios

Similarly, in practice often no distinction is made between the specification of training activities and of training scenarios. Training scenarios specify the environmental conditions for performing a particular training activity or set of training activities. There are several good reasons for distinguishing the specification of training activities from training scenarios. First, by making a clear-cut distinction between training activity and training scenario, the design of training scenarios may be more focused in that only those aspects that are *minimally* required to perform the training activities are considered. This prevents the introduction of all kinds of features and requirements that, although valid from an operational point of view, are not strictly required to perform the training activities and, ultimately, to achieve the training objectives. Of course, particular features may be important for acceptance by trainees and instructors. However, for the underpinning of training (and simulation) requirements, it is important, at least initially, to keep issues of training necessity and user acceptance separate. Of course, at a later stage additional features, i.e., features that are not strictly required for training purposes, may still be added. Secondly, by designing training scenarios on the basis of training task specifications instead of 'copying' them from operational scenarios, training time may be used more efficiently. For instance, it is usually not necessary to execute a complete flight profile from take-off to landing in order to train the skills required to respond adequately to a particular engine malfunction. Thirdly, training activities may deviate more or less from operational activities, and hence may require a training environment/scenario that is considerably different from the operational environment. There are other reasons for separating the specification of training activities and training scenarios, which will be discussed later in this chapter and in Chapter 13.

For the aforementioned reasons, the specification of training activities and the specification of training scenarios will be discussed in separate sections.

Training Activities

The specification of training activities is one of the most difficult steps in the design of a training programme. Many authors contend that different types of training objective require different approaches to training and instruction, and hence may require different types of training activity.

Several attempts have been made to develop guidelines for specifying training activities. Most of these attempts have focused on the cognitive and procedural skills encountered in educational settings. Not much has been published on the design of training activities for the generally more complex and dynamic types of knowledge and skills that are usually trained by means of training simulators. Of course, the simpler the training activity, the faster will be the skill acquisition rate (due to reduction of task load and other factors). For much the same reasons, the level of familiarity of the trainee with the training activity will affect skill acquisition rate. Other potentially relevant considerations are the amount of control that is offered to the trainee in executing his assigned training activities and the extent to which training activities enable or encourage the active involvement of the trainee. Finally, the extent to which training activities provide opportunities for applying the skills to be learned is an important determinant of skill acquisition rate.

For each training objective, one or more training activities may be specified. In practice, training activities have to be combined into one or more composite activity, especially during later stages of training. Towards the end of training, training activities may approach operational activities (depending, of course, upon the criterion levels of performance that are to be achieved with the training programme). For reasons mentioned in the introduction, it seems wise to retain explicit links between training objectives and training activities throughout the specification of training activities. One way to accomplish this is first to specify alternative training activities for each training objective and only then to combine them. Due to sequencing constraints, the number and type of training activities that may be combined will be restricted.

All operational activities can be used as training activities, although, as noted before, this may not be very efficient. Many training activities may never occur in practice. This may depend on the training strategy that is adopted. For instance, for team training one may adopt cross-training as a strategy (team members assuming the role of other team members, roles they would never assume in reality). Also, part tasks may be isolated for training purposes that in practice never occur in isolation. The extent to which this is the case may also depend on the 'depth' of skill analysis. Obviously, the higher the level of detail at which task performance has been decomposed into part tasks and skills, the more obvious deviations from operational reality may be required. Most instructors are reluctant to deviate from operational reality. It should be kept in mind, however, that, first and foremost, training activities should make sense to the trainee and be valid for the purpose of training.

The nature of training activities depends on proficiency level (e.g., beginner, advanced, or expert) and hence the stage of training. Generally, the more proficient the trainee, the more demanding the training activities will be. However, differences in training demands may also be reflected in stricter performance standards rather than changes in the nature of the training activities themselves. A more important, though still crude, way of distinguishing training activities is in terms of the types of skill that they are intended to develop. In this respect, the main distinctions are between:

- perceptual-motor skills;
- procedural skills;
- cognitive skills;
- time-sharing skills;
- team skills.

These skill types have already been introduced in Section I and in Chapter 9. Below, these distinctions will be elaborated further.

Perceptual-motor Skills

A perceptual-motor skill is one in which the primary activity to be performed involves co-ordination between perceptual inputs and motor outputs. However, there are skills that may be regarded almost exclusively as perceptual skills or motor skills, i.e., skills that involve primarily perceptual and motor activities, respectively. For instance, many monitoring/inspection and target acquisition tasks (e.g., sonar and radar tasks) can be classified as perceptual tasks, whereas many task components associated with driving, weapon delivery, and so on would be classified as motor skills. However, the distinction between perceptual and motor tasks is a matter of degree. Most tasks require a mixture of perceptual and motor skill components.

Generally, perceptual-motor skills take a large amount of effort to learn but, once learned, are relatively well retained. Adaptive training has been used in training perceptual-motor skills. Adaptive training is a technique in which the problem, the stimulus, or the task is varied as a function of how well the trainee performs (Kelley, 1969; Gaines, 1972a, b, 1974). Adaptive principles can be applied at different levels of aggregation. Most of the research on adaptive training strategies has dealt with relatively simple perceptual-motor skills and a large number of alternative adaptive training techniques have been used. Due to methodological shortcomings, these studies have yielded equivocal results (Lintern & Gopher, 1978; Mané *et al*, 1989).

Perceptual skills Perceptual skills can be distinguished according to whether they are associated with search, detection, and identification of signals or targets. Learning a perceptual skill may require a substantial amount of knowledge, and subsidiary skills associated with the range and properties of possible targets and signals, the environments in which they may appear, interactions between target and environment, sensors to be used, and options for processing information about targets and signals. Perceptual skills can be further classified as inspection, scanning, and monitoring skills. These skills are usually highly situation-specific and require a large set of cases to be learned. A problem often encountered in designing training for these skills is the lack of good training materials. The composition of this learning set is critically important and a major determinant of transfer; much depends on the representativeness and level of realism of the stimulus material. Not surprisingly, learning perceptual skills may be very time-consuming. This calls for special care in designing training. Unfortunately, relatively little research has been conducted in this area. One systematic approach that may be suited to training a range of perceptual skills is that described by Riemersma *et al* (1995).

Motor skills Motor skills can be categorised on the basis of the muscle groups that are involved in the movements (e.g., Harrow, 1972). However, in the context of human-machine systems (with the possible exception of man-borne weapon systems), usually only a subset is relevant.

Much of the research on motor skills has addressed differences between continuous and discrete tasks. The general finding is that skill on continuous motor tasks is retained much better than skill on discrete motor tasks, although the exact reasons for this effect are not clear (e.g., Hurlock & Montague, 1982).

Many experimental studies have indicated that manual tracking shows very little decay even over long-term retention intervals of months or even years (Schendel & Hagman, 1991). Even a 'warm-up' decrement on the first re-test trial can be reduced if the subject is sufficiently highly practised during initial training. However, the field orientation study on this topic in the MASTER project found evidence of skill decay in a complex manual tracking task in a real operational setting (Carver *et al*, 1996). To explain this, it is hypothesised that skill loss is dependent on tracking task complexity factors, such as control law parameters, target characteristics and engagement disturbance factors (e.g., smoke and noise). Therefore, although skill loss may not be an issue if the experimental tracking task is elementary (simple control law, steady rate targets, no disturbance effects), this may not be true if a complex, real-world tracking task is represented (Evans *et al*, 1996). To conclude, there appears to be very little skill loss with continuous task skills or skill components, at least when there are no other task complications.

In contrast to continuous tasks, there does appear to be substantial decay in the case of discrete-response perceptual-motor skills (e.g., typing). The classical finding with regard to continuous and discrete tasks can be summarised as: skill in performing a continuous-response task is retained almost perfectly and perhaps indefinitely, whereas skill in performing a discrete-response task is prone to loss or deterioration without regular practice. The problem with discrete tasks may be that they are usually 'chained' into sequences of different discrete responses — that is, they are essentially parts of procedural skills.

Procedural Skills

In a procedural skill, the primary activity to be performed involves the execution of an algorithmic sequence of discrete actions. These actions involve few decisions and are generally performed in the same way each time. Procedural skills vary in

• the amount of required planning;
• the number of steps;
• the amount of inherent cueing;
• the number of decision points or branches;
• the number of permissible sequences.

Examples of types of task that involve procedural skills are assembly tasks, maintenance tasks, system management tasks (e.g., standard monitoring and control tasks, and tasks performed during powering up or shutting down a system), and simple diagnosis and troubleshooting tasks. Such tasks are prevalent in the military domain.

Procedural skills are constantly referred to in the research literature as being not only the most difficult to acquire, but also the most susceptible to decay, even after relatively short retention intervals (e.g., Johnson, 1981). Procedural skill learning involves at least two components:

- remembering how to perform each individual step;
- remembering the sequences in which the steps are to be performed in given circumstances.

It is the latter component that appears to degrade more easily during periods of non-practice. The greater the number of discrete steps involved in a task procedure, the greater the likelihood of skill loss or decay. Furthermore, task steps that are not overtly cued, either by previous steps or by the equipment itself, are more likely to be forgotten. Yet another problem with procedural tasks in terms of retention is that many of these skills, such as emergency procedures, are used infrequently. Given that procedural task skills are the most poorly retained, there is clearly more to be gained from the rehearsal of these skills during periods of non-use.

Cognitive Skills

A cognitive skill is one in which the primary activity to be performed involves the heuristic analysis and synthesis of information. Simply stated, cognitive tasks are tasks that involve a lot of thinking, i.e. tasks that do not present a pre-determined or straightforward course of action. This aspect largely derives from the complexity or the uncertainty of the task. These properties necessitate the use of heuristics — problem solving and decision making strategies — instead of algorithms for successful performance. Examples of cognitive tasks are complex monitoring and control tasks, diagnosis tasks, problem solving tasks, and more generally all tasks involving decision making in a complex and/or dynamic situation.

The distinction between procedural and cognitive tasks is a matter of degree and mainly one of complexity. Procedural tasks are generally simpler (e.g., involving fewer steps) and are relatively fixed (e.g., containing fewer decision points). Cognitive tasks involve more uncertainty, which may derive from the amount, the complexity or the inherent uncertainty of the information provided, the complexity of the decisions that have to be made on the basis of this information, or the possible outcomes of the decisions made. By nature of their relative simplicity, procedural tasks can be characterised as deterministic and reproductive.

With respect to learning cognitive skills, it should be noted that simply learning the appropriate declarative and procedural knowledge is not sufficient. Successful performance requires that this knowledge is applied actively in a large variety of contexts. Generally, cognitive skills are built up more slowly but are better retained than procedural skills.

The extent to which cognitive skills such as situational awareness and decision making are lost or retained, and how their retention is affected by other factors, is poorly researched and is not well understood.

Time-sharing Skills

The proficiency in smoothly co-ordinating the execution of a number of different tasks is referred to as skill in time-sharing. Time-sharing refers to the ability to execute qualitatively different task components simultaneously and as such it is one of the defining characteristics of high-performance tasks. Time-sharing skills have to be practised under high task-load conditions. High task load can be induced by manipulating the system and the environment, e.g., occurrence of a system malfunction during a critical flight manoeuvre.

It should be noted that, although separate skills (perceptual-motor, procedural, or cognitive) may present no difficulties when performed in isolation, their combined execution may pose considerable training problems. The latter will be the rule rather than the exception. Especially for military tasks, these high task-load problems may be even more difficult due to the effect of stress caused by threats. Thus, skills that are relatively simple, and in terms of simulation pose no significant problems, may none the less impose substantial training and simulation requirements, by virtue of the fact that they have to be performed and hence trained in a high task-load/high stress context.

Before time-sharing skills can be trained, trainees must be sufficiently proficient on the perceptual-motor, procedural, and cognitive skills to be performed concurrently. For successful performance, this implies that individual skills have to be sufficiently automatised to ensure reliable and accurate performance under high task load conditions. As discussed in the previous chapter, the order in which constituent skills are integrated into a composite skill is very important. Special attention is required for the transitions between different stages of skill integration (van Emmerik & van Rooij, 1998) as the load imposed on trainees may easily become too high and the risk of developing inappropriate time-sharing skills may be increased. Depending on the nature of the transition, several instructional strategies may be used to deal with these risks.

Team Skills

Traditionally, selection, training, and human factors efforts have focused almost exclusively on individual task performance. However, it is increasingly recognised that many modern weapon systems require effective team performance. One impetus for this recognition is the fact that many aircraft, nuclear power plant, and industrial incidents and accidents can be attributed to inadequate team or crew co-ordination. Errors and misconceptions in executing crew procedures are more likely to occur in conditions that induce conflicts, misunderstandings, and misconceptions. These conditions are high task load conditions and conditions that cause vigilance or fatigue problems, distraction, disorientation or stress. In military training and simulation, the emergence of technologies such as networked simulation has also stimulated interest in aspects of team performance.

Team tasks are tasks that are in a way superordinate to tasks assigned to individuals and, depending on task requirements and the organisational structure of the team, rely more or less heavily on sharing of task information between the individuals who constitute the team. However, it should be noted that a team has no memory. Team skills are skills of an individual in functioning within a particular team. This implies that much of what is known about the acquisition of individual skills may be equally applicable to the acquisition of team skills.

Research on team training is still relatively scarce (Salas *et al*, 1995a). Most of the research conducted has focused on measurement of team performance (see Section IV). Although there are various ideas about what constitutes good team performance, it seems that most ideas are still too vague to be empirically tested. From a methodological point of view, research on team training is extremely difficult. Among other things, this difficulty arises from the intractability of team interactions and the associated problems of monitoring and controlling training scenarios. Considering the large variety in team sizes, team compositions, and team tasks, there are also immense problems with respect to generalisability.

Nevertheless, for some domains and aspects of team skills, training concepts have been developed, e.g., cross training and Crew Resource Management (CRM). But it is not clear to what extent these training concepts can be generalised (Verstegen, 1997). A more promising recent idea is to train with simulated team members (Verstegen, 1997). This idea is also referred to as 'agent-based training'. Training with simulated team members has the advantage that both individual and team skills can be addressed systematically. Apart from training with 'ideal' team members, simulated team members can be programmed to function in a sub-optimal way. Simulation of team members, however, is not without problems, and, considering the present lack of knowledge, it will probably take considerable effort to develop valid agents.

Very little attention has been paid to social skills retention in the military domain. It is not known whether this is because of the different nature of communication tasks performed by military personnel (e.g., effectively pre-defined procedural tasks), or because of a difference in perception of such skills within the military and non-military domains. Social skills may become more significant as increasing attention is paid to such factors as teamwork, co-operative task performance and crew resource management.

Training Scenarios

As noted in the Introduction, the training scenario constitutes the environment in which training activities are to be executed. The design of training scenarios is an important determinant of training effectiveness over and above how the training activities and the simulation capabilities of the training simulator have been specified. For instance, given the same training activities and simulation capabilities, transfer may be substantially positive or negative simply by designing good or bad training scenarios. It should also be noted that, by careful design of training scenarios, particular limitations with respect to the simulation of particular cues may be circumvented (cf. Section III). Despite the importance of good training scenarios, there is a paucity of research concerning the design of training scenarios; i.e., research that yields concrete guidelines for how to design good training scenarios.

Typically, a training scenario is run as part of a training session and is preceded by a briefing and followed by a debriefing. Among other things, during briefing the trainee is allocated his training assignment. In addition to the training assignment, the behaviour of the trainee during the scenario is determined by the appearance of the environment and by the events that occur. The course of events that may ensue will vary in response to the actions and reactions of trainees.

In the following, the issues related to the design and composition of training scenarios are discussed. This is followed by a discussion of the required validity of training scenarios.

Scenario Composition

The purpose of a training scenario is to induce and support the execution of a specified training activity or set of training activities, i.e., a training scenario may subserve the execution of more than one training activity. Conversely, more than one training scenario may be associated with a single training activity.

Training scenarios are not operational scenarios. Although it is tempting to use operational scenarios as a starting point for specifying training scenarios, as discussed in the Introduction to this chapter there are several good reasons to resist this temptation. First and foremost, training scenarios must match training activities, i.e., they should provide sufficient context for the trainees to perform their assigned training activities. This implies, for instance, that training scenarios may be very much briefer and simpler than operational scenarios, notably during the earlier stages of training. This not only renders it easier, and cheaper, to implement the training scenario but also facilitates instructional control.

It is obvious that training scenarios have important implications for simulator requirements; in fact, they should be the primary drivers of simulator specifications. For a further discussion of how training scenarios may be used as a basis for the specification of simulator requirements, the reader is referred to Chapter 13.

Ideally, the specification of training scenarios should be sufficiently explicit for subject-matter experts (SMEs) who have not been involved in the design to understand it. This can be checked by using a talk-through or walk-through as a basis for specifying training scenario content. As a first step in specifying this content, one may construct a time-line of the training activities to be executed. After this has been done, the scenario events that are required to initiate, execute, and terminate training activities may be described. For each event, the specifics of the system and the environment that are involved in the event may then be elaborated. Finally, an overall consistency check may be conducted to fill any gaps. It should be noted that, in practice, the aforementioned sequence of steps typically progresses in reverse order. A drawback to the latter approach is that it may result in under- or over-specification of training scenario components and inclusion of superfluous features. Also, the link between training need and simulator requirements may be obscured (see Chapter 13 for further discussion of this issue).

Of course, designing training scenarios at a high level of detail may be a very laborious and time-consuming process. It should be noted that not all scenario components have to be specified at the same level of detail. On the contrary, by taking the training activity, i.e. the view of the trainee(s), as the primary design focus, this will typically not be the case. An option is to elaborate training scenarios only for those training activities that are likely to be trained on a simulator, that are most critical, or that are most representative of other training scenarios, which are therefore not elaborated. Another option is to limit the level of detail or to defer further elaboration after possible implications or issues for the specification process have become clearer.

In the following, several categories of scenario components that may have to be specified during training programme design are described. These descriptions include some considerations that may be relevant for their specification. The main categories that are distinguished are associated with the *system*, *environment*, and *process* aspects of a training scenario.

System The main system component that is relevant for the trainee is his or her system interface. Main components of this interface are the so-called Human-Machine Interface (HMI) and, if this is present, the Out-of-The-Window (OTW) view. The HMI is the interface between the operator and the system that contains all the displays and controls that are available to the trainee to monitor and control the system; i.e., the parts that provide the instrument cues. The OTW view is the interface between the operator and the environment outside the system. Sometimes the two coincide. For instance, for a sonar or radar operator, the HMI is the sole interface with the underwater environment. Also, during IFR flight, pilots have only their instruments to fly the aircraft.

Environment In the case of mobile weapon systems, the representation of the environment comprises a description of the spatial layout of the terrain, the water surface, or the underwater surface. Typically the spatial configuration of specific features of these surfaces, e.g., relief, vegetation, sea states, is also specified. The representation may be a set of mathematical equations that generate appropriate signals and noise that are processed by the sensors under the control of the operator. The behaviour of the sensors, i.e., their signal processing characteristics, may also be represented by a mathematical model.

Process On the training activity level, events, actions, and reactions can be used to describe interactions between system and environment. An event is a change in the state of the system or the environment. An action is an event initiated by the trainee. A reaction is a action that is initiated in response to an event.

An important reason for the use of simulators is the fact that more training activities can be executed in less time. However, compression of training activities may compromise script plausibility. This may be less problematic if deviations from reality are explicitly addressed, for instance, by simply telling trainees or by interleaving simulator training with training on the real system. Usually this will be less of a problem for continuation training in which trainees/operators already have operational knowledge that enables them to take deviations into account. During initial training or acquisition, deviations from operational conditions may be faded out of the training programme before trainees transition to the real system, e.g., by gradually progressing towards more plausible scenarios.

A distinction can be drawn between reactive, interactive, and multi-interactive scenarios. A reactive scenario is one in which the trainee has only to react to events. Typically, only a small number of alternative courses of events may occur. In interactive scenarios, the course of events also depends on the self-initiated actions of the trainee. In multi-interactive scenarios, the course of events depends not only on the actions of the trainee but also on the actions of other participants in the scenario, e.g., other trainees/teams, agents, and computer-generated forces. Of course, the larger the range of alternative courses of actions, the larger the problem of keeping training scenarios on track. This is essential to guarantee that the intended training activities are performed and to prevent trainees from floundering. The extent to which this is considered to be a problem depends on the training strategy that is adopted. For some types of training activities and trainees, allowing for more freedom for discovery and exploration may be beneficial. Naturally, this does not obviate the need to keep track of what happens and why.

One option to control the alternative courses of events is to allow for only one or a limited number of alternative scripts. Where events threaten to take another course, corrections will have to be applied. Another option is to include a large number of alternatives. In the first case, each time the scenario is run much effort may be required to monitor and control the course of events. In the latter case, much more effort may be required to elaborate all relevant scripts. However, this effort has to be invested only once.

The way in which the control issue is resolved has important implications for the possibilities of trainee assessment, the specificity of instruction that may be achieved, and the options for automating instruction and/or for providing instructional facilities.

Dimensions of Validity

As noted earlier, 'all training is simulation'. This includes training on the real system in the 'real' environment. This statement notably applies to military training where in many cases the 'operational practice' remains an idealisation based on past experience and hunches about what the future may bring. Thus, validity is always an issue.

Validity is not an absolute concept, and one should always ask 'validity with respect to what?'. In MASTER terms, validity should be expressed in terms of the skills that can be attained rather than the level to which physical reality can, or has to, be approximated. In other words, within MASTER, training objectives are the primary standards for assessing validity. Thus, the MASTER conception of validity is broader than is customary, and also considers the composition of the training programme as a factor that affects validity.

Validity comprises two aspects: comprehensiveness and realism. The former refers to the number of skills that can be trained relative to the total number of skills that are required; the latter refers to the proficiency level that can be attained relative to the proficiency level that is required in practice.

Levels of Description in Scenario Specification

A training scenario can be specified at a level that closely corresponds to the level at which training activities have been specified, i.e., in terms of features of the system and the environment, and objects and object relations that are associated with each of the actions, events and reactions. This level of description is relatively straightforward and closely matches the level of discourse used by SMEs. To be useful as a basis for the specification of simulator requirements, specifications need to be much more specific.

12   Design of Instruction

Introduction

As noted in Chapter 9, a distinction can be made between training and instruction. Training has been defined as comprising those trainee activities that are executed in interaction with a scenario and are intended to induce or promote learning. Instructional activities have been defined as those activities executed in interaction with a training process that are intended to enhance training efficiency; i.e., instruction is regarded as a means of supporting training, and hence is subsumed under training. In this view, instruction primarily serves as a catalyst in the training process. As a catalyst, instruction should facilitate the training process without the trainee coming to rely on it.

Purpose and Principles of Instruction

The purpose of instruction is to facilitate the training process. This can be accomplished in a large number of ways, which all boil down to providing a corrective loop between the knowledge and skills of trainees and their performance. This loop may be generated internally by the trainees or externally by means of instruction. Ideally, the external loop that is provided by instruction should facilitate and complement/augment, rather than substitute for, the self-corrective loop that is established by the trainees. Ingredients of any corrective loop, whether generated internally or provided externally, include:
- criteria for assessing, and generating expectancies about, performance;
- performance measures or indicators;
- diagnostics and diagnostic rules to interpret differences between performance and criterion;
- interventions and intervention rules to improve performance.

Training objectives and training activities generally provide the criteria against which performance can be assessed. Training objectives primarily specify criteria related to the result of training, whereas training activities primarily specify the criteria for assessing the training process.

Performance measures are typically derived from the criteria adopted. Given a particular set of criteria, a large variety of different performance measures may usually be defined and used. The choice between these measures is guided by considerations of validity, reliability, sensitivity, discriminability, ease of use and cost (see the discussion of workload measures in Section IV).

To be able to interpret deviations and discrepancies between criteria and measures of performance, one should have ideas about the underlying causes. Deviations and discrepancies may merely represent noise or measurement error. To be able to choose between alternative responses, the most likely origin has to be pinpointed. Resolving such issues may require one to take the learning history of the trainees into account.

Given a hypothesised origin of a particular deviation/discrepancy, different types of interventions may be in order. Which intervention is most appropriate depends *inter alia* on trainee characteristics and the intervention history. For instance, if a particular intervention has already been delivered several times, and apparently has not yielded the desired effect, another intervention may be appropriate. Another important decision to make is when to deliver an intervention. This may involve waiting for a suitable moment to occur or it may involve creating such a moment by, for instance, postponing forthcoming scenario events. Executing a particular intervention effectively closes (and re-commences) the corrective loop.

From the foregoing it will be clear that the design of instruction pre-supposes many assumptions about the learning process that should take place, about possible obstacles, problems, and misconceptions that learners may encounter, and about the best way to overcome them. This knowledge is often difficult to obtain, notably if the skills to be trained are new or rare. Usually one is forced to draw rather heavily upon one's own learning experiences, to extrapolate and draw analogies from one's own experiences, to tap the experiences of others, or to refer to the available literature. Whatever the validity of the assumptions that are used as a starting point, it is critically important to explicate them and to document, exchange, and discuss ideas and experiences. Explication of ideas renders them amenable to testing and correction (see Chapter 14), whereas documenting, exchanging, and discussing ideas and experiences further the development of a more consistent and more comprehensive knowledge base.

In designing instruction, a useful principle is to minimise it. One reason is that instruction may add to the trainee's task load. Another reason is that minimising instruction promotes the active involvement of trainees and prevents them from relying on instructional support for their performance. However, a caveat is that research on discovery learning in simulation-based learning environments (van Joolingen, 1997) has shown that even university students have difficulty in monitoring their learning performance.

If sequencing of training objectives and the design of training activities and scenarios have been conducted appropriately, there should be minimal requirements for instructional support. Of course, what is considered minimal depends on trainee characteristics and the training strategy. With respect to training strategy, it is helpful to note that instruction is not confrontation, as instructors sometimes seem to think. At times, it may be a good strategy to confront trainees with the consequences of their mistakes. But such a confrontation strategy should not be used as an argument for giving trainees a hard time or letting them flounder by refraining from helping them when they need it. The purpose of training and instruction is to challenge trainees, not to overwhelm and frustrate them.

In most cases, the design of instruction will remain an iterative process that may continue for a long time after the initial delivery of the training programme. During this process it may be wise to change instruction only after the possibilities for improving training by other means, e.g., by modifying the sequence of training objectives, the amount of training, and the design of training activities and training scenarios, have been exhausted.

Distinction between Briefing, Tutoring, and Debriefing

Within the context of a training session, instructional activities can be distinguished in terms of whether they occur prior to, during, or after scenario execution. These activities have been labelled briefing, tutoring, and debriefing activities, respectively. Briefing, tutoring, and debriefing are closely related, and an important issue in the design of instruction is how to combine them in an optimal way. Ideally, tutoring should be invoked only if instructional support cannot be provided during briefing and debriefing.

Instruction will be specific to a particular training scenario and can be specified in the form of scenario-specific briefings, debriefings and possible tutoring interventions during training. Briefing aims to activate prior knowledge and prepare the trainees to execute the training activities. Debriefing aims to evaluate results in terms of training objectives and consolidate acquired knowledge and skills. Tutoring aims to concentrate training effort and to correct deviations and discrepancies between actual and intended performance.

Actually, briefing and debriefing may be considered as constituting two ends of a larger corrective loop, with tutoring an intermediate step. For this reason, the topic of tutoring will be reviewed after issues and considerations with respect to the design of briefing and debriefing activities.

Briefing

It is generally assumed (for instance, in research on 'advance organisers') that providing trainees with advance information (e.g., training objectives, lesson overview, and training guidelines) aids subsequent training. For instance, Ohlsson (1992) has proposed a theory in which the function of prior knowledge in skill acquisition is to enable the learner to detect and to correct errors.

Briefings may contain:

- information about the position of the lesson/scenario within the overall training programme;
- a review of the relevant learning history;
- information about the lesson / scenario (e.g., duration, breaks);
- the training assignment, which should include a statement of the training objectives and the training activities. This may include remarks about the relevance for operational performance, e.g., by pointing out analogies and links between training activities and operational performance using examples and anecdotes;

- the composition of the scenario;
- information about the way in which performance will be assessed;
- information about caveats, difficulties, and deviations from operational conditions (for instance, with respect to cueing realism);
- information about instructional strategies and tactics that will be used (e.g., augmented cues that will be presented).

Testing at the end of briefing is very important, particularly if the training scenario is complex, unusual, or has a long duration. This ensures that the trainees know what to do and what to expect, and thus prevents training effort from being wasted. Testing may be accomplished by asking questions or by letting trainees repeat the most important points (simply asking whether or not the trainees understand the briefing is not sufficient).

The form in which briefings are presented generally depends on information content, and in particular on the nature of the skills that will be trained. Some relevant considerations and issues are reviewed below.

Perceptual-motor Skills

The training of perceptual-motor skills typically involves the presentation of more dynamic and complex types of information, e.g., temporal or spatial. For these types of information, non-verbal briefing formats (simulations, animations, and demonstrations) are generally most effective. Visual demonstrations can adopt the form of imitation, in which the trainee observes another performer on the task or at work (Shebilske *et al*, 1992). Demonstrations can also be carried out using films in which task performance is shown. Such demonstrations may be augmented by highlighting particular aspects by verbal comments or by presenting the trainee with additional visual cues, thus fostering the active participation of the trainee.

The trainee apparently learns by observing and imitating another's performance. Most research on this issue is conducted within the context of observational learning theory (Carroll & Bandura, 1990). The mechanisms underlying the effect are not completely understood (Holding, 1987; Annett, 1991). Social variables such as the presence of the model while trainees perform the task, the status of the model (i.e., instructor or peer), and the skill level of the model performing the task affect the results of this kind of training. Thus, if the model is present when trainees perform the observed task, the trainees' performance on the task is better. Furthermore, observing an unskilled teacher is less effective than observing an unskilled peer, and this is less effective than observing a skilled model of either kind.

Imitation may be useful in the early stages of skill acquisition, when attentional resources are needed to perform the task and performance is error-prone and slow. Observation provides the trainee with a standard to which he can compare his performance, and reduces the number of alternative actions (Holding, 1987) and thus limits the number of interventions required during training.

Procedural Skills

Conceptual knowledge refers to an understanding of the principles underlying a device's functions, whereas operational knowledge refers to an understanding of only the procedures required to operate the device. Research has shown that, for the long-term retention of complex procedural tasks, operational knowledge should be supplemented with elaborations designed to induce enhanced processing and understanding (Farr, 1987). It is believed that including functional explanations in the briefing allows students to acquire a more elaborated mental model of the system and task. However, the question of whether or not conceptual knowledge will enhance skill retention is complicated by such factors as:

- the way conceptual information can support task performance, and in what context the task will be carried out;
- how long the task needs to be retained over periods with no practice;
- whether the difficulty of understanding the theory, and using it, is within the ability level of the trainee population;
- whether adding conceptual information to procedural instructions exceeds working memory capacity.

In general, conceptual knowledge is not necessary if the system is so simple that the user does not need this type of information to infer the correct operating procedures, or if the task is frequently carried out and the procedures can be learned by rote. Conceptual information is helpful for skill retention if it allows the user to infer the exact procedures to perform a complex task, and should include information on the system's components, the way the components are connected, and how they behave and interact. In addition, the user must be shown the strategies for applying the conceptual knowledge to meet task goals.

Cognitive Skills

For the training of cognitive skills, e.g., the application of rules and heuristics, briefings are usually delivered verbally as these skills are difficult to visualise or demonstrate. Sometimes a briefing in the form of a 'mental talk-through' or 'walk-through' of the scenario or of particular events that may occur may be helpful. In such cases a trainee talk-through might follow an instructor talk-through.

Time-sharing Skills

To the extent that the skills that have to be combined or integrated can be visualised, the remarks made with respect to the briefing of perceptual-motor and procedural skills will apply. Otherwise the remarks on the briefing of cognitive skills are applicable. However, a difference with training individual skills is that, during briefing of time-sharing skills, the focus will have shifted to dependencies between different skill aspects.

Team Skills

Often team skills are also difficult to visualise or demonstrate, and team briefings will be in a format similar to the briefing of cognitive skills, e.g., a talk-through or walk-through of the scenario or of scenario fragments. However, considering the emphasis that should be placed on dependencies between trainees, talk-throughs or walk-throughs may be combined with some form of role play.

Debriefing

The importance of reviewing results after training is widely recognised, and the effect is generally attributed to mechanisms similar to those hypothesised to underlie briefing and tutoring effects (e.g., Thatcher, 1990). There has been little or no research on the effect of briefings and debriefings, let alone the trade-offs that are involved in exploiting the interactions between these alternative approaches.

An important issue in planning and designing debriefing activities is to resolve what is to be addressed during training, i.e., during scenario runtime, and what is to be addressed after finalisation of the training scenario or session. To a large extent, resolution of this issue will depend on the position of the training scenario in the training programme and on the training history of the trainee. One may hypothesise that critical aspects that may adversely affect the ongoing training process (e.g., misconceptions, and interventions that are relatively easy to understand, of short duration, and do not require a specific response/acknowledgement from the trainee) may best be resolved during rather than after training.

Debriefings generally contain an overall evaluation of trainee performance after the training scenario has been terminated, and highlights of illustrative training events. Usually this evaluation will be in terms of a comparison of trainee performance during scenario execution with the performance criteria presented during briefing. On the basis of this comparison, possible deviations and discrepancies may have to be reviewed. As noted in the introduction, this requires determination of deviations/discrepancies to be considered significant. Ideally, such reviews should start by briefly re-iterating what has been said during briefing. This may then be followed by a review of events during scenario runtime. The level of detail will depend on the duration and complexity of the scenario. The longer the duration and the more complex the scenario, the more global these reviews will be. To a large extent, this also depends on the available possibilities for registering and reviewing trainee performance. Debriefings may be finalised by formulating a number of conclusions and associated recommendations that may be stored for future reference.

To maintain and enhance trainee motivation, it is important that during debriefing the positive aspects of performance are also brought to the fore. It may be a good strategy always to start by mentioning the positive aspects before reviewing those aspects that are amenable to improvement.

Much of what has already been said about the briefing of different types of skill is also relevant to debriefing. In most cases, debriefing will focus on the more molar, strategic, aspects of performance; more specific guidance and feedback may already have been delivered during scenario runtime. This implies, generally, that debriefings will primarily focus on cognitive, time-sharing and team skills rather than perceptual-motor and procedural skills.

Tutoring

As compared with the corrective loop of briefing and debriefing, tutoring is a corrective loop at a more molecular level. Like any corrective loop (cf. Introduction) tutoring comprises the following ingredients:

- performance criteria or standards;
- performance measures or indicators;
- diagnostics and diagnostic rules to interpret differences between performance criteria and measurements;
- interventions and intervention rules to improve performance.

The major distinction between tutoring and briefing/debriefing is that tutoring is a process that proceeds in real-time, i.e., in parallel and in interaction with the training process, whereas briefing/debriefing is a process that proceeds off-line. Consequently, in designing tutoring, timing is a major issue. Ideally, performance measurement, diagnosis, and intervention should be conducted so fast that the training process is minimally disrupted. Of course, the constraints imposed depend on the timing of the training process. To some extent this timing is under the control of the designer of the training programme, who can design training activities and training scenarios in such a way that sufficient time is available for intervening in the training process. This may also be under the control of the instructor, e.g., by providing him with the means to adapt the training scenario. For instance, instead of waiting for an opportunity to intervene, instructors may be given the means to create such opportunities by deferring scenario events, by slowing down or freezing scenario time, and so on.

The decision whether or not to intervene is not always easy. The stress associated with an intervention may impose additional load on the trainee and, as a result, the intervention may do more harm than good. One rule that may be used in this respect is always to intervene when there is a risk of error propagation, and hence of training activities and scenario progress becoming compromised. Another rule that may be used is to intervene when there is a risk that errors will be repeated or deviations persist. In this case, valuable training time may be wasted and the wrong skills may be learned.

Scheduling interventions may be a problem. Interventions may be scheduled relative to scenario time, i.e., with respect to an absolute reference, or relative to the occurrence of particular events. The latter approach is more common. A problem with event-based scheduling of interventions is deciding when to intervene after an error has occurred. Intervening too soon may prevent the trainee from correcting himself; intervening too late may reduce the impact of the intervention and may cause subsequent problems because there is less time available for correction. When multiple interventions are called for, there is a problem of which intervention to select and how interventions should be prioritised. In cases like this it may be necessary to take the learning and/or intervention history of the trainee into account.

Tutoring Interventions

Guidance and feedback tutoring interventions can be distinguished. Guidance is proactive, feedback is reactive; both constrain the degrees of freedom in the direction of the training objectives. In this respect, it should be noted that tutoring serves the same purpose as sequencing, the design of training activities and scenarios, and briefing and debriefing. The provision of guidance and feedback affects performance. The danger is that trainees may come to rely on it. This may be prevented by gradually withdrawing tutoring support from the training process, a technique called 'fading'. Fading may be made contingent upon improvement of performance, i.e., adaptive. Fading the provision of feedback towards the end of training enhances long-term retention, probably because this encourages trainees to develop self-correction strategies (Nicholson & Schmidt, 1991).

Both the content and the form of guidance and feedback may vary widely. Guidance and feedback can be more or less explicit (correcting behaviour vs. changing conditions), more or less direct (e.g., prompting vs. hinting), and more or less imperative (directive vs. suggestive). Guidance and feedback may serve different functions: to direct attention to particular aspects, to warn, to hint, to prompt, to correct, or to reinforce.

A distinction can be drawn between intrinsic and extrinsic guidance and feedback. Intrinsic guidance and feedback are inherent in the training activity and the training scenario and hence are not subsumed under tutoring. Extrinsic, or augmented, guidance and feedback are provided in addition to the guidance and feedback inherently available. The distinction between these two categories is not always clear. For instance, particular cues that are intrinsic may be amplified or attenuated beyond their normal range of variation to make them more or less salient (accented cueing and feedback).

Different kinds of guidance and feedback can be provided to enhance the training process. Frequently, distinctions are between verbal guidance, augmented cueing and feedback (Adams, 1971; Adams & Goetz, 1973; Adams *et al*, 1977; Salmoni *et al*, 1984; Winstein & Schmidt, 1989; McKendree, 1990; Schmidt *et al*, 1991; Johnson *et al*, 1993), physical guidance (Holding, 1987; Patrick, 1992), and prompting (Patrick, 1992).

Augmented cueing and feedback may be presented either before (cueing) or after (feedback) particular training events. Extrinsic cues are additional information given to trainees so that they can associate cues external to the task to the responses required by the task, and thus be able to anticipate the correct response and avoid errors. Augmented feedback is additional feedback information given to trainees to correct or improve performance. Augmented feedback or Knowledge of Results (KR) consists of information, provided externally to the trainee, about the discrepancy between the trainee's actual response and the criterion response. Augmented feedback should be provided in the initial skill acquisition phase, if task-inherent cues are too scarce or too difficult for trainees to interpret. The feedback should direct the trainee's attention to his errors and the causes of these errors. For simple tasks, simple directional feedback will often suffice (e.g., 'too slow', 'too fast', 'too far to the left', 'too far to the right'). However, more detailed feedback is recommended for complex tasks, provided that the trainee can assimilate and integrate this detailed information to plan and execute better performance on subsequent trials. If not, it may be preferable to practise the difficult components of the task separately and integrate them at a later stage. Trainees perform better during acquisition when they receive more or more accurate KR, but usually perform worse in retention tests, when KR has been withdrawn, than those trainees who received less useful KR or whose KR was progressively withdrawn during training (Holding, 1987; Schendel & Hagman, 1991).

Augmented feedback is usually distinguished from response-produced feedback, i.e. feedback that is naturally produced when a response is made. Response-produced feedback designates the sensory consequences of motor responses associated with them (i.e., sights, sounds, feelings, proprioceptive sensations). Increases in the number of feedback channels and the quality of response-produced feedback during training facilitate skill acquisition as well as skill retention. The time interval between response and feedback is important. Generally, immediate feedback is to be preferred over delayed feedback.

Physical guidance is especially important in motor learning. Physical guidance can be executed by stopping an ongoing movement (response prevention) and by physically forcing a particular movement (response forcing). Response prevention prevents the trainee from performing incorrect alternatives; response forcing provides information about what is the correct response (Holding, 1987). The relative effectiveness of response prevention and response forcing depends on the types of movement that are being trained. For serial movements such as typing, prevention appears to be more useful than forcing (Holding, 1987). The availability of knowledge of alternative responses also affects the effectiveness of these methods. Thus, a trainee trained by forcing responses has no possibility of becoming acquainted with possible alternative ways of performing the task. Hence, information about alternative movements should be inserted into the training programme (Holding, 1987).

Tutoring Models and Implementation Issues

Given the aforementioned constraints, opportunities, and considerations, there are several ways to model and implement the tutoring process:
- on the basis of the intuitions of instructors;
- on the basis of a pre-specified list of possible errors;
- on the basis of deviations from an empirical model;
- on the basis of deviations from a theoretical model.

Intuitions of instructors Most tutoring activities are based on the intuitions of instructors. It is clear that such an approach offers much flexibility. It also enables one to take into account aspects that may only be assessed by direct observation (e.g., attitude, amount of effort required). A drawback is that this approach capitalises on the didactic expertise and the vigilance of instructors. Another drawback is that instructors may be biased and may use widely divergent tutoring approaches. Because of these differences, and because biases and intuitions may largely remain implicit, it may be more difficult to compare training results and to validate training. A more serious risk of relying on instructor intuitions is much less transfer.

Pre-specified list of possible errors/deviations In many cases it may be possible to specify/predict particular errors or deviations that may occur in advance of training. These may be included in the instructor syllabus, for instance in the form of a checklist, or implemented in the form of instructor alerts that are automatically triggered when the appropriate conditions apply. Drawbacks of this approach are that it capitalises on the validity of this list, and that it may cause instructors to overlook or de-emphasise other aspects that are not listed.

Deviations from an empirical model Another way to programme and deliver tutoring activities is to compare the performance of trainees against performance of an expert or an idealised trainee. This approach may enable tutoring to proceed automatically, i.e., without the presence of an instructor, and may enable close monitoring of performance. Of course, it presupposes that there is only one or a limited number of alternative ways of performing adequately. Whether or not this is the case may be assessed by listing correspondences between the performance of experts who perform the same training activities in the context of the same scenario. A high level of correspondence is most likely to be found for activities that are relatively simple, e.g., simple motor tasks.

Deviations from a theoretical model As research on the development of Intelligent Tutoring Systems (see Chapter 9, and Verstegen, 1996) testifies, this approach is very difficult to realise even for relatively well-structured and static domains. Another related strategy is frequently to test the skills of trainees using tests that are based on a model of the training process. The tests used for this purpose may be embedded in the training scenario.

It will be clear that each of the aforementioned approaches has its advantages and drawbacks. In most cases a mix of approaches is likely to be optimal. Which mix is most appropriate will, as always, depend on the nature of the skills that are to be trained and on the composition of the training programme. The combination of tutoring strategies that is chosen will determine the nature of the implementation. Implementations can be distinguished in terms of the level of automation, i.e., the allocation of functions between computer and instructor, and in terms of staffing requirements, i.e., one or more than one instructor. In the former case, guidelines with respect to the allocation of tasks between human and machine may provide additional guidance. Where the instructor responsible for tutoring is a member of a training staff (as, for instance, in team training), allocation of tasks, communication, and consensus between training staff members become additional issues to be addressed.

13 Methodology for Training Programme Design

Introduction

In Chapter 8, current practices with respect to the procurement and specification of training simulators and the design and delivery of simulator-based training programmes were reviewed. In Chapters 9-12, a large number of issues, guidelines, and considerations were considered with simulator-based training as the criterion. By comparing these reviews, it will be clear that there is a gap between the theory and the practice of simulator-based training. It can also be concluded that there is a 'communication gap' between theory and practice: concepts and findings do not easily find their way into applications or practical guidelines, and practical problems do not drive the development of new concepts or set directions for research.

The issue addressed in this chapter is how to close this knowledge and communication gap. Within the context of the MASTER project, this issue was resolved by developing a methodology for the systematic specification of simulator requirements.

The MASTER Methodology

As depicted in Figure 13.1, the MASTER methodology comprises three related steps: Training Needs Analysis (TNA), Training Programme Design (TPD), and Training Media Specification (TMS). The distinction between these consecutive steps reflects one of the main starting points underlying the MASTER methodology: first and foremost, simulator requirements should be derived from *training* rather than operational or technical considerations. In current practice, the latter is the rule rather than the exception; approaches to (military) training and simulation are still largely determined by considerations of operational similarity, availability and affordability of current technologies.

During TNA, the training need is determined and described in terms of a set of related training objectives. During TPD, training objectives are translated into training programme requirements. Finally, during TMS, training programme requirements are translated into simulator requirements. Each of these main steps is subdivided into a number of more elementary substeps connected by means of input/output relations (see Figure 13.2).

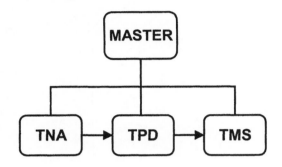

Figure 13.1. Main steps of the MASTER methodology

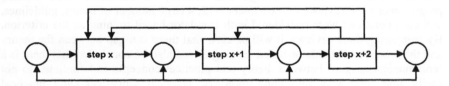

Figure 13.2. Iterative input-output relations between consecutive steps

Applying the MASTER methodology involves an iterative progression through the steps that constitute the methodology. At each step, the user is required to perform a circumscribed set of activities that invariably involves generating a particular output given particular input information, i.e., elements of the output of previous steps. The user is supported by a number of support facilities and guidelines. Also, facilities are available for documenting the activities that are performed. At each step, the user may choose, or be advised, to return to previous steps to elaborate requisite information or to resolve ambiguities. By progressing through the steps of the methodology, the user systematically builds up a relational database of all the relevant information that bears on the specification of simulator requirements. The resulting database can be used for documenting and communicating (intermediate) results.

TNA and TPD

As described in Chapter 10, the output of TNA is a set of related training objectives and a set of trainee characteristics. This information constitutes the main input to

TPD; other relevant inputs may be information on available resources and on applicable constraints that is acquired during the execution of the various TPD sub-steps. In Chapter 10 and subsequently, the issue of how the results of TNA may be used in the design of training programmes has already been discussed extensively. Therefore, the following description of the MASTER methodology will be limited to a description of the rationale and outline of the TPD methodology. This will be followed by a somewhat more extensive discussion of how the output of TPD may be used as a basis for the specification of simulator requirements.

Training Programme Design

A major problem is that the design of training and instruction strategies is very task-specific, whereas most of the guidelines encountered in the literature are formulated in a general way (although their empirical basis may be quite narrow). As already stated in the concluding paragraph of MASTER Deliverable A2.1 (Literature Review on Simulator-based Training and Instruction): 'The challenge facing this work package is to develop a training programme model and a training programme development methodology that systematises, and is consistent with, research findings and that is sufficiently explicit to provide practical guidance. *The main issue will be finding a balance between generality and specificity.*'

In the literature, several instructional design methodologies have been described (e.g., Landa, 1974; Briggs & Wager, 1981; Merrill, 1983; Reigeluth & Stein, 1983; Reigeluth, 1987; Hooper & Hannafin, 1988; Leshin *et al*, 1990; Merrill *et al*, 1991), and have been reviewed by van Rooij *et al* (1995). These methodologies have typically focused on educational (classroom) settings; none was developed specifically for the kind of skills and settings where training simulators are typically deployed, i.e., the training of high-performance skills in industrial and military settings.

In recent decades a number of methodologies, all subscribing to the so-called Systems Approach to Training (SAT), have been proposed to systematise training concepts and to support the application of these concepts (for an early example, see Branson *et al*, 1975a, b). Most of these SAT methodologies are quite general and lack procedural specificity, which makes it difficult to apply them consistently and reliably, and hence to validate them. The difficulty in applying these methodologies may also partly reside in the fact that the design of training deals with concepts that are quite abstract and, partly for this reason, the design of training is a highly iterative process.

The approach adopted within the MASTER project is to develop a methodology that comprises a step-wise procedure for the specification of training programme requirements. This methodology is specifically focused on the specification of training programmes for simulators, and hence is more restricted in scope than other SAT methodologies. Also, the TPD methodology is being implemented in a software tool. It is hoped that this will result in more explicit and consistent procedures and less terminological confusion. It is planned that further development of the prototype developed in MASTER will be realised by means of empirical validation studies with prospective users. By restricting the scope, implementing the methodology in software form, and validating the TPD methodology empirically, many of the drawbacks of earlier SAT methodologies will be circumvented.

The review of TPD will be limited to the steps depicted in Figure 13.3. It should be noted that, in their present form, each of these steps comprises several substeps (cf. Verstegen *et al*, 1998; van Rooij *et al*, 1998a).

Essentially, during TPD the 'blueprint' of a training programme is designed. As mentioned earlier, the main input to this step is the set of training objectives that is the output of TNA. Another important input is information about the group of trainees to be trained, information that is acquired during Trainee Analysis, one of the steps of TNA. This input consists of a description of trainee characteristics, e.g., learning strategies, and a specification of the available skills. The output of TPD is a specification of the prospective training programme. It should be noted that the level of detail at which the training programme is described may vary considerably. In the context of deriving simulator requirements, the design of the training programme is primarily intended as a means to this specific end; it is not intended as a training programme that is actually to be delivered. In cases where the main interest lies in designing or analysing an executable simulator-based training programme, the required levels of comprehensiveness and specificity are likely to be higher.

During TNA, training objectives have been derived by means of a systematic analysis of operational requirements and an analysis of trainee characteristics. This has largely been accomplished by a process of abstraction, in which training objectives have been extracted from the mission and task descriptions of concrete operational behaviour. During TPD, the reverse process takes place: the translation of more or less abstract training objectives into concrete *training behaviour*.

Training Design

In this step, an outline of the training programme is constructed based upon the training objectives and the characteristics of the target group of trainees. Training design includes:

- selection of general training strategies and/or learning principles that will be applied in the design, and later the delivery, of training;
- decisions concerning the sequence of training objectives;
- allocation of a range of potentially applicable training media to each training objective;
- construction of an assessment plan.

Specification of Training Activities

The goals of step 2, the specification of training activities, are twofold. First, the user develops the content of the training programme further by defining what the trainee is going to do in order to learn (i.e., the training activities that will be executed by the trainee to attain the training objectives). The second step is process-oriented: the user focuses the design process towards those training activities that are suitable for simulator training.

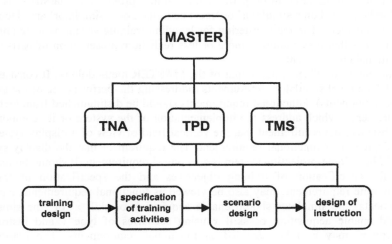

Figure 13.3. TPD steps

Scenario Design

In this step, exercises are specified that will induce the trainees to execute training activities and, ultimately, to attain the corresponding training objectives. The focus is on those parts of training that will take place in a future simulator. Scenarios provide one of the main inputs for specifying the requirements for the training system to be procured or developed, i.e., the scenarios will be used to derive functional specifications for the future simulator in the next phase (TMS). As already noted, for this purpose they do not have to be elaborated to the level of detail that would be required for implementation; a more global description might suffice.

Design of Instruction

In this step, the instructional support that might be necessary before, during and after the execution of the training scenarios is specified. The timing, form and content of instructional interventions are influenced by the chosen overall teaching strategy, the assessment plan, the kind of training activities that are to be executed by the trainee, and the scenarios. The descriptions of instructional interventions are used in the next phase, TMS, to derive specifications for the required instructional facilities.

TPD and TMS

The output of TPD constitutes the input to TMS; it consists of a prospective training programme that is to be at least partly delivered by means of a training simulator. During TPD, those parts of the training programme classified as 'may need to be trained on a simulator' or 'must be trained on a simulator' are elaborated most extensively. The main criterion for labelling training scenarios as requiring a simulator is that they require a more or less realistic representation of parts of the operational environment.

The output of TMS is the output of the MASTER methodology. It consists of a set of functional simulator requirements (addressing the performance of the system or its components). Functional requirements should be distinguished from technical requirements, which address the implementation of the system or its components. For instance, the requirement that the vertical field of view of a display system be 120 degrees is a functional requirement. The requirement that the display system should be a dome-projection system is a technical requirement. It should be realised that the specification of training objectives and the specification of training programme requirements may also be viewed as functional requirements, e.g., the statements 'the simulator should enable acquisition of skill x' or 'the simulator should enable acquisition of skill x using scenarios of type y and instruction strategy z' may also be regarded as functional requirements. The reason for restricting MASTER to the functional specification of simulator requirements is that they can be specified in a more generic way and are less subject to change.

In linking training programme requirements to simulator requirements, two principles are used: the minimalisation principle and the principle of specific validity. According to the first principle, training scenarios should represent the training environments that are minimally needed to perform the training activities. Adherence to this principle ensures that training scenarios can be differentiated. According to the second principle, simulator requirements should be explicitly linked to training scenarios. For any particular training scenario, this may imply that some simulator requirements will need to be of high operational validity, some of moderate validity, some in the form only of an abstract representation, and some not present at all.

Applying these two principles ensures that training scenarios can be distinguished in terms of validity requirements and vice versa, i.e., the required validity of requirements can be distinguished in terms of training scenarios. This enables an assessment of the comprehensiveness and the realism of the simulator requirements for a particular set of training scenarios. This also enables an assessment of which training scenarios can be used given a particular set of simulator requirements. An additional advantage of such a scenario-based specification of requirements is that SMEs usually find it very difficult to specify requirements in a general way, in the absence of a concrete context.

The output of TPD consists of a specification of a prospective training programme that must, or may, be delivered by means of a training simulator. This specification consists of an ordered sequence of:

- training objectives;
- assessment points;
- training activities;
- training scenarios;
- associated instructional specifications.

The last two components constitute the main inputs for TMS. Instructional specifications constitute the primary input for the functional specification of the instructional support facilities required to deliver training. These specifications consist of three components: briefing, tutoring, and debriefing activities (see Chapter 12). Training scenario descriptions comprise a process description, an environment description, and a description of the system (see Chapter 11).

A training simulator, and therefore its functional specification, can be decomposed into a number of components. For instance, for a comprehensive simulator the components depicted in Figure 10.1 can be distinguished.

Trainee Simulator Interface (TSI) The TSI comprises specifications of the displays and controls that the trainee needs to interact with the simulator, including a description of their spatial layout. The information presented on the displays is generated by the simulation model, which in turn is driven by the control inputs generated by the trainee. If applicable, the specification of the TSI also includes the requirements for the OTW view (see Chapter 11). The main inputs for specifying TSI requirements are the system description parts of the training scenarios.

Database   The database specification includes the tactical and physical environment. The main inputs for specifying database requirements are the environment description parts of the training scenarios.

Simulation model   The specification of the simulation model consists of a description of the dynamic behaviour of the simulator and its interaction with the simulated environment. This model constitutes the 'heart' of any simulator. The main inputs for specifying the model requirements are the process description parts of the training scenarios.

Essentially, the TSI, the database, and the simulation model are the primary simulator components that co-determine what the trainees will see, feel, and hear during training (given the initial conditions of the training scenarios and the actions and reactions of the trainees). The image system, the motion system, and the sound system (and the TSI displays) primarily serve as systems that transduce the outputs of the simulation model into physical consequences that can be seen, felt, and heard and acted upon by means of the TSI controls.

Image system The image system generates and displays the image content that can be viewed by the trainee from the OTW views of the TSI. This image content is generated by one or more image generators, and displayed by a display system in accordance with the position and orientation of the TSI, or, more specifically, the eye point of the trainees relative to the database. This position is determined by the initial conditions at the start of the training scenario and the sequence of events and reactions of trainees during training scenario progress. The main inputs for specifying image system requirements are the OTW and database requirements.

Motion system The motion system generates mechanical motion cues. The main inputs for specifying motion system requirements are the simulation model requirements. As it is very important for visual and vestibular motion cues to be timed properly, image system requirements may also have to be taken into account.

Sound system The sound system generates ambient noise and sounds. The main inputs for specifying sound system requirements are the TSI and simulation model requirements.

Instruction system The instruction system subserves the authoring and management of training scenarios, the initialisation and control of the training simulator, the delivery of instruction prior to, during, and after scenario execution, and the evaluation of training results. The specification of the instruction system may comprise not only specifications of the functionalities associated with these activities but typically also a description of the Instructor-Simulator Interface (ISI). Apart from the training requirements, i.e., the output of TPD, the main inputs for specifying instruction system requirements are the TSI, database, and simulation model requirements.

Associated with each of the aforementioned simulator components is a specific set of functional requirements. The goal that is to be accomplished during TMS is to specify the functional requirements associated with each of the required simulator components, given the training programme requirements, i.e., the output of TPD. TMS comprises three main steps: scenario selection, scenario-based specification of requirements, and comparison of requirements. For further details see Section III and the MASTER Manual (van Rooij *et al*, 1998a).

14 Optimisation of Training Programmes

Introduction

No training programme will be optimal from the start; the training process is much too complex and our knowledge too limited. A good design, however, may offer an advantageous starting position. During implementation and delivery of the training programme, much can be improved by applying revisions and modifications. This requires a systematic approach in which evaluation is an integral part of training programme development. In many respects, evaluation can be viewed as a continuation of the design process, the main difference being that empirical evidence enters the process. Like design, evaluation is an iterative process. For this reason alone, it is important to consider during design what will be evaluated and how this will be achieved. This not only focuses the design process but also enables one to take into account facilities required for evaluation.

In this chapter, the emphasis is on evaluation strategies and options for optimisation, not on measurement issues (see Section IV). Also the emphasis will be on the evaluation of simulator-based training programmes, not of individual trainees.

The Purpose of Evaluation

The purpose of evaluation is usually to check or to improve the effectiveness and efficiency of the training programme. Effiency is a function of the effectiveness of training (benefits) and the costs of the resources used for training (costs). It can be expressed as a simple ratio, but different values can be used in the numerator and the denominator. For example, transfer or retention might be used as the 'benefit', giving different ratios; and there are many different approaches to calculating costs. The efficiency ratio also depends on the integration period adopted in calculating the numerator and denominator; for example, the entire life cycle of the simulator or only a part of it. To prevent discussion, it may be wise to achieve consensus with respect to the criteria that will be used for evaluation before the training programme is delivered and evaluated. Evaluation can be conducted at various levels of aggregation, i.e., using different units of analysis. The most appropriate level will depend on the purpose of evaluation. When different levels of analysis are adopted, it is important to take dependencies between levels into account.

Evaluation can be part of an acceptance test. Checking whether the objectives of training are achieved may constitute the first test of any training programme and simulator. This may be followed up by assessments of transfer and retention. In this context, it is of interest to note that in the UK there is now a requirement for a post-project evaluation for all new training facilities that aims to measure how well they have achieved the *performance enhancements* that were expected. As noted in Chapter 7, a problem in evaluating simulator-based training programmes is to separate the effect of the training programme from the effect of the simulator. In evaluating a particular training configuration, this may be less of a problem because, more or less, the simulator can be regarded as a constant that leaves the training programme as the main vehicle for improvement.

One of the problems with acceptance tests (and evaluation in general) is determining the moment or time window that should be used as a reference for evaluation. It may take quite a long time for the training programme to settle down into a steady state and for sufficient data to become available. This implies that one should not be too quick to draw conclusions and apply changes.

If effectiveness or efficiency is significantly below expectation, one may continue the evaluation to pinpoint the causes. But even if effectiveness or efficiency is within expectation, one may want to investigate whether there is room for improvement. Whatever the impetus for continued evaluation, for efficiency reasons such evaluations should be constrained by the possibilities for increasing training effectiveness. For instance, if the duration of training is fixed, it is pointless to assess or evaluate the effects of training duration.

Another purpose of evaluation is to establish performance norms against which the performance of groups of individual trainees can be assessed. Norms can also be used to monitor training programme effectiveness and to assess the impact of changes. Establishing performance norms makes sense only if the training programme assessed is the same as that on which norms are based. This implies that norms can be established only if the training programme is relatively stable.

Evaluation may also be directed at establishing more specific trainee selection criteria or at further differentiating the training programme with respect to particular trainee sub-groups. Evaluation of retention of skills may be used to establish requirements for refresher training. The results of evaluation may also be used to improve the future design of training programmes, e.g., by checking assumptions that were made during design and, if necessary, by subsequently adapting guidelines or procedures that are part of the methodology.

The Process of Evaluation

A distinction can be made between evaluation of the training process and of the results of training. Measures of the result of training (e.g., transfer) are the terms in which training effectiveness is expressed. Process measures are training programme factors that may be hypothesised to affect effectiveness criteria. Essentially, the design of a training programme can be considered as the specification of a theory, albeit a very specific one, about what constitutes the optimal training approach for a particular training need, given specific resources and constraints. In this view, the process of evaluation is concerned with testing this theory and improving it.

Evaluation of Training Results

Several criteria can be used to assess or optimise training effectiveness: learning, transfer, and retention. The type of criterion that is most useful depends on the goal set for training and on the constraints imposed. A learning criterion is defined in terms of performance during or at the end of a training programme. An end-of-training criterion may be used to determine the extent to which the training objectives have been achieved (irrespective of the validity of these training objectives; see also Chapter 10). The fact that the training programme enables one to achieve the training objectives does not prove that training has been effective. During TNA, training objectives may not have been specified adequately, and transfer may be low, zero, or even negative.

A transfer criterion expresses the effectiveness of training in terms of performance in the operational environment after training (in a simulated training environment). Retention criteria are based on assessments at intervals after conclusion of the training programme. If retention assessments are made in terms of operational performance, they are consistent with transfer criteria; if retention assessments are made in terms of performance on the training system, they are consistent with end-of-training criteria.

Effectiveness criteria are not independent. For instance, assuming that training objectives are valid, end-of-training performance predicts transfer. Also, the better the match between the skills that have been learned during training and the skills required in practice, i.e., the better the transfer of skills, the higher the probability that the skills, as learned, are actually used and hence retained.

Performance in the operational environment is always assessed subsequent to the end of a training programme. The time interval between end of training and first application of the acquired knowledge and skills may be quite long, especially in the military domain. This implies a potential confounding between evaluations in terms of transfer and those in terms of retention. An alternative viewpoint is to look upon transfer and retention as aspects of the same phenomenon: retention being related to temporal aspects and transfer to similarity aspects.

Effectiveness criteria may be combined with costs to yield efficiency criteria. Efficiency criteria relate the benefits or gains of training to the costs (in terms of resources such as time, money, and trainee drop out). The challenge in designing training programmes is to maximise the benefit/cost ratio given a particular training need (and given budgetary, logistic, organisational, and technological constraints). This may be accomplished by increasing benefits, by reducing costs, or both. These strategies imply different approaches to evaluation, as discussed later.

Process Measures

As noted earlier, the design of a training programme constitutes a theory of how training should be conducted. Depending on the principles used, it may be regarded as a more or less pure instantiation or operationalisation of more general ideas of what constitutes good training. The more specific and explicit the design, the more testable the training programme.

From the reviews in Chapters 10-12 and from the preceding paragraph, it can be concluded that the same types of factors affect most of these criteria, albeit in different ways and to different extents. Notably, (1) the sequencing of training activities, (2) the type of training activities, (3) the similarities between training and operational environments, and (4) the timing and nature of the guidance and feedback that are provided prior to, during, and after training may be potent determinants of training effectiveness.

Depending on the way in which these factors are manipulated, they may be confounded. For instance, several training programme factors that promote transfer, e.g., variability of practice, may decrease skill acquisition rate and vice versa: uniformity of training conditions may further skill acquisition rate but may limit transfer. Also, providing augmented guidance and feedback during training may improve performance but impede learning (i.e., result in spurious learning effects) and, consequently, transfer and retention. The reverse, augmented guidance and feedback resulting in poorer performance during training, may also occur, e.g., due to the extra load that is imposed on the trainee.

Evaluation can be conducted by comparing different groups (cross-sectionally), or by comparing the same group at different stages of training (longitudinally). The former takes less time but does not control for pre-existing differences between groups. Often a combination of these approaches is appropriate. Whatever approach is chosen, it may take a considerable amount of time before one has sufficient data to be able to conduct an adequate evaluation, notably if trainee throughput is low. Instead of setting up a data acquisition programme for each evaluation separately, one may register data on a regular basis. Of course, this will require specific data measurement, storage, and analysis procedures and facilities.

In most cases, the purpose of evaluation is not merely to analyse the effectiveness and efficiency of the training programme but to improve it. To ensure that the changes that are applied are improvements, it is important to adopt a systematic policy. One important strategy is to set priorities for improvement, e.g., by ordering possible improvements on the basis of expected impact or ease of implementation. An important rule is to make sure that the changes that are applied can also be evaluated. This implies that changes should be applied sequentially and not simultaneously. Another important rule that may be useful is always to ensure that changes that have been applied can be reversed.

Adopting a sequential approach to optimisation implies that evaluation can take a large amount of time. Also, many people may be involved in this process. To keep track of the process, it may be necessary to employ a system for change management that tracks when, why, how, and by whom changes are applied.

Qualitative and Quantitative Evaluation

Evaluation can be conducted in a qualitative way, simply by recording incidental comments of trainees, instructors, and SMEs. Such a passive informal approach may be combined with more active and formal methods, e.g., structured interviews, checklists, and questionnaires administered periodically to trainees, commanders, and managers. In this respect the TPD methodology may be used as a basis for developing instruments for evaluation and as a qualitative reference for evaluating responses.

Quantitative evaluation One of the advantages of using simulators for training is that they offer many possibilities for performance measurement (Vreuls & Obermayer, 1985; Sanders, 1991). However, as noted by Vreuls and Obermayer (1985), and again more than ten years later in Chapter 8 of this handbook, these possibilities and the associated possibilities for automating instruction and for more objective training evaluation are rarely exploited. Many alternative performance measures, and guidelines for their use, are described in Section IV of this handbook. However, the primary rationale for defining performance measures is the additional insight that they give the trainee, the instructor, or the evaluator into the training process.

Although it may be very tempting to make quantitative assessments of the training process, several caveats should be noted:

- any performance measure is a statistical measure and therefore subject to unreliability;
- performance and learning effects may be confused, e.g. an improvement in performance during training may be due to the (augmented) guidance and feedback that are provided instead of being a learning effect;
- different criteria may be used to evaluate learning. The choice of criteria determines effectiveness and efficiency estimates;
- learning effects may be determined by multiple factors that may be partly unknown and that may interact in complex and unpredictable ways;
- learning effects are typically non-linear, which makes it more difficult to make extrapolations;
- learning effects are affected by individual differences.

In principle, statistical methods may be applied to analyse relations between performance measures. However, these analyses can become quite involved and require special expertise and large amounts of data.

15 Discussion and Conclusions

In this section, an attempt has been made to organise the available knowledge, both theoretical and practical, with respect to the use of simulators for training and, more specifically and extensively, with respect to the design of training programmes for simulator-based training. The main conclusion that can be drawn from this review is that there are still many gaps between theory and practice. For several reasons, the development of a methodology for training programme design is proposed as a means of closing these gaps. It is believed that this methodology may serve a variety of purposes and target groups.

Research The TPD methodology may serve as a means of organising available expertise and, hence, identifying knowledge gaps and setting priorities for research. Thus, the TPD methodology may function as a bridge between theory and practice, between researchers and practitioners.

System design The TPD methodology enables early consideration of training implications of design alternatives, and hence may provide a means to evaluate them. Thus, it may function as a bridge between system designers and training designers.

Simulator design One of the basic tenets of the MASTER approach is that simulator requirements should be determined by training programme requirements. This implies more explicit and more specific training programme requirements that are determined in advance of the specification of simulator requirements. The TPD methodology may enable the timely specification of such requirements.

Simulator procurement The result of applying the TPD methodology may be used as a means of assessing the training implications of procurement alternatives. Thus, the TPD methodology may diminish the currently dominant role of operational or technological considerations.

Delivery and implementation of simulator-based training programmes The TPD methodology is not only useful as an intermediate step in the specification of requirements for new, or to be acquired, training simulators, but may also be of benefit for analysing and re-designing existing training programmes and hence improving their effectiveness and efficiency. Also, by bringing together the state of the art with respect to training programme design, the TPD methodology (and relevant chapters of this section) may be used as a basis for developing training courses for simulator instructors.

Section III
Training Media Specification

16 Introduction to Training Media Specification

Introduction

Although this handbook addresses specifically the use of simulators as training media, all available media should be taken into account. In Chapter 10, a distinction was made between CBT, SBT, and RBT. Due to technological developments, the distinctions between different media are blurred. Many capabilities previously available only on high-end simulators are now available on desktop systems for desktop prices. Also, many real systems are equipped with embedded training facilities. It is not easy to keep up with these developments. Every selection rule and media categorisation scheme is at risk of becoming obsolete. Different organisations will have different training needs and constraints, and hence different rules and categorisations may apply. Technological developments cause changes in system concepts and operations and thus changes in training needs. These developments make it all the more important to specify training and training programme requirements accurately. In principle, one might simply require suppliers to provide a training solution. However, it is not easy to formalise and test whether a supplier has succeeded in meeting a particular training need. It is usually not sufficient to specify training or training programme requirements. Additional, more detailed, media requirements are necessary, if only to ensure that training media match the existing infrastructure.

The issue addressed in this section is how to translate training programme requirements into functional simulator requirements. As will be shown, resolving this issue requires knowledge about skills, requisite cues, and their implications for simulation. Before reviewing the available knowledge, the research on which this knowledge is based will be discussed briefly.

Research Issues

In the previous section on TPD, an attempt was made to define skills, and different types of skill were distinguished. Clearly, a skill is an attribute of a person. A cue, on the other hand, is an attribute of the task environment. These concepts are not independent: skill is required to be able to use a cue, and a cue is only a cue for those who have the skill to use it. Each skill that has been specified at a sufficient level of detail can be linked to particular cueing requirements. Here a 'cue' is defined as a modality-specific unit of information. Defining 'cue' as modality-specific renders it somewhat more specific than skill. Also, since they are attributes of the environment, it is possible to define cues partly in physical terms. Although this issue will not be pursued further here, the concept of 'cue' may allow us to define the concept of 'skill', and hence the interface between person and environment, more accurately.

Individuals differ in skill proficiency, and hence cue sensitivity. However, individual differences may also exist with respect to the types of cue that are used ('cue utilisation'). This implies that the mapping between skills and cues will often not be one-to-one.

Another problem with linking skills to cues is that many skill domains are not well researched. What is known about cues has mostly been obtained from rather isolated laboratory studies. Moreover, most applied studies have been conducted in the domain of flight skills; as noted in the introduction to Section II, many have used a transfer-of-training paradigm, and have focused on relatively crude assessments of simulator fidelity. Some have confounded the effects of training and simulation. It is therefore impossible to determine whether the results obtained are due to differences in training approach, to differences between simulator and simulated system, or both.

Applied studies are strongly technology-driven. For example, many earlier studies on motion cueing used technologies that have been superseded by more advanced technologies. Such studies (notably those that reported null results) may have to be replicated (see, for instance, the recent review of research on motion cueing by Bürki-Cohen *et al*, 1998). Most applied studies have used rather subjective assessments (e.g., Cooper-Harper ratings). Although current technologies permit relatively unobtrusive and objective measurements of human and system performance under operational conditions, for a variety of reasons it remains very difficult to gain access to operational personnel and systems and to obtain real performance data. Such data are essential for finding out which cues are used.

Resolving these conceptual, methodological, technological, and organisational problems requires a more integrated research approach, comprising laboratory, simulator, and validation studies. Such an approach requires a more common terminology, and interfaces between training research, research on human perception and performance, and simulation technology. Even if such an approach is initiated, the problem remains that skills change in response to new system concepts and technologies. This naturally has consequences for the types of skill to be trained and the types of cue that are relevant and need to be simulated. For instance, there is a growing need for team, supervisory, and remote control skills.

Fortunately, there are some constraints. One set of constraints can be derived from our extensive knowledge of the capabilities and limitations of the human perceptual system. Another derives from knowledge of the characteristics and limitations of human information processing capabilities. Both types of knowledge are increasingly being used in task and system design as, due to extension of technological capabilities, pressures towards optimal human performance continue to increase. These pressures restrict and delineate further the operational cues that operators use.

Owing to our lack of knowledge, the impact of technological developments, and the specificity of training needs, the need to resolve specific issues during the specification of simulators will remain; in other words, most of the issues addressed in this section have not been definitively resolved. Nevertheless, a systematic approach may help to ensure that the correct issues are addressed. Some ideas for such an approach to the specification of training media will be presented. First, however, existing knowledge will be reviewed.

Skills and Cues

For training to be effective, the cues (features or parameters in the environment) used by the operator to perform his tasks should also be present during training. The type and number of cues that are used depend on the task goal, the task strategy, the skill level of the operator, and the environmental conditions. They may also depend on specific operator knowledge of a particular region and on situational awareness at any given moment (people are notoriously opportunistic in trying to achieve their goals).

Cues can be classified as 'instrument' and 'non-instrument'. An instrument or equipment cue is a parameter of the HMI that the trainee and operator must use as an aid in performing their training activities and tasks. A non-instrument cue is a modality-specific parameter of the physical environment that the trainee or operator uses. Instrument cues may be redundant, complementary, or continuous with respect to non-instrument cues. Instrument cues are relatively well documented in system documentation and manuals, and can be subdivided further into display cues and control cues (e.g., control force feedback). Since it is relatively simple to specify and simulate instrument cues, our main concern in this section is with the specification of non-instrument cues. From the definition given, it should be clear that what counts as a cue depends on the training activity or task to be performed, and, even more specifically, on the trainee or operator who executes it. Another useful distinction is between onset, sustained cues, and stop cues. This distinction refers to the occurrence of events and the maintenance of particular states.

Skill Type and Cueing Realism

For some task categories and skill types, full realism is much easier to achieve than for others. Some of these dependencies and their implications are reviewed below for different skill types.

Perceptual and motor skills Perceptual-motor skills impose the highest demands on simulation (Boer, 1991). Owing to the larger number, variety, and dynamics of the non-instrument cues involved, perceptual-motor skills take longer to learn and the level of realism is more difficult to achieve, if it can be achieved at all. This difficulty is partly due to our as yet incomplete understanding of which non-instrument cues contribute to performance and partly to technological limitations in simulating relevant non-instrument cues. Mismatches between the cues generated by the simulator and those available on the real system may result in skills not transferring completely, or even transferring negatively, to the real system. To counteract these hazards, careful simulator tuning is always required and, if possible, an adequate balance should be maintained between training hours spent on the simulator and the real system.

Procedural skills With respect to training procedural skills, a distinction should be made between learning to recognise the conditions for initiating a particular procedure and learning to execute (and terminate) the procedure. The latter is generally much easier, although retention is relatively poor and frequent recurrency training is required to maintain skills at adequate levels. The difficulty in learning when to initiate particular procedures depends on whether or not procedures are triggered by instrument or non-instrument cues. For many standard operating procedures described in operator manuals, instrument cues are available. However, in some cases non-instrument cues may provide additional or earlier information about whether or not a particular emergency procedure should be executed. Learning the timely recognition of such cues is much more difficult and requires a high level of cueing realism. Non-instrument cues may also be relatively more important in the execution of emergency procedures and in handling degraded system modes.

Cognitive skills The main training focus for cognitive skills is to learn to analyse and integrate different types of information and to use the result in monitoring, planning, and decision making. Most of the information used in exercising cognitive skills is in the form of instrument readings and radio communications. Consequently, a high level of cueing realism is relatively easy to achieve. None the less, circumstances should be replicated sufficiently accurately to induce the appropriate cognitive sets and to learn to deal with the dynamics and complexities of real-life conditions.

Time-sharing and team skills Although the learning of time-sharing and team skills does not directly lead to requirements with respect to realism, in an indirect sense training these skills certainly has implications for the realism required. The amount of transfer will depend upon the extent to which these skills are trained under conditions and task loads that are representative of real-life conditions. A specific requirement of time-sharing skills is that they may demand more attention to be paid to accurate synchronisation of cues. For training particular team skills, e.g., obstacle avoidance, the use of common external spatial references between crew members may require cues to be perceived with specific spatial and temporal accuracy. This has implications for image simulation, e.g., multiple image generators, a larger viewing volume, and separate display systems.

With increased automation, the shift towards procedural and cognitive modes of control will continue. Situational awareness and crew co-ordination will assume a more important role. The specification problem may become more difficult; with the increasing complexity, situational specificity and interdependency of tasks, there will be an increased emphasis on TNA and TPD.

Cue Taxonomy

Typically, cues are classified according to modality, such as visual, aural, and body-centred (van Rooij *et al*, 1997a). These categories can be further sub-divided, respectively, into:

- monocular (e.g., accommodation, known size) and binocular (e.g., optic flow, motion parallax);
- monaural (e.g., loudness) and binaural (e.g., time differences and frequency 'colouring');
- vestibular (e.g., linear and rotational acceleration), tactile/haptic (e.g., skin pressure, temperature), kinaesthetic (e.g., joint position, muscle tension) and somatosensory.

The main use of smell is in signalling malfunctions caused by, for instance, overheating and fire. The human olfactory system is not as sensitive as that of some other species, but in many cases it will be able to provide an early warning. One of the oldest senses in evolutionary terms, the olfactory system has links with the limbic system, which moderates basic emotions. This explains why under stressful conditions certain smells such as smoke may contribute to a state of agitation.

When training of emergencies is considered, the application of some basic smell generators may provide additional realism. Generally, however, smell cues are not considered essential. Other cues listed in Table 16.1 will be covered in detail in subsequent chapters of this section.

Relations and Interactions between Cues

In addition to skill-related correlation in the use of cues, in many cases natural correlations exist between different cues. For example, luminance has an effect on the perception of colour, contrast, and detail. These changes may alter the availability or relative informativeness of the cues. Cues may mask other cues or render them less salient. For instance, a loud noise may mask the perception of other, potentially more informative, sounds. In addition, cross-modal cue interactions occur frequently and can be exploited for simulation purposes. For instance, in motion simulation, knowledge about vestibular, visual, and sound cues is used to induce motion sensations. In combining cues, great care must be taken to avoid mismatches or conflicts between cues, otherwise serious problems may arise; for instance, a mismatch between visual and vestibular cues may induce a condition called 'simulator sickness'.

Table 16.1. Taxonomy of non-instrument cues

Visual		Auditory	
Monocular	**Binocular**	**Monaural**	**Binaural**
Accommodation (distance [short range])	Stereo-vision (distance [short and mid range], shape)	Loudness of known source (distance)	Time differences, frequency 'colouring' (direction of sound sources)
Known size (distance)	Interocular rivalry (relative distance [short and mid range])	Echoes (obstacle proximity)	
Occlusion (distance ranking, object shape)	Vergence (distance [short range])	Spectral composition (system status such as rotor-frequency)	
Linear perspective (distance, relative height)		Speech (verbal communications)	
Texture (distance, object shape)			
Shading (shape, lighting conditions)			
Shadows (shape, lighting, height)			
Aerial perspective (distance [long range])			
Colour (distance [long range], object separation)			
Optic flow/motion parallax (distance, shape, heading, motion detection, time-to-contact)			

	Body-centred		Smell
Vestibular	**Tactile**	**Kinaesthetic/ somatosensory**	
Sacculus, utriculus (linear acceleration: surge, sway, heave, vibrations, body orientation, collisions)	Skin pressure sensing (vibration, accelerations)	Joint position sensing (body attitude)	Olfactory signals (smoke, exhaust fumes)
Semi-circular canals (rotational acceleration: pitch, roll, yaw)	Skin temperature sensing (cabin temperature)	Muscle extension and force sensing (body attitude, accelerations)	
		Internal pressures (accelerations)	

Given the large number of different cues, interactions, and factors affecting whether and how the operator exploits them, specifying cueing requirements is a difficult task. Therefore, the safest strategy seems to be to vary relevant cues by training under different conditions; in other words, to use a cue-diversification strategy. This can be accomplished by designing scenarios that force trainees to use different types of cue, by explaining cue-utilisation strategies, and by alternating or interleaving simulator training with training on the real system. Whatever strategy is chosen, in all cases a set of cues has to be specified; the better this specification, the more effective the training.

In subsequent chapters, our current knowledge with respect to cues and their implications for functional simulator requirements will be reviewed. Each chapter centres on a specific simulator component:

- Databases and simulation models.
- Human-simulator interfaces (including simulation of audio cues).
- Visual cueing and image systems.
- Vestibular cueing and motion systems.

The issue of how to use this knowledge in the scenario-based specification of functional simulator requirements will also be addressed.

17 Databases and Models

Introduction

Databases are used to store a geometric representation of the environment in which the system is immersed. The behaviour of the system in this environment is specified in terms of a mathematical model. At the start of a training scenario, this model is initialised to a specific state and to a specific position and orientation relative to the environment. Changes in system state and position and orientation occur by means of inputs to the model. These inputs may originate from the control inputs of the trainee or from the environment. The output of the model may be a change in the state of the system, a change in orientation/position of the system relative to the environment, or a change in the environment. The trainee, via instrument cues and non-instrument cues, perceives these states and changes in states. Cues are generated by the different available cueing systems, e.g., the Trainee-Simulator Interface, the sound system, the image system, and the motion system. Thus, all information flow during the execution of a training scenario is initiated and sustained by interactions between the database (the environment) and the simulation model (the system).

Which interactions the trainee can perceive is determined by his senses and the sensors that are available to him. Sensors extend the range of the human senses. Obviously, the types of sensor that should be available to the trainee may have implications for the database and the simulation model. Electro-magnetic (optic, infrared, radar, radio), and acoustic and sonar sensors can be distinguished. Sensor performance characteristics are determined by sensor settings (position/directivity, sensitivity, bandwidth, frequency resolution, temporal resolution) and by the characteristics of the medium (air or water) in which they are immersed. Characteristics of the medium, e.g. the atmosphere in which the system and surrounding objects are immersed, may be rendered using a variety of techniques. For example, the effects of wind may be implemented as part of the simulation model, and clouds may be implemented as database objects. In this chapter, considerations and trade-offs with respect to the specification of databases and simulation models will be reviewed. Issues associated with the specification of cueing systems will be covered in subsequent chapters.

Databases

The environment can be specified in terms of surfaces, objects and media, and the characteristics of these entities. Surfaces and objects and their characteristics are typically modelled in terms of database requirements. Media and sensor characteristics may be modelled as part of the database or the simulation model.

Surfaces and Surface Characteristics

A database contains geometrical and other information that the cue generator (e.g., an image generator) will process to produce cues (e.g., scenes or scene properties) in real time. This will include at least an organised structure of polygons. Polygons are plane surfaces enclosed by three or more straight sides. Each polygon can be assigned a colour and intensity value, and a certain texture. In this way, terrain and soil type such as sand, clay, grass and concrete can be added to the basic terrain. To be able to interface the database to the simulation model, additional information, such as colour, texture, shading, and sensor-specific characteristics, may have to be attached to these surfaces, or a separate database may have to be built that incorporates this information. Databases can be characterised in terms of their type, size, and resolution.

Database type Training scenarios may be divided into two general categories: geo-specific (e.g., mission rehearsal) and generic (e.g., skill acquisition). In the case of general training, a purely generic terrain may suffice. A generic set of relevant landscapes such as flat, lightly undulating and hilly areas, mountains, swamps, deserts, forests and populated and industrial areas may be provided.

Mission rehearsal requires accurate representation of an existing terrain. To acquire such a database it is necessary that tools be provided that can convert a number of standard geographical and/or cartographical database formats and aid in the decoration of the terrain with objects based on aerial photographs and CAD drawings.

Many image systems are now capable of accepting real-world (geo-specific) data in a standard form. A series of photographs from a satellite transiting a geographic area can be transformed by existing software programmes into 2D real-world imagery. This imagery can then be formatted using standards such as Digital Feature Analysis Data (DFAD) and Digital Terrain Elevation Data (DTED), so that the real-world information can be used by any appropriate image system. Military mission rehearsal using realistic visual imagery of terrain and cultural features is therefore feasible for any part of the world, irrespective of its accessibility by ground or by aircraft.

If the appropriate geo-specific data are available in the proper format, building a geo-specific database may be faster. Also, for geo-specific areas, maps are already available and there is less risk of inconsistency. The use of geo-specific scene arrangements may enable validation of training scenarios by comparing performance under real and simulated conditions.

Database size The size of the database is determined by the speed, duration, and direction of system movement. For slow aircraft and helicopters, many manoeuvres may be performed on an area of 10×10 km^2. An area of 500×500 km^2 may be required for extended flying with fast jets. For driving, a minimum requirement is probably a gaming area of 10 km^2, although driving a 50 km route on an express highway, with a desirable viewing distance of 3 km, leads to a required area of the order of 300 km^2. For sailing in a channel, a trip of 5 km is a minimum requirement (Schuffel, 1986). Combined with a minimum visibility of, say, 2 km ahead and 1 km laterally, one arrives at a minimum area of 15 km^2. For coastal navigation in an area of 400 km^2, with visibility of 50 km, an area of 5000 km^2 is required. In oceans, an outside world image is required only for the detection and identification of other ships, and checking for collision hazards. Of course, much depends on the training scenario and on the monitoring and control options that are exercised during scenario execution. For instance, trainees may be prevented from wandering off the intended course.

The size of the terrain to be modelled has an effect on (a) the amount of data that is required to build the database and (b) the amount of work required to build the database. It should not have an effect on the rendering speed.

Database resolution Terrain data consist of terrain height values and of terrain and soil type information. The height information is a set of elevation values specified on a regular or irregular grid. The spacing of the grid points is the *resolution* of the database. Practical resolutions for flight simulators are between 1 and 100 m grid spacing. For driving, a higher resolution is required. The type of terrain to be modelled and the type of skill to be trained determine the basic grid of the database.

A rather flat or slowly undulating terrain, with few high spatial-frequency features such as steep sides of canals or hills with steep slopes, can be described with map data on a grid of 100 x 100 m. If there are a few high-frequency features in such a terrain, these can be modelled as objects, and placed on the terrain at the required location. A very hilly terrain, with steep canyons and many outcroppings, requires a much higher resolution grid (a few metres) to be modelled correctly. Terrain data of such a resolution will be more difficult to acquire. If terrain data are not available at the required resolution, one may have to revert to using a lower resolution and adding all the high-frequency terrain features as objects.

For certain training activities, the trainee will have to be able to see a range of levels of detail, such as ditches and canyons and their sides/walls, small hills, steep rock faces, tree trunks and branches, power lines, and small roadside structures. The first types of structure are essentially parts of a terrain map, the second types are objects. If a trainee must carry out operations very close to the terrain (e.g., nap-of-the-earth flight or rescue operations) the elevation map must have a high resolution, that is, the grid of height values should have a spacing of a few metres. If a pilot has to carry out a reconnaissance task, a terrain map resolution of 30-50 m may be sufficient.

Database resolution may vary over the database, with particular areas for training being modelled to high resolution. Between training areas, low resolution or even reliance on a generic database may be acceptable. An example is a commercial aircraft simulator, where the gaming area will normally be specified to include the whole world, but only key airports and their surrounding areas will be modelled in detail in the database. This allows other airports to be added later as the requirements change or as others use the database.

Objects and Object Characteristics

An object belongs to a defined category of database elements, grouped together for the purposes of scene management. A specific number of polygons and/or light points or strings may be grouped in this way. Techniques for rendering objects vary widely in level of sophistication and hence in cost. A simple building may be included as a single object, whereas a complex model such as an aircraft may be modelled in the form of several objects (one for each wing, one for the fuselage, and so forth). Object information consists both of natural objects such as trees and of cultural objects such as roads, buildings, and bridges. Objects may also be classified as stationary or moving. Moving objects in general are those that move on their own behalf, not as a consequence of the movement of the vehicle simulated. For driving and gunnery simulators, and in certain cases also for flight or ship simulators, the presence of moving vehicles in the scene is required. The number required is strongly task-dependent. From analysis of video records of road traffic scenes, it appears that a maximum of 10 moving cars occur in the frontal scene simultaneously (Haug, 1990). If pedestrians are included, too, even the busiest traffic scenes can be represented by 16 moving objects (FAAC, 1989).

Imaging of moving vehicles requires that one take account of the following requirements: they must correctly occult, or be occulted by, other objects; and they must move in accordance with vertical irregularities in the terrain. A cast shadow moving with the vehicle promotes its localisation. Additionally, it may be important to be able to vary the heading and speed of one or more of the vehicles independently.

The environment may contain semi-autonomous objects, e.g., enemy forces and animals (for instance, whales can be mistaken for a submarine). Objects may be controlled by built-in intelligence (agents such as Computer Generated Forces), by training staff members (e.g., Semi-Automated FORces [SAFOR]), or by other crews linked to the same scenario environment by means of a distributed network (networked simulation).

One may distinguish moving parts on stationary or moving objects and animation effects. Objects with moving parts are denoted as articulated objects: for example, radar antennae and windmills, rotors of flying helicopters, wheels on moving cars, and pedestrians' legs. In fact, all objects that move according to a predetermined trajectory within a restricted part of the scene (including traffic streams on a highway) can be seen as articulated objects (Wyckoff, 1989). Fixed sequences in change of object appearance, such as explosions and moving parts on objects, may be represented by storing the sequenced object versions, and calling them successively in real time. The transitions can be smoothed by means of the transparency feature (cf. next chapter).

In addition to the visual appearance of objects, a host of object characteristics may have to be modelled, e.g., signatures (radar, thermal, sonar, acoustic), available sensors, countermeasures, communication facilities (radio, data links), weapon systems, combat identification (friend/foe), vulnerability, and behaviour rules such as rules of engagement.

Media and Media Characteristics

Aerodynamic characteristics and processes (temperature, air density, humidity, air pressure, wind, precipitation, electro-magnetic phenomena) may affect visibility and the flight behaviour of the system (turbulence, wind effects, icing). Atmospheric states and effects may also influence signal transmission characteristics and sensor performance, and hence detectability (e.g., by radar). Similarly, acoustic properties of the underwater environment are affected by numerous parameters (salinity, temperature, depth, precipitation, sea state, bottom characteristics) that interact in complex ways to yield a specific transmission loss and sound velocity profile. However, in contrast to atmospheric effects that may also produce visible effects, these properties are typically represented entirely in mathematical terms. Naturally, the geometric properties of the underwater environment and the echo profiles and noise signatures of surface and underwater objects are stored in databases.

Interactions

Obviously, numerous interactions may occur between objects, between objects and terrain, and between terrain and media. Interactions between objects include characteristic behaviour patterns/manoeuvres of objects working together, e.g., as in formation flight, effects of collisions between objects, and weapon effects (weapon impact and detonation effects). Terrain-object interactions include dynamic terrain features such as the appearance of tracks, explosions, and craters, construction of minefields/obstacles, effects of collisions with terrain surfaces or objects, appearance of dust, smoke, or water trails, rotor and propeller translucency, and down-wash. Terrain-medium interactions include effects of climate, season and time of day. Effects of rain and temperature on the terrain may have to be taken into account, since they may affect the mobility of ground vehicles. Fog, humidity (haze), and precipitation may restrict visibility; wind force and direction may also affect visibility (dust storms, snow storms) and may yield visible effects on terrain features. Again, whether and to how much detail these interactions should be simulated depend on the training scenario.

Interfacing, Modelling, and Management of Databases

Interfacing with other simulator components As noted before, to interface with other parts of the simulator (vehicle model, instrument indications) it should be possible to acquire certain types of information (height above terrain, ranges, surface type) from the database.

Interfacing with other simulators In the case of networked simulation, compatibility between databases of networked simulators is an important issue. For example, accuracy/fidelity with respect to location of objects, appearance of objects and features, and levels of detail should be within specified tolerances. Another important issue is the delay in data exchange that may occur between simulators that are widely separated.

Database modelling and management facilities Inputs for, and outputs of, database modelling are stored in databases. Modelling and managing these databases require specific facilities. The output of database modelling provides the material for scenario authoring (a topic that is covered in the next chapter). This authoring material may comprise specific terrain databases, libraries of terrain features and objects, and options for choosing between different simulation model options or parameter settings. Database modelling and scenario authoring are activities that are performed at different levels of detail and guided by different considerations. Ideally, therefore, database modelling and scenario authoring should be kept separate. An additional advantage is that changes in database formats and features do not affect the authoring level. Moreover, by separating database specifics from the authoring process, scenario authoring may be performed by subject-matter experts/instructors.

Simulation Models

The simulation model defines a mathematical model of the vehicle and should be capable of reproducing the vehicle motion at all relevant points within its operational envelope and, in some cases, outside the envelope. The model output is used to control the image system, the motion platform system, and the sound system, and to provide instrument cues. The major parts of a simulation model are:

System-Medium Model

The system-medium model describes the relationship between the reactions of the medium and the motion of the system. The nature of this model is a set of motion equations reproducing the dominant features of the forces and moments acting on the system frame. The model is based upon a number of descriptions in terms of motion, and may include:

- medium-dynamic terms, e.g., aerodynamic, surface mechanical, or hydrodynamic, considering forces and moments of the physical components of the vehicle frame (hull, body or fuselage; wheels, tracks) due to the dynamics of the medium. These terms are resolved into the degrees of freedom;
- gravitational terms representing the weight of the system, and the moment of the weight about the centre of gravity;
- control terms describing the forces and moments due to operation of the controls;
- power terms determining the forces and moments on the frame due to the engine. For a proper representation, a detailed model of the entire power generation, transmission, and propulsion chain may be required;
- external disturbance terms, e.g., aerodynamic terms describing the external forces and moments acting on the frame (for instance, turbulence and wind effects);
- other terms, e.g., forces and moments due to specific states and events associated with loads and undercarriage.

Engine Model

The engine model produces motor rpm as a function of the trainee's demand for power. This parameter is also used to drive, for instance, the sound system and motion cueing devices.

Models of the System and Engine Control Systems

These models describe the connections between the trainee controls and the system control interfaces in mathematical terms. These connections may be mechanical, hydraulic, and electric/electronic systems.

Models of System Components

These models describe the functioning of the hardware and software associated with on-board systems, e.g., avionics systems, control loading, and sound. This may include normal functioning as well as system failures.

Model limitations The simulation model should represent all relevant dynamic aspects of the system. The mathematical modelling is extremely complex, time consuming and costly. Therefore, it is essential to model only those aspects that are relevant. Training requirements directly affect the complexity of the model: the training objectives to be achieved and the training scenarios to be used determine what is relevant. Thus, both what is trained and how training is conducted directly affect the modelling requirements. Two examples from the helicopter domain may serve to illustrate these points.

During low altitude or nap-of-the-earth flying tasks, the presence of the ground close to the rotorcraft influences the airflow and the effective rotor lift capabilities ('ground effect'). This may increase the model complexity considerably. Low-speed flying requirements also impose a high demand on the model's output accuracy. In particular, during hovering, the pilot's handling qualities have a large impact on system behaviour. It appears, however, that it is difficult to match a general mathematical flight model with rotorcraft characteristics over the full flight envelope. Therefore, additional specific models may have to be developed and included in the model.

For part-task training, a model developed and validated for a particular task, range of flight speed, and limited set of atmospheric conditions may suffice. The model will not be generally applicable, since it is partly linearised about some set point. Full-mission training, however, requires an extensive model, validated for a wide range of speed, rotorcraft configurations, and atmospheric and environmental conditions.

Validation As stated above, the complexity of the simulation model may vary considerably. In particular, for crew training in which evaluation of crew performance depends on the handling qualities, it is important that the model respond as accurately as possible. Since operators are highly sensitive to aspects of the task and environment, model errors may be perceived directly. Therefore, each model should be tested extensively and validated using operational data for the real system. The manufacturer of the system may provide such data.

It should be noted that a mathematical system model is valid only for the manoeuvres for which it has been originally developed. The purpose of a training simulator is that the trainee learns to use the controls in the simulator in the same way as he would in the real system. The purpose of validation is to prove that this assumption is true. In fact, validation of the model indicates whether the general mathematical model matches the system characteristics over the full operational envelope. Therefore, it is highly important that full insight be gained concerning the validity of the simulation model.

Validation can be performed in several ways. For limited applications, such as part-task simulation, operational data can be checked by comparison of model output data with results of particular system tests, e.g., wind tunnel data. However, full-mission simulation relies on extensive validation based on real data, for instance by comparison of responses to control inputs in the simulator with responses to equivalent control inputs measured during real operational tests with the actual system. The data should reflect system performance during normal as well as extreme operating conditions.

In the aviation domain, regulations with respect to simulator validation have progressed furthest. For instance, the Federal Aviation Administration (FAA) has issued a document commonly used for approval of simulator systems, known as *Advisory Circular AC 120-63: Helicopter Simulator Qualification* (1994). This document is widely accepted as a guideline for simulator approval, and has removed some of the subjectivity from simulator inspections. AC 120-63 describes the minimum simulator requirements for qualification. For acceptance of the flight model, the document includes, for example, effects of:

* aerodynamic changes: change in helicopter attitude, aerodynamic and propulsive forces and moments, altitude, temperature, gross weight, centre of gravity location and external load operations;
* ground reaction: reaction of the rotorcraft upon contact with the landing surface;
* ground handling characteristics, including crosswind, braking, deceleration and turning radius;
* aerodynamic modelling of ground effect, effects of airframe icing, interference of rotor wake and fuselage, influence of rotor on control and stabilisation systems and representation of side slip.

With respect to the use of such guidelines as a basis for simulator *specification*, some notes of caution are in order. Qualification requirements reflect the specific state of knowledge and technology at the time of writing. Also, training requirements may be very specific and may impose similarly specific requirements not captured by general qualification standards. Of course, if the simulator is to be used for obtaining FAA training credits or pilot qualification levels, these requirements should be taken into account.

Comparing the results of tests in the simulator with performance data obtained from the real system constitutes an objective test of the simulator model performance. For example, the test requirements, tolerances and flight conditions are also listed in AC 120-63:

- engine start and acceleration operations;
- power turbine speed trim;
- minimum radius turn;
- rate of turn vs. pedal deflection or nosewheel angle;
- taxi;
- take-off with all engines or one engine inoperative;
- hovering;
- vertical climb;
- trimmed flight;
- descent;
- autorotation performance;
- landing with all engines or one engine inoperative;
- autorotational landing;
- cyclic and collective/pedals handling.

During validation, it must be possible to perform and verify such tests. All the means for recording the model response for comparison with data from the operational system should be available.

18   Human-Simulator Interfaces

Introduction

This chapter addresses the interfaces provided for personnel who have to interact with the simulator: trainees and instructors. These interfaces are referred to as Trainee-Simulator Interfaces (TSIs) and Instructor-Simulator Interfaces (ISIs), respectively. The section on TSIs focuses mainly on instrument cues, but also includes a review of aural cueing and the simulation of sound.

Trainee-Simulator Interface

For general guidelines on the design of controls and of displays, the reader is referred to Chapanis (1972) and Heglin (1973), respectively. Here, we address only the specification of TSIs. Some elements of TSIs in the broad sense are discussed within other sections of the handbook. For example, specifications of the HMI for the instructor station are discussed later. Similarly, image and motion system requirements are covered in detail elsewhere. This section, then, is concerned only with specifying the requirements of the TSI. Common themes addressed at each level of the specification are the physical fidelity of simulation, transfer of training, and the target audience.

Specification of TSI Requirements

Clearly, the specification of TSI requirements will vary from case to case. The basis for the simulation and thus the TSI will be the training scenario. In particular, the identification of the required perceptual cues will be based on the particular scenarios selected. This will determine the nature of much of the design of the TSI. The tasks to be trained, the objectives of the training programme, and the skill levels of the trainees will all have a bearing on the TSI requirements.

Working environment The working environment for the simulator requires some attention, although it is not strictly a TSI issue. The environmental factors worthy of consideration include lighting, noise, temperature, and air quality. In particular, the thermal load on the trainees must be considered. Trainees may be surrounded by electronic equipment producing heat, without the same provisions for forced cooling of equipment (and personnel) found in the military vehicle that is being simulated.

Augmented feedback The amount of feedback available in the simulator can be manipulated to aid training. This can vary from giving more or qualitatively different feedback, to giving less than normally occurs in the operational system, which results in a form of overtraining. The number and quality of various cues made available to aid learning can be moderated during training. This may involve gradual withdrawal, or a staggering process. The cues may be more or less salient than those encountered in the real world. Other possible modifications include degraded motion, changes in sound and vibration levels, and time lags in displays such as helmet mounted displays (HMDs). The rate of alarms and warnings presented in a simulator is often greater than in the real system. To aid the learning of kinaesthetic cues, larger or smaller responses than those on the operational equipment can be used. Menu structures, such as those on multi-function displays, may include extra information to help navigation during learning.

Embedded training Embedded training is sometimes available in operational equipment. The considerations of the HMI for such simulations should be the same as for simulators. Although the physical interface will be correct, all the other aspects of simulation must be considered. For example, the visual system representations, such as targets, time of day and weather effects, will still need to be designed properly.

Trainees Knowledge of the users (trainees) of a particular system is useful in determining the design, selection and training requirements of new systems. This is known as a target audience description (TAD). Relevant characteristics include educational level, training, computer literacy and anthropometry. It should be recognised that the TAD may change during the life of the simulator, due, for example, to restructuring of branches of the armed services.

The competency of trainees may have a bearing on the level of TSI fidelity adopted. TSIs may need to be adaptive; if trainees are fairly naive with respect to a system, initial training may require some intermediate interface rather than a full-blown version. Similarly, trainee competency may determine whether or not a motion system is desirable for initial training.

The anthropometry of the users will be important in the design of simulators. The system must also be useable when the operators are wearing protective clothing. This includes Nuclear, Biological and Chemical (NBC) clothing and respirators; cold weather clothing, including gloves; and spectacles.

Physical Fidelity

In accord with the overall MASTER methodology described earlier, the principle of specific fidelity may be applied to the design of the interface. This states that fidelity requirements should be explicitly linked to training scenarios. The training scenario will dictate which simulator components will be required to be of high fidelity, of moderate fidelity, or only an abstract representation, if any. For the training of reasoning skills or other cognitive abilities, for example, complete physical fidelity of the TSI is often not required. Here functional fidelity may be sufficient. However, if the specific purpose of training is the learning of perceptual-motor skills or human-system interactions (how individuals interact with particular control and display layouts), a realistic environment may be required to guarantee training credibility and consistency. Physical fidelity may be required if negative transfer is to be avoided. For example, if displays and instruments in aircraft simulators are not updated with those of the real aircraft, transfer of training may well be compromised. If the goal of training is not specifically linked to human-system interactions, alternative TSI designs may be implemented that offer cost savings. Touch-sensitive screen controls, for example, are often cheaper and easier to implement than switches, buttons, or knobs.

Considerations of fidelity may be overridden by prevailing health and safety regulations. For example, the UK MoD has a Health and Safety policy that Visual Display Equipment (VDE) such as personal computer screens needs to be adjustable in position. This also applies to VDE used in simulators, even if the real equipment is not adjustable in terms of distance from the eye.

The fidelity of TSIs may have a bearing on the motivation of trainees, and thus the transfer of training. In general, a realistic control environment is more likely to lead to greater motivation during training. But a growing body of research has indicated that low-fidelity part-task training devices (such as game playing) may promote better conditions for the motivation of trainees.

Rest breaks when using a simulator requiring visual attention may be more important than when using the system being simulated. For desk-based visual display equipment, frequent rests are recommended. Pheasant (1986) states that, for a task that is reasonably interesting under satisfactory conditions, five minutes' rest per hour is adequate. Where conditions are poor and the task dull or stressful, a rest pause of fifteen minutes may be more suitable.

Kinaesthetic and tactile requirements The mediation and fidelity of control laws for continuous controls such as knobs and joysticks need to be carefully addressed. During the design of a training simulator, the designer must consider the nature of input controls. Skill training is mode-specific. The mode of control (hand, speech or foot) in the system should not be replaced by another mode in the simulator. The training of the operation of a certain control by hand does not automatically mean that this function will easily be performed by foot. For example, it is evident that adequate control over the footbrake in a car does not mean that the operator can adequately operate the handbrake.

The resistance of controls should be replicated in a simulator, because the feedback or feel of a control depends on this. At least three forms of feedback are related to controls: the amount of displacement, the amount of force applied, and the effect on the system (e.g., vibration, acceleration or sound). Feedback is often redundant, and operators use different forms under different circumstances. For instance, an operator may identify a control by touch if it cannot be seen. During simulator design, the designer should attempt to identify these forms of feedback and implement them in the simulator. Again, the different types of feedback should not be confused.

One method of learning the physical locations of controls is often referred to as 'reach and teach'. A physical mock-up of the cockpit or other workstation is used. It needs no functional capability; it can be a 'cardboard cockpit'. However, the location and shape of the controls need to be accurate. The trainee can be taught to find these controls in the dark so that only kinaesthetic cues are used to locate and distinguish them.

Sound cueing and sound systems Aural cues cannot be ignored and therefore are frequently used as warning signals. Apart from such aural (instrument) cues, operators use naturally occurring aural cues in control; for example, engine noise levels in helicopters provide a primary cue for control of engine speed. To act as a cue, rather than merely background noise, a sound must be detectable and should inform the operator of the state of the vehicle, a change in state, or a control input. Auditory information may be relevant in a complementary sense, enhancing and verifying information derived from another sensory modality, but sound can also mask or conflict with other relevant cues from the same or different modalities.

Simulation of sound is an important aspect of training simulators. It increases the sense of immersion in the simulation, and it may convey important information about the system (e.g., in the case of malfunctions/battle damage) and the environment. Sound may also act as a distractor and a stressor and thus add to the workload of the trainees. Trainees have to learn to cope with these aspects during their training. Apart from directly adding to the fidelity of a simulation, sound may be used to mask undesirable sounds (e.g., sounds caused by platform motion).

It should be noted that, although simulation of sound requires considerable expertise, it is not really a cost driver and, probably for this reason, within the area of military training and simulation little or no research has been conducted on this topic. Following are some general facts and considerations with respect to aural cueing and the simulation of sound.

Aural cues can be classified as speech or non-speech signals. Due to the high noise levels present in most vehicles, most speech communication takes place by means of intercom systems that are either a fixed part of the interface or mounted on headsets (often built into helmets). To increase the speech-to-noise ratio and provide some noise protection, most headsets are designed to attenuate or exclude environmental sounds. The best way to 'simulate' the speech transmission and attenuation characteristics of intercom systems is to use the same systems in the simulator and to use the simulated sounds as input to these systems. Due to noise protection regulations, the level and duration of noise exposure may be restricted. In such cases, operational signal-to-noise ratios may still be approximated to maintain consistency with operational speech communication conditions.

Sounds are perceived as having a characteristic loudness (intensity), pitch (fundamental frequency), and timbre (spectral composition). These monaural cues enable listeners to identify their source. Listeners are able to detect characteristic frequency and temporal modulations in sounds and, hence, in the state of the sources. Whether or not these variations and changes are detected depends largely on signal-to-noise ratios. As noted earlier, these ratios should be approximated as closely as possible.

The loudness of a sound source is attenuated with distance (inversely quadratic). Thus, the loudness of a known sound may act as a cue for distance. Moving sound sources are characterised by a shift in pitch and loudness that may inform listeners about their speed and direction.

Listeners are able to determine the direction of sounds reasonably well by means of binaural cues. These include differences between the ears in the time of arrival and in the 'colouring' of the sound spectrum due to the listener's head ('head shadow'), the shape of the auricles ('ear shadow'), and the ear canal.

Sounds are reflected by surrounding surfaces that have specific sound absorption characteristics, and are changed by the distance and orientation of these surfaces relative to the source. The resulting reverberations modulate the emitted sounds in a way that is characteristic of a particular environment, i.e., each environment has its own acoustic characteristics that determine how emitted sounds are perceived.

Sounds combine logarithmically. The effect of adding sounds on the overall sound pressure level depends not only on the intensity but also on the spectra of the sounds. Sounds, especially at high intensity and low frequency, may induce vibrations in the environment and may cause surfaces and objects to resonate. Sounds can be stored in a database of samples. During sound generation, which is largely driven by parameters of the simulation model, sounds may be mixed and sound effects may be added to reflect properties of the acoustic environment and of the transmission medium and of the transducer.

Reverberations and resonance characteristics of the environment may be simulated either by including objects and surfaces with the same characteristics or by digitally adding reverberation and resonance effects to the generated sounds. For the presentation of background noise, a minimum of four speakers will generally be necessary. These speakers should be mounted in such a way that the emitted sound is sufficiently reflected to create an omni-directional impression, and should have sufficient dynamic range and power. Additional speakers may be required to simulate the location of specific sound sources.

With sound presentation via headsets, most of the 3D characteristic of sounds is usually lost. If these characteristics must be preserved, they can be simulated. For optimal simulation of 3D sounds, transfer functions for individual trainees should be obtained.

In the near future, developments in the area of noise protection (e.g., Active Noise Reduction), automatic speech recognition, and the use of 3D audio displays are likely significantly to affect aural cueing and sound simulation requirements.

Conclusions

It is clear from the above that the overriding issues that need to be addressed in the design of TSIs are:

- the requirement for physical fidelity;
- the implications for transfer of training;
- the needs and competencies of trainees.

Specifications regarding the physical fidelity of TSIs are likely to have the greatest implications for financial costs. A modular and flexible design of the simulator and training programme will allow functions and capabilities to be added more easily.

Instructor-Simulator Interface

To support the delivery of training programmes, training simulators are equipped with instructional facilities. Usually these facilities are implemented in an Instructor Operator Station (IOS). Facilities for authoring training scenarios are often also provided, as are administrative and evaluation facilities. The nature of the facilities required will depend on:

- *The characteristics of the training programme*, which, apart from the training and instruction strategies chosen, will depend on the domain: a training programme consisting of a highly structured sequence of pre-programmed short training scenarios requires different facilities from a training programme composed of a small set of loosely-defined training scenarios that are varied or adapted during runtime.
- *The number of instructors*: an instructor who has to deliver a training programme to a group of trainees will require different facilities from an instructor who works on the basis of one-to-one tutoring.
- *The didactic background and expertise of instructors*: in most cases, the responsibility for simulator-based training rests with instructors who are specialised in delivering training on a particular simulator. Instructors are almost always military personnel, usually experienced operators who have been extracted from operational units and who have been assigned to their duties. However, they may also have been selected for their expertise in the domain to be taught (for example, experienced pilots as instructors for a flight simulator) or for their didactic qualities. Sometimes 'instructor' is a general function for which all kinds of experienced military personnel can apply. Although most instructors undergo a basic course in didactics, they are often not explicitly trained for their particular function. The didactic course may be quite short, sometimes not more than a couple of days, with an emphasis on general didactic principles. Instructors often have to learn how to teach on the job, coached by other members of the instruction group. The same holds for acquiring expertise in operating the simulator. Only in a few cases are specific simulator training courses designed for instructors.
- *The distribution of tasks between instructors*: it should be noted that instructors are frequently responsible for other tasks, including: acting as a participant in training scenarios, either indirectly (e.g., controlling enemy forces) or directly (e.g., acting as an Air Traffic Controller); development and maintenance of the

training programme; providing classroom instruction; administrative and organisational duties; and technical maintenance duties. These tasks are sometimes assigned to specific people (instructors often work in a group, mostly 3-10 persons, and have regular work meetings), but in most cases instructors have to combine several or all of these tasks. In some cases, the commander of the unit to which the trainees belong is responsible for the delivery of training. Here, instructors assume the role of system manager and provider of training facilities, and thus support the unit commander. This is often the case in tactical trainers. More rarely, trainees deliver their own training. For example, within limits, experienced pilots may be responsible for their own refresher training.

- *The characteristics of the simulator*: the term 'simulator' refers to a wide variety of different systems that represent different levels of comprehensiveness and sophistication. This implies that the range and sophistication of the facilities required to operate these systems will differ correspondingly.
- *The number of trainees*: this is affected by whether simulator-based training is focused on the training of individual trainees, crews, or groups of trainees/crews.
- *Trainee characteristics*: the trainee population ranges from novices to highly-skilled experts, and from low educational levels to academic degrees.

To a large extent, the nature of the facilities that are available determines the effectiveness and efficiency of training independently of the quality of other simulator characteristics. For instance, given the same image system, database, motion system, and so on, the training capability of two training simulators is determined by the facilities that they offer. Unfortunately, many training simulators, especially the older types, have a very limited set of facilities. This is surprising, because generally the cost of these facilities is negligible compared to other simulator features. But, even in more modern systems, the range of facilities is rather limited and not well matched to training programme and instructor requirements. One of the reasons is that the specification and procurement process is biased towards fidelity rather than instructional aspects, and focuses on cost-drivers (to the neglect of 'benefit-drivers'). Of course, the availability of the facilities is a necessary but not a sufficient condition for simulator-based training to be effective and efficient. Much also depends on the composition of the training programme and on the capability of the instructors to exploit the possibilities of these facilities to their full advantage.

The literature with respect to the use and effectiveness of instructional facilities is very limited (Flexman & Stark, 1987; Sticha *et al*, 1990). Most of the literature is limited to flight simulators and focuses on tutoring aspects. Only a few studies are available in which instructional features have been empirically evaluated. Most of the knowledge about instructional features is based on anecdotal reports and subjective assessments. Polzella *et al* (1983, 1987) systematically examined the use and perceived utility of various instructional facilities. Polzella *et al* (1987), for example, surveyed 543 Air Force flight simulator instructors on the use of instructional features that allowed for varying task difficulty, performance monitoring, and feedback. Although the level of use of instructional facilities was affected somewhat by hardware and software unreliability, implementation time, functional limitations, and design deficiencies, the perceived training value of an instructional facility was the most important determinant of its use. Perceived training value is a function of familiarity, which in turn is determined by instructor training. This implies that:

- instructor opinion on the utility or desirability of particular instructional features may be biased;
- instructor training should be an important issue during the implementation of any simulator.

Given the paucity of research on facilities, most of this review is limited to an inventory of general principles and examples based on considerations gleaned from Section II, incidental research reports, findings from field orientations, and available expertise.

Authoring Facilities

Authoring facilities permit design, editing, and management of training programmes and associated automated tutoring features in advance of training sessions. They may provide simulator instructors with a high-level design environment enabling them to:

- set the gaming area and terrain characteristics;
- position objects;
- select events, e.g., meteorological effects or system malfunctions, and their occurrence;
- define performance measures, standards, and logging requirements;
- pre-program automated cueing and feedback and instructor alerts in terms of objective decision rules.

Standardisation and authoring of training scenarios For many reasons, standardisation and authoring of training scenarios in advance of training sessions have distinct advantages over *ad hoc* scenario management. However, training scenarios may differ considerably in complexity, duration, and interactivity. For more complex and interactive scenarios, especially when there is little experience in using them, scenario progression and the behaviour of trainees are difficult to predict. Experience accumulated may be used to adapt and re-author scenarios and to modify, standardise, or automate the way in which they are delivered. This may reduce the need to apply changes during scenario runtime. Although instructors generally prefer to have the option of applying changes and overruling automated scenario proceedings, they should be aware of the consequences. Changes may add to the workload, particularly if they have implications for other scenario aspects or for subsequent system behaviour or scenario events. Runtime changes also impose a responsibility for checking and maintaining consistency between different aspects of the scenario: it is not always easy to understand the consequences of changes for other aspects of scenarios. Another drawback is that runtime modifications may reduce the possibilities for comparing performance across trainees: preferably one should be able unambiguously to interpret differences in performance in terms of differences between trainees, not in terms of differences between scenarios.

Authoring can be viewed as involving two types of activity: definition and tuning. In authoring a training programme, one can either work from scratch or adapt an existing item.

Definition Separate sets of facilities/interfaces may be required for authoring the different components of a training programme: training scheme, training scenarios, briefing, automated tutoring, and debriefing. As always, the exact specifications of these facilities will depend on (1) what has to be trained, (2) who has to be trained, (3) the training and instruction strategies that are to be used, (4) who will deliver the training, and (5) the specifics of the training medium.

Tuning Tuning consists of matching the training programme to its design criterion, e.g., its training objective, by means of an iterative testing and debugging process. It is likely to be the most difficult and time-consuming, and the functionalities that are required to support these activities require special attention. In many cases, the facilities required are the same as those required for scenario management (see subsequently).

To a relatively large extent, authoring is a trial and error process that requires many iterations, and it may take considerable time to tune a training programme, scenario, or instructional intervention optimally. Therefore, it is usually desirable that a separate facility be available that enables authoring in parallel with the delivery of training.

Storage and database requirements It should be possible to store the results of the authoring process in a database for subsequent retrieval at the start of training sessions, thus relieving instructors of much of the effort of initialising the simulator and the training session. Such a facility also enables documentation and configuration control of training programme components, and the accumulation of expertise. The latter is an important advantage, particularly in view of the high rate of personnel turnover in military establishments. It also allows the re-use of components in other training programmes. By storing pre-authored training scenarios in a database, appropriate learning experiences can be achieved by selecting training scenarios that elicit them, rather than by *ad hoc* modifications during runtime, as is often the case.

The training schemes specify the relations and sequencing of training objectives for specific groups of trainees. Training objectives are linked to particular training scenarios, and so the training schemes also specify the relations and sequencing of training scenarios. Thus, the structure of the training schemes and the format of training scenarios may be used as the basis of the database that is to contain the training programme. Separate sets of facilities/interfaces may be required to author training schemes, training scenarios, and automated instructions (briefings, interventions, and debriefings).

The main difficulty in specifying the functionalities required for authoring training programmes resides in identifying, at each level of design, those aspects that are relatively invariant and hence can be predefined and stored in databases, and those aspects that require flexibility and must be resolved interactively, i.e., at the interface that is used for authoring. The choices made determine the complexity of the interface and the size and structure of the database. It should also be noted that facilities may be required to protect the database against unauthorised access or modifications. The requirements for these facilities can be derived on the basis of an outline or blueprint of the prospective training programme and by means of 'talkthroughs' or 'walkthroughs' of idealised authoring sessions with those who will be assigned to the task of authoring.

Instructional Facilities

In practice, different types of simulator configuration may be encountered, such as stand-alone, convertible, and networked. These configurations may be used in different ways, and by different combinations of trainees and instructors. Examples include one-to-one (one trainee-one instructor), many-to-one (as in crew training or the training of groups of trainees in parallel), one-to-many (as in individual training of C³I-skills), or many-to-many (different varieties of group and team training). In this chapter, instructional facilities are discussed without regard for how many instructors will use them or the allocation of tasks among them. However, one should be aware that the requirement for instructors to collaborate may involve additional facilities, notably with respect to communication and to authorisation/prioritisation rules. In describing optional instructional facilities, the main distinctions that will be used are those between individual, group, and crew training. It should be noted that these types of training may be delivered on the same simulator.

Scenario Management

Scenario management facilities enable the instructor to configure and control the simulator so that simulated events occur in accordance with a specific training scenario. Training scenarios are structured sequences of events intended to provide the trainees with practice on various tasks. Although there is some overlap with instructional facilities, especially tutoring facilities, these facilities will be reviewed separately.

Initialisation

At the start of a training session, the simulator needs to be initialised. In addition to specific start-up checks that test whether the simulator is functioning properly, this involves setting initial conditions of the training scenario to be run. These settings can be entered manually or by downloading a pre-authored scenario or scenario settings from a scenario database. The latter option is usually preferable, since it tends to be more reliable and quicker. At this stage, information concerning the trainee or crew and the instructor may be entered. This information is useful for administrative and evaluation purposes. For group instruction, it may also be necessary to configure trainee consoles/mock-ups. After initialisation has been completed, the training session may start.

Real-Time Scenario Control

During the execution of training scenarios, unforeseen events may occur that require the intervention of the instructor. For instance, a trainee may have misunderstood his training assignment and cause the training scenario to wander off its intended course of events. Particularly for more complex training scenarios, events may occur that were not envisaged at the design of stage. A new training scenario may also contain bugs, or simulator malfunctions may occur. In all these cases, it is highly desirable that deviations are noted and corrected in a timely manner so that no valuable training time is lost. This requires specific scenario view and control options. In many existing simulators, training scenarios are only partially pre-authored, thus requiring instructors to devote much of their time to scenario management. The training scenario may require the instructor to play particular roles as part of the training scenario. The instructor must have the necessary facilities for playing these roles.

Scenario View Options

During training, the instructor should be able to monitor the simulated system, the environment in which it is operating, and the events that are to take place. The nature of the facilities required depends upon the specific circumstances and instructor preferences. However, a number of generic recommendations for system, environment, and event view options can be suggested.

System view options The instructor should be able to inspect system status at all times during the scenario, including all relevant system displays and the settings of controls. These system views should contain all parameters under the control of the instructor, and their content should be selectable by the instructor.

Environment view options Monitoring the system environment requires a bird's eye view of the gaming area. In addition, trajectory plots or waypoints of moving models may be displayed. A useful option is zoom in/out of particular parts of the gaming area. Equally useful is the option to project information overlays over particular areas, such as the action radius and line-of-sight information, and the opportunity to apply information filters. Options for inspecting specific environmental entities or parameter settings (e.g., atmospheric conditions) are also indispensable.

Event view options Event time lines (history, preview) may be presented so that the instructor can anticipate forthcoming events.

Scenario Control Options

The options for control of the scenario are described below.

System control options These options refer to facilities to change system parameters during runtime, including the possibility of initiating system malfunctions.

Environment control options   Similarly, these options represent the ability to change aspects of the gaming area, the environmental conditions, and properties of entities. For instance, entities may be repositioned, deleted, or inserted, and their properties may be modified.

Event control options Overall scenario progress may be controlled by features such as play, rewind, forward, stop, pause, reset, and halt. Some of these facilities may also be applied to particular events, rather than the scenario as a whole. For instance, the occurrence of an event may be postponed or re-scheduled.

All changes to the scenario that are applied by the instructor during a training session should be logged for administrative and re-authoring purposes.

Options for Role Play

Simulation of other actors such as enemy forces is often rather limited. Sometimes, the instructors have to play these roles, and hence require information that enables them to provide the trainee with appropriate inputs. Different types of role can be distinguished. If the instructor is to act as a crew member, a remote control unit may be required enabling him to control instructional facilities from the corresponding crew member position. The instructor may also act as an operator located outside the vehicle, e.g., a commander of a different unit or an ATC operator.

Simulation of threats (adversary weapons, aircraft, ships, and so on) is important in mission training. Computer-controlled adversaries are computer models that allow for the simulation of enemy system performance. Computer adversaries can be fully automated, or partly under the control of the instructor (SAFOR). Where conflicts may arise, the instructor must be able to overrule the computer.

Shut-Down Options

After a training session is complete, the instructor must shut down the simulator. At this stage, a further task is to save the results of the training session for debriefing or administrative purposes.

Briefing

Briefings may have to be delivered to individual trainees, groups of trainees, or crews. Individual briefing can be delivered in the simulator, which may be equipped with facilities for automated delivery of briefings or demonstrations. The same applies when groups of trainees are trained simultaneously but individually in separate simulators. Here, however, facilities for delivering group briefings will usually be required (e.g., a briefing room with audio-visual presentation facilities). Ideally, these facilities should be located near the location of training. Briefing of crews may be more involved than individual and group briefings because of the higher complexity of crew training scenarios and because of the potential need to present separate briefings for different crew perspectives.

Tutoring

As with scenario management facilities, view and control options can be specified for the tutoring facilities required to deliver guidance and feedback during scenario runtime. These facilities are generally complementary to those described for scenario management, the main difference being that tutoring facilities are more trainee-oriented. Again, tutoring of groups and crews will generally require facilities additional to those required for tutoring of individual trainees.

Tutoring View Options

For training and instruction to be effective and efficient, trainees must be provided with timely and accurate guidance and feedback. In addition to having access to information about scenario progression, the instructor should be able to monitor closely the behaviour of the trainee. Which aspects of trainee behaviour are most relevant will depend on the specifics of the scenario and the training history of the trainee. Generally, the following types of view facilities can be distinguished: Outside-The-Vehicle (OTV), TSI, trainee, and history views.

OTV view The OTV view contains the view of the environment as it is seen from within the simulator mock-up. Preferably, the instructor should be able to see this view from the same perspective as the trainee; for crew training, viewing of the environment from different crew position eye-points is therefore necessary, and can be accomplished automatically using a head-tracker.

TSI view The instructor should be able to view displays and instrument readings that are available to the trainee through his TSI. A useful facility is to 'slave' the instructor view to the settings for the trainee. If the instructor wants to view settings other than those currently displayed, this facility enables him rapidly to switch back to the settings of the trainee. The instructor should also be able to view the trainee's handling of controls, by means of direct viewing, video cameras, or logging and display of the position of controls.

Trainee view The instructor should be able to see the trainee's direction of gaze to determine the aspects of the environment or interface to which attention is being given. There are, of course, different ways in which this may be accomplished, such as use of video cameras or locating the IOS at a position where the instructor can maintain eye contact with the trainee.

In addition to facilities that permit a direct view of the trainee, it is extremely useful to have facilities for the automated recording of performance measures. The measures required in any particular case will depend on the training objectives. Even if adequate training objectives are available, it is highly likely that the need for new performance measures will be suggested by training experiences. Thus, it should be possible for instructors to define and use new performance measures.

History view The measurement and logging of performance enable instructors to plot particular performance measures against scenario time or as a function of particular events or actions. This information may be useful in comparing current performance against training history. Such a facility also provides many options for delivering automated guidance and feedback.

A history view may also include an overview of results obtained during previous training courses or scenarios. This kind of information may be useful at the start of a training scenario to determine the requirements for briefing and tutoring. For instance, it may enable an instructor to assess what the trainee already knows and what his weak spots are.

The instructor should be able to switch smoothly between different views. The views presented at any particular time may be pre-programmed according to preference, thus relieving instructors of the need to apply settings during runtime.

Test facilities The simulator may also be equipped with the facility to insert or embed tests into the training scenario to diagnose trainee performance. For instance, such a facility may be useful in determining whether a particular error should be interpreted as an action slip or as the result of a misconception.

Tutoring Control Options

Instructors may be given the opportunity to apply changes to the TSI, such as changing display settings, instrument readings or control parameters. They may also be able to take over particular controls from the trainees. The latter may be useful when delivering part-task training on a full-mission simulator, or for demonstration purposes.

Instructors should be able to mark and annotate scenario segments for logging and debriefing purposes. Adding annotations may be too time-consuming during runtime. It may therefore be useful to specify a list of pre-defined annotations from which instructors can select. This relieves them of the task of entering information, but leaves the opportunity to add particular reminders and cues.

During scenario runtime, the instructor will need means of communicating with trainees. The facilities required depend on the types of interaction anticipated. Audio and video facilities are helpful when the instructor is not in direct contact with trainees. Audio communications can usually be delivered in parallel with other scenario proceedings. Their advantage is that, unlike visually presented communications, they cannot easily be ignored or overlooked: they automatically attract attention. Visual communications can take a variety of forms, ranging from presentation of alphanumeric information on a separate communication display to presentation of, or highlighting of, information in the OTV or MMI displays. Generally, this mode of communication is more obtrusive. An alternative, more direct, means of communicating with trainees is to use response-forcing, e.g., to demonstrate control handling procedures.

The availability of automated performance measurement and logging facilities offers the opportunity for automated guidance and feedback. The possibilities range from automated performance alerts (the delivery of trainee or instructor alerts whenever performance exceeds pre-specified performance tolerances) to sophisticated tutoring dialogues and adaptive strategies such as fading.

Debriefing

Debriefing facilities for individual, group, and crew training can be distinguished. Debriefings of groups of individuals trained on the same or similar scenarios will usually require comparisons between individuals. Debriefings of crews usually require the use of different crew perspectives.

Debriefings vary in detail from global performance outcomes to detailed review of playback of training events that require accurate synchronisation between information sources (simulator and video/audio recordings, and performance logs and annotations) and rapid access to different parts of the recordings. Playback may be continuous (with the option to pause, rewind and forward), or based on fixed time increments, scenario events, or markers or debriefing cues inserted by the instructor during runtime.

Debriefings may be delivered in the simulator or in a separate room. For group and crew briefings, a specially designed debriefing room is typically used. Debriefing rooms should be located near the simulator and should be equipped with the appropriate presentation facilities, including those allowing results to be printed in different pre-defined report formats.

IOS Design

Most instructional facilities required during runtime (scenario management, briefing, tutoring, debriefing) are integrated into an Instructor Operator/Operating station (IOS). IOS requirements are determined by (1) didactic requirements, (2) simulator configuration, and (3) ergonomic requirements. As has been pointed out in preceding sections, these factors are inter-dependent. Most of the didactic requirements have already been mentioned. The discussion below primarily addresses simulator configuration and ergonomic requirements. IOS requirements for simulator control are also briefly discussed.

IOS design and simulator configuration In the simplest case, the IOS is located adjacent to the TSI in the simulator mock-up. In flight simulators, this configuration is called an on-board IOS (Rolfe & Staples, 1986), and can be used for individual and crew training. From an instructional perspective, an on-board IOS has the advantage of enabling direct view of the behaviour of the trainees. In essence, it permits a more natural interaction between instructor and trainees, including direct perception of non-verbal cues such as gestures, and is generally preferred by instructors.

An alternative is to locate the IOS separately from the trainee interface/simulator mock-up ('off-board IOS'). Achieving the same 'naturalness' of interaction may require more extensive facilities, and hence may be more expensive. There are several reasons for choosing this configuration. Mounting the IOS on a motion platform increases the payload and may result in additional cost. Moreover, the presence of the IOS displays on-board may cause undesirable lighting effects and interfere with the training of night operations using night vision goggles. However, some regulatory authorities (e.g., the Federal Aviation Administration) require an on-board IOS, and extra seats for use by officials.

It is possible to use a system that combines the characteristics of on-board and off-board configurations. Communication between off-board and on-board instructors is maintained by means of audio channels on a headset. Here, on-board instructors are typically responsible for the tutoring of trainees and give commands to the off-board instructors, who are primarily responsible for IOS handling. Different allocations of tasks are also possible. For instance, off-board instructors may also have the responsibility for tutoring trainees and invoking the assistance of on-board instructors when trainees require on-site assistance or when their workload becomes too high. The latter arrangement may be used for training groups of individual trainees or groups of crews simultaneously. Group tutoring requires specific IOS facilities (van Delft *et al*, 1996).

For more complex types of training, such as tactical training of teams, instructor tasks are usually more specialised, and more elaborate IOS facilities are required. Different instructors may be assigned to the tutoring of separate teams, and may require their own separate IOS facilities. Separate IOS workstations may be needed to control specific aspects of the simulation (e.g., control of enemy forces). In addition, higher levels of instructional control will usually be required to manage and harmonise tasks. Owing to the greater complexity of scenarios and the associated management overhead, most of the guidance and feedback for these types of training is provided at the beginning of training sessions and during debriefing, also known as After Action Reviews (AARs).

Ergonomic requirements   Ergonomic requirements include those related to the Human-Machine Interface (HMI) and those related to simulator controls and instructor position.

As always in designing HMIs, a trade-off is necessary between flexibility and ease of operation. A general guideline is that instructors should be able to allocate as much as possible of their time to their primary activity of instruction, and minimise the time required to handle the IOS. Time-critical instructional tasks, such as initiating system malfunctions or marking scenario fragments for recording, should be assigned to Special Function Keys (SFKs). Instructional tasks that are less time-critical may be menu-driven or under the control of Multi-Function Keys (MFKs). In all cases, care should be taken to minimise the number of control actions required by the instructor. A keyboard for entering alphanumeric data and a mouse for arranging windows and selecting pre-defined options will usually also be required. As noted earlier, a hand-held remote-control panel may be useful if the instructor also has to act as a crew member.

A uniform and standardised way of presenting information is highly conducive to efficient IOS handling. This requirement is especially important given the large amount and variety of information that may have to be monitored. One option is to use a large 'glass' area incorporating either several displays or large monitors in combination with software windowing techniques. For example, the IOS may contain displays assigned to managing the environment, managing system parameters, and observing trainee performance (instrument panels, performance measures, video).

Customisation of the HMI to instructor preferences may be desirable, and the HMI may be adapted to the requirements of particular training scenarios. For instance, facilities that are not used for a particular scenario may be switched off or disabled. The information required for scenario-customisation of the HMI may be derived from didactic analysis of the training process, from the results of trial runs, or from available training results stored in log files.

With respect to requirements for simulator controls and the instructor position, an intercom system is required that enables communication between instructor and individual trainees (point-to-point) and between instructor and crew (conference). During training sessions the instructor may also need to be able to communicate with maintenance personnel outside the simulator.

The temperature, overall sound level and ambient lighting of rooms in which the IOS and the TSI are located should be under the control of the instructor. The instructor should also be able to switch particular simulator components, such as the motion system, on or off (an emergency stop is usually obligatory).

The instructor position should have a comfortable adjustable seat with armrests. If the IOS is mounted on a moving base, the seat should be fixed to the ground; safety belts may be required. In some cases it may be desirable to move the seat to different positions by means of a seat rail. Most simulators are also equipped with specific test and demonstration facilities. Generally, these facilities will also be operated from behind an IOS.

Automation

Automated instruction has distinct advantages over instruction delivered by humans: increased consistency, reliability, speed, and accuracy. However, most simulators provide little automated instruction during training sessions. Generally, human tutors deliver instruction during training or in a debriefing session.

Ideas for automated instruction can be drawn from the fields of Computer-Based Training (CBT) and Intelligent Tutoring Systems (ITS).

Computer-Based Training Computers can be used in many ways in the context of training: to simulate the task environment (simulators), to take over low-level or routine tasks (tools), to manage the logistics of education (Computer Managed Instruction), to administer tests and keep the scores, to facilitate educational research, and also to provide instruction and training to students. A number of terms have been used for these systems, including Computer-Assisted Instruction (CAI), Computer-Assisted Learning (CAL), Computer-Based Training (CBT), and Computer-Based Instruction (CBI). Authors have used these terms with slightly different definitions to include either all computer systems involved in training and instruction or only a subset. Here the term Computer-Based Training (CBT) will be used for all computer programs actually delivering training and instruction in a particular domain.

A subset of CBT programs is based on simulations of the real world. These simulation-based programs usually have lower physical fidelity than simulators. They often provide a more abstract, functional simulation rather than mimicking the exact physical properties of the task environment. Most CBT systems are quite straightforward branching systems: the student is presented with some domain knowledge, followed by a number of questions or exercises to make sure that he has understood the information presented and can apply it in different contexts or environments. The errors students might make are foreseen, and feedback or remediation is pre-programmed. Most CBT systems are relatively brief, and deal with only a restricted well-structured domain. The major goal is to teach specific tasks or knowledge efficiently. Hence CBT systems are designed for a specific domain and a specific group of students. They are often based on the knowledge of experienced teachers in the domain, rather than on theories of instruction. Technical issues are important: CBT systems must respond rapidly, be attractive to students, and run on affordable and widely available machines (Larkin & Chabay, 1992).

Intelligent Tutoring Systems   Most of the research on tutoring has been conducted in the context of the development of Intelligent Tutoring Systems (ITSs). The purpose of these developments is to design computer programs that teach in a more intelligent way. Researchers have tried to achieve this goal by applying tutoring concepts derived from the research literature on training and instruction and by applying techniques from the field of Artificial Intelligence (AI). A desired outcome is provision of individualised and flexible tutoring resembling that delivered by human tutors. The main goal of ITS research is to test and evaluate tutoring principles and alternative ways of implementing them.

ITSs are considered more flexible than traditional CBT programs because they adapt their training and instruction to the particular student. Designers have typically followed a modular approach, segregating the different types of knowledge:

- knowledge about what is being taught is contained in the *domain model*;
- knowledge about the strengths and the weaknesses of the particular student working with the system at a particular moment is contained in the *student model*;
- knowledge about instructional strategies and tactics is contained in the *pedagogical model*;
- knowledge about the way to exchange information with the student is contained in the *interface module*.

To be truly intelligent, all four components should be fully developed and integrated. Most ITS studies are focused on a specific research issue, and hence most researchers have concentrated on one component and designed the others in a very rudimentary way or even not at all. Therefore, many well known ITS systems have never been used in practice, and only a few have been evaluated with students.

Most of the research on ITSs is conducted in the context of relatively homogeneous and well-structured tasks (e.g., problem solving) that do not possess the dynamic, time-critical, and time-sharing aspects that characterise the high-performance tasks typically trained on more advanced simulators. Given the complexity and dynamics of high-performance tasks, it is questionable whether current analytical approaches are appropriate; their labour-intensity alone may preclude their application.

In short, for most simulators, aiming for complete automation of instructor tasks does not seem a feasible option. However, between manual control and complete automation, a large range of options may be adopted to increase efficiency. Many of these options have already been mentioned.

Even if automation cannot be achieved, standardisation offers considerable advantages that may reduce training costs. For instance, training scenarios, instructional strategies, and the HMI of the IOS may all be standardised. These steps will substantially reduce instructor familiarisation time and the time to author training scenarios, they will facilitate evaluation by enabling comparisons across scenarios, and they will provide many opportunities for semi-automated instructor support.

Facilities for Administration and Evaluation

Administrative facilities are those required for scheduling training activities or, more generally, for managing the logistics associated with simulator-based training. Again, their requirements depend largely on factors such as the nature of the training programme and the simulator configuration.

Administrative facilities are also required to manage the results of training. If the evaluation of results comprises assessment of transfer or retention of training, the results must be augmented by data obtained after training, i.e., on the job. Analysis of results may be used to re-author or re-schedule training activities, or to evaluate trainees.

Administrative facilities assist in the entry, storage, viewing, editing, processing, backup, security, and printing of data. Often, general-purpose software packages are sufficient. However, this will depend on the level of detail and the nature of the data formats. Administration and evaluation facilities may be linked or integrated with authoring facilities. If the results are used for re-authoring purposes, for example, they can be organised in terms of training programme characteristics.

Specification of Requirements

Although general guidelines and options have been specified in this chapter, guidance in the choice and design of facilities is required. Despite specific requirements associated with the domain of application, the simulator configuration, and the user group, a feasible solution is to provide requirement checklists and general guidelines in the context of particular specification problems. The resultant requirements can then be iteratively compared with other requirements, and can be cross-checked with prospective users, e.g., by means of talk-throughs or walk-throughs of scenarios.

19 Visual Cueing and Image Systems

Introduction

The importance of visual cues, i.e., visual sources of information, is that almost all relevant operations with mobile weapon platforms on the ground and in the air depend on them. The primacy of vision compared to the other human senses is obvious. The multitude and complexity of cues that can be processed by the human visual system exceed those of any other sensory system by several orders of magnitude. Vision is also the only way to perceive complex information at considerable distances from the observer, and is essential in vehicle control, target acquisition and weapon delivery. There are few exceptions, such as basic instrument flight and beyond-visual-range engagements, where OTW visual cues play a secondary role in ground vehicle or aircraft operations.

In simulators, the OTW visual system is equally important. The question addressed here is not whether an OTW system is needed, but the type of visual cues needed, how realistic they must be to attain the required skill level, and how they should be translated into simulator requirements. Image systems, it should be noted, generally constitute the main cost driver.

In addition to work conducted within the MASTER project (de Fontenilles *et al*, 1997), the main findings presented here are derived from van Rooij *et al* (1997b), literature reviews on quality criteria for simulator images by Milders and Padmos (1991) and Padmos and Milders (1992), an overview of visual cueing requirements in flight simulation by Buffet (1986), work on visual space perception by Cutting (1997), and work on scene detail and stereoscopic vision by Clapp (1985a, b, c, d).

The image system provides the outside-world image: visual information on the simulated vehicle's position and motion in its environment and on the position and motion of objects in the environment.

One complete channel of an image system consists of the following consecutive subsystems: database, image generator, and display (Baarspul, 1990; Yan, 1985). More channels can be combined to obtain a larger field of view. The database (see

Chapter 17) contains a digital representation of the visual aspects of the vehicle's environment.

This chapter primarily considers cueing requirements and issues associated with the generation and display of images. First, considerations and trade-offs with respect to image systems are reviewed, followed by a detailed overview of visual cues and their implications for simulation. In the final section of this chapter, MASTER findings from a survey of user experiences with respect to image systems will be summarised.

Image Generation

The image generator produces the image to be displayed from the current viewing position and direction. Its overall performance may be characterised by its update frequency and its image delay. The update frequency is the frequency with which a completely new image content is generated. The image delay is the time from determination of the virtual camera position and direction in the database to the complete display of the corresponding frame. Overload is a condition in which an image generator is required to process more than its capabilities allow. It can be caused by attempting to create too many polygons, light points, pixels, transparencies, occulting calculations, or dynamic models. Overload management is the deployment of strategies to reduce the effect of overload. Generally, it will automatically reduce the number of polygons and/or lights in a given scene, although some systems respond by reducing the update frequency.

Image generation is accomplished in a number of consecutive processing steps executed by separate subsystems: the scene manager, the geometric processor, and the display processor.

Scene Manager

The scene manager, or object manager, determines which objects and parts of the terrain from the available database are potentially to be displayed (the active database) and the level of detail, given the position and orientation of the 'virtual camera' that represents the eye (or head) orientation of the operator. Therefore, its position and attitude are coupled to the position and attitude of the simulated vehicle. The eye point or camera point is the point in space from which the scene manager calculates images with the correct perspective. Many image generators are capable of simultaneously making calculations for several eye points, such as those of different crew members, and for several sensor positions. For debrief purposes, many eye points may be presented — enemy crew stations, threat sites, or the 'bird's eye-view' (a plan view of the battlefield or engagement taken from height). The position and orientation of the virtual camera should always closely follow the motion of the vehicle as calculated by the simulator model, so that the direction and distance of scene elements, as seen by the operator, are compatible with earth-locked reference.

Level of Detail (LoD) For image systems, the term 'level of detail' refers to a method of scene management in which a high LoD is used in the foreground, gracefully degrading to a low LoD in the distance. This prevents 'feature popping', whereby a cultural feature such as a building suddenly appears in the scene as the eye point moves towards it. The mechanism employed is to increase the number of polygons and light points used for a feature image as the distance of the feature from the eye point is decreased. The greater number of polygons helps to establish a more complex shape. In the case of buildings, windows, doors and even surface detail such as bricks will be added as the eye point moves closer. Some image systems use their transparency feature to fade in new Levels of Detail and to fade out old ones ('Fade Level of Detail').

Automatic LoD switching can be provided to prevent overload, if modelled in advance in the database. It is possible to exclude targets from LoD switching. Switching between levels should be performed gradually. Fixed sequences in the change of object appearance, such as explosions or smoke, can be presented smoothly using animation effects.

Moving models The term 'model' is used to describe 3D moving entities within a database (each of which requires detailed modelling). In specifications for image systems, the system capacity will often be given in terms of the maximum number of 'moving models', including aircraft, missiles, ships, and ground-based vehicles. Vehicle structures that are in reality visible in the field of view should be displayed. Special attention should be given to structures potentially used by the operator as aiming points to aid accurate spatial orientation.

The scene manager may report:

- the Height Above Terrain (HAT) of the own vehicle and other moving objects within a given temporal and spatial accuracy, e.g., within one update cycle with an accuracy of 5 cm;
- all collisions of the vehicle and other moving objects with structures that hit the collision volumes within one update cycle, with a specified accuracy. A distinction can be made between soft collisions (such as aircraft touchdown) and fatal crashes;
- the distance from the virtual camera to specific database elements (line of sight ranging), controllable from the simulation computer;
- whether specifically marked database elements are within the field of view (threat detection).

Geometric Processor

The geometric processor calculates the projective transformations from the database objects to the image plane. It removes objects or parts of objects that fall outside the field of view or are occulted by objects closer to the virtual camera. The magnification, i.e., the ratio of visual angles between database elements as seen by the observer to corresponding angles as perceived after projection, should be 1.00 at all locations within the field of view.

Surfaces at varying distances in the same line of sight should correctly occult each other in all directions of the available field of view. Occultation must be achieved through software, and specific calculations are needed for correct lines-of-sight with respect to terrain and objects on and above the terrain. Incorrect occultation gives false visual effects, such as revealing features of ground that would be hidden in the real world. Some image generators are limited in the numbers of layers or levels of occulting, and occulting performance is related to the processing power and priority mechanisms. Occultation is also called hidden-surface removal, and can be achieved by various priority and buffering systems.

Priority is the process that determines the relative priority of features in a scene. In the real world, occulting of one object by another happens naturally and automatically; whereas in an image system this process has to be handled mathematically by appropriate algorithms. One of two methods is generally used: a Z buffer or a Range (R) buffer. The Z buffer is a priority technique whereby the Z distance (depth) of a polygon is compared at the pixel level to those features that have already been processed. An R buffer uses slant range instead of the Z component. The R buffer has advantages for large horizontal fields of view, where a Z buffer may run out of resolution. Occulting should be done automatically, without complicated provisions in the database. This may require an R buffer rather than a Z buffer technique.

A polygon is a two-dimensional shape within a visual database that can be coloured, shaded and textured, and whose position is defined by the co-ordinates of its vertices (corners). The geometric processor calls up the polygon structure of a scene from the scene manager and renders it in correct perspective ready for transmission of the processed data to the display processor. Although the polygonal surface itself is inherently two-dimensional, it may be placed in a visual scene in a three-dimensional orientation. Because of the number of ways of specifying a polygon, the definition of polygon count used should be considered when analysing the characteristics of a specific image system. It is usually expressed as number of polygons per frame per channel; for example, 2000 four-sided polygons at the required update frequency.

Display Processor

The display processor, or video processor, scans the image plane and transforms it into discrete picture elements (pixels). A possible value is 1024 by 1024 pixels per channel. The processor calculates the colour of each pixel, possibly including shading or fog effects. It may also take care of features such as spatial anti-aliasing (without compromising spatial resolution) and texture.

The display processor may be able to display scenes in full daylight, in dull daylight, in dusk, or at night. The colour, intensity and source position of sun or moon illuminance may be dynamically controlled by the simulation computer. The colour and luminance of earth and sky should be properly rendered at each time of day, horizon effects included. The colour palette to be displayed simultaneously per time of day condition may amount to 1024 colour-brightness combinations (from a possible 16.7 million), excluding atmospheric, shading and texture effects.

Realistic scene illumination by the vehicle lights should be provided. Realism includes a correct beam pattern and approximately correct luminances of surfaces, depending on their distance and orientation with respect to the lights. The appearance of a light point, such as a flare on the battlefield or an approach or runway light in aircraft simulation, will depend on its intensity and hue (colour) as modified by distance, atmospheric visibility, and directionality, rather than by perspective and size as with polygons. Light points will therefore be described in the database in terms of geographical position, intrinsic intensity, colour and, where relevant, directionality of light. Calligraphic scanning is often used in display systems to produce intensely bright, sharp, light points, although display systems using a high number of raster lines often dispense with calligraphy and paint light points as a cluster of bright pixels as part of a normal raster scan (especially at close distances). A Light String is a data format used for storing a large number of light points, rather than resorting to defining each light point separately. Light Strings can be straight or curved, or produce a given density of lights randomly distributed over an area.

Per channel per frame, the image generator may display a large number of light points, possibly 4000. Light points should be traded with polygons at a ratio of at least 2 to 1. Displayed light point intensity should realistically decrease as a function of distance (inversely quadratic) and atmospheric extinction. Directional light points may be provided, for which the intensity is a programmable function of the viewing angle. Special-purpose sources may include flashing and intermittent lights. At close range, the larger light sources should have a smooth transition into self-luminous surfaces.

Shading is the technique of varying the colour and intensity of a polygon in accordance with its angle to a defined light source, frequently a simulated sun in combination with the sky acting as a diffuse illuminant. The orientation of the polygon to the discrete light source is calculated; the more the angle deviates from the perpendicular, the lower the luminance of polygon colour.

Flat shading or Gouraud shading of polygons should at least be provided, depending on the position of the sun (or other illuminants such as landing and anti-collision lights). Phong shading may replace Gouraud shading if the same refresh rates are delivered. Cast shadows of critical objects may be provided, if not automatically then by means of semi-transparent polygons.

Texture is a reticulated visual effect involving a contrast pattern within an other-wise evenly coloured or shaded polygon or surface. In image systems, texture is generated mathematically or by means of digital photography, and stored in the form of a library of texture maps. Texture effects produce visual cues additional to the basic scene content using polygon modelling. This not only enhances realism but is also particularly important in training tasks where the own vehicle or platform is moving with respect to the background scene. Here, the peripheral vision cue of vection (see subsequently) is strong, and gives important cues of speed, and, for aircraft, height and velocity vectors, that are independent of cues involving conscious comparison with recognisable objects in the visual scene.

Textures may be static or dynamic, the latter produced by moving one or more texture-maps with respect to the surface being textured. This can be used to produce visual effects such as rotor-wash, sea states, and corn or long grass blown down-wind.

Geospecific or real-world texture is a texture map derived from real-world data such as satellite and reconnaissance photography. Such texture maps do not tessellate at the edges, but can be fitted together such that the joints are not visible (similar to joining paper maps).

Texture mapping (i.e., modulation of luminance, colour and transparency) should be supported on surfaces in any position and orientation. At least 256 maps of 128 by 128 texels may be provided, or a proportionately higher number of smaller maps. A texel (TEXture ELement) is the smallest element or cell that forms a texture pattern or texture map. Per polygon, at least four different maps can be displayed to provide far/near effects. Aliasing of texture patterns should be prevented. Dynamic textures such as clouds and sea state may be supported.

In meteorology, visibility is understood as the distance at which a black object's contrast is attenuated to the threshold of seeing (often taken as contrast 0.05). The international definition of fog is a visibility of less than 1 km; mist is a visibility of between 1 and 2 km, and haze corresponds to visibility of 2-5 km. Fog and mist are generally assumed to be composed principally of water droplets; haze and smoke consist of smaller particles. This has implications for sensors such as thermal imagers (TI/FLIR), operating in the far-infrared at wavelengths of about 10 microns, which are capable of penetrating haze and some smokes because their particle size is smaller than the wavelength. The IR radiation is therefore not significantly deflected or absorbed by the particles.

Generally, the attenuation of object contrast as a function of atmospheric extinction (expressed as meteorological visibility) and distance (through clouds, fog, haze, rain, snow) should be realistically displayed (approximating Allard's and Koschmieder's laws), in all directions of the available field of view. Realistic variations in local extinction, depending on the location and height distribution of clouds and ground fog, may be applied, and lightning effects may be provided.

Display Systems

The display system (DS) presents the outside-world images to the trainee. Former displays were mainly calligraphic or vector-scan, well suited to depicting lights in night-time scenes. Current displays are mainly of the raster-scan type, which are able to show full-colour daytime scene images. The outside world picture is often termed the Out-of-The-Window (OTW) display, and is assumed to be viewed either directly by eye in the normal visual band at wavelengths of 0.4-0.7 microns or via sensors. Sensors include intensifiers such as Night Vision Goggles (NVGs) and low-light TV operating in the near IR between 0.7 and 1 micron, thermal imagers (including forward-looking IR) operating in the far IR at 10 microns, and radar displays operating at millimetre wavelengths and above.

Characteristics of Display Systems

Field of view (FoV) The FoV is the area of image produced by a display system, normally expressed as horizontal and vertical arcs with respect to the Design Eye Point (DEP) of the system. The FoV provided by the DS should be as large as the functional FoV of the operator. The latter may be limited by vehicle windows and other features. If parts of the vehicle such as the window frames are used by the operator as aiming points aiding spatial orientation in critical manoeuvres, they should also be incorporated in the display.

Viewing region and distance   In principle, the observer has a correct view of the display only from one point in space. At other locations, distortion and inhomogeneity of image luminance may occur. The viewing region is the area (or, more precisely, the volume) of space around the DEP within which the image can be seen without noticeable distortion or colour or luminance change. The viewing volume should allow for trainees' normal head and body movements. Generally, collimation yields a viewing region of about 10×10 cm^2, except for collimator-projector combinations. If there is more than one observer and/or several metres of moving room (as on a ship's bridge), the viewing region must be relatively large. This is generally achieved by projection of the image on a distant screen.

For non-collimated images, the horizontal and vertical dimensions of the viewing region are proportional to the viewing distance, given a permitted distortion of the frontal image channel. If one accepts a maximum parallax distortion of x deg, it can be determined that the minimum viewing distance is equal to the required width or height (whichever is the greater) of the viewing region multiplied by 57/x. (The resulting distance will be expressed in the same units as the width or height.) For driving simulators, if one accepts a parallax distortion of 1 deg, a minimum viewing distance of 2.9 m is required to allow head movements of 5 cm.

Collimation   Collimation consists of aligning the light rays emitted by the display so that they are parallel with one another, thereby placing the observed display image at optical infinity and creating the illusion of depth in the scene. In simulators, this is usually accomplished using a concave mirror (AGARD, 1981). Collimated images of more than one channel can be combined almost seamlessly. A large collimated image may be obtained with a projection system in combination with a large hollow mirror (Kent, 1990; Todd, 1988). Collimation enhances realism in flight or ship simulators, although the image itself remains two-dimensional.

Collimation is useful if objects of interest are at distances of more than about 15 m. However, a serious disadvantage may arise when using a collimated image for driving simulators, in which the lower part of the scene often represents a distance of a few metres in reality. This may conflict with the optically large distance of the image. Consequently, a collimated image may give an unwanted illusion of large eye height, and disturb perception of the distance of nearby objects. Moreover, perspective errors will occur for nearby objects if several observers simultaneously view the scene.

Iavecchia *et al* (1988) and Roscoe (1989) observed in flight simulators a systematic overestimation of depth in collimated images. They therefore recommended an image magnification of 1.25. Meehan and Triggs (1988) also suggested this level of magnification for simulator images. But, as suggested by Padmos and Milders (1992), this may not be a satisfactory solution for driving simulators.

Luminance The maximum raster luminance should be at least 20 cd/m^2, which can be displayed over the central 5° × 5° area of the FoV. For reading instruments, a higher luminance may be preferable. Luminance at the edges should be at least 60% of the central luminance. The highlight luminance (i.e., the luminance of small light points) should be at least twice as high as the maximum raster luminance.

Colour Correct, homogeneous colour rendering should be provided, independent of mean luminance. Colour convergence error (i.e., the alignment error between the three RGB channels) should be less than 5 arcmin centrally and 10 arcmin at the edges.

Geometry error The geometry error of the DS should be less than 1°. If larger errors occur, the IG should compensate through non-linear image mapping.

Contrast ratio The contrast ratio (the luminance ratio of centres of neighbouring white and black fields of a displayed checkerboard pattern with field size of about 4°) should be at least 10:1, and more if detection of dark objects in dark parts of otherwise bright scenes (e.g., trucks stationed near a wood edge) is critical.

Addressable resolution An addressable resolution of at least 20 pixels/degree is required. For critical detection tasks, higher resolution is necessary. As a rule of thumb, the addressable resolution should be *0.14 × object distance ÷ object size*. Given the number of pixels per channel provided by the IG and the DS, the required resolution limits the FoV per channel. For 20 pixels/degree, the FoV per channel cannot be more than 50° × 50°, given a 1024 × 1024 pixel structure per channel.

Refresh rate The refresh rate (also called frame rate) is the rate at which a whole frame of the display is written. It should be the same as the update frequency, e.g., 60 Hz.

Channel matching Near the borders of display channels, there should be a match for geometry, luminance and colour. Geometric mismatch should be less than 5 arcmin; luminance mismatch should be less than 10% of mean luminance; chromatic mismatch should not be perceptible to the operator. Adequate edge blending should be provided.

Maintenance The stability of the DS should be high enough to preclude the need for frequent complicated adjustments (e.g., of geometry and colour convergence).

Types of Display System

Monitor, projection, and helmet-mounted displays (HMDs) can be distinguished.

Monitors Monitor-based OTW displays are generally referred to as 'windows', each driven by its own image channel, with the exception of side-by-side crew seating where each crew member may have a display window directly ahead using a common image source. Direct view on monitors is often not practical, firstly because of the short viewing distance (52 cm to obtain a diagonal field size of 60° for a monitor with diagonal size 60 cm), and secondly because of the relatively large separation areas between monitors if more than one image channel is used (many monitors will be required to provide a large FoV at an acceptably large viewing distance).

Projection Front or rear projection systems are available. The advantage of rear projection is that contrast and luminance may be higher than with front projection, but it is difficult to avoid a hot spot (a conspicuously higher luminance in the image centre). With plane projection screens, separation areas between channels are likely to be visible. On curved screens, edge blending can be applied to avoid this, but special measures are required to avoid image distortions. With projection on approximately spherical domes, very large field sizes may be obtained.

Front projection may be an option for the FoV around the horizon, but is probably not feasible for nearer or lower areas, because of blocking of the projector beams by the vehicle structures and the trainees' bodies. Moreover, with a large projected field the contrast ratio (see below) decreases because of stray light.

There are two methods of dome projection for crews: real and virtual. In a real dome, the scene is projected on a screen inside a dome of a fixed diameter. Virtual dome projection can be achieved by collimating lens systems or hollow mirrors, simulating projection on a virtual dome of a fixed diameter. Dome projection is often used to allow more than one trainee in the same scene. An example is training ground-to-air teams using man-borne missile systems such as the Stinger. A problem with this type of projection is that there is only one viewing point for which the projection is completely correct; for other trainees, there will be distortions of the projected image in the form of a different viewing direction and a different position and distance for a particular object in the environment. De Vries (1997) analysed this problem and formulated as a guideline that, for a two-person crew who are 1 m apart, dome radii of 5-8 m are acceptable.

Helmet-mounted displays HMDs are used in some simulators. Potential advantages are compactness, large available FoV, the possibility of stereo presentation (if two IG channels with separate camera points are presented), and a large viewing volume. The HMD is one of the most complex computer peripherals yet devised. A very small display, attached to the head, is projected by means of a complicated optical lens system on the retina. The two basic forms are the immersive display, excluding any vision of the actual physical surroundings, and the 'see-through' form in which the display can be superimposed on the actual environment in a transparent or a non-transparent form. In the latter case, only an external view of the surround of the display is possible. The technology is rapidly evolving from liquid crystal displays to field emission displays, overcoming some of the limitations of current LCDs that impose a trade-off between FoV and resolution. A solution to this trade-off problem is to have higher resolution in the area of interest: the foveal part of the projection. This can be static, or dynamically linked to eye movements. Possible problems with HMDs are limited spatial resolution, limited instantaneous FoV, inaccurate compensation of the virtual camera position and direction for head movements (non-linear and delayed head tracking), inability to see instruments and control devices, and visual strain due to accommodation and convergence problems.

Visual strain is a major problem associated with use of this technology. For an immersive head-tracked virtual environment, the strain is caused by the constant accommodation on the virtual plane of projection, the lagging behind of images with head movements, and jitter of the images. This is aggravated by the low resolution of many displays, causing the viewer to attempt to compensate by focusing when the projected image does not allow this. The problem of accommodation is the most difficult to resolve. The causes of eyestrain with 'see through' HMDs are different, since the image plane is merely an object in the environment allowing freely changing accommodation. Technology-induced lag and jitter are also absent, since no use is made of head tracking.

When the projected image comes from a hand-held video-camera, e.g., used as a disconnected rifle sight, the image will move and jitter according to the movements of the camera sight, and will move over the real scene when the head is rotated. This can induce the 'opto-kinetic' reflex; the normal response of counter-rotating the eyes to keep the fixation steady at a certain point. The need to suppress this reflex is a determinant of eyestrain. A further factor is the requirement actively to focus the attention on the projected image or parts of the environment. In the case of a monocular HMD (in which the image is projected to one eye only), binocular rivalry may induce strain. The wearer of the HMD may thus be tempted to avoid motion of the camera or the head even when the task requires such motion. Another negative effect is attention capture, the tendency to fixate attention solely on the displayed image. This may result in inadequate monitoring of the real environment.

Other Display Options

In addition to OTW views, electro-optical devices may have to be simulated. These include rear-view mirrors, telescopes, image intensifiers (night-vision goggles), thermal imagers, and range finders.

Rear-view mirrors   In a driving simulator, rear-view mirrors may be useful, although mirror discipline may also be taught using small green/red lights at the mirror locations controlled from the instruction console. For mirrors, separate image channels are required, with fields of 20×15° for the side mirrors and 35×15° for the interior mirror (Haug, 1990). Effects of mirror magnification or distortion, if desired, are more flexibly represented using the image channels rather than optically. Demands for spatial resolution and update frequency may be lower than in the main channels; luminance may be a factor of two lower. In addition to rear-view mirrors, rear-view cameras may have to be simulated (for instance, in the case of some tanks).

Telescopes   In ship simulation, the use of a real telescope is not practicable, because of the image system's limited spatial resolution. Simulating a telescope must be performed using a separate image channel with an appropriate magnification and field size.

Image intensifiers and thermal imagers Electro-optical devices, such as image intensifiers and thermal image telescopes, provide monochrome scene images. In the latter devices, objects of higher temperature than their surround are depicted with higher luminance. Especially in military training, simulating these devices may be useful. Because object contrasts and colours using these devices are very different from those in daylight with normal vision, special provisions have to be implemented in the database and the image system to use the same database for visual and electro-optical observations (Green & Grayston, 1989; Wyckoff, 1989).

NVGs Real NVGs may be used in the simulator with filters covering the projectors. Because NVGs are very sensitive in the infrared, the filters should block the visible spectrum while transmitting sufficient infrared light. The crucial factor is that typical projectors emit very little energy in the infrared range compared to the visible range. A simpler way to simulate NVG vision is to use mock-up goggles. The noise characteristics, reduced image resolution, and appropriate image contrast need to be simulated in the image.

Range finders In tanks and helicopters, a laser pulse is used to determine the distance to an object. Several image systems have the facility to output the distance of an object pointed at (Wyckoff, 1989).

The Human Visual System

The way in which the visual system processes its input is sometimes described as using 'a bag of tricks'. The visual system can be thought of as using a large number of specialised sub-units, each tuned to a specific type of information (*cue*) contained in the input. Cues are constrained by lens characteristics, receptor density and sensitivity, and so on. An overview of the resulting capabilities and limitations is presented below, followed by discussion of the visual cues themselves.

Perception of Colour, Contrast and Detail

The luminance range in which the visual system operates lies between 10^{-6} and 10^8 cd/m^2. Luminance level has an effect on the perception of colour, contrast, and detail. Generally, perception is enhanced as the luminance increases.

Colour discrimination begins at 6×10^{-2} cd/m^2, but is optimal between 10^2 and 10^4 cd/m^2. The perception of *contrast*, here defined as the luminance difference between adjacent areas divided by the average luminance, is optimal at luminances of 300 cd/m^2 and higher, at which contrasts as low as 0.02 can be perceived. Perception of detail is denoted as *visual acuity*, the inverse of the smallest perceptible angular detail of objects expressed in arcmin^{-1} (1 arcmin, or minute of arc, equals 1/60°, or 2.91×10^{-4} rad). With optimum contrast, optimum acuity is reached at luminances of about 10^3 cd/m^2 and higher, and ranges then from 1.0 to 2.0 arcmin^{-1} (corresponding to detail sizes of 1 to 0.5 arcmin, respectively) for the majority of the working population. S-cones (retinal cells that are sensitive to blue light) discriminate *flicker* up to 35 Hz. M- and L-cones (green- and red-sensitive cells, respectively) detect flicker up to a frequency of 60-70 Hz.

Implications for simulation Given the extreme luminance range in which the visual system operates, a bright display system is preferable. The natural range cannot be achieved, but is unnecessary since the visual system operates in such a way as to compress this range logarithmically. Moreover, the visual system is able to adapt itself to very low luminance levels.

Most monitors are able to yield a luminance of at least 50 cd/m^2, and luminance levels of 100-300 cd/m^2 are quite common. Projection systems may reach lower values, as low as 10-20 cd/m^2 when their light is spread over a large projection surface to achieve a large field of view. What is required depends partly on the training environment. A dark background allows for lower luminance ranges of the display system, but this may render the instruments unrealistically dark.

Parameters such as recognition distance and conspicuity are impaired as a function of the discrepancy between visual acuity and the resolution of the image display. Most image display systems have resolutions that are at least a factor of five lower than optimal visual acuity. For current display systems, a resolution of 2-3 arcmin (20-30 pixels/degree) is deemed acceptable.

The contrast ratio should be at least 10:1, or 40:1 if detection of dark objects in dark parts of otherwise bright scenes (e.g., trucks stationed near a wood edge) is critical. To prevent fatigue and irritation, the display refresh frequency should be close to or above the flicker fusion frequency, i.e. at least 60-70 Hz.

Foveal versus Peripheral Vision

Perception is optimal in the central 2 degrees of the retina (the fovea), at least for lighting levels above twilight. Visual acuity drops off strongly outside the fovea. At eccentricities of 20 degrees, it is only about 0.3 arcmin^{-1}.

Implications for simulation It is possible to have a high-resolution inset devoted solely to the fovea (the 'Area-Of-Interest' (AoI) technique) and a larger background at a lower resolution, but this requires accurate eye- and head-movement detection. For a very large FoV, it may be useful to have an AoI system in which a restricted projected field follows the trainee's head movements (the scene being kept stable with respect to the earth through the image generator) or a projection screen gain considerably larger than 1.

Perception of Depth and Motion

For adequate control of a vehicle, perception of depth in the scene, as well as perception of self-motion and motion of other vehicles, is generally required.

Depth Cues

The 3D space is perceived by means of 2D images on the retinas. The image cues that are used in depth perception can be divided into binocular, static monocular, and dynamic monocular cues.

Binocular Cues

Retinal disparity The primary binocular cue is retinal disparity, the difference in the location of object images on the retinas of the eyes. At distances of less than 1 m, depth differences of less than 1 mm may be perceived stereoscopically.

Stereopsis Because the eyes' optical centres are a few centimetres apart, the projected images on the retinas contain slight projection differences (called disparities) that are characteristic of the depth structure of the viewed scene. Human stereo vision is well developed. Stereo acuity is about 5-15 arcsec, which is better than the resolution with which fine detail can be resolved in 2D. We can calculate the just noticeable difference (jnd) at a certain distance (the minimum distance by which two objects must be separated in depth to perceive the depth difference). Beyond 50 m, the jnd becomes so high that the stereo cue is useless for most vehicle co-ordination tasks.

Implications for simulation The resolution needed to achieve the described levels of accuracy is beyond the capabilities of most current display systems. For instance, HMDs are in use with a resolution in a range of 2-20 arcmin, which is at least eight times lower than human resolution capability. For judging distances between vehicle and close obstacles, current display devices are insufficient. At distances up to 20 m, the full unrestricted resolution of the human visual system is required.

Interocular rivalry When one object occults another, parts of the occulted object will be visible with one eye but not the other. Thus, the visual system has to deal with conflicting information. It does this routinely, and usually successfully. The extent of the conflicting area, however, serves as an additional depth cue. The larger the separation of the two objects, the larger this area becomes. The same happens when both objects become closer to the observer. The useable range of this cue is comparable to that of stereo vision, and is similarly impaired by the resolution of the displays.

Implications for simulation The same requirements as for stereo vision hold.

Vergence The lines of sight of both eyes converge reasonably accurately on the point of interest. When the observer changes fixation towards a closer object, the angle between the two lines of sight (the vergence angle) increases. When the observer selects an object farther away, the vergence angle decreases. Hence, vergence is a cue for distance, and research has confirmed that it is used by the human visual system. For example, space and shape perception from stereo vision is distorted when the vergence angle is independently manipulated. Vergence is a highly inaccurate cue, and its applicability is restricted to a few metres.

Implications for simulation Vergence and accommodation are tightly coupled in the visual system, and any conflict between them (as is often found in HMDs) may be a source of discomfort. There are some reports that prolonged decoupling of vergence and accommodation in HMDs may result in long-term disturbances in their natural co-operation. It seems advisable to use HMDs only to display far objects, applying lenses to set the accommodation at optical infinity.

Static Monocular Cues

These cues may be perceived from a single stationary viewpoint. Static monocular cues are plentiful. The most important are:
- relative angular object size (the retinal image of an object decreases with distance);
- gradient of object or texture density (at larger distances, there are more objects and details in the same angular area);
- interposition (a closer object partly occults a more distant object);
- linear perspective (parallel structures, such as road verges, are convergent on the retina).

Other monocular cues are height in the visual field (the closer to the horizon, the farther); light and shadow effects; atmospheric haze; amount of detail visible; and relative luminance (a brighter object seems nearer). Ocular accommodation is a monocular depth cue that works only at distances smaller than 2 m.

Accommodation   Accommodation is the focusing of the eye lens on an object of interest. It is achieved by flattening the lens using a system of delicate muscles and fibres. Beyond about 6 m, the focal length of the eye lens does not change. Most psychophysical research shows that, although we are able to use accommodation as a cue for distance, it is effective only up to about 1-2 m. Moreover, accommodation as a cue is relatively inaccurate, errors typically being 10% or higher. Generally, in flying tasks accommodation plays a minor role (except for older people who have difficulty in accommodating and are not able to switch quickly from looking at their instruments to the view outside). In a simulator, accommodation may lead to cue conflicts if the projection screen is close and the simulated distance is large, or vice versa.

Implications for simulation   Accommodation conflicts in simulators may be expected if visual presentation is by means of HMDs or uncollimated displays at close ranges. Displays showing objects closer than 6 m should preferably not use collimation, which puts those objects at optical infinity. See-through HMDs should not change the optical distance of objects within the TSI. If projection is used, the screen should be located at a distance beyond the accommodation range.

Known size   This is a rather abstract cue, whose use is learned over the course of several years. The principle is simple: the visual angle subtended by familiar objects of known size (e.g., trees, houses, people) is proportional to their distance. Using this knowledge, distances can be roughly estimated. Generally, observers find it difficult to judge the spatial layout of their surroundings if they are devoid of familiar size cues.

Implications for simulation   To use this cue, the visual database should contain numerous familiar objects of standard size. Preferably, several levels of details of these objects for different depth ranges should be provided, or at least such an option should be available.

Occlusion or interposition Generally, objects covering other objects are perceived as closer to the observer. This is a very strong cue; known size cues, for example, are overruled by erroneous occlusion cues. These circumstances are very rare, however, and slight movements are sufficient to eliminate the illusion, but this finding illustrates the importance of correct occlusion calculations in image generators. Occlusion does not generate a continuous scale of depth as in the case of known size: it merely rank orders objects in depth.

Implications for simulation Occlusion of objects should be managed correctly and quickly. Occlusion of several layers of transparent objects should also be handled correctly.

Linear Perspective This term is often used incorrectly. Linear Perspective in general describes the behaviour of projections from a central viewpoint of a three-dimensional scene to a two-dimensional projection surface. However, in perception research it is most often used to describe certain phenomena and rules that follow from central projection, such as:

- parallel lines converge to vanishing point at the horizon;
- the horizon is the collection of all vanishing points and is at the same height as the viewing point;
- objects above the horizon are higher than an observer viewing horizontally;
- the closer earth-bound objects are to the horizon, the farther they are from the observer.

Known Size and Texture cues are members of the Linear Perspective family. Psychological research has confirmed that humans use these cues. A well known example is the Ames room, whose walls and windows are distorted in such a way that people positioned in different parts of the room appear to change size. Clearly, the Known Size cue can be overruled by other perspective cues.

Implications for simulation Most image generators use central projection, and hence all perspective cues will be present automatically. However, projection screen position and calculated viewing position should be compatible, since otherwise perspective distortions will result. The calculated perspective projection must be applied correctly, and should not cause geometrical distortions when viewed by the observer. Preferably, with multiple observers, each should have his own point of view.

Texture Many surfaces contain a texture with elements that, although irregular, can be adequately specified with a few parameters such as average size, separation and orientation. The value of these parameters in the projection depends on the distance and orientation of the object. In continuous surfaces (grasslands, ploughed fields, woods, waves) this leads to texture *gradients*, of which there are three types:

- the density gradient: the number of surface elements per visual angle varies with distance and orientation;
- the size gradient: this is comparable to the known size cue, but refers to variations of the characteristic size of elements *within* an object;
- the foreshortening gradient: the ratio of the size of an object along the line of sight to the size of the object perpendicular to this line changes with the orientation of the surface.

Implication for simulation All these texture cues are present if texture is mapped onto objects accurately. A projection of a texture on a surface in a way that does not account for its orientation leads to spurious information. Texture should be able to vary between 100% opaque and 100% transparent in a reasonable number of steps, and it should be possible to define textures for different viewing distances. Preferably, texture memory should be sufficiently large to support several hundred full-colour maps for objects, and terrain maps in which repetition is not immediately apparent at ground level and at different height above ground level. To increase flexibility, it should be possible to load texture at will. Dynamic texture (moving one or more texture maps with respect to the surface being textured) implements effects of moving waves, or corn or long grass being blown downwind.

Shading The term 'shading' refers to the distribution of brightness along an object depending on the observer's line-of-sight, the angle of incidence of light, the orientation of surfaces, and the reflective properties of the object. Shading is the most important source of shape information in photographs.

Implications for simulation The lighting models used in most image generators offer only simple approximations to real shading. The simulator should at least support flat shading and Gouraud shading. Preferably, the interaction of various light sources should be accounted for.

Shadows When one object partly obscures another object or the ground plane, such that it receives less light than its surroundings, it is said to cast shadows. The shape of the projected rim of an object contains important information concerning its three-dimensional shape. The length of the shadow relative to the length of the object reveals the elevation of the light source, which is useful input to the shape-from-shading calculations performed by the brain. Shadows are also very useful in estimating the height of flying objects, since the proximity-to-the-horizon cue (see Linear Perspective) is valid for ground-bound objects only.

Implications for simulation Unfortunately, many image generators do not calculate cast shadows. A partial solution is the use of semi-transparent planes that closely follow important objects in a scene. This is effective when the shadows are cast on a flat surface, but unsatisfactory for more complex shapes. Preferably, the simulator will at least be able to generate shadows for a limited number of key objects. The shadows should be influenced by searchlights and so on.

Aerial perspective When light travels through the atmosphere, it is attenuated by particles of moisture and dust. The attenuation increases with distance travelled; hence, the closer the objects, the brighter they appear. This yields a rough measure of distance that is used in human vision. A well known phenomenon is that distances appear to be shorter on an unusually clear day.

Implications for simulation Atmospheric effects (haze, fog, clouds) should be realistically modelled. Realistic variations in local extinction, depending on the location and height distribution of clouds and ground fog, should be applicable. Preferably, effects of rain, snowstorms and smoke should be modelled.

Colour Since the attenuation of light mentioned in the previous section is slightly wavelength-dependent, the light emitted by or reflected from distant objects undergoes a slight colour change. This is a weak cue for distance.

Implications for simulation Colour can be used to improve the separation of adjoining objects in the visual fields. It improves the usability of the occlusion cue. In general, since the brightness range of simulators is rather restricted, colour can be used to restore the saliency of objects to a more natural level. Human colour discrimination abilities are generally better than most image generators can provide. An acceptable choice is 1024 colours from a total of 16.7 million (with 8-bit colour resolution for each constituent base colour). To create effects of different light sources and times of day, it should be possible to switch between several prepared colour tables. The atmospheric model will preferably yield realistic sun and sky colours depending on the time of day.

Dynamic Monocular Cues

A powerful dynamic monocular depth cue is motion parallax: if there is self-motion through a scene, static objects outside the direction of movement that are closer to the observer move faster over the retina than more distant objects (Rogers & Graham, 1979). Similarly for a moving object, if there is some independent estimate of its real speed, its speed at the retina provides a cue for distance. For objects in or near the direction of self-motion, speed of change of the monocular depth cues mentioned earlier may also provide distance cues.

Motion Cues

There are cues for the perception of motion of objects in the scene, and of self-motion.

Object motion Object motion is generally perceived most easily if there is a motion component that differs from the direction of gaze. Movements with retinal speeds between about 0.03 arcmin/s and 200°/s may be perceived. The whole retina is sensitive to motion; but the periphery is sensitive only to faster movements. Motion in the periphery often instigates head movements.

Object motion in depth may be perceived by changes in angular size or texture density or by lateral retinal speed. A measure called *tau*, the rate of change of angular size, is directly related to the time taken to hit an object to which the observer is moving (time-to-contact). There is compelling evidence that such a measure is used by many species including humans. It is of the utmost importance in approach, landing and other steering tasks.

Self-motion Self-motion may be perceived by cues similar to those mentioned for object motion. The more objects visible in the scene, the more accurate the perception of self-motion will be. To estimate the direction of self-motion, observers may make use of the so-called *optic flow*, the pattern of motions generated by objects in the visual field. If the optic flow is sufficiently dense, it is a very good source of object shape information as well.

Implications for simulation To have a well defined optic flow field, the visual scene should contain numerous traceable features: surfaces should be richly textured, and the number of objects should be sufficient and well distributed. Perception of apparent motion is improved if the number of defining frames is increased. A minimum update rate of 25-30 Hz is required. To be able to separate ego-motion from object-motion, the image delay between ego-motion onset and the resulting movement on the display should be small, not more than 50-70 ms.

User Opinion on Image Systems in Flight Simulators

In the MASTER project, structured interviews were conducted at 21 training establishments with 39 pilot/instructors and 10 trainees, to compile an inventory of user experiences with respect to the use of image systems in flight simulators. Each system examined, from the simplest to the most sophisticated, had flaws limiting its training potential. Examples of critical tasks that depend heavily on the quality of the image systems are landing, carrier and frigate operations (French SEM), Air-to-Ground and Air-to-Air visual target acquisition, vertical/short take-off and landing (V/STOL) operations (UK Harrier), low-level flight, and in-flight refuelling. Some of these tasks were unable to be trained on the simulator, even if that was its intended purpose. Associated critical visual parameters mentioned by users are field of view, peripheral cues, depth cues, altitude cues, scene detail, texture and image resolution. More insight into the results is given in the following paragraphs, and a summary is provided in Table 19.1.

Some of the simulators have no image system. Most of these were installed in the 1970s, the most recent dating from 1985. Some are equipped with platform motion or devices such as a stick shaker. The Tornado GR.1 simulator (1980), for example, is equipped with platform motion, g-suit and a HUD, but not an OTW view. The general instructor opinion is that an image system can enhance training on such devices, e.g., for transition to visual flight at minimum decision height during instrument approaches. Simulators with a FoV of (typically) 50 degrees horizontal and 40 degrees vertical have been installed until recently, using CRT screens. Most often, no platform motion is used, but motion cueing devices such as a g-seat and g-suit are present. These systems are applied across the full range of pre-operational and operational courses, including weapon utilisation training, mission rehearsal, and tasks such as terrain following and bomb delivery.

Table 19.1. Summary of simulator visual systems

Aircraft	Year	FOV Horizontal/ vertical	Type of training	Example of visual critical task mentioned	User opinion
Harrier GR.5	1992	240° x130° (8 m. dome, HUD, eye slaved AOI, high res. projected targets)	Full mission, all courses	Formation tactics, basic V/STOL (currently not possible)	Preference for the whole scene to be high resolution, lack of peripheral cues for altitude
Hawk	c1976	—	Pre-operational	Transition to visual flight at minimum decision height during instrument approaches	Limited use for existing training due to lack of visual system
Jaguar	1974	FOV unknown, model board with camera and mirror projection (three screens)	Operational (refresher, currency)	Co-ordination flying not supported	FOV too narrow (partial loss of picture at extreme bank angles), change of colour contrast due to ageing of paint on model board
F-16 A	1982	c120° x40° three monitors, low detail (land mass satellite data), high res. targets, HUD	Conversion, currency (11 different courses)	Low-level flying (no capability)	FOV too small for closed patterns near the field and lack of detail
C-101		—	Refresher for non-operational pilots, instrument flight only	Instrument flight	Skill acquisition could be improved by incorporating visual systems
F-18		FOV unknown, visual system + HUD	Pre-operational, to support initial solo flights on the type	No answers available	No user opinion available
Mirage F.1	1978	— (simulator is deployable)	Full range of courses	Instrument flight and procedures	Limited use

Table 19.1 (continued)

Aircraft	Year	FOV Horizontal/vertical	Type of training	Example of visual critical task	User opinion
Mirage 2000-C	1992	360°x 360° (8 m dome)	From type qualification to formation leader	Target acquisition, weapon delivery	Poor ground target acquisition, no real ranges
Mirage 2000-D	1996	53.3° x 40° (direct view CRT)	Weapon system utilisation	Low level flying, target acquisition, and weapon delivery	FOV and image resolution too limited
Mirage F.1-CT	1992	40° x 40° (collimated front imaging CRT)	Full mission, from type qualification to formation leader	Target acquisition and weapon delivery	FOV too limited; Visual A/A targets not realistic
C-160 Transall	1995	220° x 50° (five channel collimated projection)	Operational	Low altitude navigation, A/A refuelling, landing, formation flight	Visual definition is too limited for tactical low altitude navigation
SEM	1994	36°H x 27°V	Mission rehearsal and procedures	A/G-attack	Too limited for landing circuit, formation flight, co-ordination, self defence, A/G weapon delivery
Tornado GR.1	1980	HUD only	Conversion to type	Landing and selection of targets	Visual system would enhance training
Tornado F.3	c1985	No OTW	Mission and emergencies, BVR engagements, conversion, continuation, refresher	Radar/visual intercept (currently not possible)	A visual system is required

Tasks that, according to the users, cannot be trained well on such systems include Air-to-Air target acquisition, Air-to-Ground attack, low-level flying, landing circuit, formation flight, co-ordination and self-defence, although the simulator syllabus sometimes also covers these tasks. The general comment is that the FoV is too limited and that an upgrade of the image system would enhance training.

Three simulators with a medium-to-large FOV were visited: the Jaguar simulator (1974, three-screen configuration), the F-16A simulator (1982, three screens, 120°H x 40°V) and the C-160 TRANSALL simulator (1995, five-channel collimated projection, 220°H x 50°V). The visual systems are combined with platform motion and/or motion cueing devices. The simulators are mainly used for operational training at the squadron level. The Jaguar simulator does not support

Air-to-Air missions (no co-ordination flying is possible) or tactical/strategic aspects. The model board visual does not support extreme bank angles.

The F-16A simulator is used for emergency procedures not trained in the air for safety considerations. This also holds for deep stall training. The terrain represented on the visual contains few cultural and natural features or objects, e.g., no buildings, trees or moving objects. The 2D projection on the monitors was thought to give a limited depth perspective unsuitable for low-level flight. The FoV was considered too small for flying closed patterns near the field.

The C-160 TRANSALL simulator is also used for operational training (full range of courses, including crew training), Air-to-Air refuelling, landing and formation flight. According to the users, it is not suitable for tactical low-altitude navigation, since the visual system lacks resolution. For this reason, instructors would prefer an upgrade of the image system.

Two simulators with a dome projection system were visited: the Mirage 2000C simulator (1992, full sphere FoV, 8 m dome) and the Harrier GR.5 (1992, 240°H x 130°V, 8 m dome). Both simulators are equipped with a HUD and represent g-effects by dimming the visual display.

The Harrier simulator has a six degrees of freedom synergistic motion platform as well as g-suit, g-seat and rudder pedal shaker. The Mirage simulator is equipped with g-suit and g-seat. It is used for operational training, but shortcomings are the lack of wing men, no night attack training, and poor ground target acquisition. The Harrier simulator has full mission capability and is used in conjunction with other training devices. Students spend only limited time on this simulator (on average 20% of real aircraft time for most of the courses). There are high-resolution projected targets and an eye-slaved Area of Interest (24°) display that can also be head-slaved (40° AOI) if eye-slaving is not possible for some reason. Important tasks for the Harrier are formation tactics and basic V/STOL. The latter task is currently difficult, mainly because of the lack of peripheral cues for altitude. There is a preference for the whole scene to be high resolution, rather than only an Area of Interest.

20 Haptic, Kinaesthetic and Vestibular Cueing

Introduction

Body-centred cues include haptic, kinaesthetic, and vestibular cues. These types of cue are most relevant for aircraft handling, less relevant for ground vehicles, and least relevant for vessels. Hence, the research literature is concerned mostly with aircraft handling, and most of the examples in this chapter are similarly drawn from aviation. Little attention will be given to haptic and kinaesthetic cues: the vestibular system is most important, and will be considered in detail.

A description of the relevant sensory physiology is beyond the scope of this handbook. A general overview can be found in several texts, such as Cacioppo and Tassinary (1990). An overview of applied experimental literature relevant to the fidelity of flight simulators appears in Cardullo (1994).

In a review of the literature on motion cueing research (de Fontenilles *et al*, 1997), two main experimental approaches were distinguished:

- Performance research (or backward-transfer research), most often experiments in which the task performance of *experienced* operators on a specifically configured simulator is compared with the performance of the same operators on the criterion vehicle (e.g., an armoured vehicle or aircraft).
- Transfer-of-training research, most often experiments in which (1) a 'control' group of trainees is trained on a simulator configured without motion cueing and (2) an 'experimental' group is trained on a simulator with motion cueing. Subsequently, the performance of the two groups on the criterion device is compared, to test for a difference in training effectiveness between the two simulator configurations.

Numerous variations in types of experiment (multiple experimental groups, quasi-transfer experiments) were noted. Although performance research may yield interesting results concerning motion cueing fidelity and the optimisation of flight simulator motion systems, it usually does not provide data on skill acquisition and the training effectiveness associated with simulator configurations.

As noted in the introductory chapter of this section, much of the earlier work on motion cueing was conducted with systems that have been superseded by superior technologies. Thus, earlier findings may either be obsolete or need to be replicated. Moreover, many motion cueing devices currently in use are based on older technologies. User opinions on the utility of motion cueing may sometimes reflect the limitations of these technologies rather than the importance of motion cueing *per se*. In general, non-visual motion cueing becomes especially important when the operator is required to operate in a closed-loop, high-gain manner.

Most of the findings and guidelines reported in this chapter are derived from laboratory research on motion perception, transfer-of-training research, and surveys of user experiences (reviewed by Bles *et al*, 1991, and extended in the MASTER project). In this chapter, findings and guidelines with respect to motion cueing will be reviewed, followed by an overview of cueing systems. Later, a synopsis is given of results from MASTER experiments and a user survey.

Motion Cueing

Different cue complexes may mediate information about motion. For instance, vertical acceleration may be signalled by a particular combination of visual, vestibular, kinaesthetic, and auditory cues. The exact type or combination of cues used in practice to satisfy particular information needs may differ widely. This depends on the availability of cues, but level of expertise is also an important determinant of the selection and usage of cues. Knowledge about cue relations is limited, since most of the research has focused on the interactions of a small number of cues under laboratory conditions. Since the transmission speed of information from the vestibular and the kinaesthetic system to the brain is typically less than 50 milliseconds, it is clear that motion cueing via these systems is of importance in situations critical for rapid control responses such as equipment malfunctions and high-gain control tasks.

Haptic Cues

The haptic system is the sensory system that is formed by the innervation of the skin and by specific skin transducers. Several types of nerve cells and transducers can be distinguished; their roles are in some instances unclear, but as a whole they result in the temperature and pressure sensitivity of the skin. Skin pressure sensing may support information from the vestibular system, especially since the latter may easily become saturated.

Pressure applied by means of clothing with inflatable pockets or by other means will improve the recognition of vehicle motion and attitude. G-seats provide cues by adjusting seat pressure according to the simulated accelerations. Cabin temperature may be considered as part of the simulation. It should be easily adjustable both under simulator and instructor control.

Kinaesthetic Cues

Since the body has an elaborate distribution of afferent neurons, the brain has a large array of measures of body posture and relative positions of body parts that can be influenced by vehicle status. The measures include pressure on organs due to accelerations, signals concerning applied force from muscles, and information about limb and joint position. The force on the muscles in the neck is an important source of information about the orientation of the body in the gravity field.

Vestibular Cues

The vestibular organ in the inner ear is sensitive to accelerations in all six degrees of freedom. The organ consists of the semicircular canals for detection of angular accelerations and the otoliths for the detection of linear accelerations. Both systems have thresholds below which acceleration is not detected, and they become saturated after prolonged exposure to above-threshold accelerations. This has important consequences in blind-flying aircraft (leading to the danger of spatial disorientation) and in motion simulation technology. Because of the motion thresholds of the vestibular system and the motion characteristics of aircraft, the vestibular system is unable to register the real motion of the aircraft. This may lead to spatial disorientation accidents in conditions of poor visibility, if the pilot is not using the flight instruments properly.

In simulators, detection thresholds for motion are exploited in a technique known as 'acceleration-onset cueing'. This means that the motion platform of the simulator is moved at the onset of an acceleration, accompanied by the correct visual motion information, leading to a saturated self-motion sensation. When this sensation is sustained by the ongoing visual motion information, the motion platform can be moved back gently to its original position (wash-out), which is not detected by the subject flying the simulator. The motion platform is then ready for the next acceleration to occur. This system is quite satisfactory if the vestibular and visual cues are properly timed, otherwise simulator sickness may arise (cf. subsequently).

Relationships between Vestibular and Visual Cues

Information conveying a sense of self-motion is normally derived from sensations received from both the visual and vestibular systems. These systems respond to different cueing aspects of the same event. Vision is good at detecting position, attitude, velocity and slow changes in these variables. On the other hand, the vestibular system detects the onset of angular and linear acceleration that accompanies bodily motion.

Not all simulators have an image system. The visual sense, however, is dominant in man and can override vestibular inputs. Illusions may occur as a result of stimulation of the vestibular system without reference to visual cues. If an aircraft accelerates in the line of flight, the vestibular system experiences a sustained linear acceleration. This can be confused with the naturally occurring sustained acceleration of gravity. In certain cases, the gravity vector is overlaid by the acceleration vector to produce a resultant force at an intermediate angle, inclined backwards. This becomes the reference acceleration, and is regarded as the vertical. The pilot will feel as if he and the aircraft are in a pitch-up attitude, unless there are appropriate visual cues to counteract this impression. Similarly, sustained deceleration gives rise to a sensation of pitch-down.

Not all simulators have a motion platform. When a sensation of self-motion is induced by the visual system alone, the phenomenon is known as *vection*. Apparent motion of a full visual field without whole body motion is at first perceived as no self-motion and a moving surround. After a few seconds delay, however, the visual field appears to slow down and even stop. An illusion is then experienced of self-motion in the direction opposite to the former apparent motion of the visual field.

For vection to work well, it appears to be important that the background extend to the sides of the observer and therefore surround him. This is perhaps because peripheral cues are most important in sustaining a sense of self-motion.

Vestibular Cueing and Simulator Sickness

One speaks of *simulator sickness* when certain simulated motions result in the syndrome of motion sickness, whereas experiencing the same motions in reality would not induce motion sickness. Thus, the cause of simulator sickness must be discrepancies between the simulated and real motion. Symptoms of motion and simulator sickness are: nausea, vertigo, sleepiness, sweating, pallor and saliva flow. Clearly, simulator sickness will disturb the intended learning processes, due to the concomitant apathy, headache, depression, disorientation and fatigue. The cost may be even higher when the after-effects are also considered. The main after-effect is a disturbance of balance of posture, which requires the prohibition of certain activities (such as car driving) for periods of up to 24 hours.

For training, there are two very negative effects of simulator sickness. Not only is learning in a particular session disturbed, but a more general distrust and aversion may develop in the trainee community with regard to training in simulators. A second, even more detrimental, effect is that the trainees learn to avoid the development of simulator sickness by adopting behaviour patterns that are less than optimal in the real-life task. In this case, simulator sickness may induce negative transfer of training.

Simulator sickness cannot be dismissed as a problem affecting only some trainees. The incidence is as high as 60%, or even 100% in certain driving simulators.

Causes of Simulator Sickness

As with 'natural' motion sickness, simulator sickness is caused by a mismatch between sensed and expected motion cues. The discrepancy can originate in information from different sensory modalities (visual and vestibular), particularly in fixed base simulators, but also within a single modality, such as the two components of the vestibular organ: the otoliths and semicircular canals. This is most likely in a moving-base simulator, due to the inherent limitations in maintaining naturally occurring correlates between these two different types of information.

Another factor playing a role in motion and simulator-induced sickness is low-frequency vertical movement (between 0.2 and 0.4 Hz). In the simulator, such movements may be due to the wash-out phase of acceleration onset cueing, and are thus artificial. In tasks such as dog fighting, wash-out phases will often necessitate this kind of motion.

The following characteristics known to induce simulator sickness can be defined, with associated recommendations:

- Time delays leading to cue mismatches. These can be avoided by minimising transport delays and frequency-dependent phase lags or leads.
- Motion resonance of the order of 0.2-0.4 Hz in the vertical direction. Simulator resonance in this frequency band should be avoided or minimised.
- Wide fields of view: vection-inducing displays are more likely to induce sickness. Narrow fields of view are preferred, if this does not interfere with the tasks to be performed.
- Lack of motion cueing or unsatisfactory motion cueing. Motion and force cueing systems with sufficient bandwidth and minimal acceleration noise should be employed, together with appropriate wash-out algorithms to eliminate false motion cues.

Motion System Guidelines

The current state of knowledge on motion system effectiveness is insufficient to determine categorically whether or not a motion system must be implemented in a training simulator. Similarly, research on non-platform motion cueing devices has not yielded enough evidence to draw final and general conclusions about their contribution to training effectiveness. However, guidelines are available that assist in determining whether a motion system is required, and in identifying its desirable features. The requirement for a motion system must be considered in relation to:

- the tasks to be trained: If the task to be trained does not include a component of motor skill, then a motion platform or other motion cueing system is not required;
- the trainee's experience: Experienced trainees may be trained without a motion system, because they are familiar with the actual system and how it moves, and can transfer successfully to the real system. However, the prevalence of simulator sickness is such circumstances may cause complications, and there is a danger with air systems simulators that inappropriate control strategies may be developed;
- the type of training: Novice trainees *may* benefit from the inclusion of a motion system, particularly if they have had no previous experience with the real system. However, high-fidelity motion systems do not seem to be fundamentally necessary for most *initial* training. Fixed-based ground vehicle simulators appear to be quite efficient for this purpose;
- when training is frequently switched between the actual system and a simulator, a motion system is less important.

Types of Motion

Manoeuvre and disturbance motion can be distinguished. Manoeuvre motion represents the natural movement of a vehicle in response to the operator's commands. These motions are therefore expected. They provide sensory feedback about the appropriateness of control actions, and allow the operator to generate more lead and gain than visual cues, and hence more quickly correct inappropriate control actions. This reduces the occurrence of operator-induced oscillation.

Disturbance motion results from turbulence, wind gusts, irregularities in the road surface, failures of the vehicle, and so on. These motions can be further subdivided. *Uncorrelated* disturbance motion is perceived as being essentially random in frequency, direction and amplitude, but virtually always present. Engine vibration is an example. *Correlated* disturbance motion is a consequence of events that are of immediate interest to the operator and require his prompt attention. These motions are unexpected.

Manoeuvre Motion Cues

In stable, conventional aircraft, manoeuvre cues are of relatively low frequency, and can generally be provided visually: a motion system is not required. In unstable or marginally stable aircraft, such as VTOL (Vertical Take-Off and Landing) aircraft or helicopters, prompt attention is required by the pilot to maintain control. In these cases, manoeuvre cues should be provided by a motion system. Tasks for which such cues are important include:

- helicopter hovering;
- helicopter nap-of-the-earth flight;
- target tracking;
- air-to-air refuelling;
- low level terrain following;
- VTOL manoeuvres.

In the hover mode of helicopter and other VTOL operations, the pilot probably uses motion cues as the primary or initial source of information about changes in the position, movement and attitude of the aircraft. Visual cues that would reflect these small, but rapidly occurring, changes tend to be noted by the pilot later than motion cues, and thus would possibly be inadequate for aircraft control. The pilot might even be unable to hover in a VTOL simulator that lacked manoeuvre motion cues simulated by a platform motion system. Hence, appropriate manoeuvre motion cues for these simulator tasks would probably enhance training, but large displacements do not appear to be required.

A general rule for aircraft simulation is that, for high-gain, closed-loop tasks (manoeuvring of marginally stable aircraft, recovering from turbulence, air-to-air refuelling and other formation flying tasks), a motion system should be procured. To simulate the high-frequency manoeuvre cues associated with helicopter hovering, it may be sufficient to use a g-seat rather than a motion platform. To simulate the high-frequency manoeuvre cues associated with the following tasks, a motion platform and/or a dynamic seat may be required:

- helicopter nap-of-the-earth flight;
- target tracking;
- air-to-air refuelling;
- low level terrain following.

The presentation of low-frequency cues associated with sustained high-g manoeuvres must be accomplished by means other than platform motion. Platforms are not capable of providing useful acceleration cues (>0.1 g) for manoeuvres with a period of 2 seconds or more. This can impair training fidelity, especially in air-to-air operations and perhaps also in air-to-ground operations.

In low-level fixed-wing operations, the strong vibrations increase the workload significantly and can reduce performance. Using a vibration system in addition to other motion cues can lead to an increase in training effectiveness.

In air-to-air tracking tasks, the nature of the tasks themselves will affect the usefulness of providing manoeuvre motion cues. These cues cannot be fully exploited in tasks that are essentially sustained in nature (those that have few dynamic components, causing the motion platform to remain largely static, such as a loop). Therefore, the whole range of tasks to be trained should be examined before deciding whether manoeuvre motion cueing is a worthwhile investment.

The training of air-to-air tracking tasks that require manoeuvres that are *not* predominantly sustained in nature may benefit from the provision of manoeuvre motion cues. Without manoeuvre motion cues, trainee pilots tend to over-control the aircraft, especially in tracking tasks, and make large sweeping control inputs that are not representative of those produced in real flight. Similarly, trainees tend to be slower in responding to changes in direction when motion cueing is not provided, as they wait until the changes are apparent in the visual system.

Depriving pilots of manoeuvre motion cues during training means that, during the first few flights in the aircraft, they will have to re-develop control strategies and learn to use unfamiliar feedback cues. Pilots trained with manoeuvre motion cues will already have developed the appropriate control behaviour and will transfer more easily to the real flight environment. Experienced pilots may be able to achieve acceptable performance using a fixed-base simulator, but they will develop control strategies that are very different from those used in real flight.

The mid-frequency components (0.1-2.0 Hz) are relevant to manual control activities. During fighter aircraft manoeuvring, accelerations in the range of approximately 8-12 g and onset rates up to 10 g/s are possible. For helicopters, the range of manoeuvring frequencies is roughly 0.5-10 rad/s. For large aircraft and helicopters, relatively low acceleration amplitudes are attained.

Disturbance Motion Cues

Most disturbance motions are characterised by small amplitudes. Cues representing failures of the aircraft possess a relatively high-frequency content. The higher-frequency vibration components of a motion environment act as a stressor, making the performance of certain tasks more difficult. To simulate the high-frequency disturbance motion associated with aircraft pre-stall buffet, engine/rotor vibrations, runway/road vibrations, turbulence or wind shear/gusts, a motion platform, seat shaker or stick shaker should be considered.

Motion Cueing Devices

A motion system should be procured if a Training Needs Analysis (TNA) indicates that:

- motion is required because it provides essential cues to the trainee to learn to perform the task correctly;
- motion is essential because it provides characteristics of disturbances that can degrade performance, and thus need to be practised so that appropriate strategies can be mastered.

Principles of motion cue simulation Acceleration-onset cueing is a term denoting the motion cueing principle used by a simulator motion platform. The initial acceleration of the vehicle being simulated is replicated closely by the platform but, because of its limited throw, the continuing motion of the real vehicle cannot be reproduced. Thus, after the initial acceleration, the response is gradually decreased, eventually to zero (the wash-out phase). The motion platform is then reset to the neutral position, but at a rate below the sensory threshold of the trainee. Fortunately, the body sensors (inner ear, muscle-and-joint feedback, etc) principally react to accelerations rather than steady-state motions, and have thresholds below which they do not react. Thus, the way in which the body signals motion to the brain should match acceleration-onset cueing in a simulator. In this respect, the latency is a crucial parameter. Latency is defined as the time between stimulus and reaction. In simulation applications, it refers to the time delay, normally measured in milliseconds, between initial input and an output that is clearly discernible to the trainee. Latency is sometimes also called transport delay. Some authorities, however, distinguish between latency and transport delay, using latency in the sense of the time delay additional to the reaction time of the vehicle being simulated, but this requires a detailed knowledge of the vehicle dynamics and can be controversial. Here, the terms latency and transport delay are taken as identical: the time delay between initial input and a discernible output.

Trade-offs with motion systems In a sophisticated mission simulator, the motion platform itself is unlikely to be a major cost driver, but the design of any other system mounted on a motion base must be compatible with the maximum accelerations experienced. This imposes a limitation, particularly for wide-FoV visual display systems.

G-Seats, however ingeniously designed, will never be able to replicate six-DoF motion in the same way as a large-throw platform, and so any training role requiring cues of real motion needs one of the many high quality, low latency platforms on the market. A solution is to use a very large projection dome into which the whole simulator and its motion platform can be placed, thus avoiding any limitation of dome construction due to a motion platform.

Face validity A realistic motion system can enhance trainee motivation. According to most learning theories, this should lead to improved training performance. In formal studies, pilots have been reported as liking the presence of a moving base for 'face validity' and, indeed, to maintain adequate performance. But these studies refer mostly to more aggressive and high precision flight paths. Even when performance is a little lower in a simulator without a motion system, one may argue that the pilot's performance, although not optimal, is perhaps sufficient. The need for a motion system is therefore questionable. One option is to ask experienced pilots to evaluate handling qualities during the most demanding lessons in an existing simulator with and without the motion system.

Regulations and training credits In civil aircraft regulations, only a device with a motion platform is called a Flight Simulator; devices without motion platforms are known as Flight Training Devices and are allowed fewer training credits than a Full Flight Simulator.

Motion Platforms

The provision of a high-fidelity motion platform may reduce the incidence of simulator sickness, particularly for skilled pilots for whom simulator sickness is most prevalent. It has been suggested that simulator fidelity requirements increase as the tasks to be trained increase in difficulty and approach the performance limits of the operator/vehicle system. Fidelity requirements may also differ for skill acquisition versus skill maintenance training. Therefore, the minimum acceptable fidelity level may vary according to training application. It may be cost effective to establish fidelity requirements for the worst case condition in which the simulator is likely to be used. The following motion platform characteristics should be considered:

Delays Most motion systems exhibit transport delays and frequency-dependent phase lag or lead. The total delay is the sum of these effects. These delays should not be confused with simulator model delays, which are inherent in the system being simulated.

Frequency response This refers to the amplitude and phase relationship between a sine wave input signal and the acceleration output signal. An expression for the frequency response takes into account the delays mentioned above.

Envelope This covers the operational limits of the platform's displacement, velocity and acceleration.

Positional accuracy This simply refers to the accuracy and tolerance to which the simulator achieves a demanded position.

Dynamic threshold This is the time required for the output acceleration to reach 63% of a step input acceleration command. This parameter is often included under signal transport delays, and may also be reported as attainable acceleration onset rate.

Signal delays It is well established that operators do not benefit from badly timed motion cues: *no motion is better than bad motion*. However, if properly timed, even minimal vestibular stimulation can reduce the visual vection onset (self-motion sensations with a wide FoV) from several tens of seconds in the no-motion case to the more realistic value of tenths of seconds.

Visual-motor compatibility Delays in the motion system relative to the visual system, and vice versa, should be avoided, as they can lead to cue mismatches, and in turn to lower performance and transfer of training, and possibly to simulator sickness. However, the motion system should not be delayed deliberately to match the timing of the visual system, or vice versa. It is more important to present the trainee with feedback from the motion and visual systems that is as timely as possible.

A cockpit motion system is unable to replicate with high objective fidelity the motion effects of highly manoeuvrable combat aircraft, because of the vast manoeuvring frequency spectrum that can be achieved. However, for large aircraft and helicopters, a significantly greater proportion of the aircraft's manoeuvring frequency spectrum can be reproduced. The following guidelines apply to both fighter and cargo aircraft:

- To ensure appropriate handling qualities in the simulator, the sum of aircraft model delays and added simulator delays should not exceed 150 ms.
- To minimise delay effects on pilot performance in the simulator, the sum of aircraft model delays and simulator delays should not exceed 200 ms.
- To promote good transfer of training, the sum of aircraft model delays and simulator delays should not exceed 300 ms.

Wash-out filtering of a motion platform ensures that it returns to its neutral (mid-point) position at an imperceptible rate. With small excursion platforms, wash-out filtering can acceptably be provided by a high-pass, first-order filter between the signal that represents a given vehicle acceleration and the signal that commands the corresponding platform acceleration. Such a filter smoothly removes the sustained excursion from the actuator command. Sustained surge and sway accelerations can be produced by pitch and roll motion of the platform.

The way in which a motion system can best be driven remains unclear. False inputs to the operator, exceeding his perceptual threshold, either from mechanical noise or wash-out, have a detrimental effect on transfer of training.

Types of motion platforms A breakthrough in motion platform technology was achieved in the early 1980s when second-generation six-DoF synergistic platforms became available. The modern 'industry-standard' six-DoF platforms show considerable improvements in terms of the latency (transport delay) of the motion platform.

A synergistic motion platform has three mounting points on the floor under the simulator, from each of which two jacks, displaced from each other at an angle, are connected to the simulator cockpit base plate. By correct programming, all six DoF can be obtained from such a platform design. It should be noted that, because of the arrangement of the jacks, in a synergistic platform the amounts of movement possible will be greater if only one DoF is used at a time. However, frequently the movement requires, say, pitch, roll, heave and surge (Table 20.1) to be applied together.

Table 20.1. Degrees of Freedom (DoF) nomenclature

Type of Motion	Name of DoF (Flight Simulator Terminology)	Description of motion	Axis of Rotation or Motion	Scientific Symbol for Acceleration
Angular/rates	Pitch	Pitch rate	Lateral	Ry
	Roll	Roll Rate	Longitudinal	Rx
	Yaw	Yaw rate	Normal (vertical)	Rz
Linear/movement	Heave	Vertical (up and down)	Normal (vertical)	Gz
	Sway	Lateral (side to side)	Lateral	Gy
	Surge	Longitudinal (fore and aft)	Longitudinal	Gx

The usefulness of simulator motions for various aircraft requirements may be summarised as follows :

- *Surge*: of little use except in VTOL aircraft.
- *Sway*: can be used to simulate high-frequency side forces and for the elimination of spurious side force in roll.
- *Heave*: unless a large excursion is required, use of a g-seat or seat shaker to simulate heave motions should be considered.
- *Pitch*: useful when training tracking tasks.
- *Roll*: useful when training tracking tasks.
- *Yaw*: useful when simulating high-frequency Dutch roll, VTOL aircraft control, and system failures.

Synergistic motion platforms yield better dynamic performance, higher reliability and lower power consumption than *Cascade* platforms. However, their disadvantage is the high level of interaction between actuators and degrees of freedom.

The most satisfactory operation of the six-post synergistic platform in a fighter aircraft simulation is obtained by avoiding use of platform vertical motion and reserving the available actuator travel to reproduce the other degrees of freedom more effectively. However, vertical travel may be used to good effect for buffet, turbulence and vibration simulation.

Cascade motion platforms have the advantage that movement in any one degree of freedom is independent of movement in any other. With Beam motion platforms, there is no surge degree of freedom, i.e., no longitudinal movement along the X-axis. Surge can be simulated by pitching the platform to provide a surge-gravity tilt component. Approximately 6 metres of heave (vertical/Z-axis) and sway (lateral/Y-axis) are possible.

Centrifuge type simulators are mostly used for g-tolerance and disorientation training. However, the US Naval Air Warfare Center uses a centrifuge as a motion platform for its Dynamic Flight Simulator (DFS). This simulator incorporates a reconfigurable full-scale cockpit within a gimballed cab, which allows the inclusion of sustained g-loading cues. It is best used for simulation of high-stress or hazardous flight scenarios, including sustained high-g air combat manoeuvring, highly agile manoeuvring, high angle of attack departures, and out-of-control flight and spins.

Non-Platform Cueing Devices

Some of the cues or elements of cues that operators experience cannot be reproduced by motion platforms (e.g., sustained accelerations). For this reason, a number of specific devices have been developed to supplement or replace the range of motion cues induced by platform motion systems.

Research on non-platform motion cueing devices such as dynamic seats, g-seats, and seat-shakers has not yielded enough evidence to draw definitive conclusions about their contribution to training effectiveness.

Motion seats Motion seats are specially designed simulator devices attached to crew seats and designed to give cues of motion including vibration and acceleration. The principal acceleration cueing provided is normally for Gz (acceleration along the vertical axis), in which case the device is called a G-Seat.

G-seats G-seats were originally designed to provide *sustained* acceleration cues that cannot be produced by platform motion systems. This is achieved by means of tactile stimulation representing postural and skin pressure changes that are indicative of whole-body acceleration in the aircraft.

The seat pan and backrest cushions of a modern g-seat are constructed from arrays of inflatable pneumatic bellows. The seat pan bellows have an operational stroke of approximately 3 cm, while the backrest bellows have an excursion capability of approximately 2 cm. Such a design stimulates the buttocks, thigh and back with a pressure profile that is appropriate to simulate aircraft accelerations. Further, this device is able to provide increased buttock pressure and lowered skeletal position at the same time, the phenomena that are expected to accompany $+G_z$ manoeuvres.

G-seat cues for lateral and roll motion may be reinforced by mounting thigh panels on either side of the seat pan. These stimulate the thighs through pneumatic bellows. Further cue enhancement can be provided by the use of a lap belt to provide the illusion of XZ-plane acceleration through uniform extensions and contractions on each side of the belt. Some g-seats have a bandwidth of 0.5 Hz, which is inadequate to provide onset cues. With more advanced control systems, 5 Hz is possible.

Dynamic seats A g-seat can also be enhanced by actuators providing pitch, roll and yaw. Such a *dynamic seat* is also capable of providing onset cues. This will inevitably result in an incompatible pilot location with respect to the rest of the cockpit.

Vibration systems An example of a vibration system is the seat shaker. Vibration systems are used to supplement vibration cues from motion platform systems at frequencies of 3-20 Hz. A main reason for using such systems is that it is inadvisable (because of wear and tear and structural damage) to subject the motion platform system and cockpit/cabin to vibrations with frequencies higher than 5 Hz. Moreover, actuators for motion platform systems possess resonant frequencies at about 10 Hz. It is therefore desirable to avoid these frequencies in the platform.

The seat shaker is used in fighter aircraft simulators to reproduce stall buffet, Mach buffet, landing gear rumble, speed brake, gun firing and other vibration cues. It can also be used to provide discrete cues such as touch-down bump, gear up/down lock, ordnance strike, ordnance launch and certain malfunctions. The seat shaker usually provides just one degree of freedom — vertical vibration cues. Pre-stall buffet appears to be an important cue for air combat manoeuvring. When these cues are provided by a seat shaker, pilots can spend more time keeping their opponent in sight than looking at their instruments for precise angle of attack data.

A seat shaker may also be used to provide vibration cues for certain ground-based and naval simulations. In helicopter simulations, it provides the 'n per rev' vibration from the rotor; often a multi-degree of freedom vibration cue is provided.

The seat shaker has the disadvantage of causing relative movement of the operator in the cabin, although the amplitudes of the excursions may not be very large. A further limitation is its ability to provide only onset cues, mostly limited to one degree of freedom. Therefore, a cue mismatch may result. This problem can be resolved by adding rotational degrees of freedom to the seat shaker to stimulate more appropriately the operator's vestibular system.

G-suit The presence and operation of a g-suit in a flight simulator will enhance the realism of the simulation, and provide the pilot with sustained (low-frequency) cues for the g-loading of the aircraft. Obviously, the g-suit does not provide the onset of high-g cues, but provision of pseudo high-g cues is more important for tactical fighter pilot training. In air combat manoeuvring and close air support missions, acceleration profiles with amplitudes of about 10 g and onset rates of 10 g/s can occur.

MASTER Research Findings

A number of findings from the MASTER project are reported below: the results of a number of transfer of training studies, and findings from a survey of user opinion on motion cueing in flight simulation.

Transfer of Training Studies

A series of experiments was performed using a similar experimental design, but varying vehicles, simulator types, and so on. A 'high end' simulator configuration was compared to a 'low end' configuration. The high-end configuration included all possible options, whereas the low-end simulator contained only components considered as standard applications.

Three fixed-wing experiments were performed to examine the training value of platform motion cueing for aircraft manoeuvring. The experiments included three different aircraft models, pilot experience levels, and training tasks. Two groups were formed within each experiment: one group trained with motion and the other without motion. The three experiments shared the following features:

- a between-subjects experimental design to investigate and measure learning and transfer effects for motion/no-motion conditions (12 pilots for each experiment);
- *manoeuvre motion* studied. Effectiveness of platform motion using disturbance motion has been demonstrated before, and a new study would merely replicate this effect. But effects of platform motion using manoeuvre motion have rarely been found;
- a quasi-transfer design, since transfer to real flight proved to be impossible due to military restrictions.

The range of subjects used included relatively inexperienced general aviation pilots (EF2000 training) and very experienced former operational pilots (F-16 and Tornado training). To assure learning curves, the training tasks and simulator configuration were adapted to the entry level of the subjects. For the EF2000 training, three tracking tasks were selected and the simulator was operated with auto-throttle and rudder stabilisation. After each practice run, the pilots received knowledge of results (KR) on root mean square (RMS) error and were coached (if necessary) by an instructor. F-16 pilots also received KR on deviations from ideal parameters. The Tornado pilots were instructed only to optimise the appropriate parameters, but no coaching was provided. The Tornado simulator did not include pilot's OTW view, and each group of pilots had to transfer to the other condition. Hence the motion group in this case also had to transfer to a different motion cueing situation (no platform motion), which allowed a crosscheck on changes in robustness of the skills acquired in both conditions. Table 20.2 provides a summary of the experiments.

Given the variations in experimental set-up, the results were strikingly similar. On most tasks, the pilots achieved good learning progress, which indicates that the training adaptation to initial skill levels was successful. Throughout the training, pilots trained with motion cueing tended to perform worse than pilots trained without motion cueing, especially for experienced pilots in the early training trials. Motion cueing did not lead to faster learning. On transfer, the lack of motion during training had at most a temporary negative effect. Table 20.3 provides an overview of the results.

Based on performance data only, the conclusion would be that the training value of motion cueing for manoeuvring is low and therefore should not be recommended; this conclusion, however, is not supported when the cross-transfer results of the Tornado experiment and the differences in pilot control strategies are more closely studied.

Table 20.2. Summary of experimental conditions in fixed-wing experiments

	EF2000	F-16 MLU	Tornado
Performed by	BAe, DERA	NLR	CAE, GAPH
Pilot experience & background	General Aviation pilots, no experience with military aircraft	Former operational F-16 pilots (< 5 years out of service)	Operational Tornado pilots
Simulator	6 DOF & Dome, generic aircraft model	6 DOF & g-cueing & Dome, high res. Insert, F-16 aircraft model	6 DOF & g-cueing & HMD visual, Tornado aircraft model
OTW visual	Active	Active	Not active
Training tasks	Tracking basic manoeuvres - loop - turn - pull up	Aerobatics - vertical reposition - double Split S - pop-up weapon delivery	Aerobatics - barrel roll - 5 barrel rolls - Cuban eight
Instructional principle and feedback	Instructor coaching with use of KR on RMS	Self instruction with use of KR on parameter deviation	Guided (to parameters) self instruction without KR
Transfer	To configuration with motion, performing: - same tasks (4x)	To configuration with motion, performing: - same tasks (1x) - VRP with different parameter values (1x)	For Motion group: to configuration without motion to configuration without motion & HUD for Non-Motion group: to configuration with motion to configuration with motion & without HUD
Measures	Flight path stick inputs workload	Flight path, speed parameters etc. stick inputs workload EPOG	Flight path, speed parameters etc.
Domains of additional research questions	Comparison of tasks	Transfer of skill to a different task setting	Transfer to situation differing in information available

Table 20.3. Summary of results of the experiments

	Ef2000	F-16 MLU	Tornado
Pilot performance	(RMS)	(parameter deviations)	(parameter deviations)
Motion	NM tended to perform better than M during Loop and Turn training	NM tended to perform better than M (especially in the first session of VRP and POP training)	NM tended to perform better than M on speed control; otherwise no clear differences
Learning	Good learning progress	Good learning progress	Good learning progress only on the first task (Barrel Roll)
Learning* motion	Generally no group difference in learning	Generally no group difference in learning	Generally no group difference in learning
Transfer	- NM initially worse than M during Loop transfer - no group difference during Turn transfer - both groups improved during Pull-Up training	Generally no group difference; NM performed worse only on the first transfer test (VRP)	- M performed better during transfer for Barrel Roll with lack of motion than vice versa - M performed better on transfer (Barrel Roll 5) to information-poor situation - no group difference on transfer for Cuban Eight
Scanning	N/A	During DSS training, NM tended to use more information from the instruments. M tended to be more head up	N/A
Control inputs	- NM tended to larger amplitudes and delays in roll input compared to M - M deviated less on pitch than NM (analysed for first session with RMS)	- NM started with stronger input corrections than M, but adapted quickly - On transfer, NM again had to correct more strongly	- (Derived from roll rate variance) NM input was initially worse than M - both groups improved roll control on transfer to information poor situation
Pilot workload	Workload higher for NM during training, and even more so during the transfer test.	- On DSS training, NM allocated more effort than M, and after transfer less effort was needed than during training - On POP transfer, NM allocated more effort than during training, during which NM relaxed earlier than M	N/A

Note. NM = Non-Motion group; M = Motion group; N/A = Not Available

In the Tornado experiment, transfer results indicated that pilots trained with motion acquired more robust flying skills. This trend was observed in the pilot control input data of all experiments. Pilots trained without motion appeared to provide stick inputs with a delay, and a higher gain (needing stronger correction) than the group trained with motion. The workload scores confirmed the additional effort. Experienced pilots (F-16 and Tornado), however, could adapt to the lack of motion cues by modifying their control strategy (based on analyses of stick input frequency spectra and roll rate variance). They used relatively smaller corrections but their control strategy did not transfer well to a task with motion cues (F-16 experiment). The amplitude of corrections increased again (consistent with more effort being allocated to the transfer task). For the Double Split S, the workload trends were not consistent with the control input behaviour, but this may be a result of a shift in perception strategies for the non-motion group during the Double Split S training.

On the basis of performance, behavioural and workload data, the following coherent interpretation emerges: without motion cueing, inexperienced pilots put more effort into input control, but the applied control strategies tended to lead to better performance. On transfer, the control strategies appeared to be initially disturbed by the motion cues, but rapid adaptation to the situation was possible. The experienced pilots trained without motion followed the same process, but the overall control strategy was more efficient since it required less effort. The control skills therefore seem to be flexible, although adaptation time is required, similar to the case of transferring to another aircraft.

In the same series of experiments, a study of battle tanks was performed. Gunners had to operate their equipment in a moving tank with or without motion systems. The results showed that motion does not seem to be critical for transfer, but again the phenomenon of adapting control skills was reported: more experienced trainees needed to adapt to the no-motion conditions. The overall results bore a resemblance to the disorientation known to occur during simulator sickness: after adaptation, it is possible to perform again. In these studies, it was once again confirmed that human operators are flexible to changing working and controlling conditions. There were, however, clear indications that the control skills found in the real world differed from those in the simulator.

The relation between experience and flexibility seems to follow an inverted-U. Both lack of experience (novice control level, no automated skills) and high levels of experience (based on multiple aircraft, each with different handling qualities) allow for some flexibility, as was found, although for different reasons. In the first case, the internal model had not yet been established and was still in the phase of trial and error. In the second case, pilots had adopted more, and better quality, modes of handling the aircraft familiar to them. An analogy is experienced truck drivers who transfer regularly between light and heavy vehicles. The trainees of interest are those with an intermediate level of expertise (say, used to a single aircraft). They can be compared to a recently certified driver who is unwilling to drive another car. If the inverted-U notion is valid, it predicts less flexibility in adapting control strategies (which forms a hypothesis for a possible future study). Transfer experiments using fine-grained input control measures should be able to support or refute this hypothesis. The use of such measures is of great benefit in improving the level of understanding of control skills and their shaping factors. An illustration is a recent study on possible benefits of force cueing (dynamic seat, g-suit, seat pan bladder, etc.) for simulators without platform motion (Heintzman *et al*, 1997). Pilot inputs were recorded and analysed in detail. The results revealed that such cueing 'will cause the pilot to perform and behave in the simulator similar to the aircraft'. Considered with the MASTER studies, the conclusion that such measurements should be mandatory seems warranted.

User Opinion on Motion Cueing in Flight Simulators

Within MASTER, structured interviews were conducted at 21 training establishments using flight simulators. Emphasis was placed on the operational air-to-ground role of the aircraft. The simulators visited covered a range of 25 years, some being full-mission high-fidelity devices and others being deployable pro-cedure trainers equipped neither with a motion nor a visual system. Additionally, some training establishments with part-task training facilities were visited. An overview of the results is given in Table 20.4. The aircraft tasks most frequently mentioned as having the greatest requirement for platform motion were:

- emergencies training;
- air-combat manoeuvring;
- low-level manoeuvring.

Formation flying, weapon delivery and ship-deck landing were also mentioned frequently. Important physical system parameters cited included:

- six degrees-of-freedom of the platform;
- responsiveness;
- time lag.

Users were in general neutral-to-positive in their opinion about the usefulness of mechanical motion cueing devices such as g-seats, g-suits, dynamic seats, seat shakers, stick shakers and rudder pedal shakers. Some users were reluctant to wear g-suits or use the g-seat.

Simulators without platform motion, such as the French Mirage simulators that came into service relatively recently, are used for the full range of training courses. Motion cues seemed to be considered secondary in importance to visual cues, with the exception of Instrument Flight. From the user opinions, it can be concluded that the need for motion cues is in general:

- of secondary importance;
- determined not only by the specific task but also by individual preferences.

Arguments in favour of motion emphasise that situational awareness is affected in head-down situations or that handling turbulence and wind shear on final approach necessitates its use in pre-operational training. In roughly half the cases, users indicated that an upgrade to platform motion was desirable.

Simulators with three-, four-, and six-DoF platform motion from the 1970s-1990s were examined. Users of the Tornado GR.1 simulator (1980), equipped with a three-DoF platform and used for conversion to type, considered the motion platform to be adequate.

Table 20.4. Motion systems

Aircraft	Year of Sim.	Motion systems installed	Type of training	Example of motion critical task mentioned	User opinion
Mirage 2000C	1992	G-seat, g-suit	From type qualification to formation leader	Emergencies, weapon system training	G-seat is not considered to be very important (rating of 3 on scale of 1-10)
Mirage 2000D	1996	—	Weapon system utilisation	Low-level manoeuvring, self-defence	Users do not specify an opinion or requirement
Mirage F.1-CT	1992	G-suit	Full mission, from type qualification to formation leader	Dog-fight, Air-Ground weapon delivery, landing, take-off	Upgrade of motion environment is desirable
C-160 Transall	1995	Platform: 6 DOF	Operational	Low altitude navigation, landing	Platform motion seems adequate, though not most important for skill acquisition
SEM	1994	Platform: 4 DOF, G-suit, stick shaker	Mission rehearsal and procedures	Dog-fight, ship-deck landing	Opinions differ on platform motion, other motion devices considered unimportant
Tornado GR.1	1980	Platform: 3 DOF, G-suit	Conversion to type	Emergencies, IF, EW, turning at low level	Motion cueing is adequate
Tornado F.3	1985	G-suit, seat shaker	Mission and emergencies, BVR-engagements, conversion, continuation, refresher	Basic manoeuvring (turning, climb and descent)	Platform motion needed, currently situational awareness when head down believed to be affected
Harrier GR.5	1992	Platform: 6 DOF, G-suit, G-seat, seat shaker, rudder pedal shaker	Full mission, all courses	IF	Platform motion not realistic, seat shaker provides good cues
Hawk	c1976	Platform - unknown DOF, G-suit	Pre-operational	Demonstration of turbulence and wind shear	Platform motion not realistic
Jaguar	1974	Platform: 3 DOF, g-seat (simple cushion)	Operational (refresher, currency)	Co-ordination flying, manoeuvring	Platform motion not realistic (system lag)
F-16 A	1982	G-suit (trousers only), G-seat (pan, belt, shoulders), seat shaker (gun effects)	Conversion, currency (11 different courses)	Emergencies, Air-to-Air-tasks	Platform motion could give an advantage for some tasks, other devices adequate (high g-cueing limited)
C-101	Unknown	—	Refresher for non-operational pilots, instrument flight only	Not asked	Not asked
F-18	Unknown	G-seat	Pre-operational, to support initial solo flights on the type	Not asked	Not asked
Mirage F.1	1978	—	Full range of courses	Not asked	Not asked

The C-160 TRANSALL simulator (1995) users also considered their six-DoF system satisfactory, but rated control loading systems as more important. The users of three other simulators (Harrier, 1992, six-DoF, Hawk, 1976, and Jaguar, 1974, three-DoF) characterised the platform motion of their simulators as unrealistic, at least for some tasks such as VSTOL operations (Harrier). The Jaguar simulator suffers from time lag, which makes it more difficult to fly than the real aircraft.

Most users considered realistic control loading/control feel highly useful for training of manual flying skills. Its importance was rated about 9 on a scale of 1-10. Note that, in simulators of fly-by-wire aircraft, control loading can be implemented with full engineering fidelity.

Conclusions

Recent technological developments have significantly improved the capabilities of motion platforms. Most of the research has been limited to using 'older platforms' and facilities. Problems associated with such platforms are low bandwidth capabilities, limited excursions and relatively long time delays. The latter factor, in particular, is a limitation in relation to the response times of the human sensory system. Given these limitations, the following benefits have been reported for motion systems:

- Performance and control behaviour is consistently improved for disturbance motion types of task. Hence, all corrective manoeuvring in relation to external influences will benefit.
- More unstable vehicles will benefit more from motion systems. The more agile the aircraft, the more relevant a motion system will be.
- Manoeuvring skills developed with motion cueing are closer to those observed in the real system, but real-life data are very limited.
- User acceptance is neutral-to-positive, depending on the type of vehicle.

The results of the transfer of training studies are more difficult to summarise. In many cases, it proved impossible to gain access to the real systems, leading to the use of quasi-transfer experimental designs. Furthermore, the performance measurements lacked detail and did not permit a clear understanding of the actual skill-specific cueing requirements. More recently, operator input strategies have been studied in the training context by means of spectral analysis of frequencies, phase lags, and so on. These types of data consistently point to more realistic control behaviour as a function of motion cueing during manoeuvring tasks. However, such data also indicate that experienced crews are quite flexible in adapting their input strategy to the simulator configuration in an attempt to achieve good performance scores, although such strategies may not be optimal for real-life performance. More studies in the real vehicle are therefore required to specify the training and cueing requirements for configuring the simulator to the control strategies and not the other way around.

21 Methodology for Training Media Specification

Introduction

The MASTER methodology supports the process of deriving simulator requirements from operational requirements by means of an iterative progression through a number of steps. To re-iterate, the methodology comprises three main steps: Training Needs Analysis (TNA), Training Programme Design (TPD), and Training Media Specification (TMS). During TNA, the training need is determined and described in terms of a set of related training objectives. During TPD, training objectives are translated into training programme requirements. Finally, during TMS, training programme requirements are translated into simulator requirements.

In Chapter 13, the input-output links between TPD and TMS were described. From the preceding chapters in this section, it will be clear that the specification of simulator requirements requires different kinds of expertise: knowledge of the domain (skills, organisational requirements and constraints), of training and instruction strategies and techniques, of human perception, and of simulation technology. A methodology for TMS must encapsulate this expertise, and support users in applying the expertise to their own training problems. It should also provide an interface between users of different backgrounds. Clearly, this calls for a systematic approach. In this chapter, the rationale for such an approach will be outlined, with an overview of the issues and trade-offs involved in the process of TMS.

Training Media Specification

The output of TPD constitutes the input to TMS. It consists of a specification of a prospective training programme to be delivered by means of a simulator. More specifically, it comprises an ordered sequence of:

- assessment points;
- training scenario descriptions;
- associated instructional specifications.

The last two components constitute the main inputs for TMS. In Chapter 11, the design of training scenarios was discussed from the viewpoint of training programme design. In the context of TMS, however, the issues are considered from the viewpoint of cueing realism. Although training considerations should lead cueing considerations in the scenario design process, compromises may have to be made in practice. Hence, frequent iterations between TPD and TMS may be required.

A training simulator, and therefore its functional specification, can be decomposed into a number of components. For instance, a full-mission simulator might comprise a TSI, an ISI, a database, a simulation model, an image system, a motion system, and a sound system. Associated with each component is a specific set of functional requirements. The goal of Training Media Specification is to specify the functional requirements associated with each of the required simulator components, given the training programme requirements. This is accomplished in three main steps: setting up a specification scheme, specifying requirements, and assessing requirements.

Setting up a Specification Scheme

Specifying simulator requirements may be a very laborious job, and it may be necessary to impose restrictions on the specification process. This step is intended to reduce the amount of work by explicitly considering:

- which training scenarios to use as the basis for specifying requirements (norm scenarios);
- which simulator configuration, i.e., which set of requirements, to use as a starting point for specifying simulator requirements.

The result of this step is a specification scheme.

Specifying Requirements

During this step, the actual specification of requirements is conducted, according to the specification scheme determined in the previous step. Together with the minimisation principle, the principle of specific fidelity (see Chapter 13) ensures that training scenarios can be distinguished in terms of simulator requirements and vice versa. This enables an assessment of the level and the nature of the fidelity required for a particular set of training scenarios, and helps to determine which training scenarios can be used given a particular simulator specification. Obviously, due to the strong inter-dependencies between simulator components, specifying simulator requirements will be a complex and highly iterative process that draws upon different types of expertise.

Assessing Requirements

After a set of training scenarios has been processed, it may be necessary to pause and compare requirements across training scenarios in terms of factors such as comprehensiveness and realism or 'functional fidelity' (see Chapter 11). Comprehensiveness is defined as the range of training scenarios that may be performed with a particular set of simulator requirements, i.e., a particular simulator specification. Realism is defined as the extent in which a particular set of simulator requirements enables approximation of real-life behaviour (behavioural realism) or real-life cues (cueing realism). In short, comprehensiveness represents the breadth, and realism the depth, of simulation.

At this stage, consideration of constraints and issues not strictly related to training may also enter the specification process. These may include, for example:

- computer and software requirements;
- interfacing and networking requirements;
- housing requirements;
- safety requirements;
- maintenance requirements;
- management requirements;
- standards, testing and certification requirements.

The output of TMS is a set of functional requirements. The reason for restricting MASTER to the *functional* specification of simulator requirements is that they can be specified in a more generic way and are less subject to change. (This is also why the estimation of simulator costs was not addressed within MASTER.) Of course, the requirements can be used to compose a Request For Information (RFI) or Request For Proposal (RFP). The RFI/RFP may be used to obtain up-to-date cost estimates, information on feasibility, and assessments of possible technical requirements. In evaluating responses to an RFI or RFP, the functional requirements may be used as evaluation criteria.

Only after functional requirements have been specified and implementation issues addressed can trade-offs be considered with respect to the type of training media that will be required.

Scenario-Based Specification of Simulator Requirements

In Chapters 17-20, several guidelines were provided with respect to the specification of cueing and simulation requirements. Although useful, these guidelines do not prescribe how and when they should be applied in specifying the functional simulator requirements for a particular training scenario. This specification involves elaboration and translation of the elements of a training scenario in terms of cueing and simulation requirements.

An approach will be outlined that may serve as the basis for such a specification, and thus for the TMS methodology (proposed by Kappé in van Rooij *et al*, 1998b). The approach will be illustrated by means of examples drawn from the domain of helicopter flight. These examples will provide a feel for issues to be resolved during the specification process, and an impression of how the knowledge presented in preceding chapters may be applied in a particular case.

Simulator Requirements for Helicopter Flight

In some training scenarios, such as nap-of-the-earth flight, the helicopter pilot primarily depends on visual and vestibular information; a high-fidelity simulator is required to train these tasks. In other scenarios, such as in those primarily involving cruise flight or take-off, fewer cues are utilised, and a less sophisticated system may suffice.

In defining the type of simulator needed for a particular scenario, one could analyse the cues required to execute the training activities. Unfortunately, few data are available on the cues that a pilot may use when performing a particular task or training activity. Even when the cues are known, it is not always obvious how many should be presented or how they should be measured. If the type and amount of cues *can* be specified, how do they relate to the functional specifications of a simulator? Specifying the resolution, colour depth or field of view required for accurate perception of a cue is a problem in itself.

Instead of relating training scenarios to simulator specifications via cues, we suggest an additional step: the specification of the vehicle parameters that are controlled during the execution of a task or training activity. Parameters might include the position and orientation of the helicopter and their first- and second-order derivatives (translation, rotation and linear and rotational acceleration). The use of vehicle parameters has several advantages. First, it allows a task to be defined in terms of subtasks that do not depend on cues. Pilots often know which vehicle parameters are controlled in a task or training activity, but they may be unaware of the cues that are utilised to assess information on these parameters. For instance, when hovering, accurate control of the orientation of the helicopter is important to maintain position. Which cues are utilised in this process is not directly relevant (to the pilot), and may differ between pilots. Second, vehicle parameters allow the available cues to be clustered. It seems simpler to relate functional specifications to such a cluster of cues than to each cue individually. Third, in contrast with some cues, vehicle parameters can be quantified: for example, when hovering at 10 ft, the change in lateral position should not exceed 3 ft. Finally, in a simulator, vehicle parameters are often used as performance measures. If tasks are defined in terms of such measures, it may be simpler to assess training effectiveness.

To summarise, it is suggested that cues may not be the ideal intermediate step when relating tasks to functional simulator specifications. It is difficult to define which cues are required, and how they are related to functional specifications. As an alternative, it is proposed that the vehicle parameters controlled by the pilot should first be identified. Decomposing a task or training activity into vehicle parameters is more straightforward. The relation of vehicle parameters and functional specifications is more straightforward, and vehicle parameters can be quantified much more easily. When using vehicle parameters as an intermediate step, the specification process may be broken into four steps:

- The first step is to determine which vehicle parameters are controlled in a certain task, and how relevant a vehicle parameter is for task performance.
- The second step is to determine which cues are utilised when assessing information on a certain vehicle parameter. This results in a cluster of cues that may be used to assess information on a vehicle parameter.
- The third step is to relate vehicle parameters (and cue clusters) to functional simulator requirements, resulting in a list of functional requirements for each vehicle parameter.

- The final step is to relate tasks to functional simulator requirements, using vehicle parameters as an intermediate step.

Step 1 At the first step, the vehicle parameters controlled during the execution of a task are determined. Since some tasks may require more accurate control of a vehicle parameter than others, a weighting factor (0, 0.1, 0.25, 0.5, 0.75, 1) is used to indicate its importance. Determining which weighting factor should be assigned is sometimes relatively simple (e.g., in cruise flight or for an instrument take-off). In other cases, interviews with pilots may be required (for instance, in hover, sling-load operations or emergency situations). When a weighting factor is assigned for each vehicle parameter and for each task, a table of tasks and vehicle parameters is obtained, with a weighting factor for each cell.

Although it is important that the weighting factors are assigned correctly, they are only an indication of the relevance of a certain vehicle parameter. That is, a parameter with a weighting factor of 0.1 is not ten times less important than one with a weighting factor of 1; it is clearly, however, much less important.

Step 2 At the second step, a list is compiled of all relevant cues, and then a cluster of cues is assigned to each vehicle parameter. A list of all cues potentially available was presented in Chapter 16. When assessing information on a vehicle parameter, the pilot can use several cues. The particular subset of cues used depends on the flying environment and the preferences of the pilot. Thus, a cluster of cues can be assigned to each vehicle parameter. Table 21.1 shows the cues for each vehicle parameter. The co-ordinate system that is used has an x-axis of lateral direction, a y-axis of longitudinal direction, and a z-axis of vertical direction.

Step 3 In the third step, vehicle parameters are related to functional requirements. Step 3 is the most difficult, since there are virtually no data available in the literature on the relationship between vehicle parameters and functional simulator requirements. Therefore, this step involves the application of several rules of thumb that have emerged from knowledge of perception and from the current state of simulation technology. For each vehicle parameter we will discuss some of these rules of thumb.

In the perception of position, a large cluster of size and depth cues is involved. Most of these cues are related to linear perspective (e.g., ground intercept angle, horizon ratio). Most simulators accurately present such perspective cues. Other cues are texture-related, such as density-, size- and foreshortening-gradients. Some pilots use very specific cues to initiate a manoeuvre, such as cow pats, the blades of grass in a meadow, or the bark on trees. Obviously, accurate presentation of these cues requires texture with several levels of detail. The transition from one level of detail to another should be modelled to coincide with the normal appearance of such details. Known size also plays an important role in the perception of position. To use this cue, objects should have a prototypical size, and should be presented at a high enough level of detail to enable recognition by the observer. Interposition and occlusion require many objects to be present in the environment, so that there is a reasonable chance that two objects will be presented at the same location in the visual field. Some pilots may use the position of a landmark below the helicopter relative to a vehicle reference (for instance, at the edge of the instrument panel) as a cue to position. Since the visual effects of a change in position are largest just below the helicopter, a large field of view (chin windows) will improve positioning performance. In sling-load operations, highly accurate position control is required to hook up or deliver a load. Since the altitude of the pilot is relatively high during this operation, information on position is decreased. Here, a large field of view and high resolution are especially relevant for accurate positioning.

Table 21.1. Cue clusters and vehicle parameters

Vehicle parameter	Unit	Cues	
Position	x (m) y (m) z (m)	Accommodation Occlusion Known size Linear perspective Horizon ratio Ground intercept angle Splay angle Compression rate Texture	Density gradient Size gradient Foreshortening gradient Visibility of specific detail(s) Interposition/coincidence Aerial perspective Colour Expansion Motion parallax
Translation	x= (m/s) y= (m/s) z= (m/s)	Expansion Motion parallax	Edge-rate Flow-rate
Linear acceleration	x=> (m/s^2) Surge y=> (m/s^2) Sway z=> (m/s^2) Heave	Sacculus, utriculus Internal pressures	Muscle force Skin pressure
Orientation	x axis (deg) y axis (deg)	Sacculus, utriculus Position of the horizon	Orientation of the horizon Position in the visual field
	Z axis (deg)	Position in the visual field	
Rotation	x axis (deg/s) Pitch y axis (deg/s) Roll	Translational flow Rotational flow	Sacculus, utriculus
	Z axis (deg/s) Yaw	Translational flow	Rotational flow
Rotational acceleration	x axis (deg/s^2) y axis (deg/s^2) z axis (deg/s^2)	Semi-circular canals	Internal pressures

Observers may also use information contained in the optic flow as a cue to spatial position. In the perception of optic flow, the visual system makes use of specialised neuronal circuitry that allows direct perception (Gibson, 1950) of spatial position. This process does not depend on the mental processes (recognition, identification) involved in high-level visual perception of position. In optic flow, information is contained in the streaming of objects, not in the objects themselves. Consequently, perception of optic flow depends less on the complexity of objects and more on an adequate update rate (Kappé, 1997). The issue of whether depth perception is based upon optic flow or on pictorial size and depth cues has been discussed extensively in the literature. Recently, there seems to be a growing consensus that both sources of information play a role in perception.

As a rule of thumb, accurate perception of position necessitates complex images with many detailed, textured objects and surfaces. Sling operations, and other tasks that require highly accurate control of position, require a wide field of view (with chin windows) and a high resolution. Since optic flow is also involved in the perception of spatial position, a sufficient update rate is mandatory.

The cues involved in the perception of translation are all related to optic flow. Correct perception of optic flow does not require many objects or textures. It is known that only a few objects are required for accurate perception of the direction of translation. Ten random dots in a 30 x 40 deg field of view are sufficient for accurate perception of heading (Warren *et al*, 1988). Kappé (1997) has shown that translation can be perceived just as accurately in a relatively simple environment, provided that a large field of view is presented. However, accurate perception of optic flow does require a high update rate. The rate required depends on the distance-to-speed ratio. When this ratio is small, i.e., when moving fast at low altitudes such as in nap-of-the-earth or contour flight, an update rate of 60 Hz or more is desirable (Haber, 1986). A reasonable minimum seems to be about 30 Hz (Käppler, 1986).

As a rule of thumb, accurate perception of translation can be based upon relatively simple images, which are presented with a large field of view and updated frequently.

In the perception of linear acceleration, vestibular and somato-sensory information is of primary importance. A sensation of linear acceleration can be brought about in two ways. The first is by moving the platform. Since a moving base with a linear excursion of more than a few decimetres is exceptional, this method can be used only for simulating the short, transient, linear accelerations due to disturbances and steering corrections. There are indications (Condon, 1990) that a moving base may improve vehicle handling performance in nap-of-the-earth flight.

The second method allows simulation of the more prolonged accelerations that occur in high-speed curves and other complex manoeuvres. In a simulator, changing the orientation of the entire simulator platform, including the displays, can bring this about. The vestibular system registers that the gravity vector is no longer oriented vertically, while the visual system registers a constant orientation. The resulting percept is a linear acceleration.

As a rule of thumb, short, transient linear accelerations due to disturbances and steering corrections can be simulated veridically, but the continuous linear accelerations that may occur in some manoeuvres can only be imitated. When helicopters are equipped with an automated flight control system (AFCS), control stability is substantially improved. In most tasks, the AFCS system is fully functional, and the need for a sophisticated motion platform is precluded. A high-end motion platform is required only in special circumstances, such as in sling-load operations, disturbances, or during an AFCS malfunction.

The perception of orientation is dominated by visual information, although vestibular information on the orientation of the gravity vector is also involved (Groen, 1997). In the visual perception of the pitch and the roll angle, the horizon plays an important role. The position of the horizon in the visual field provides important information about pitch angle, whereas the orientation of the horizon with respect to the vertical provides information on the roll angle. In a simulator, a large pitch angle could cause the horizon to disappear off the display. Therefore, the field of view should be large enough to keep the horizon in sight. Perception of the yaw angle relies on distant landmarks such as church towers, mountain ranges, and the sun. Since discriminating between landmarks may be difficult for the pilot, the database should provide enough landmarks to induce similar difficulties.

The vestibular system or, more specifically, the otoliths, may also provide information on pitch and roll angles, by registering the orientation of the gravity vector. Due to linear accelerations, the orientation of the gravity vector may change, resulting in disorientation or vertigo. To avoid vertigo, pilots are trained to ignore vestibular information and base their attitude judgements on instruments and visual information only. In some situations, however, the vestibular system does provide veridical information on pitch and roll angles. Whenever linear accelerations are absent, such as in hover or in linear cruise flight, the vestibular system can be used to assess pitch and roll.

As a rule of thumb, adequate perception of pitch and roll requires a large field of view, a horizon, and a sufficient amount of landmarks. Vestibular information on pitch and roll can be used only in the absence of linear accelerations, such as in hover or cruise.

The primary source of information on rotation of the helicopter is translational and rotational optic flow. In theory, there may be two sources of rotational optic flow: local flow, generated by a rotation of the helicopter in respect to the virtual viewing direction; and global flow, generated by a change in virtual viewing direction. In the former, the viewing direction of the eye does not change with respect to the computer-generated environment whilst the helicopter is changing orientation. In the latter, the viewing direction does not change with respect to the helicopter. A change in orientation will result in global translational and rotational optic flow generated by the entire environment. Which of these two components is observed depends on the rotational acceleration.

The semicircular canals provide information on rotational acceleration. Using this information, sudden disturbances in orientation of the head are compensated, so that the viewing direction of the eye is stabilised and optical smear is reduced. The vestibular system is concerned mainly with fast and vigorous accelerations (the vestibulo-oculomotor reflex) whereas the visual system compensates for slow rotations and rotational accelerations (the opto-kinetic reflex). Sudden vigorous rotational accelerations primarily occur during disturbances, whereas slow and gradual rotations are normally generated by control commands.

As a rule of thumb, a moving base is required whenever the helicopter is subjected to rotational disturbances. The rotational accelerations generated by control commands are generally much smaller, allowing them to be perceived using visual information only.

In Step 3, a table is compiled of vehicle parameters and functional specifications. Using the rules of thumb, for each vehicle parameter and for each weighting factor a set of functional simulator specifications can be assigned. Some specifications are relevant to almost all simulators, such as resolution or refresh rate of the display. Others are not relevant to the perception of a particular vehicle parameter, an example being the properties of the moving base in the perception of position.

Step 4 The final stage in the process is to combine the tables that resulted from Steps 2 and 3. In Step 2, a table was composed of tasks and vehicle parameters, with a weighting factor for each cell. The table developed in Step 3 related vehicle parameters to functional simulator requirements, with a set of functional specifications assigned to each of the six weighting factors for each vehicle parameter. The process of combining the two tables is as follows. First, for each task and each vehicle parameter, the weighting factor with the highest value (of the x, y and z axes) is determined. There is now a set of six vehicle parameter/ weighting factors for each task. Using the results obtained during Step 3, a set of functional simulator requirements can be assigned to each of these six combinations. All that remains to be done is to collapse these six sets of functional specifications into one envelope, by determining the maximum or minimum value for each functional specification. The result of this operation will be a table with functional specifications for each task.

Concluding Remarks

Relating tasks to be trained to functional simulator requirements is not a simple operation. There are not enough data available in the literature to allow the specification of a simulator to be accurately determined. The cues used may vary between environments, tasks and pilots. The relationship between cues and functional simulator requirements is rather obscure. Nevertheless, using the method described in this chapter, an educated guess can be made on the functional simulator requirements to train a particular task. The advantage of this method is that it uses simple and basic measures. Vehicle parameters are commonly used in describing a task, they can be quantified easily, and they allow cues to be clustered into convenient groups. A second advantage of this method is that it is transparent. By using tables, the relations between the different steps (tasks, vehicle parameters, and functional requirements) are clear, and the origins of a functional specification can be traced. However, it should be noted that the method still relies on rules of thumb to derive functional specifications. The current state of simulator research simply does not allow more refined methods to be used.

Of course, this proposed approach does not capture all the cues that may be relevant. For instance, cues associated with the search, detection, and identification of objects and with the tracking of moving objects are not addressed. However, these cues might be readily accommodated by supplementing the intermediate set of vehicle parameters with moving object parameters and by mapping them onto each other. The essence remains clustering of molecular cues in terms of more molar skill and system parameters, as an aid in translating training requirements into cueing and simulator requirements. It is believed that this will facilitate communication between domain experts, training specialists, and simulation engineers.

22 Discussion and Conclusions

It will have become clear that training and training programme requirements have direct and far-reaching consequences for the functional specification of simulator requirements. For example, opting for a training strategy such as discovery learning necessitates a larger gaming area and perhaps also higher database resolution and a more sophisticated simulation model. Clearly, too, the creation of convincing illusions requires knowledge of the capabilities and limitations of the human perceptual system and of simulation technology. On the other hand, applying simulation technology and working around its limitations require knowledge of cues and their interactions. The latter knowledge is also a prerequisite in designing training scenarios, controlling scenario execution, tracking trainee performance, and optimising scenario tuning. Monitoring and controlling scenario execution and trainee performance may prevent trainees from wandering outside the intended training scenario envelope. Such a more highly directive approach may result in considerable savings in terms of simulator requirements. Scenario tuning allows simulator settings to be optimised for particular training activities. This may greatly enhance the effectiveness and efficiency of simulator training.

Matching training programme requirements to simulator requirements involves a number of translations. Each requires different kinds of expertise. Much of the available evidence has been reviewed here. Although there is considerable knowledge, it is not always in a form that enables all users to appreciate and exploit it fully. A problem in making this knowledge more accessible to users (subject matter experts, training specialists, and simulation engineers) is that they may have quite different backgrounds and interests. Moreover, the knowledge that is required in any particular case may be highly specific. This is one of the reasons why the specification process is likely to remain a highly iterative process requiring considerable expertise on the part of the user. It is not easy to keep track of such processes. Specific user support guidelines and tools will be needed to retain a clear focus throughout, to trace the evolution of the specification process, and to re-use results.

Although many useful guidelines are available, knowledge gaps remain that can be traced back to conceptual, methodological, technological, or organisational problems. In principle, many of these problems are surmountable. But this will require a common integrated approach.

In military simulation and training, knowledge is a highly dynamic, if not volatile, commodity. New operational concepts emerge that require new skills and new cues to be simulated. At the same time, technological developments continue to expand the possibilities of simulation. To keep up with these developments, a conceptual framework and methodology are required of sufficient abstraction and with sufficient coherence to tie together ideas and developments. Such a framework and methodology may provide an interface and a common perspective for those working in this area, and may help to organise and make accessible available expertise and to absorb new findings and developments. It may also assist in setting priorities for research and development. As one of the results of the MASTER project, ingredients and a blueprint for developing such a framework have been given. These cues, it is hoped, will be sufficiently inspiring to stimulate further work in this challenging area.

Section IV
Training Evaluation

23   Performance Measurement

Introduction

Two major uses of training evaluation can be distinguished: determination of the best method of delivering training, and assessment of the progress made by individual trainees. This section summarises the results of reviews of the literature, examination of current military practice, and experiments relevant to evaluation issues.

The work of the MASTER project included development of psychometrically sound, objective performance measures that can be applied to training, and demonstration of the useful role of workload measures. The available measures are summarised below, and the results of experimental evaluations are described. A clear requirement is for increased attention to the development of measures of unit rather than individual performance.

Although MASTER was concerned primarily with training, it was necessary to consider selection issues. Trainability testing, for example, is an important element of the training process, and errors at this stage may prove extremely costly. As will be seen, many European military establishments currently fail to apply rigorous measurement and data analysis procedures during both selection and training.

All simulator-based training depends upon effective transfer to the corresponding weapons system. This section only briefly addresses the long history of theoretical research on transfer, concentrating instead on the methodological issues in the measurement of transfer. Skill retention is also a key consideration of training programmes, since there may in some instances be a long interval between training and the requirement to exercise the acquired skills operationally. The need for refresher training can be assessed only if valid measures of the retention of training are available.

A standardised battery of generic performance and workload measures was produced as part of the MASTER project. This battery represents a set of core measures that can be applied to many military tasks.

Importance of Performance Measurement

The following questions might be asked during the development and administration of training programmes:
- To what extent is a particular applicant trainable?
- What is the rate of learning of a particular trainee?
- How much training is required to achieve mastery of a particular task?
- What are the effects of changes in the training regime on rate of learning?
- How often is refresher training required?
- Should realistic stressors be introduced during training?
- To what extent does training on a simulator transfer to performance using the real weapons system?

All these questions require sound methods of measuring performance. Failure to evaluate performance adequately will have profound implications for cost, effectiveness and safety. Selection of an unsuitable applicant for flying training, for example, may lead to wastage of more than 3m Euros in training costs; failure to provide sufficient refresher training may seriously compromise mission effectiveness; and improperly trained personnel are more likely to be involved in accidents.

Requirements for Performance Measurement

There is a requirement for valid performance measures that can track and monitor the skill acquisition process and verify that performance meets pre-determined criteria. Determination of performance standards is therefore an essential aspect of the development of training programmes. But it has been noted (Vreuls & Obermayer, 1985) that even sophisticated training simulators often have entirely inadequate systems for performance measurement. Sanders (1991) suggested that one underlying reason may be lack of interest in human performance issues among engineers responsible for simulator design, who devote more attention to physical fidelity. Sanders identified three problems of performance measurement:
- The nature of the skill: perceptual-motor skills are easier to measure than cognitive skills, such as decision making, that may be associated with little overt activity.
- Timelocking of responses to external stimuli: In complex tasks, the external events that triggered particular actions cannot always be clearly identified.
- Definition of optimal performance: In decision-making or even flying tasks, it may be difficult to define clear and unequivocal criteria for optimal performance.

Booher (1990) criticised the concept of objective performance measures, arguing that they do not allow for measurement of meaningful tasks in realistic environments. He suggested that data gathered by a computer can represent only low-level phenomena, such as switch closure, rather than the preceding complex process of perceiving and deciding, and that there may be no clear structure of rules for the systematic integration of low-level measures into a global index. It is argued here, however, that careful analysis of performance data, such as the decomposition of reaction time, can reveal much concerning covert cognitive processes.

Berliner *et al* (1964) specified a two-stage process for identifying performance standards. The first involves selection of the specific behaviours of interest, typically those required for successful achievement of the job; Berliner *et al* suggested a classification system to identify commonalities across tasks during this process. At the second stage, the required levels of proficiency must be specified, perhaps using the achievement of highly accomplished operators in the simulator as the criterion.

Performance must be compared to the required standard to determine whether the trainee is sufficiently competent or more training is required. Vreuls and Obermayer (1985), however, noted deficiencies in the predictive validity of performance measures in training, and a lack of quantitative criteria to assess the importance of performance changes and to relate such changes to overall system or mission effectiveness. They suggested that the following issues should be considered:

- operational figures of merit (measures of system effectiveness related to tasks and operating environments);
- automated performance measurement able to cope with changing human strategies;
- performance diagnosis to determine the source of trainees' errors;
- the strategies that may be adopted during task performance;
- the development of skills to the level of expert performance rather than a minimum standard.

Level of Analysis

In psychology, experiments initially followed the 'small and simple' paradigm, in which attempts were made to study individual elements of performance such as memory or motor control. This paradigm is open to criticism (Sanders, 1984, 1991). For example, the delays in responses made in rapid succession, as found in laboratory studies of reaction time and attributed to a psychological refractory period, do not occur in real-world activities such as skilled typing or piano playing. Further, even simple laboratory tasks do not allow us to study single mental processes in isolation. Although the problems of this approach might suggest that the study of complex tasks is preferable, Sanders noted that this too is problematic. Performance on such tasks is difficult to measure and may involve a large number of variables, and studies at this level often fail to improve understanding or produce only trivial results.

The approach taken in MASTER was therefore to produce a method for mission and task analysis that would result in associated skill taxonomies. These methodologies were intended to direct those charged with training design to the performance measures most meaningful for training.

Objective versus Subjective Measures

Both subjective and objective measures have a role in training programmes. Subjective measures represent the opinion of the trainee or of a subject-matter expert such as an instructor, and may be based upon a rating scale. Objective measures are collected directly from performance, such as deviation from a required track.

Subjective measures tend to be easier to use and less expensive to obtain than objective measures. Expert evaluation by a trained observer can take into account specific situational circumstances, knowledge of the individual trainee's experience and abilities, expectations of a typical trainee at a particular stage of training, and the types of mistake likely to be made. The observer can also form an assessment of performance in real time, continuously updating and integrating information from a number of sources. However, subjective assessments are liable to be influenced by biases, pre-conceptions and memory limitations. Moreover, a summary judgement may be unduly influenced by significant performance peaks or troughs, and inter-rater reliability may be low. Such difficulties led Obermayer and Vreuls (1972) to conclude that objective performance assessment was required to achieve training research goals. Several possible objective measures were explored and validated in MASTER.

In the context of training, performance measures should fulfil the following roles:

- monitoring the progress of the trainee by evaluating learning and attainment;
- indicating sources of learning difficulties;
- providing feedback to the instructor and/or trainee;
- allowing comparison with criteria specified at the beginning of training;
- measuring transfer of training;
- measuring skill retention;
- evaluating training and sequencing methods;
- assessing the effects of physical system parameters;
- assessing the effects of stressors and high workload.

Objective and subjective forms of feedback   Consideration of the timing and specificity of the feedback offered to the trainee is essential to maximise the effectiveness of training. Knowledge of performance during training, especially if objectively measured, can have positive effects on both performance and motivation (Wainwright & Hone, 1995). Spiker *et al* (1997) suggested that the capacity of simulation to provide objective data after the event is considerably more useful than subjective and peer-dependent feedback. However, the kind of feedback that an instructor provides is considered important. The MASTER study by van Rooij *et al* (1996) canvassed opinion on this topic, and reported that trainees wanted more feedback than performance scores alone.

Types of Performance Measure

The most appropriate performance measure will be determined by the nature of the training task. However, several common types of measure can be identified. Perhaps the most widely used are reaction time (RT) and error rate to discrete stimuli, which provide a summary of the output and efficiency of information processing. A simple method of selecting performance measures is to classify the task according to whether it places demands primarily on input processes (detection and recognition of stimuli), central processes (storage and manipulation of information) or output processes (such as manual or vocal responses). For example, in a tracking task there is greatest interest in manual control processes. Measures relevant to different types of task are described below.

Monitoring

For tasks involving stimuli that are clearly above the threshold of detection, RT and accuracy measures are usually sufficient. However, tasks involving detection of very weak signals require special analysis, by means of Signal Detection Theory (SDT). In SDT (e.g., Green & Swets, 1966; Egan, 1975), it is assumed that noise is present on each sensory channel, and that its magnitude is normally distributed (since noise is by definition random); the presentation of a stimulus causes a translation of this distribution along the axis of sensory activity by an amount proportional to the intensity of the stimulus. Performance under these circumstances can be influenced not only by the quality of the signal but also by bias in the observer.

SDT is applied only to cases in which there is overlap between the 'noise' and 'signal plus noise' distributions. It is useful for the analysis of performance on monitoring or vigilance tasks (e.g., the detection of sonar signals or signals on noisy analogue radar displays). The operator's task is to decide whether the current level of sensory activity originates in the noise distribution (no signal) or the signal plus noise distribution (signal present). Thus, SDT could be applied to a subject sitting in a quiet, dark room waiting for a weak auditory or visual stimulus, but not to a subject required to detect the illumination of a 40-Watt lightbulb under such conditions. In other words, SDT is applicable in any situation in which signal and noise cannot be easily discriminated. Typically, signals are reported 'present' or 'absent' by the operator, and there are four possible outcomes: hits, misses, false alarms and correct rejections.

SDT rejects the notion of a simple sensory threshold beyond which all stimuli are detected. Rather, it assumes two important determinants of performance: d' (discriminability) and ß (response criterion). The measure d' indicates the distance between the means of the noise and signal plus noise distributions; it is affected not only by task variables such as stimulus intensity and display quality but also by subject variables such as fatigue. The measure ß, however, indicates the strictness of the subject's criterion for deciding that a signal has been presented; for example, if ß is high the subject will commit few false alarms but will miss a high proportion of signals. The most appropriate ß will be determined by the characteristics of the task. If the operator must ensure that all signals are detected and there is little penalty for false alarms, a low criterion is appropriate; if, however, false alarms are costly and detection of all signals is not imperative, a higher criterion should be adopted. Although d' and ß can be computed mathematically, tables are available to derive these measures from the observed proportions of hits and false alarms.

In real-world environments, the response criterion (ß) may be biased by a particular operator's beliefs and knowledge concerning the probability of a signal or event. For example, doctors will adjust their response criterion in diagnosis according to their knowledge of the frequency with which a disease occurs within the population (Lusted, 1976). In a military context, a pilot's expectation of the presence of hostile aircraft in a particular area could result in an increase in false alarms, even to the extent of mistaking a friendly for a hostile aircraft.

Reaction Time and Accuracy

RT, defined as the interval between presentation of a stimulus and execution of a response, is one of the most common measures of human performance.

RT improves with practice, and can be used as an index of level of attainment during training, particularly for sub-tasks that involve responses to discrete stimuli. There are two major categories of RT: simple and choice. In simple RT, only one stimulus-response pairing is used. In choice RT, two or more stimuli are presented, each with an associated response. Naturally, choice RT is usually longer than simple RT, and tends to increase with the number of stimuli and responses.

RT is affected by a number of task-related variables, including the presence of a warning before the stimulus is presented, the length of the 'foreperiod' (i.e., the interval between the warning and stimulus), the variability of the foreperiod, and the compatibility of stimuli and responses. In training, these variables should match as closely as possible the characteristics of the operational system.

RT represents a measure of the time required for all the mental processes involved in detecting, interpreting and responding to a stimulus (including the programming of the movement required). Since the pioneering work by Donders (1869), attempts have been made to decompose RT into its components (e.g., detection and discrimination), as the basis of 'chronometric' analysis of mental processes (Posner, 1978). Sternberg (1969), for example, decomposed total response time using the 'Additive Factor' method, which identified at least five different stages of processing: (a) stimulus processing or encoding; (b) response choice; (c) motor programming; (d) motor activation; and (e) response execution.

When there is particular interest in the motor component of a skill, movement time (MT) of the hand or arm should be recorded separately. MT is defined as the time between initiation and completion of the response to a stimulus (Singleton, 1953; Bjorklund, 1992; Jensen, 1982; Baker *et al*, 1986). When the subject has to use muscles specific to the response task, electro-myography (EMG) can be used to measure MT. If, for instance, the subject has to react by pressing a button with his index finger, the EMG of the *interosseous dorsalis* can give the onset of the movement (Geraats, 1991).

As with RT, MT has been found to be affected by a variety of task-related variables such as temporal factors (Teichner, 1954; Wilkinson, 1969; Welford, 1968, 1980). For example, a short foreperiod generates a general preparedness in the motor system to respond rapidly, whereas longer foreperiods decrease preparedness (Bjorklund, 1992). Unlike RT, however, MT is not affected by time on task, suggesting that slowing of sensorimotor performance owes more to the effects of fatigue on perceptual/cognitive than on motor processes. Attentional strategy appears to have an effect on MT (Henry, 1960; Ona, 1990). When instructed to focus on the movement required in a response, subjects show shorter MTs but longer pre-motor RTs; on the other hand, when subjects are instructed to focus on both the stimulus and the movement required, improvements are found both on the perceptual/cognitive component of RT and on MT (Ona, 1990).

Fitts described the relationship of MT with movement amplitude (A) and target width (W) as follows:

$$MT = a+b \ \log_2(2A/W)$$
where a and b are constants

This relationship (Fitts's Law) describes a speed-accuracy trade-off in movement, and can be considered an index of difficulty. Movements of equal difficulty can be created using different combinations of distance and target width.

These laboratory results are relevant to training, since it is important to know which task factors prove difficult for trainees. Is the performance for a tank gunner suboptimal for reasons associated with visual target identification or difficulties with handling the controls in a smooth manner? The manipulation of stimuli such as targets, type of terrain or weapon automation support, as defined in the training scenario, can assist in identifying the limiting factors for trainee performance.

In the MASTER experiments described later, a simple measure of percentage errors was found to satisfy the psychometric and practical criteria defined for use in training programmes. However, under some circumstances it may be desirable to analyse errors in greater detail for diagnostic purposes.

Decision Making

Decision making is a complex human activity for which it is difficult to set unequivocal performance criteria. In many military weapon systems, the operator's tasks are highly proceduralised and involve selection of actions from a relatively well-defined range of options. Thus, rule-based rather than knowledge-based behaviour (Rasmussen, 1986a, b) is of particular relevance.

Although understanding of decision-making processes is incomplete, there is evidence from aviation that decision-making skills can be trained. In response to research by Jensen and Benel (1977) showing that decision errors were implicated in many aircraft accidents, training courses in Aeronautical Decision Making (ADM) were developed. Diehl (1991) confirmed that decision-making skills improved following such training. There is interest in two aspects of decision making (e.g., Jensen, 1995): rational judgement or 'headwork' (based on examination of the available evidence, diagnosis of problems, and risk assessment), and motivational judgement or 'attitudes' (influenced by the individual's biases and personality, and sometimes leading to apparently irrational decisions). Berlin *et al* (1982) identified five hazardous attitudes encountered in aviation: anti-authority, resignation, impulsivity, invulnerability, and macho.

Recently, there has been interest in 'naturalistic decision making' (NDM), which emphasises that, under time pressure in risky and rapidly changing situations, experienced decision makers do not adopt the lengthy procedure of examining each possible course of action in turn to find the optimal solution (e.g., Klein *et al*, 1993). Klein's recognition primed decision making (RPD) theory (Klein, 1989), for example, suggests that experienced operators use their past experience rapidly to find a satisfactory solution rather than necessarily the optimal one (so-called 'satisficing' behaviour).

Although the NDM approach offers promise, it is not yet sufficiently well advanced to incorporate into training programmes, and difficulties with measuring aspects of decision making remain.

Subjective reports Sanders (1991) points to the use of verbal reports as a means of making explicit the underlying cognitive processes. The verbal report approach has several variants, the major distinction being between a) retrospective and concurrent verbalisation, b) verbally and non-verbally coded information, and c) whether or not the instructions interfere with the original task. Ericsson and Simon (1980) showed that, when subjects report on verbally-represented issues, the original internal processes change little in terms of content or speed of processing. If, on the other hand, verbal recoding is required due to the information being in the form of images or automatised perceptual-motor representations, then the original flow of processing may slow down and the verbal reports may be incomplete or incorrect, especially where recoding is hard to accomplish.

The more objective measurement of decision making has been addressed in two major ways: examination of the outcome, and examination of the decision process.

Consideration of the outcome of decisions: accuracy of choice Hudgens and Fatkin (1985) introduced rewards and penalties for making the correct or wrong decision. Adoption of a scoring procedure enabled comparisons to be made between runs. Grether and Wilde (1983) used frequency of selection of dominant alternatives as a measure of decision quality to identify whether the correct decision had been made. Rothstein (1986) investigated consistency of decision-making behaviour: did the decision maker make the same judgement or choice when later faced with the same stimuli?

Consideration of the processes involved in decision making Payne and Braunstein (1978) investigated the number of alternatives and risks of decisions. The process-tracing method (a method for viewing decision processes) was used in a gambling task. A number of measures were derived: amount of processing; selectivity of processing; degree of alternative-based (different risk dimensions) vs attribute-based (same risk dimension/different gamble) processing. Bettman *et al* (1990) adopted a method of controlled process-tracing: number of times information was returned to; average time spent on items; effectiveness (maximisation of accuracy) vs efficiency (minimisation of effort) of the decision process; and decision latency. In the MASTER project, a novel automatic method of error analysis during simulator-based training was tested. This method considers the following types of error:

- Interpretation errors: the trainee may fail correctly to interpret all the elements relevant to his decision making, and will therefore follow an inappropriate plan or schema.

- Planning errors: even if the trainee correctly interprets the situation, he may incorrectly sequence the actions related to his short-term intentions.
- Execution errors: correct interpretation and formulation of appropriate intentions do not guarantee error-free performance; the trainee may still incorrectly execute the actions required to perform the task. Examples of execution errors include errors of omission, inversion (of the order of actions), repetition, insertion, 'finger errors' (if switches are located close together), delay, and mode (a type of error relevant to modern multi-modal displays).

Continuous Manual Control

Manual control is typified by the 'tracking' task, in which the subject attempts to maintain the position of a moving cursor on a target using an appropriate control device such as a joystick. Usually, the cursor is subject to perturbation by a forcing function (cf. flying in a cross wind). Many sub-tasks in military vehicles and weapons systems can be considered tracking tasks. For example, in attempting to fly straight and level using the attitude indicator, the pilot must maintain the position of the horizon bar (cursor) on the fixed aircraft symbol (target) using the control column (control device).

Three major types of tracking task can be distinguished: compensatory, pursuit, and critical instability tracking. In compensatory tracking, the target is stationary, and only the error (distance of the cursor from the target) is displayed; this is analogous to a pilot attempting to maintain the position of a moving horizon bar on the fixed aircraft symbol, or a driver attempting to keep the needle on the 70 mph marker of the speedometer while experiencing variable headwinds. In pursuit tracking, both the cursor and the target move; this is analogous to attempting to keep a weapon sight centred on a moving target. In critical instability tracking, a positive feedback system is used in which the subject's error is magnified, and complete loss of control is possible. This type of tracking, used in the USAF Criterion Task Set, is analogous to balancing a stick on the end of the finger: if a particular level of error is exceeded, control of the stick is irretrievably lost.

In tracking tasks, a number of control laws may affect performance, such as control order (the response to a control input as change in position, velocity, or acceleration), lag (delay between control input and system output) and gain (the magnitude of the effect of a given control input). However, these characteristics will be determined by the system under consideration, and, since they are independent of the performance measures used, they will not be considered further here.

Tracking measures are typically based on sampling the distance between the actual and desired position of the cursor at frequent intervals. Many measures can be derived from these data (Poulton, 1974), the most common of which are modulus mean (MM) error and root mean square (RMS) error (Hammerton, 1981). MM error is simply the mean of the absolute values of the error scores:

$$MM = \Sigma \, |x|/n$$
where

$$x = \text{individual error scores}$$
$$n = \text{number of observations}$$

RMS error, on the other hand, is based on squared error values:

$$RMS = \sqrt{(\Sigma x^2/n)}$$

RMS error was adopted in the MASTER project, since it is the more widely used, and penalises inconsistent performance. For example, individual error values of 2, 4, and 3 would lead to a greater RMS error than values of 3, 3, and 3; MM error, on the other hand, would be the same in each instance.

The actual measurement of tracking performance is not simple, and requires good co-ordination between the scenario design and the measurement tools. Consider a pilot flying a 360-degree 'rate one' turn. This manoeuvre might be performed perfectly, but not initiated at the right moment. The distance from the desired tracks would thus be consistently, but artificially, counted as very high, depending on the time offset. The offset effect must be corrected before analysing the execution of the manoeuvre itself. This can be done by hand, but a computer would require a manoeuvre recognition module to do so automatically. The complexities involved can be handled in a laboratory, but are more difficult to interpret in real training situations.

Current Applications of Performance Measures

Wigdor and Green (1991) reported the outcome of the work of the Committee on the Performance of Military Personnel, established in 1983 to address joint-service job performance measurement. Although there is a clear distinction between measurement of job performance and training performance, it is likely that similar principles will be applicable to each. Wigdor and Green described the steps in developing job performance measures:

- definition of the job content universe: all tasks and behaviours required to perform them;
- definition of the job content domain: a smaller set of essential tasks;
- specification of the domain of testable tasks: tasks for which measurement is feasible;
- development of performance measures: suitable tasks translated into test items.

According to Wigdor and Green, the job content universe can be defined using task analysis, trait analysis (based on human abilities), task-by-trait analysis, or cognitive task analysis. The approach adopted by MASTER included most of these elements: (operator) task analysis for military vehicles and mobile weapons operations; consideration of the abilities required to perform these tasks; and a skill taxonomy that considered the cognitive processes required by the tasks. Examples of performance measurement in training are provided later in this section in the context of selection, transfer of training, and skill retention.

Most measurement of the actual *processes* involved in the performance of individual trainees or teams is currently still subjective. More objective measures can be found with respect to the *outcomes* of task performance.

Process Measures

Process measures usually take the form of assessments by subject matter experts of how well a task is executed in terms of 'correct' actions and behaviours. Often based on behaviourially anchored rating scales, such measures include the Team Observation Measurement System (TOMS) described by Meliza *et al* (1994) or scales developed from the Team Dimensional Training (TDT) model (McDevitt, 1998). An alternative approach uses a checklist format — sometimes with weightings for key items or groups of items — that records either correct actions or errors. Error checklists provide more immediately useable and standardised feedback to trainers and trainees, whereas SMEs often feel more confident in identifying what has been done wrong than what has been done right. If such a bias is not controlled, negative feedback may become dominant. However, a weakness of error checklists is that they do not help to identify errors of omission.

Outcome or Product Measures

Measures of outcome or product are more readily provided objectively. For most simulators, and especially for interactive simulators using digital data, software packages are available that record, aggregate, analyse and present data flexibly and effectively. The US Unit Performance Assessment Software (UPAS) reported by Meliza *et al* (1992, 1994) provides a suite of research tools. Using Distributed Interactive Simulation (DIS) protocols, it analyses the time-stamp data in a protocol data unit to provide a range of useful measures. It also incorporates a sophisticated training interface, and allows the user to identify:

- the tasks to be trained;
- the individual or group of individuals to be assessed;
- the timescale or event to be assessed;
- the measures to be collected (e.g., hit/kill ratios; time to first shot; hits received);
- the type of output (e.g., graph, table, display of critical events as a series of freeze-frames).

Subsequent developments (e.g., 'STRIPES') have incorporated additional features, and the UK has developed a package called Exercise Analysis for Collective Training (ExACT; Kelly, 1995). Although ExACT lacks the training interface, it incorporates some important new measurement features. It includes the facility to combine the data components into any new combination or metric. More importantly, it records both positional and time-stamp data in a protocol data unit, enabling generation of a number of new metrics (e.g., the dispersion of a tank platoon on the ground, the lines of inter-visibility between tanks and targets, or the arcs of fire or areas of dead ground from a given position). In many instances, the appropriate measures or metrics for collective performance are still a matter of debate; tools such as UPAS and ExACT provide a means of generating and collecting objective measures that may be subjected to meta-analysis (examination of trends across various sets of data).

Visual Monitoring and Feedback Facilities

A key feature of DIS is that the digital format provides the capacity for more complete and accurate capture of events. The scenario, the entities, the actions of participants and computer-generated forces, and the effects of those actions can all be recorded on disk or tape. They are not replayed with one viewpoint as in a video, but are reconstructed by the system and can then be viewed from any position or perspective. This means that enhanced facilities are available for performance monitoring, for diagnosis and assessment, and for feedback. The fact that events can be seen from any viewpoint provides a potentially useful teaching facility. For example, it could be used for training:

- optimal location of sensors;
- concealment strategies (for example, trainees could see how they appear to an enemy gunner, or how to plan routes to maximise concealment from radar);
- co-ordination of battlefield assets;
- situational awareness (trainees could be taught what kinds of information are important).

As well as enhancing feedback processes, these types of visual facility can provide more accurate and reliable assessments. Assessors can view performance in slow time, note the relative position of players at key events, consider how a group moves together across the terrain, and then give a detailed diagnosis of strengths and weaknesses. Visual playback can also be provided to resolve ambiguities or to settle points of disagreement.

Evaluation of Performance Measures

On the basis of a literature review, the MASTER skill taxonomy, and the military functions identified as relevant to the project, candidate generic performance and workload measures were selected for further scrutiny. The general strategy adopted was to identify performance measures suitable for each specific type of task, and workload measures applicable to any task. The performance measures selected were RT for discrete responses; accuracy of discrete responses; root mean square (RMS) error, and responses to a decision-making questionnaire. A measure of team performance was also tested.

Experiment 1 used a task designed to include elements of the operational tasks of navigation and co-ordination. The navigation element included the tasks of knowledge of map position and the planning of routes, to enable the assessment of skills such as matching and decision making; the co-ordination element involved three tasks: planning, exchanging information and adjusting plans, to assess the skills of decision making and communication.

Experiment 2 was based on tasks developed to address the functions of mobility and weapon delivery, and included presence or absence of feedback to subjects to determine its effects on learning. Subjects flew a route from waypoint to waypoint over simulated terrain, maintaining heading and altitude within pre-specified limits, and tracked a target aircraft by means of a head-tracking device incorporated into their helmet, eventually performing weapon delivery.

In Experiment 3, subjects performed a target acquisition task; included were elements of the operational tasks of searching, detecting, identifying and evaluating new tactical situations. A modified version of the electronic map task developed by the UK Army Personnel Research Establishment (now part of the DERA Centre for Human Sciences) was devised. Subjects were required to detect and respond to symbols presented on the map display, identifying them as a 'target' or 'non-target' and indicating the direction and level of threat of those perceived to be targets. At the end of some runs, subjects were asked to report how they had made their decisions regarding the overall threat level represented by the targets.

Experiment 4 addressed self-defence, using a validated threat assessment task. Hostile aircraft were represented as travelling at a range of speeds and of relative closure angles to the subject's own aircraft. On each trial, the subject's task was to decide which of three hostile aircraft presented the most immediate threat. Task difficulty was manipulated using two different display types: a textual display and a pictorial form of display shown in previous studies to simplify threat assessment.

In Experiment 5, system management was addressed using the Multi-Attribute Task (MAT) Battery developed by NASA to simulate piloting tasks. The MAT battery comprises several task elements performed concurrently; those used in the experiment were tracking, monitoring, and resource management. A further communication task was available, but was not used in this experiment. In the compensatory tracking task, the subject was required to keep the target located in the centre of a window using a joystick; in the monitoring task, the subject monitored four vertical scales and two lights for changes in system state; and in the resource management task, the subject turned pumps on or off to maintain the level of fuel in two tanks.

The RT measures were found to be sensitive to training, and it was recommended that they be used in tasks requiring discrete responses. Accuracy of discrete responses was also used successfully as a measure of learning (see Figure 23.1). The RMS error in continuous manual control tasks was similarly found to be useful. The decision-making questionnaire was difficult to score, and would have little value in training programmes.

The recommended measures all satisfied a range of psychometric and practical criteria, such as validity, reliability, sensitivity and ease of use. Many of the measures reached asymptote even during the relatively short training periods employed in the experiments. There was little evidence, however, that the feedback concerning performance had a beneficial effect on learning, with the exception of learning the light monitoring task.

In other experiments, Farmer *et al* (1997) tested the proposed automatic method for detection of omission, inversion and delay errors in a simulated flight task. It was found that this technique was successful, and that it could be used as an automated method of assessing trainee progress. Moreover, examination of the types of errors committed by particular trainees could permit training to be tailored to individual requirements. In these experiments, there was evidence that the provision of feedback to trainees did enhance their performance.

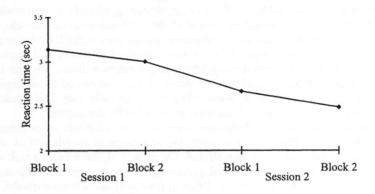

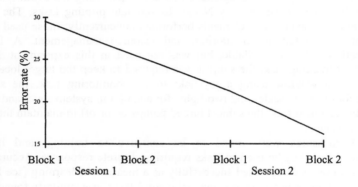

Figure 23.1. Reaction time & error rate for threat assessment in Expt. 3

The outcome of these experiments guided the construction of a standardised battery of performance measures, and the findings were incorporated in the MASTER software tools. Most of the measures will be easy to derive from simulator-based tasks, and will incur little additional cost. The generic nature of the measures will, however, necessitate translation to the particular domains of application to be readily understandable by the trainee. A tank gunner needs no information on overall RT, but information on time elapsed between using the laser to acquire distance and initiation of the actual shot. If the shot took so long that the measured distance lost its validity, the projectile would over- or undershoot the target.

24 Workload Measurement

Importance of Workload Measurement

Training in complex, multiple-component tasks must extend beyond the attainment of a criterion level of performance to that of 'overlearned behaviour'. Such a learning state is characterised by automatisation of sub-skills and freeing of mental resources to cope with other concurrent demands or stressful circumstances (in simplistic terms, greater 'spare mental capacity'). Conventional measures of performance are insensitive to changes during overlearning, whereas many workload measures are specifically designed to indicate spare capacity. The term workload in the context of training is defined as the 'effort' that an individual has to invest to achieve a certain level of performance. In the context of scenarios or tasks, workload is often referred to as reflecting the *external* demands imposed by the situation. For experienced operators a high external workload does not necessitate a high individual workload, due to the extensive level of practice. The same conditions, however, may result in overload for a less experienced operator or a trainee.

Practice on a task leads to the development of automatic 'motor programmes' that place minimal demands upon central cognitive processes. Schneider and Shiffrin (1977) demonstrated a clear shift from 'controlled' to 'automatic' processing with extended practice that was apparent in greatly improved performance.

For all complex military tasks, it is essential that training produce maximum automaticity of behaviour. Such behaviour is classified as skill-based in Rasmussen's (e.g., 1986a, b) system, and is distinguished from the rule-based and knowledge-based behaviour that requires more conscious consideration of information. However, one of the major disadvantages of skill-based behaviour is that it is associated with certain types of error, described by Reason (1990) as 'strong but wrong' behaviour. In other words, a highly practised activity is likely to be performed proficiently but may not be appropriate to the situation. Most absent-minded behaviour occurs when the individual performs inappropriate but well-learned behaviour when conscious attention is directed elsewhere (e.g., pouring milk into the sugar bowl).

Types of Workload Measure

Workload measures must satisfy the criteria shown in Table 24.1. Since no single measure is likely to satisfy all these criteria, and since mental workload is multi-dimensional in nature (Kramer, 1990), a battery of measures is often used. The major categories of workload measure (see Aasman *et al*, 1987; Schick & Hahn, 1987; Wilson, 1993) are described below.

Table 24.1. Criteria that workload measures should satisfy

Criterion	Description
Validity	The measure must genuinely provide an indication of mental workload
Reliability	The measure must yield consistent and replicable scores under given conditions
Sensitivity	The measure must discriminate with sufficient precision between different levels of external workload
Task-independence	The measure should be applicable to any training task
Acceptability	Trainers and trainees must consider the measure to be acceptable as an index of workload
Selectivity	The measure should be unaffected by variables other than workload, or these effects should be controllable
Diagnosticity	There may be a requirement that the measure indicate the precise source of unacceptable levels of workload
Bandwidth	The measure should be sensitive to a sufficient range of variations in workload
Intrusiveness	The measurement procedure should not interfere with performance on the training task
Ease of use	The measure should be easy to administer by the trainer, and should not produce unacceptable demands for data analysis

Performance-based Measures

Performance on the primary task (in this context, the training task) can reflect the effects of level of workload, at least prior to overlearning. However, primary task measures, such as RMS error and RT and errors to discrete stimuli, represent global rather than diagnostic measures of workload, giving little indication of which of the capacities or resources are affected by changes in demand (Eggemeier, 1988). Performance on a secondary task can be used as a measure of the demands of the primary task. Some of the secondary tasks used in workload studies are described below.

Interval production Subjects find it increasingly difficult to tap at a constant rate as workload increases.

Time estimation The passage of time is progressively underestimated as workload increases. Elapsed time will, on the other hand, be overestimated when assessed afterwards.

Random number generation Under high workload, subjects instructed to produce a series of random numbers tend increasingly to resort to well-learned sequences (e.g., 1, 2, 3); this decrease in the degree of randomness can be quantified mathematically.

Probe reaction time Under high workload, reaction time to a discrete external stimulus is likely to increase. This secondary task can consist of a straightforward reaction task, such as an 'oddball', but may also include memory search elements. An auditory version of Sternberg's (1969, 1975) memory search task has been used, for example, with a fixed memory set of four letters. An extended version uses mental counting to create a more continuous load on short-term memory. This Continuous Memory Task (CMT) has been standardised and was successfully applied to training and selection issues, such as the assessment of trainability of candidate pilots and the effects of anxiety and stress on performance (Jorna 1989a, b; Jorna & Visser, 1991).

Subjective Measures

A common method of assessing workload is to use rating scales. However, one difficulty associated with workload measurement is that little attention has been given to the underlying structure of mental workload (Farmer, 1993a, b). Although it is generally agreed that workload is multidimensional, the nature of its dimensions remains elusive. This is illustrated by the different number and types of rating scales used in multidimensional subjective techniques such as the Subjective Workload Assessment Technique (SWAT) and the NASA Task Load Index (TLX). Subjective workload measures have been applied most often to aviation environments, but in general would be suitable also for land- and sea-based tasks. Examples include:

Modified Cooper-Harper and Bedford Scales These are 10-point unidimensional scales based on a decision-tree, derived from a scale originally devised for the assessment of aircraft handling qualities; they are easy to use and have face validity.

Instantaneous Subjective Assessment (ISA) The subject presses one of five buttons to indicate level of workload. This is a relatively unobtrusive method, but only a rough estimate of workload is derived.

Subjective Workload Assessment Technique (SWAT) Ratings are obtained on three subscales; scoring using this method is fairly complex.

NASA Task Load Index (TLX) One of the most commonly used techniques, generating ratings and importance weightings for six subscales such as mental demand and frustration.

Rating Scale Mental Effort (RSME) This uni-dimensional scale originates from the effort scale 'beoordelingsschaal mentale inspanning' (BSMI) developed in the Netherlands (Zijlstra & van Doorn, 1985). The RSME asks for the amount of effort that has to be invested during task performance. Guidance is provided by textual labels to improve the consistency of the ratings. The response is given on a vertical axis ranging from 0 to 150.

Defence Research Agency Workload Scales (DRAWS) Four workload factors were derived from an extensive set of workload data obtained for a wide variety of tasks. The factors are input demand, central demand, output demand, and time pressure. A separate scale represents each factor.

Physiological Measures

A wide variety of physiological measures has been used, many of which are based on the notion that the operator's level of arousal will increase under high external workload. Physiological measures have the following advantages: they can be obtained continuously, they do not necessarily intrude into the operator's primary task (Wilson, 1993), and in some instances they provide even more information when coupled with performance measures. Their disadvantages are that they may be difficult to obtain under operational conditions and they sometimes reflect factors other than workload (Kakimoto *et al*, 1988). The major types of measure are discussed below.

Heart rate (HR) and heart rate variability (HRV) HR is often used as a simple index of mental workload, since it generally increases when the task becomes more demanding. A disadvantage is that HR measures can easily vary with physical effort, emotions and stress. In fact, Lee and Parks (1990) found that even minor motor actions such as finger tapping led to increases in HR. Averaging of the inter-beat-intervals will reduce the resolution of the HR measure over time. Variability in HR appears to be more sensitive to changes in mental demands, particularly if spectral decomposition of the data is conducted. In various laboratory experiments (Roscoe *et al*, 1978; Mulder, 1980; Mulder & Mulder, 1981) power in the mid-frequency band (0.07-0.14 Hz) of the HRV spectrum diminished during tasks that required mental effort. HRV has produced results where average HR has failed to do so (Jorna, 1991). Besides a reported sensitivity to the mental effort associated with task execution, HRV has been reported to be sensitive to changes in emotional responses as a function of repeated exposure to threatening or risky working environments. Such an adaptation process is commonly denoted as 'coping', indicating a learning process in handling tasks under special circumstances. An example is the coping process associated with military working environments as reported for military divers (Jorna, 1984) and pilots in training (Jorna, 1993). An extensive review of HRV responsiveness to both task and environmental factors can be found in Jorna (1992). Recent work has indicated that HRV measurement supports more objective workload assessment for complex cognitive tasks such as air traffic control (Hilburn *et al*, 1995, 1996a, b; Jorna, 1997b) and tactical co-ordination in maritime patrol aircraft (Zon *et al*, 1999). As respiration is known to affect HRV, additional respiratory measures are needed as a control measure, and speaking should be monitored or even prevented to enable accurate interpretation of HRV data.

Event related heart rate response Heart rate changes can be investigated in relation to specific task or scenario events. A response to a system failure is expected to normalise as a function of repeated exposure to the event. This technique has been used in laboratory experiments. Recent work applied it to the flight deck environment and demonstrated sensitivity to different display configurations of data link systems (Jorna, 1997a).

Blood pressure (BP) Veldman (1992) found that BP increased as a consequence of the effort required during task performance. BP must be measured continuously, using, for example, the 'Portapress', which receives a signal from cuffs around two fingers of one hand (Imholz *et al*, 1993). These two fingers cannot be used for task-related activities during measurement, because their bending would produce artefacts; hence, BP measurement may be rather intrusive.

Respiration Wientjes (1993) found that mental effort and mild stress are generally associated with an increase in respiration rate (number of breaths per minute), a decrease in tidal volume (the volume displaced during each breath) and an increase in minute ventilation (the volume of air displaced per minute). Graded variations in mental effort are accompanied by clear respiratory changes. Respiration rate provides very little physiologically meaningful information unless it is combined with volume measures.

Electroencephalogram and event-related potentials The brain's electrical activity detected at the scalp is a composite signal reflecting the activity of many neurons and brain structures. This spontaneous or ongoing activity can be plotted as a voltage x time function, resulting in an electroencephalogram (EEG). The EEG can be subjected to spectral analysis to determine the power in a number of relevant frequency bands, such as 4-7 Hz (theta), 8-12 Hz (alpha), and 18-30 Hz (beta). In general, the energy of low frequency EEG spectral bands, such as alpha, increases during prolonged and continuous performance (Parasuraman, 1986). Event-related potentials (ERPs) represent the responses of the brain to a discrete stimulus and can be distinguished by latency, amplitude, polarity, topography, and sensitivity to experimental manipulations and instructions (Mulder, 1986). The P300 (positive polarity, with 300msec latency between the onset of the stimulus and the beginning of the ERP) has received special attention. There are a number of methods by which the P300 may be recorded. It is also possible to assess the workload of a task by determining the P300 elicited by the task itself. This is called the P300 to the primary task. The results of several studies (Kramer *et al*, 1985; Donchin *et al*, 1987) have revealed an increase in the amplitude of the P300 as a result of an increase in task difficulty, and the ability of the P300 component to reflect differences between two levels of workload (Isreal *et al*, 1979).

Pupil size Pupil size is influenced not only by visual parameters but also by stress, arousal, and mental processing of information. The autonomic nervous system controls this response, which is entirely involuntary. Changing pupil diameter is a task-evoked response that provides a very sensitive index of workload (O'Donnell & Eggemeier, 1986). Dilation has been observed to increase with increasing cognitive workload, during both perceptual and reasoning tasks. Recent studies of complex air traffic management tasks have confirmed such sensitivity (Hilburn *et al*, 1996a, b, c).

Blink pattern Blink rate seems to vary with the difficulty of a task and to be related to muscle tension (Roscoe *et al*, 1978). Wierwille and Eggemeier (1993) described a number of studies in which a relationship was found between blink rate and visual workload: blink rate decreased with increases in visual processing demands (Krebs *et al*, 1977; Sirevaag *et al*, 1993). The inverse relationship can be attributed to attempts to minimise the likelihood of missing important information (Baumstimler & Parrot, 1971).

Biochemical measures The hormones nor-adrenaline and adrenaline, known as catecholamines, are secreted by the medulla and tend to augment the action of the sympathetic nervous system (SNS). Catecholamines have been used as indicators of short term stress, workload, and fatigue. To measure the level of catecholamines, blood, urine, or saliva must be collected. This last technique may also be of value for assessing short-term workload (Roscoe *et al*, 1978; Farmer *et al*, 1991). Cortisol gives an estimate of the state of a person over relatively longer time periods. Farmer *et al* (1991) reported greater cortisol excretion among civil air traffic controllers during busy periods.

Muscle tension and electromyography Tucker and Williamson (1984) suggested that effort manifests itself through the motor control system. The amplitude of the EMG increases linearly with the force exerted by a muscle, and the EMG spectrum changes as a muscle fatigues (exhibiting dominance of the lower frequencies). Therefore, EMG can be used as an index of physical workload by determining the absolute force necessary for system operation (Boff & Lincoln, 1987). Little research has been reported using this technique. The available results reveal that EMG reflects changes in workload, but that it measures the somatic system and is only peripherally related to mental workload (Lysaght *et al*, 1989).

A combination of these types of measure (performance-based, subjective, and physiological) will be a more powerful method of evaluating workload. For example, if two concurrent tasks vary in difficulty, subjects may devote more energy to performing the more difficult task and hence produce comparable levels of performance on each task. However, their subjective ratings for the tasks will probably differ, and physiological data may be able to confirm whether more effort was invested on the more difficult task. If performance decrements do occur, it is important to be able to identify their sources, which may include factors such as overloading of one or more specific resources, or operator motivation. Therefore, it is advisable to combine primary task techniques with other evaluation techniques, such as physiological measures and effort ratings.

Current Applications of Workload Measurement

In one of the few training studies to include workload measures, Paas and van Merrienboer (1993) described how the relative efficiency of training can be calculated by transforming into Z scores (i.e., by standardising measures that have different units) the units of percentage correct (performance) and the units of mental effort (measured by rating scales, psychophysiological techniques or dual-task methods). Relative condition efficiency is defined as the relation between mental effort and performance in a particular condition relative to a hypothetical baseline in which efficiency equals zero. When effort and performance Z scores are plotted, the relative condition efficiency is calculated as the perpendicular distance from a given point to the zero-efficiency line. In this way, a comparison can be made between the efficiency of different training conditions.

There have been many studies of workload in non-training environments, particularly in aviation. Heart rate measures have frequently been used, for example, to assess workload in simulators or in real flight. Further, they have gained acceptance as part of the criteria for government certification of several commercial aircraft (Blomberg *et al*, 1993; Roscoe, 1987; Speyer *et al*, 1988; Wainwright, 1988). Heart rate variability has also been used to measure workload in-flight (Wilson, 1993; Sekigucchi *et al*, 1979; Jorna, 1993). Although mid- and high-frequency band activity has been found to decrease during highly demanding segments of air-to-ground missions, neither band could distinguish between flight components (Wilson 1993; Veltman & Gaillard, 1993). Wilson (1993) did, however, find a significant decrease in HRV (0.1 Hz component) when pilots also performed a memory task compared to performing the flying task alone.

Jorna (1991) investigated HRV during a series of standard flight manoeuvres in a simulator with secondary tasks introduced. The results revealed differences between some but not all flight phases. Three physiological states could be identified that seemed to be associated with progressive loads:

- being attentive but not performing a particular task or flight manoeuvre;
- performing a flight manoeuvre in one dimension, such as maintaining heading by compensating for disturbances;
- handling tasks or manoeuvres with dual-task characteristics, such as performing descending turns (monitoring rate of turn and rate of descent in combination). A similar HRV response was found when handling a standard secondary task in addition to a one-dimensional tracking task.

Veltman and Gaillard (1993) measured blood pressure during a military flight task in a fixed-base simulator. The pilot's task was to follow a target aircraft. During half of the flights, the subject pilots had to perform a secondary task in addition to their flying task. Systolic blood pressure was significantly higher during the dual-task condition, but no significant difference was found between the flight phases.

Evaluation of Workload Measures

The workload measures selected for the MASTER experiments were the Bedford scale; RSME; DRAWS; Probe RT; heart rate; and heart rate variability (power at 0.1 Hz). The subjective workload measures were found to be task-independent, and could therefore be used to assess progress during any training task. Of these measures, DRAWS was considered to be most sensitive, but for a simple assessment of overall workload either the Bedford scale or the RSME was acceptable. All the subjective measures satisfied a wide range of psychometric and practical criteria.

Although Probe RT was shown to be sensitive to training in some experiments, it had a number of disadvantages. For example, a possible trade-off between speed and accuracy, and the opportunity for subjects to adopt different allocations of attention between the primary and secondary task, would create difficulties of interpretation. Since the Probe RT measures did not appear to offer information unavailable from the subjective measures, their use was not recommended in training programmes. Neither heart rate nor heart rate variability was found to be a suitable measure of workload in the training tasks studied. These measures seem, however, to reflect the motivational state of the trainee, since individuals who are continuously striving for the best performance will always exert the highest level of effort. This response can, as an example, be observed in situations with high levels of competition or with selection phases to be passed, such as during military aviation training.

These experiments permitted a battery of workload measures to be compiled for use in training programmes. Unlike performance measures, the workload measures can be used for any task.

25   Team Performance

Importance of Team Performance Measurement

A team may be defined as 'a distinguishable set of two or more people who interact dynamically, interdependently, and adaptively toward a common and valued goal/mission/objective, who have each been assigned specific roles or functions to perform, and who have a limited life span or membership' (Salas *et al*, 1992). The crews of mobile weapon systems conform to this definition of a team. Although each member of the team must be trained in 'taskwork' (the technical skills required to perform the task), there is evidence that teamwork must also be addressed, since it has an important influence on effectiveness. Teamwork has been defined as 'the way team members interact with each other to achieve team goals and adapt to varying circumstances and situations' (West, 1994). An important element of teamwork is the development of 'shared mental models' (Cannon-Bowers *et al*, 1993; Pascual *et al*, 1998; McGahan *et al*, 1998), common understandings held by team members about each other and about the tasks that they perform.

Requirements for Team Performance Measurement

Team performance measures could be used to answer the following general questions: Should operators be trained on their individual tasks before being put into the crew environment? Should training be conducted at the level of the crew from the outset? Should training of crew skills be conducted separately from the training undergone in crews? The requirements for team performance measures have been summarised as follows (Cannon-Bowers & Salas, 1997):

- They must address individual competencies, team competencies at the individual level, and team competencies at the team level. If remediation (e.g., to improve communication) is best delivered at the individual level, then measurement should occur at this level.
- They must address both processes and outcomes. The latter, although important, do not indicate the reasons for poor team performance, and hence cannot be used in isolation to determine how training should proceed.

- They must describe, evaluate and diagnose performance. In complex dynamic tasks involving much covert cognitive actitivity, the description of performance may be difficult. However, accurate description is necessary to allow evaluation. Even evaluation is not sufficient, since the causes of inadequate performance must be able to be identified.
- They must support remediation. For example, it must be possible to use the measures to provide feedback to trainees that will improve their performance.

Types of Team Performance Measure

The competencies required by team members were identified by Cannon-Bowers *et al* (1995) in the form of knowledge, skills and attitudes. Knowledge included shared task models and team role interaction patterns; skills included adaptability and mutual performance modelling and feedback; and attitudes included team orientation and team cohesion. Cannon-Bowers and Salas (1997) emphasised that team training often requires dynamic assessment, and argued that team performance measures used in training should be different from those used in other circumstances: a key requirement was the ability to use such measures to formulate remedial action (in the form of feedback, knowledge of results, or subsequent instruction).

Cannon-Bowers and Salas identified a need for measures of both individual and team performance. Some skills, such as communication, may be best measured at the individual level, whereas others, such as shared task models, may require analysis at the team level; the most important consideration is the level at which remedial action will be taken.

Dickinson and McIntyre (1997) described the use of the critical incidents technique to construct teamwork measures. This method was used in workshops to obtain descriptions of examples of teamwork from experts in anti-air warfare team tasks. The categories of teamwork used to elicit responses were: team orientation, team leadership, communication, monitoring, feedback, back-up behaviour, and co-ordination. The responses were then transformed into task-oriented statements, from which decision rules were derived to identify behaviours that corresponded to particular aspects of teamwork. Later, the statements were re-assigned to teamwork components, in most instances being correctly assigned to the component that they were originally used to represent. These statements formed the basis of the teamwork measures (e.g., the statement 'is aware of other team members' performance' was used as one measure of monitoring).

The authors recommended the use of both numerical scales and checklists. For each component of teamwork, a behavioural observation scale is constructed, comprising items constituting that component. A behavioural summary scale is used to rate overall teamwork skill on each component. Finally, a behavioural event checklist is used to record scenario-specific critical events that call for teamwork.

Kokorian (1995), on the basis of an extensive literature review, proposed a Military Crew Competence Model (MCCM) in which the variables affecting team performance could be divided into 'external conditions imposed on a crew, and the internal processes and functions through which crews work towards their objectives'. The external conditions comprise 'structurals' (crew characteristics such as individual abilities, training and experience) and 'contextuals' (the physical conditions in which the crew is expected to operate). The internal processes reflect the ways in which the crew approaches tasks and missions, and comprise four elements:

- Co-deciding: the crew's collective ability to plan forward in time, set milestones for measuring performance, anticipate problems, prepare contingencies and plan ahead for workload management.
- Communicating: the communication structure established by the crew, the content and style of communication, including non-verbal elements, and the timing and relevance of information given.
- Controlling: the self-monitoring and collective-monitoring of performance against mission milestones, including maintenance of an overview of the mission, scheduling/time management, adapting to changes in situations, and crew member support.
- Cohesion: the process by which the crew establishes 'a shared identity and a shared commitment to achieving mission and task goals' (Kokorian, 1995). The processes of crew decision making, communication and controlling all contribute to crew cohesion, which in turn reinforces these processes among the crew (Figure 25.1).

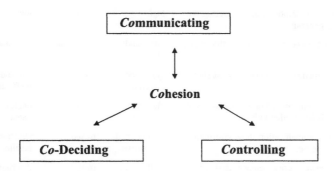

Figure 25.1. The four co-processes of crew competence

The Crew Competencies Questionnaire (CCQ), designed to measure these variables, comprises three sections. The first two measure external influences (mission conditions and crew characteristics) and the third measures internal influences (crew actions in terms of co-deciding, communicating and controlling). The CCQ comprises statements with three response choices, ranging from positive or effective descriptors to negative or less effective descriptors (see Table 25.1). The statements in the crew action section are based on the behavioural indicators of crew performance identified in the literature review by Kokorian (1995).

Measures of Processes

Some studies of crew processes have considered the flow of information between crew members. Information can be analysed for content, such as its accuracy, completeness, relevance to the task, timeliness, and usefulness. Each of these considerations will be dependent upon the context in which it occurs. Measures of crew communications and co-ordination can be derived from analysis of recorded tapes. Cannon-Bowers *et al* (1992) suggested analysing this information using scales such as the Air Crew Observation and Evaluation Scale. This assesses the frequency and quality of co-ordination behaviours on seven behavioural dimensions: communication, situational awareness, leadership, assertiveness, decision making, mission analysis, and adaptability.

Table 25.1. Examples of CCQ items

Statement	Response boxes		
Updates on overall progress with the task/mission were provided...	regularly	occasionally	rarely
Awareness among the crew of each other's progress on individual contributions was...	high	mixed	low
Co-ordination of each member's actions during the task/mission was generally...	high	inconsistent	low
Responses to crewmembers' requests for information tended to be...	quick and clear	inconsistent	slow and vague
Responses to crewmembers' requests for assistance tended to be...	quick and effective	mixed	late and ineffective
The content of crew communication (what was said) during the task/mission tended to be...	clear and relevant	mixed	unclear and vague
The style of crew communication (how information was given) tended to be...	positive and supportive	mixed	negative and/or hostile
Communication between crewmembers during the task/mission tended to be...	well organised & co-ordinated	mixed	disorganised/ unco-ordinated
Encouragement between crewmembers was exchanged...	frequently	occasionally	rarely
In general, the crew tended to...	keep ahead of the action	stay up with the action	fall behind the action

Reasons for poor communication can be determined using measures of individual performance. For example, it might be found that incomplete information passed from one operator to another was attributable to high workload. Each crew member can provide a rating regarding the quality and quantity of information received from other members. The same type of analysis could be performed for other aspects of group performance, such as actions performed by members or crew decision-making processes.

The use of structured interviews may be appropriate for measuring crew processes, but only with clear guidelines available regarding the specific questions that can be asked. The interview should be used to gather data on the operator's perceived performance, the number of problems encountered and their context, and assessment of the crew's success in achieving defined objectives.

Another possible method of measuring team processes is to create inter-dependence in two-person crews, with each crew member having specific tasks in addition to overlapping functions. Low-fidelity flight simulators can be used in this respect. Both individual and crew performance can then be analysed. Cannon-Bowers *et al* (1992) used this paradigm in the air environment. In a study of aircraft tasks, separate responsibilities were given to individual crew members. The pilot controlled the heading and attitude of the aircraft, whilst the second team member selected weapons and helped to restore the aircraft to stable positions if the aircraft was out of control. Inter-dependence was created by situations in which performance of the sub-tasks of each crew member was essential. Such overlapping sub-tasks involved monitoring airspeed, heading, radar and threat indicators. Communications were taped for future analysis. Specific performance goals were identified, such as following certain routes or operating within given time limits.

The effect of different types of inter-dependence between teams can also be studied using an experimental reaction time paradigm. Morrissette *et al* (1975), for example, studied the performance of two teams working under a division of labour organisation and a redundancy organisation with respect to the monitoring of displays. The task consisted of detecting critical signals presented randomly on circular milk-glass windows. Long detection times were found under the division of labour team organisation but not under the redundancy organisation.

Examples of measures of processes at the team and individual level are shown in Table 25.2 (see Cannon-Bowers & Salas, 1997).

Table 25.2. Team and individual process factors that should be considered during training (from Cannon-Bowers & Salas, 1997)

Team level	Individual level
Shared task models	Assertiveness
Cue/strategy associations	Information exchange
Task organisation	Task-specific role responsibilities
Compensatory behaviour	Task procedures
Collective efficacy	Cue/strategy association
Dynamic re-allocation of function	Mutual performance monitoring
Task interaction	Flexibility

Measures of Outcomes

The following measures of the outcomes of crew activities can be identified:
- ratings of proficiency based on observations of crew performance;
- time to complete tasks;

- accuracy;
- number and type of omitted and uncompleted tasks;
- frequency counts on other variables;
- measures of knowledge, e.g., tactical knowledge test for infantry rifle squads (Dyer, 1984);
- deviation from 'ideal state'.

Examples of measures of outcomes at the team and individual level are shown in Table 25.3 (see Cannon-Bowers & Salas, 1997).

Table 25.3. Team and individual outcome factors that should be considered during training (from Cannon-Bowers & Salas, 1997)

Team level	Individual level
Mission/goal accomplishment	Accuracy
Aggregate latency	Latency
Error propagation	Errors
Aggregate accuracy	Safety
	Timeliness
	Decision biases

Expert Evaluation

Expert evaluation is increasingly being used as a measure of crew effectiveness. The expert can be asked to make both qualitative and quantitative judgements. A system of measuring team effectiveness was described by Connelly and Johnson (1981) in terms of 'summary performance measures' and 'system performance measures'. Summary measures were formulated subjectively and reflected the judgement of an individual or group in determining the objective of the mission and relevant factors such as desired safety conditions. The subjective data were converted to quantitative form. System performance measures revealed the effect upon summary performance of each constituent mission task, and the effect of instantaneous and interval performance on the performance of the entire mission could be estimated mathematically.

Meister (1985) suggested that attribute evaluation, in which certain dimensions or qualities in performance are identified and scaled, can expand upon the limitations of performance evaluation. One example is the Instructional Quality Inventory method used in the military training environment.

Issues related to the reliability of expert ratings of both crew and individual performance should be addressed when selecting or evaluating measures based on such ratings. One such issue is the effect of ratee and rater characteristics on performance-related judgements, an instance of which is the 'halo' effect in which the evaluation of an individual on one dimension influences evaluation of the same individual on another, independent dimension. Huber (1987), for example, found that ratee characteristics directly influenced overall performance ratings and hence the subsequent compensation, training and promotion recommendations made.

More specifically, a ratee who had previously obtained a high overall performance rating was likely to receive a more positive current performance rating. The significance of these findings is that performance judgements and recommendations for future training may be based on a subjective perception of the trainee that is relevant to past performance, not to the situation at hand.

Current Applications of Team Performance Measurement

The capacity to combine process and product measures provides a significant development for trainers. The examples in Table 25.4 from a simulated exercise of close air support (CAS) show how subject-matter experts' ratings of team behaviours (firepower synchronisation and manoeuvre synchronisation) improved over time in the simulator and how these correlated with objective measures of firepower (hits, kills, and engagement times).

Despite such recent attempts to measure team performance, however, Joyner (1996), in a survey of military training courses, found that few explicitly defined team-related competencies. Such competencies were recognised as important, but were considered difficult to train and to measure. Those team competencies that were identified were assessed subjectively. A similar problem exists in crew resource management (CRM) training courses, initiated by airlines in response to well-publicised accidents attributed to poor crew co-ordination (e.g., Cooper *et al* 1979). In a review of CRM training, Farmer *et al* (1998) drew attention to the lack of underlying theory of team processes and of objective measures of team performance.

Table 25.4. Improvement in performance during an exercise
(February 1995 MDT2 CAS training exercise)

Measure	Exercise day			
	2 (Defence)	3 (Offence)	4 (Defence)	5 (Offence)
CAS kills	3	5	7	9
CAS misses	3	5	5	2
Average engagement time (min)	4	3	2	1.5
Fire support synchronisation factor	1	2	3	3.5
Manoeuvre synchronisation factor	1	1.5	1.5	1.5

One obstacle to the development of team performance measures is that, of more than 4,000 team studies, fewer than 5% had been conducted on real teams performing realistic tasks (Guzzo & Shea, 1992). Moreover, measurement of non-observable aspects of teamwork such as shared mental models is not well advanced (McGahan *et al*, 1998), although some progress is being made in this area (e.g., Kraiger & Salas, 1993).

The Crew Competencies Questionnaire (CCQ), reported by Kokorian (1995), was tested in the MASTER project as a possible means of measuring teamwork skills during training. The experimental evaluation of the CCQ addressed face validity and criterion validity in a flight simulation, the latter expressed in terms of correlation with actual team performance. Usability was also investigated, with respect to perceived ease of questionnaire completion and inter-rater reliability.

Ten teams of three subjects were formed, each comprising a team leader and two pilots. Each pilot operated using a 'fly box', a control box with a joystick to allow flight through the database. In addition to the CCQ, a CCQ Utility Questionnaire (CCQU) was devised, and subjects also completed the Familiarity with Aviation Terminology Questionnaire and provided basic biographical information and details of simulator/flying experience. The familiarity questionnaire was designed to tap any knowledge/experience that might give experienced subjects an advantage in completing their mission over their more naive colleagues. Hence, in addition to aviation and navigational terms, their experience of computer games involving the use of a joystick was measured. The measurement of this familiarity enabled better control over the experiment in that the effects of familiarity could then be removed when determining the relationship between team performance and team cohesion as measured by the CCQ.

The pilots were required to fly around an area of the Hasparren database to locate 20 specified features indicated on a map, including water towers, factories and castles. Other features, such as radio towers and airfields, which they did not need to locate, were also indicated. The task was to locate as many of the 20 features as accurately as possible during the mission, automatically recording their location by pressing a trigger on their joystick. The trigger action resulted in the display of the targeted feature's latitude and longitude on a separate screen. The team leader's task was manually to record this latitude and longitude on a given record form when it appeared on his display screen. The mission consisted of ten 3-minute runs, the team being given 5 minutes to plan its strategy for the first run, 2 minutes to plan for each following run, and 1 minute after every run to review it.

All teams were initially given exactly the same information; however, pilots were given some information that the team leader was not given, and vice versa. Only the team leader was initially given a map, which was explained in detail. The ten teams underwent the experiment successively over one week, each observed by two experimenters. Subjects were taken to a briefing room and introduced to each other. The nature of the experiment was explained, and each team was given an identical team briefing. Based on the responses given regarding aviation familiarity, computer games played, and simulator experience, the roles of Team Leader, Pilot A and Pilot B were allocated. To maximise consistency across teams, the most experienced subject was always selected to be the team leader, the second most experienced was Pilot B and the most inexperienced Pilot A.

After reviewing runs 1 and 5, subjects were requested to complete Section 3 of the CCQ. After the final run, subjects were asked to complete all sections of the CCQ. Experimenters also completed the CCQ at these times.

The teams were divided into high and low performers, and statistical analysis was used to determine whether these two groups could be differentiated using the CCQ scores. The hypothesis based on Kokorian's model was that, the higher the CCQ scores, the better the team performance. In this study, this did not prove to be the case. The difference in performance between the high and low groups was not mirrored by a similar differentiation in the CCQ cohesion scores. However, there was a difference in the trend of cohesion scores between the two performance groups: the high group's cohesion scores showed an upward trend from the first to the fifth run, levelling out a little at the last run; the low performance group's cohesion scores remained effectively constant throughout the mission. The individual elements of cohesion — co-deciding, controlling and communication — confirmed the finding of improvement over time for the high performance group. These improvements were apparent for each stage of each run, i.e., planning, executing and reviewing. In contrast, for the low performance group, no CCQ score changed significantly, indicating that these subjects did not appear to adapt their team behaviour according to the demands of the situation.

These results implied that there was no simple association between level of cohesion and level of performance. Rather, openness to changing the approach to co-deciding, communication and controlling according to the task demands appeared to result in better performance.

The findings reflected previous observations (e.g., Parker *et al*, 1959; Kirchner, 1965) that supervisor ratings tend to be less lenient than self-ratings. However, on all other comparisons, no significant differences were found between different roles. On the whole, individuals were relatively consistent in their ratings, and it was concluded that the inter-rater reliability of the CCQ was reasonably high.

Most raters (subjects and observers) found the CCQ reasonably easy to complete and easy to understand. However, most also felt that the choice of responses available did not adequately cover the range of responses that they wished to give. With regard to the CCQ's appropriateness to the mission set, there was a very wide discrepancy of responses.

It was tentatively concluded that the CCQ could be used as a measure over time to show change in team cohesion, and that this would reflect team performance. It was recommended that the response choices be increased to five per statement and that response choices measuring more than one behaviour be eliminated.

26   Applications

Assessment of Candidates for Training

Importance of Trainability Measures

With the introduction of new technology and enhancements in capabilities, the control, navigation and management of weapon systems have become increasingly demanding of the operator, particularly in aviation. These systems require increasing levels of cognitive skill, and often impose high stresses upon the operator's physiological systems. Moreover, training of operators of sophisticated systems is a major cost factor in military budgets. It is therefore necessary to give a high priority to selection of candidates who will prove to be trainable. The criterion of trainability is usually the trainee's success, judged either by assessment at the end of training or by performance on the job itself (Patrick, 1992). Predictions are assumed to improve as the number of common elements between the assessment and the criterion to be predicted increases; this is known as the 'point to point correspondence' (Downs, 1989). There are three main elements of trainability tests in which point to point correspondence should be achieved: the content of the work sample (the task to be learned); the methods of teaching and learning; and the general environment in which learning takes place.

Types of Test

A large variety of personnel selection procedures has been developed, including interviews, psychometric tests (including tests of cognitive ability and self-report measures of personality), biodata (biographical information about the candidate's life history), handwriting analysis, work sample tests and trainability tests. Selection tests can be classified as 'signs' or 'samples' (Wernimont & Campbell, 1968). A sign test is a more traditional test in which inferences are drawn about the psychological characteristics (signs) needed for successful job performance; the sample approach, on the other hand, focuses on the job tasks, and designs selection procedures that provide representative samples of the actual behaviour needed for successful job performance. Work samples and trainability testing are examples of sample selection tests. Tests that allow the prediction of trainees' performance, particularly whether they will successfully complete their training and perform well in the operational environment, are a necessity for a successful training programme. Patrick (1992) argues that both trainability tests and work sample testing address trainability, since they assist in the selection of those people who will benefit most from training.

Psychometric tests Psychometric tests are based upon generic psychological principles and measurement theory. The attributes that they attempt to measure are derived from psychological constructs such as psychomotor ability or spatial orientation. Under optimal conditions the selection of variables is guided by a requirements analysis of the corresponding job workplace. In psychometric tests, the complex requirements of the workplace are represented by one-dimensional variables, which involve the essential elements of the characteristic of interest; these variables may be weighted according to the particular requirements of the job. However, it is difficult to represent job requirements in terms of a set of psychometric variables. Moreover, since the candidate during initial selection does not have specific knowledge of the job, testing must address the underlying aptitude rather than the specific job requirements.

Paper-and-pencil testing, or a computerised version thereof, represents the classical method of aptitude testing. Such testing is necessarily more or less static in nature, although some aspects of dynamics or variation in task complexity can be incorporated by using slides or movies in combination with multiple-choice test formats. The presentation of test material on computer-based devices gives the advantage of recording and evaluating a large amount of performance data, but problems of representing the complexity and dynamics of real tasks remain.

Performance assessment using psychometric tests is based upon the characteristic distribution over the target population. The distribution itself is derived empirically, and ideally takes the form of a Gaussian (normal) distribution. The distribution is an important factor in determining the sensitivity of a test, i.e., the ability to discriminate between candidates. If particular measuring dimensions show different distributions, they cannot be directly compared or combined. This problem can be solved, however, by a z-transformation in which the measured values are converted into standard scores expressed in terms of the number of standard deviations by which they deviate from the mean.

Work samples In a work sample test, a sample of test elements or behaviours that occur in performance of the actual job or task is administered to potential trainees; thus, the test situation closely resembles the requirements of the real job ('phenotypic similarity'). Work sample tests are usually administered to experienced subjects; they need carefully planned instruction if administered to inexperienced applicants.

Work samples play an important role in personnel selection. They are applied as complete test procedures in assessment centres (together with psychometric tests), in apparatus tests and in simulation-based tests. Methodological pre-requisites for effective work samples are:

- a high degree of standardisation of task presentation;

- tasks and performance criteria that can easily be observed and evaluated;
- the application of methodically derived rating systems;
- the use of well-trained raters.

The cost of development or modification of work samples is very high, and administration of testing may require the use of expensive high quality simulators. It is very difficult to decide which psychological characteristics of the applicants are really measured. Unlike psychometric testing, a small number of multi-dimensional tasks are used, making evaluation of particular aspects of behaviour difficult. Assessment of candidates and evaluation of the tests are carried out in most cases by subjective expert rating, based on experience. Ideally, test evaluation should follow standardised criteria derived from theory and defined operationally; several raters should perform the evaluation as objectively as possible, and should reach a consensus.

Work samples have been used in the military environment in conjunction with conventional predictors of performance, to increase the predictive ability of measures. In the US Army, for example, work sample tests include table-top tank gunnery simulators, the Tank Crew Gunnery Skills Test, and a mini-tank range. Criterion data are obtained from the unit's annual tank gunnery qualification exercise and consist of measures such as total crew score and frequency of successful stationary precision engagements. The tests used by Campbell and Black (1982) included gunner tracking, target acquisition, and operation of the M1 fire control computer. The criteria were training test scores, main gun firing hits and instructor evaluation of proficiency.

Trainability tests In trainability tests, as in work sample tests, tests involving task elements that occur in performance of the actual job are administered, ideally based on a detailed and systematic job or task analysis. The distinguishing feature between work sample and trainability tests is that the latter additionally involve some training on these task elements. Performance in trainability tests is assessed during or at the end of the mini-training period (Patrick, 1992). The major objective is to determine how subjects with no prior experience on the task benefit from standardised training, the underlying assumption being that the ability to learn the tasks allows prediction of success in training.

For a trainability test to be developed, the job or task must be amenable to behavioural description. In many jobs, such as those involving managerial decision making, job and task performance cannot be described in behavioural terms. Moreover, predictive validity attenuates over time (Downs, 1989): the longer the period between testing and follow-up (or performance at work), the lower the predictive validity. The performance shown in training may be contaminated by warm-up effects, and thus fail to give a pure indication of learning. Trainability tests are better predictors of motor skills than of cognitive and verbal tasks (cf. Taylor, 1975). Moreover, they are critically dependent upon the quality of the instructor/assessor.

Trainability tests offer coefficients in the region of 0.50 (Patrick, 1992), and a rigorously designed trainability test developed for the Royal Air Force produced coefficients of 0.78-0.91 (Elshaw & Lidderdale, 1982). Similar scores were obtained for a pilot selection test that was developed for the Royal Netherlands Navy but was also used for civil aviation selection. The test assesses trainability by exposing candidates to multiple sessions with pursuit tracking tasks with preview, and assessing progress in manual control behaviour and dual-task capabilities as a function of learning (Jorna, 1989a). As a general rule, it has been found that the greater the complexity of the task, the better it discriminates between applicants and therefore the better it will predict. For example, trainability tests designed for British Airways apprentice electricians were too simple to be predictive; when a more complex test was devised, statistically significant results were obtained over two years (Robertson & Downs, 1979).

Simulation-based testing Simulation-based testing combines the advantages of work samples and psychometric procedures. By applying modern electronic and computer techniques, the task presented can correspond closely to reality (i.e., have high fidelity) and can be standardised to a high degree, and the objectivity of data recording and data evaluation can be ensured.

Assessment centres Assessment centres combine work samples with expert ratings and psychometric tests, and require at least one day for administration. This method is increasingly gaining acceptance in the selection of executive personnel and in the field of personnel development (Schuler & Funke, 1989).

Test batteries In general, the Armed Services use extensive batteries of tests in their selection procedures (Bartram, 1987), including paper-and-pencil tests, personality tests or biographical inventories, psychomotor and information-processing tests, and screening by means of flying or simulator grading. Military selection involves not only the decision to employ individuals but also their classification into one of many military occupational specialities. In the United Kingdom, assessment is based on general test batteries that permit both selection and classification, with emphasis on aptitude rather than achievement. The pattern of tests represents general ability, comprising several factors (mathematical, verbal, spatial, practical knowledge). Owing to time constraints and costs, trainability and work sample tests have been used only for limited forms of entry such as pilots. In the US, many selection procedures are derived from the Armed Services Vocational Aptitude Battery (ASVAB), considered to be a general measure of trainability despite its emphasis on aptitude (Campbell & Black, 1982).

Measurement

The aspects of performance most commonly measured are:
- psychomotor ability;
- attention and concentration;
- multi-tasking ability;
- ability to cope with workload;
- ability to cope with other stressors;
- spatial abilities;

- information processing, sometimes based upon reaction time measures;
- operational capabilities.

Teamwork and social interactions are rarely considered in current selection systems. Work samples are typically used as predictors of future job performance. Criteria include job proficiency or success in training, as measured by supervisor ratings, speed and accuracy, completion of training, or grade in training. One of the most common methods of assessing trainability is by the use of rating scales and specific error checklists (Robertson & Downs, 1979). Five-point rating scales are typically used, based on subjective evaluation by a trained assessor. Robertson and Downs reported that this form of assessment has proved to be at least as successful as more objective and behaviourally anchored error checklists.

Three types of response formats for work sample evaluations have been identified (Smith, 1991): global ratings, usually on a Likert-type scale; behavioural recording forms, on which an assessor rates performance using specific examples of good and poor task behaviour developed by job experts; and behavioural checklists, in which the candidate's behaviour is described rather than evaluated.

In most psychometric tests, standard scores based on normal distributions are available. For trainability tests and work sample tests, however, this is not the case, due to the specialised nature of each job. Downs (1989) argues that the trainability test population may not be distributed normally either in its ability to learn the required skill or in its motivation. Thus, standard scores with recommended cut-off points are not available for trainability tests. Instead, there are expectancy charts based on predictive validity coefficients that show the likelihood that the applicant will successfully complete training based on the trainability test score.

Learning curve analysis Learning curves can be considered along with trainability and work sample testing as a form of predictive tool, in which curve fitting formulae can be calculated to estimate performance increases associated with learning (Coker, 1990). The Research and Training Center at the University of Wisconsin-Stout has developed training guides and computer software, allowing the applicant's performance data in the form of a learning curve to be plotted and used to extrapolate training potential. One study used learning curve analysis to predict performance, subjects performing the same work sample for five consecutive work days. Mathematical formulae for predicting future performance from performance on the work sample were compared; a reliable method was found of predicting the mean of trials 200-250 on the basis of the means for trials 1-50. A Performance Analyser and Trainer (PAT) computer-based system was developed that collected data on work sample performance and calculated a learning curve. One problem of the learning curve approach is that some people might reach a higher level of skill than suggested by their performance on the trainability test or by analysis of the learning curve.

Use of dual-tasks in prediction One of the requirements in many military tasks is that operators be able to work on several tasks concurrently. Whether an operator can process tasks and information concurrently is therefore likely to be a determinant of trainability. Within the military domain, dual-tasking often involves the necessity of tracking (e.g., following a target, or keeping a vehicle within specified tracking parameters) in combination with another task (often auditory). Jorna (1989a, b), for example, carried out a study in which trainability of pilots was assessed on the basis of dual-task performance (pursuit tracking and a continuous memory task). Dual-task performance was related to the level of 'pilot aptitude' as assessed by traditional selection, a flight simulator test and the results of advanced flight training. Prior flight experience did not relate to adequate dual-task performance. Jorna (1989a, b) developed a PC-based version of the task procedure, known as the 'PILOT' test (Processing Information in Loading Or Time-sharing conditions). Although not a conventional 'work sample', the use of dual-task testing is likely to prove useful in the prediction of training success since it relates to the skills required in the flying task. Thus this study demonstrates how a 'laboratory' task can be used in the prediction of training success.

The miniature training and evaluation approach A variation on the basic concept of trainability and work sample testing is miniature training courses. Within the US Navy, this is known as miniature training and evaluation (MTE) testing. Like trainability testing, the MTE concept involves training military personnel to perform certain tasks and then testing performance on the tasks. It is assumed that, regardless of scores obtained from standard aptitude tests, recruits who can learn to perform a sample of tasks of a Navy rating will be able to perform all of the rating's tasks. A battery of MTE-based tests was used to predict the fleet performance of personnel. At the first follow-up (9 months), use of the battery in conjunction with the standard aptitude tests led to predictive power more than double that of aptitude testing alone.

Flying grading Flying grading is probably the selection test closest to trainability testing. This typically involves 10-15 hours' flying over several days for each candidate, and is economically viable only when the candidates have already undergone some form of selection. Bartram (1987) suggested that computer-based testing analogous to whole- or part-task simulations could be used, to provide cost effective training from which the most capable trainees could be selected. Bartram described an automated testing system for pilot selection, MICROPAT, in which tracking tests and tests of information management ability were developed. The MICROPAT system can simulate the approach and landing of an aircraft and can therefore be used in flying grading trials. Within this system, training programme candidates receive a one-hour training session, after which they are given the controls and their trainability is assessed.

Prediction

One of the most important psychometric criteria is predictive validity. The results of the test are compared to a criterion value, such as success in training or measures of job performance. For work samples, coefficients of predictive validity of up to 0.45 have been reported; for simulator-based pilot selection systems, values of about 0.65 have been obtained.

The coefficient of predictive validity cannot exceed the reliability of the test, and poor reliability may underlie some of the disappointing results for validity. The use of simulators provides a degree of control that helps to improve reliability and hence validity.

Predictive validity coefficients for aptitude tests are generally low, about 0.30 (Patrick, 1992). It was because of such shortcomings that work sample and trainability tests were devised. Particularly for occupations with high operational requirements, e.g., sales representatives, policemen, board members, air traffic controllers, and pilots, success can be better predicted by dynamic testing such as simulator-based testing or work samples (cf. Schuler & Funke, 1989).

Psychometric tests are more common than work samples and trainability tests. Sometimes, the same tests have several functions, being used as psychometric, work sample, and trainability tests in different contexts. In the field orientation survey of the MASTER project, there was often a lack of empirical data. Where data were provided, the samples for computing reliabilities or predictive validities were sometimes too small to be meaningful.

The reliability data collected in the survey were partly in test-retest form, and partly in inter-rater form. Test-retest reliabilities tended to be low, often below the value of 0.7 regarded as the minimum acceptable for practical use (Lienert, 1989). Predictive validities ranged in most cases from 0.20 to 0.40, but some, such as that for the Royal Navy Observer grading, were significantly higher.

Some of the selection systems were restricted to one particular task type, whereas others, such as TASKOMAT (Boer *et al*, 1987), encompassed a wide range of tasks. Most, however, allowed presentation of additional tasks to measure multi-tasking capabilities and the ability to vary workload or introduce other stressors. In most instances, instruction and data evaluation were not fully automated. The test duration reported ranged from 45 minutes to 8 hours.

A striking finding was that European establishments are using different systems to select for the same job role. Moreover, most institutions seem to be content with only minimal statistical verification and optimisation of their systems.

Current Applications of Selection Measures

To set psychometric testing, work sample testing, and trainability testing in context, it is necessary to consider the stages at which each is relevant. The military training process can be conceptualised in terms of five different stages, which usually occur sequentially:

- initial selection;
- allocation to trades or specialisation;
- screening for training courses;
- individualising the training process;
- assessing training progress.

The type of test used varies from fully validated psychometric tests to informal instructor assessments. Generally, psychometric tests are found in the first three stages of the training process. Work sample testing and trainability testing are usually located in the third and fourth. A test can be both psychometric and work sample in nature, as indicated by responses to the MASTER field orientation questionnaire.

The literature review and field orientation indicate that simulation-based selection systems are used only for relatively highly-skilled roles such as pilot or air-traffic controller. A basic problem of these systems is that they are considered to be more efficient if they are very specific to the role in question; they therefore tend not to be applicable to other professional groups.

Recommendations

The ability to present computerised tests permits recording of detailed performance data. However, these tests may still fail to match the complexity or dynamics of the real tasks that they address. There is therefore a requirement for research on the following issues:

- limitations of static tasks in predicting qualification for dynamic tasks (e.g., drivers, operators using complex man-machine interfaces, pilots, air traffic controllers);
- the extent to which psychometric testing can be applied to dynamic tasks;
- methods of combining static and dynamic task elements for diagnostic testing and training progress assessment.

Future research in the field of work sample testing on simulators should consider:

- criteria to establish content validity;
- criteria for the assessment of the behaviour of applicants;
- methods of integrating data to produce a single value;
- procedures for assessing teamwork and crew co-ordination.

Issues to be investigated for simulator-based testing include:

- comparison of the validity of static and dynamic tasks;
- the relevance of pure behavioural data compared to that of performance data;
- use of theoretical models of human information processing;
- development of simulator-based models to predict team abilities and crew co-ordination;
- development of dynamic tasks taking account of psychometric requirements.

Transfer of Training

Importance of Transfer Measurement

Transfer of training (ToT), also known as transfer of learning (Patrick, 1992), was defined for the purposes of the MASTER project as 'the gain in learning a task as a result of previous learning (learning gain)'. The notion of transfer is central to simulator-based training, which is based upon the assumption that learning will transfer positively from a simulator to a real weapons system. Transfer assessment is used to validate training programmes rather than to assess trainees. It might be predicted that transfer would be a direct function of the realism or the fidelity of the simulation; however, Lintern (1991) noted that 'the design of an instructional strategy is based on the assumption that a planned departure from identity can enhance learning and transfer, or at least can make instruction more cost effective'.

Transfer is also important when personnel are required to operate a system after gaining experience on a different system. Rayman (1982), for example, described the negative transfer between the A-7 and A-10 aircraft. As pilots convert from older to newer aircraft, negative transfer increases the risk of errors and therefore the number of possible accidents. Rayman recommended the standardisation of cockpits, or at least a comparative analysis between old and new cockpits to determine the elements on which negative transfer could occur.

Common Experimental Designs to Measure Transfer

Transfer research has involved the use of several different types of experimental design, the most common of which are outlined below.

Classic design The most common design involves the comparison of an experimental group with a control group. Both groups are initially tested on task B. The experimental group then undergoes training for task A, while the control group is not subject to any form of manipulation. Both groups are then retested on task B. The difference between the performance scores of the two groups is a measure of the transfer of training effect.

Transfer of learning This design is similar to that above, but the learning effect rather than performance is tested. The experimental group is trained on task A, whereas the control group undergoes no form of training. Both are then tested on the extent to which they learn task B.

Self-control transfer design When a control group is not available, the self-control transfer design can be used in which the subject acts as his own control, with performance data taken prior to and after the training manipulation.

Pre-existing control design This design can be employed where a control group is not available for concurrent testing: data are used from a previous training programme. However, this type of design should be employed with caution due to possible changes in circumstances such as training programme modification or use of different instructors.

Uncontrolled transfer design In this design, there is no control group and measures of performance are taken after a particular training programme. This design lacks scientific rigour, and is not recommended.

Backward transfer design Experienced operators are used; if performance is as good on the training device as in the real environment, backward transfer is said to have occurred. Stewart (1994), for example, used this paradigm to validate a reconfigurable simulator using both objective and subjective measurements. The problem with this design is that, although the skills of experienced operators can transfer backwards, the skills of a trainee will not necessarily transfer forward (Rolfe & Caro, 1982). Backward transfer studies therefore need to be supported by other tests of training device effectiveness. As Larsen *et al* (1991) note, the prediction of forward transfer is not the purpose for which backward transfer studies are generally proposed.

Quasi-transfer studies   Quasi-transfer studies involve measuring the trainee's performance on a criterion task in the simulator. This enables training effectiveness to be established before the simulator is used as practice for real flight. There is evidence that quasi-transfer studies are valid tests of training effectiveness. Lintern *et al* (1990) found that training on a criterion task in the simulator was a valid indicator of performance in the operational environment.

Bi-directional versus uni-directional transfer   Performance of a group trained on one device is compared to the initial performance of a second group on a second device, and conversely the performance of the second group trained on the second device is compared to the initial performance of the first group on the first device (Smith & Hagman, 1993).

Blaiwes *et al* (1973) identified several types of difficulty associated with transfer designs:

- the specific details of operational situations vary from trial to trial;
- trainee variables, such as age, experience, and previous training, may act as confounding factors;
- crew composition may change;
- the training syllabus may change;
- the experimenter may be unable to exert sufficient control over real training programmes.

   Thus, in many instances it will be difficult to compare the results of transfer studies, and hence to provide training guidelines on the basis of generalisation of research results. Moreover, Waag (1991) stressed that ToT evaluations require that improved performance be demonstrated in the real environment. Although such studies have been reported (Miller *et al*, 1985; Hughes *et al*, 1983), they are relatively rare, and are both difficult and time-consuming to conduct. Many problems may arise, such as lack of experimental control, insufficient sample sizes, insufficient training time in the simulator, insufficient training time for evaluation in the real system, or use of insensitive performance measures.

Alternative Methods for ToT Assessment

Holistic approach   The holistic approach was designed as a time-saving tool, particularly when dealing with many transfer factors (Westra, 1982). It refers to 'a philosophic point of view in the conduct of behavioral experiments that emphasises the importance of accounting for as many potentially critical variables as possible, whether equipment, environment, subject, or temporal, controlled or uncontrolled'. Hence the only way to obtain accurate and precise experimental information that will generalise to a wide variety of operational situations is to include all the potentially critical factors in the same experiment and ensure that the range of values for each factor in the experiment encompasses those anticipated operationally, now and in the future. Because of the large number of factors included, the number of possible combinations is enormous, although fortunately not all conditions require testing. This approach has the advantages of being informative, easily generalisable (highly ecologically valid), and economical. Its major drawback is that one factor combination is tested on only one subject. However, it is particularly useful in the early stages of a simulator design programme, when many alternatives should be considered.

Differential transfer   Reisweber and Lintern (1991) introduced the concept of 'differential transfer' that occurs when one of two or more training regimes is relatively more effective at enhancing sensitivity to the critical properties that support performance in the task. Training manipulation can therefore induce differential enhancements in sensitivity to perceptual properties. The experimenter can manipulate many transfer factors using a large number of subject groups and assess the differential transfer effect, thus identifying conditions that could be used to define optimal training programmes.

Experimental design for ToT and cost effectiveness assessment   Many so-called 'ToT experiments' have a double goal: to assess transfer and to evaluate time or cost savings. Larsen *et al* (1991) emphasise that a good estimate of cost effectiveness is possible only if the researcher carefully records the non-productive training time spent in the simulator.

Design for knowledge transfer assessment   This is a melting pot of methods used by psychologists for knowledge elicitation: observation, interviews, videotapes, self-confrontation, and so on. Grau (1989) and Figarol (1991) used this methodology in their field studies. The use of observations, interviews, questionnaires and examination of technical documentation is useful but extremely time-consuming. They must be reserved only for research purposes or for simulation requirement definition.

Indices of Transfer

Savings   The most common way of measuring transfer of training is to measure the 'savings' in time taken to learn the target task to a criterion of performance (when prior training has been given), in comparison with the time taken for a control group to learn the target task to the same criterion of performance (where no prior training has been given). This can be expressed by the following formula:

$$\% \text{ Savings} = 100[(B2\text{-}B1)/B2]$$

where:

B1 = number of training sessions or hours to learn task B after training on task A (i.e., for the experimental group)

B2 = number of training sessions or hours to learn task B with no prior training on task A (i.e., for the control group)

Where the prior training has resulted in a saving of time taken to reach the criterion performance of the target task, the transfer is said to be positive. However, prior training can also inhibit learning of the target task, with trainees taking longer to achieve the criterion performance. The transfer in such cases is said to be negative.

Percent transfer measure The classic transfer of training model assesses the extent of transfer brought about as a result of a particular training device or programme compared to a control group. The control group either undergoes no experimental manipulation or receives training on another device (for the purposes of comparing devices). One of the most common methods of calculating the increase in proficiency or decrease in time required to achieve the same proficiency by the experimental group relative to the control group is the Percent Transfer Measure, defined as:

$$\% \text{ Transfer} = 100[(Tc-Te)/Tc]$$

where:

Tc refers either to the time in training to criterion proficiency or to the proficiency level of the control group
Te refers to the time in training to proficiency or the proficiency level of the experimental group, having received prior practice on another task

Consider the following example (Ross & Allerton, 1991). If a control group has an average time to first solo of 15 aircraft hours, and an experimental group has an average time to first solo of 10 aircraft hours plus 3 simulator hours, then the percentage transfer would equal:

$$100[(15-10)/15] = 33\%$$

Hence, 33% of the skills required to achieve a standard equivalent to first solo can be achieved on the simulator. But this measure is not entirely accurate, because 'it does not consider the amount of practice on the prior task' (Roscoe & Williges, 1980). Additionally it does not take into account the difference in cost between the simulator time and the aircraft time.

The transfer effectiveness ratio One point that must be remembered is that, whilst the use of simulators may produce more efficient learning on the real task, the amount of time (and cost) associated with the simulator training may actually be greater than training on the real task. The training effectiveness ratio (TER) therefore takes account of the amount of training for experimental and control groups to reach a criterion of performance. For example, trainees who have received training on a simulator may make a saving of 4 hours when learning the target task, in comparison to control trainees who have received no prior training. However, if the simulator training required a greater investment of time than the 'saved' 4 hours, the simulator training has actually proved to be less efficient (in terms of time) than training in the actual task environment (even though transfer is positive). Roscoe (1971) suggested that there would be diminishing returns in simulator training, and Patrick (1992) argued that percent transfer is a negatively accelerating curve that reaches 70% after 15 hours in simulator training. The 'incremental transfer effectiveness function' (Roscoe, 1971) shows that each subsequent hour of simulator training contributes less transfer than the last.

The Transfer Effectiveness Ratio (TER; Povenmire & Roscoe, 1973) provides a ratio of the savings, in time or trials, to be gained by using a training device before learning to operate the real system. TER is expressed in the following way:

amount of savings/transfer group time in training programme

When applied to simulation training, the TER has similarly been given as:

$(TE_{-sim} - TE_{+sim})/TE_{insim}$

where:

TE_{-sim} is the training effort needed to learn the task without the use of a simulator

TE_{+sim} is the amount of time to learn the task with some training in the simulator

TE_{insim} is the amount of effort required to learn the task in the simulator

This equation has also been called the Incremental Transfer Effectiveness Function, since it describes the incremental savings in learning a criterion task in the simulator. If the amount of time spent in the training programme is exactly equal to the amount of savings, the TER will equal 1. If, on the other hand, the transfer group spends longer in the training programme than the amount of savings made, training will be less efficient than for the control group and the TER will be less than 1. Although such a TER indicates lower efficiency in terms of the total time taken to learn the task, it does not necessarily mean that the training programme should be discarded. The training programme may be cheaper to run than training in the real environment, and simulator-based training is likely to be indispensable where initial training in the real environment is too dangerous.

There are problems in using the TER. For example, the numerator reflects the difference between scores for the experimental and control groups, and Boldovici (1987) has argued that difference scores do not reflect where trainees began or finished and compound the unreliability of the two scores from which they are derived. Moreover, comparisons of gains for the two groups provide no indication of how much, if any, of the gain was ascribable to training. Sources of error should be controlled by experimental design to increase the validity of the numerator in the transfer effectiveness formula.

First-shot measures A first-shot measure can be distinguished from savings measures (Hammerton, 1967). First-shot measures are used when the criterion of interest is not the savings that can be made in time or expenditure, but the achievement of near-perfect performance on the first trial of the trained task. One example where first-shot performance needed to be as close as possible to perfect was the lunar landing (Patrick, 1992). One of the problems associated with the study of first-shot transfer is that in many situations it is not possible to use a control group (as in the lunar landings) due to the fact that subjects cannot be trained to use such vehicles *ab initio*. Hammerton suggests that the question that needs to be asked is: given a certain amount of learning with the simulator, how much of it will be retained on first transferring to the real situation?

The cumulative transfer effectiveness function When plotted, the ratio between the total savings on the criterion task and the total time spent on the prior task results in a curve known as the Cumulative Transfer Effectiveness Function (Roscoe, 1971). The formula compares the time, trials or errors of both experimental and control groups to reach criterion (as in the Percent Transfer formula). The difference lies in the numerator, which is the total time (or errors/trials) required by the experimental group, rather than by the control group, to reach criterion.

The training cost ratio The training cost ratio (TCR) complements the training effectiveness ratio, taking into account the financial costs of the training programme (e.g., Gainer *et al*, 1991; Dohme, 1991a, b). This is expressed as follows:

cost of operating simulator/cost of operating actual equipment

The cost effectiveness ratio In some cases, the cost of using a simulator may be greater than that of using a real vehicle for training, in which case the training may as well be conducted in the real environment. In other instances, the use of simulators is likely to be less costly and less dangerous than giving initial training in the real environment. The cost effectiveness ratio (CER) is given as:

TER/TCR

CER values greater than 1.0 indicate that cost-effective training can be achieved (Rolfe & Caro, 1982). According to Blaiwes *et al* (1973), two factors affect cost effectiveness: the physical fidelity of the training device, and the amount of transfer resulting from the training. But Cross (1991) emphasises that 'good estimates of cost effectiveness are possible only if the researcher is careful to record the non-productive training time spent in the simulator'. Simulator failures can quickly increase the financial cost.

Damos (1991) claimed that traditional measures of ToT (e.g., savings, percentage transfer) have two major shortcomings: they fail to take into account the amount of prior practice (training), and they provide a global estimate of transfer. She supported the use of a curve-fitting method to determine ToT. This method requires the investigator to find the best-fitting equation for the transfer data of each group in the experiment. The parameters of the equation provide estimates of the rate of improvement, the beginning level (i.e., the performance level before any practice), and the asymptotic (final) level of performance on the criterion task. Such a method requires a sophisticated statistical package and knowledge of advanced mathematical techniques. Its advantages are that it provides a more fine-grained approach than traditional formulae to analyse transfer of training, it provides estimates when no control group is available, and it facilitates the assessment of training programmes. Damos gives an example of the fitting equation. For a visual inspection task, the equation has an exponential form:

$$dv = c.e^{g * x} + h$$

where:
c, g and h are the parameters to be fitted
x is the trial block number
dv is the dependent variable

In this equation, the beginning level represents the y-intercept of the exponential function and is the sum of the c and h parameters. The asymptotic level is represented by the h parameter. The g parameter represents the rate of improvement.

Despite the advantages of curve fitting, the scientific community has failed to adopt this technique because:

- it appears time-consuming, expensive and complicated;
- it is not easy to use by managers and other individuals in decision-making positions;
- there is a lack of direct evidence for the relative merits of curve-fitting versus traditional ToT formulae.

Types of Transfer Measure

If two training devices or types of programme produce equal amounts of transfer, it is necessary to choose between them using other criteria. One such criterion is based upon what a trainee learns on each training device/programme and its relevance to the operational task. Rose et al (1987) highlight several other such criteria:

Acquisition of skills and knowledge The amount of required knowledge and skills can be evaluated. The assessment of the content and relevance of a training device can be part of the evaluation of effectiveness, particularly where empirical assessment of transfer is not possible.

Acquisition efficiency Acquisition efficiency refers to the amount of time taken to acquire the necessary knowledge and skills to perform a task. However, this information is already accounted for in the transfer effectiveness ratio.

Transfer efficiency Features that enhance transfer may not necessarily enhance knowledge or skill acquisition. Rose *et al* (1987) give the example of a training device with a feature that permitted simulation of environmental conditions found in operational situations. Although this feature would enhance transfer to these situations, its use would probably slow the rate of skill acquisition or learning while using the device.

Several rating methods can be used to evaluate the transfer effectiveness of a training device. One purely qualitative method relies on a comparison of the device to a real aircraft made by experienced pilots. The comments of the experienced pilots are then compared to a control group who receive no simulator exposure but are tested on the real device. The rating method described by Adams (1979) has two parts, including an engineering evaluation of the simulator and an assessment by an experienced pilot, and indicates the similarity to the corresponding real aircraft. Several problems can be identified with this measure. First, it is a measure of transfer only in so far as it contains an evaluation of the physical fidelity of the simulator to the real aircraft. There is a false assumption that the amount of transfer is positively related to the physical fidelity. Secondly, Adams notes evidence that suggests that pilots are unable objectively to discern the similarities between simulator and aircraft with ratings reflecting their experience. Thirdly, ratings and flying performance are not always positively correlated, so that simulator handling can be shown to be degraded by the ratings but performance does not in fact change. Finally, this method assumes that it is necessary for a training device to encompass all the elements of a real aircraft, whereas the evidence suggests that too much detail can interfere with learning basic skills (Rose *et al*, 1987).

Although several studies have used expert ratings to measure qualitatively the transfer of training, some authors (e.g., Waag, 1991) think that the use of expert opinion as a means of estimating transfer is of dubious scientific validity. Edwards and Hubbard (1991) used a qualitative measure to assess the training potential of the Air Intercept Trainer (AIT) as applied to initial qualification of F-16C pilots. The quality of the training was assessed using a five-point scale for measuring performance (0 = lack of ability, 1 = limited ability, 2 = essentially correct, 3 = correct and skilful, 4 = high degree of ability). Trainees were rated by instructors on five categories of tasks. The objective was to achieve level 3 proficiency in each intercept. Although this was not a classic transfer of training study (its aim was to determine the training effectiveness of an advanced design, part-task trainer in an Air Force operational training unit environment), the authors believed that their results demonstrated the transfer effectiveness of the AIT training.

Nullmeyer and Rockaway (1985) adopted a qualitative measure of transfer of training, using selected flight performance parameters. Instructors rated deviations from desired values of specific parameters in the critical tasks (approach, landing, engine-out go-around). The number of instructor inputs was one of the indications of level of performance. Guckenberger *et al* (1993) also used the subjective ratings given by instructors as qualitative measures.

Another qualitative measure is Relative Training Effectiveness (RTE). Rolfe *et al* (1985) used a method created to decide the point at which a student should convert from an elementary trainer to a more advanced type of aircraft (Bazzocchi, 1979; Russel, 1980; Cook *et al*, 1984). According to the authors, the judgement of an experienced instructor can be expressed as a quantitative measure, which is based on simple factors, but compounded in a way that may be obscure even to the author of the process. The analysis proposed suggested an explicit algorithm. This method linked two different types of factors: characteristics of the aircraft that are objective and quantifiable, and individual exercises to form a subjective judgement. A sample of experienced pilots was asked individually to assess, on a four-point scale, the importance of each aircraft characteristic (0 = the characteristic is of no importance to the exercise, 3 = the characteristic is vitally important to the exercise), in the teaching of each exercise in the syllabus.

To determine the degree of transfer, it is necessary to measure performance accurately. Hays *et al* (1992) performed a meta-analysis of 247 studies of transfer of training. With respect to performance measurement, they found that subjective performance measures such as instructor ratings were more sensitive to training effects than those obtained with objective measures such as instrument readings.

As preparation for a transfer of training study, some crucial questions must be answered:

• What is the objective of the study (transfer of training measure, transfer of learning, cost effectiveness assessment, simulator evaluation, or fundamental research)?
• What type of transfer will be evaluated (forward, backward or quasi-transfer)?
• What are the resources available for the study?

The combined answers to these questions will for the most part determine the most appropriate experimental method. Quantitative measures are commonly used by psychologists and training specialists. They are easy to understand and to record in the majority of training programmes. More sophisticated approaches such as curve fitting are used to a lesser extent. The widespread use of these traditional techniques does not mean that they do not have shortcomings. The main shortcoming is the lack of data on the nature of knowledge or strategies learned by the trainees. Qualitative measures have to be used to assess such data, but are rarely used in transfer studies to assess the trainees' performance. Qualitative measurements are often a result of subjective assessments by experienced instructors. By taking into account their knowledge and the criteria they use for evaluating students, the inherent subjectivity of the results could be either reduced or in some cases eliminated. Knowledge elicitation using instructors would provide more informative qualitative measures and would result in more relevant results.

The errors that trainees make when performing a task could also be taken into account. Errors can be transferred from one device to another. Their occurrence can constitute a reference point in assessing transfer effectiveness or in evaluating simulator design.

Examples of transfer measurement are given below, illustrating some of the major factors that have been found to affect the transfer process.

Simulator fidelity Hays (1980) argued that 'Fidelity is the degree of similarity between the simulator and the equipment which is simulated. It is a measure of the physical characteristics of the simulator (physical fidelity), and the informational or stimulus and response options of the equipment (functional fidelity)'. Allen *et al* (1986) found that functional fidelity was a very important determinant of performance, influencing solution times and inter-response times. Physical fidelity also had an effect on performance, since persons trained on lower fidelity simulators took longer to reach correct solutions.

Fidelity as a measure of transfer To measure the training effectiveness of a simulator, Hays (1980) proposed the calculation of TER in nine different situations corresponding to the crossing of two variables — physical fidelity and functional fidelity — each of which could be low, medium, or high. This procedure would furnish trainers with alternative levels of fidelity at different stages of the learning process.

Inter-device transfer Smith and Hagman (1993) examined and measured the positive transfer of training between two devices. The following issues were addressed:

- Examination of evidence for bi-directional versus uni-directional transfer of training.
- Testing whether training measures on one device correlated with subsequent test scores on the other device.
- Computation of the correlation between test scores on the two devices. This is not a strict test, because correlation does not necessarily mean that training on one device improves scores on the other. Nevertheless, it is reasonable to expect that, if transfer is to occur, then scores on the two devices should correlate.
- Transfer of training may depend on other variables such as age, rank, or amount of real device experience. For this reason, the predictability of one device scores were examined by combining these variables with the other device scores and vice versa.

Additional research with larger sample sizes and longer training intervals is needed to draw firm conclusions concerning the transfer of training from one device to another.

Current Applications of Transfer Measurement

In the questionnaire-based field orientation survey of current military practice conducted as part of the MASTER project, three factors were cited by the interviewees as important means of improving transfer of training from the simulation systems to the real world: physical fidelity, dynamics and use of feedback. It was noted that simulators with poor physical cues or unrepresentative dynamics sometimes deliver negative transfer.

Although instructors have some understanding of transfer issues, transfer is seldom assessed during training programme design. Data are usually collected to provide a measure of success in satisfying training goals rather than of transfer. When transfer is considered, it is always assessed subjectively, either by subjective instructor assessment or by verbal interrogation of the trainee. Formal methods of transfer measurement are difficult and time-consuming to apply in real training programmes, and there is an understandable tendency to avoid exposing trainees to experimental programmes that may prove to be ineffective.

Measures such as cost or time savings are rarely objectively measured, and formal studies comparing the training programme in use to other programmes are not conducted. The questionnaire responses show that training programmes evolve on the basis of experience, with little regard for theoretical considerations. Because of the lack of theoretical background, there is often confusion between learning and transfer of training.

A possible method of collecting data on transfer of training is to obtain feedback on the trainees' abilities once they are exposed to the real environment in an operational unit. However, training establishments do not usually receive feedback with respect to the trainees' operational performance, unless they fall below the standards expected by the military unit.

There is a lack of co-ordination between the scientific community and those involved in designing and delivering training. Efforts must be made to recognise practical constraints during scientific research, and theoretical data should be used to inform training programme design. Designers and training managers should be aware of the need to introduce assessment into the design process before the simulation system is used operationally.

Skill Retention

Learning is most often associated with the initial phase of acquiring a skill, whereas 'retention' relates more specifically to the ability to reproduce an acquired skill after a period of non-performance. For several decades, researchers have been interested in the measurement of skill retention. Although numerous theoretical approaches have been proposed, there is still no widely accepted method of measuring the rate of skill decay over time.

Importance of Skill Retention Measurement

The period between the completion of training and subsequent performance of the trained skill is conventionally referred to as the 'retention interval'. Significant decay of skill during a retention interval, before it is required in operation, is obviously problematic. Hence, adequate skill retention is potentially a key criterion of training programme success. Skills in which retention is of particular importance are those in which there may be long intervals between training and operational performance, or between one performance and the next. These include skills that are used only in emergencies and other rare situations. Long-term retention is also of importance whenever skilled personnel are temporarily re-assigned to another task (as can occur with job rotation), when there is an interruption in career service, or when job assignments are sporadic (as can easily occur with reserve forces). There may also be skill deterioration under operational conditions if performance errors are allowed to go undetected and uncorrected. The problem of skill retention and loss is of particular concern in the military context for a number of reasons. First, operational conditions often demand reliable, rapid and accurate task performance under stress at what can often be very irregular intervals. Secondly, the increasing reliance on automation in tasks that once required constant operator involvement can lead to the degradation of skills through lack of practice. Finally, because of the relatively high cost of most military training, the failure of operators to retain skills can have considerable financial implications.

Skill retention is traditionally plotted against time since original learning, forming what is known as the retention curve. The classic retention curve is negatively accelerated, falling quickly following skill acquisition and declining more slowly thereafter. Accurate prediction models for skill loss could serve as a basis for defining the time intervals for refresher training. They could also be used to identify the particular tasks that are prone to skill loss, enabling the training specialist to include measures to counter this loss during initial training. Clearly, the development of mathematical models to predict the course of skill decay would be invaluable to the training specialist; however, because of the intangible nature of the subject area such models have proved difficult to formulate.

Several researchers have used the term 'forgetting function' to describe memory decay over time; however, this term is not strictly correct, since we cannot measure what has been forgotten, only what has been retained. Further, failure to remember material at a particular instant does not mean that it has been forgotten: it may be remembered at a later time under different testing conditions.

The assumption that a single function can be derived to predict skill retention in a variety of tasks, populations and retention intervals has obvious appeal, but there is little evidence for the existence of a single 'generic' function. Research has shown that many factors influence the rate of skill decay, and the complex interactions between them are the primary reason why progress in this area has been hindered. Each retention study is conducted under slightly different conditions, leading researchers to derive apparently conflicting conclusions. Although the conclusions may be contradictory, they may each be valid for the specific conditions being investigated. Hence, rather than attempting to derive a single generic retention function, it is more appropriate to derive a series of functions tailored to different conditions.

Traditionally, retention functions have been either theory- or empirically-driven. Some researchers (e.g., Wickelgren, 1972) derived theoretical models from first principles by describing the underlying memory mechanisms involved in retention, and then attempted to fit the model to empirical data. Recently, a more empirical approach has been adopted using curve-fitting techniques to account for particular sets of retention data. Theory must be developed to account for the mathematical curves with the best fit. Although this approach can serve to constrain and provide a framework for theory, it also introduces its own complications due to the nature of mathematical modelling. An infinite number of mathematical functions can be derived, and often *several* functions can be found to fit a set of empirical data. In addition, various transformations of the fundamental data can be performed, which can also affect the goodness of fit of various functions. If it is found that several functions can accurately describe a set of data, the 'correct' function is difficult to identify.

Requirements for Skill Retention Measurement

The majority of studies of skill retention have focused either on a specific type of skill learning (such as perceptual-motor skills) or on a specific domain of application (such as naval missions). Several earlier reviewers criticised the existing research literature for focusing on learning, retention and recall in the laboratory without considering the relevance of task variables and other 'real-life' factors (e.g., Prophet, 1976; Schendel *et al*, 1978; Hurlock & Montague, 1982). The results were often difficult to generalise and lacking in face validity. Experimental tasks lacked 'real-life' meaning and relevance for the subjects concerned. Later research has attempted to address this problem, but there still remains a paucity of empirical data on actual operational performance.

Hurlock and Montague (1982) reviewed the research literature on skill loss with particular reference to implications for navy personnel management practices. One of their main concerns was that there was a lack of data on skill loss and skill retention in the field, as opposed to in the laboratory. One reason for this has been the low availability of on-the-job performance evaluation tests: 'Without more precise qualitative and quantitative performance assessments, it is impossible to know when or to what degree a skill has deteriorated. It is also impossible to determine whether a preventive or corrective action has been effective. These conditions are unlikely to change soon' (Hurlock & Montague, 1982).

Although performance (recall) testing is the most direct way to identify skill deterioration in the field, it is both costly and intrusive. It can also be very difficult to develop a test that objectively indicates the extent to which the demands of a task are being met. In addition, Hurlock and Montague (1982) reported a difficulty in drawing a clear distinction between practice and non-practice periods. Most of the reported research is based on simple experimental tasks, performed, for the sake of scientific validity, under highly controlled conditions. Within these experiments, there is a well-defined training period followed by a well-defined retention interval. In practice, however, practice and non-practice periods are less distinct. It is possible that isolated elements of a skill could be developed over time through job experience before the more complex skill itself is required; it is also possible for skills to be degraded even during periods of repeated on-the-job performance if feedback is absent or inadequate.

Schendel and Hagman (1991) point out that any attempt to measure retention must entail the use of at least two recall tests: one *immediately* following training, the other at the end of the retention interval. The lack of an immediate post-training test is, they argue, a common failing of retention experiments. Farr (1987) suggests that retention testing conditions can be optimised by:

- employing consistent retention measures (either free recall or recognition);

- conducting tests in contexts similar to original learning;
- measuring savings on relearning.

Type of Measure

Many types of dependent measure are used in retention studies, some of which can be collected using the same retrieval test. Each measure offers its own advantages and disadvantages. The most frequently used measure (presumably because of its simplicity) is *percentage correct*; however, this has the disadvantage that it cannot distinguish between degrees of overlearning at 'perfect' (100% correct) performance. The second most frequently used measure is d', derived from information theory and discussed earlier in this section. This measure accounts for the possibility of false alarms and overcomes the limitations of *percentage correct* scores. The *percentage correct* and d' measures were compared in a study by Wixted and Ebbesen (1991) to determine whether they generated different retention curves. Although the measures generally yielded the same functions, they deviated at extreme scores (0% and 100 % correct).

Ebbinghaus (1885/1964) proposed the *savings* measure, which considered the number of trials or time required to regain an initial mastery level. This measure relies on the assumption that the more that is recalled on the first relearning trial, the fewer the number of trials required to reach initial mastery. However, many studies have shown that subjects who achieve a very low retention score on the first trial can achieve a very high savings score.

Other more novel measures have been developed, such as the *need odds* measure proposed by Anderson and Schooler (1991). This assumes that items in memory are assigned a weighting according to the probability of their being required in the future. A retention function can be produced relating *need odds* to recall latency and accuracy.

It is not yet clear from the literature whether the type of dependent measure *does* affect the shape of a retention function; however, this possibility cannot be discounted.

Retention Functions

Many researchers have attempted to fit mathematical functions to data sets to develop models that predict the course of skill decay. Simple retention experiments (e.g., the Brown-Peterson experiments) provide data to which the retention curve can be fitted. Having developed a retention function, the researcher then proceeds to explain the function through theory. A variety of retention functions have been developed, and those most frequently used are discussed in the following sections.

Exponential function   The exponential function, the most common retention function, was first proposed by Ebbinghaus (1885/1964). It has been successfully used in several short-term memory experiments (e.g., Wickelgren, 1974) and has the advantage of being relatively simple in mathematical terms. An exponential function implies that during each unit of time a constant proportion of the items left in memory is lost. This function has been favoured by researchers because it is widely used to describe other psychophysical phenomena such as spatial discrimination. White (1985) likened the process of direct remembering to that of direct perception. He claimed that, just as spatial discriminability declines at a constant rate with spatial distance, so too does retention. White's exponential decay function assumes that the rate of decay is independent of the initial discriminability of the stimulus (in this case the degree of original learning), which contradicts many other theories of direct remembering. Loftus (1985) and Slamencka and McElree (1983) assumed an exponential function in their discussion of retention curves.

Logarithmic function The logarithmic function, favoured by early researchers (e.g., Luh, 1922), assumes that retention has a linear relationship with the *ratio* of time, with equal ratios of time leading to equal amounts of skill decay. For example, this function assumes that, if there is a 10% reduction in retention performance between 3 and 4 seconds, there should also be a 10% reduction between 30 and 40 minutes.

Although the logarithmic function is one of the simplest in mathematical terms, it is not effective at very short or very long time intervals. At long time intervals, the logarithmic function requires that retention values are *negative* (as opposed to reaching an asymptote) and at short retention intervals (e.g., when time equals zero) the retention value nears infinity. However, as noted by Ruben and Wenzel (1996), immediate recall occurs not when time equals zero but rather after a very brief period, and so the boundary difficulties associated with this function have not caused it to be dismissed as a potential function for describing retention.

Power function According to Anderson and Schooler (1991), the power function is the most versatile of all the retention functions. They claimed that it can describe memory decay at a wide range of retention intervals (a few seconds to a few years). The power function assumes that the *ratio* of retention has a linear relationship with the *ratio* of time, i.e., equal ratios of time lead to equal ratios of skill decay. It differs slightly from the logarithmic function, which assumes that equal *ratios* of time lead to equal *amounts* of skill decay. The power function has been used to describe other judgements of perceptual magnitude such as loudness and brightness. Wixted and Ebbesen (1991) conducted an experiment in which they used a variety of measures of retention (recall and recognition scores) and memory tasks (words, faces and graphics), and tested different species (humans and pigeons) at different retention intervals (seconds, days and weeks). They found that, in all cases, the best fitting function was the power function. However, the boundary problems associated with the logarithmic function apply also to the power function. The function assumes that, as time approaches zero, retention performance nears infinity; it is therefore suitable only for describing data that do not have an upper limit of performance (e.g., d' and *need odds*). Consequently, it is not suitable for describing the percentage of correct responses, as this measure *does* assume an upper limit of performance.

Exponential-power function Wickelgren (1974) advocated an exponential-power function to describe memory trace decay in his single-trace fragility theory. He postulated that when the trace is in short-term memory it rapidly decays following an exponential function. As the trace becomes consolidated into LTM, it decays following a power function. To validate this function, Wickelgren conducted a simple recognition experiment and attempted to fit a series of retention functions to the data. He tested the linear, exponential, logarithmic and power functions, and found that only an exponential-power function was able to produce a good fit to the data.

Sticha *et al* (1983) used Wickelgren's single-trace fragility theory as the basis for a set of integrated models, which were developed using SAINT, a network simulation tool. Learning and retention models were developed to predict the effects of training and skill decay on task performance. These models assumed an exponential-power function of decay. Models of eight procedural tasks were developed and the predictions, showing the course of learning and subsequent decay, were validated against actual data and found to be closely correlated. The researchers claimed that the model would enable training specialists to predict the course of learning and skill decay, allowing them to optimise training schedules and refresher training; however, they conceded that the model required more extensive validation. Such computer-based models would indeed be invaluable to training specialists, and the model developed by Sticha *et al* represents a positive step towards achieving this objective. However, as with all such models, its validity relies on the credibility of the underlying theory, and at this stage the theory relating to skill retention cannot be considered definitive.

Need probability function   Anderson and Schooler (1991) developed a theory-driven retention function in which the course of skill decay follows a power function. Memory is assumed to have been adapted over the years to the environment, and consequently to have developed a means of using past history to estimate whether an item is likely to be needed in the future. Each memory trace has a *need odds* value that represents the strength of a memory trace. The time taken to examine a trace with a *need odds*, q, is proportional to the number of memory traces with *need odds* greater than q. The function assumes that the *need odds* of individual traces decay as a power function of time.

This function differs from the empirical curve-fitting functions described earlier because it accounts for the effects of practice on retention. The function assumes that the strength from individual presentations of an item is additive and forms the total strength; the greater the level of practice, the greater the trace strength and the slower the rate of decay. The function also accounts for the effect of different presentation schedules on retention. Anderson and Schooler demonstrated that the spacing between repetitions of an item during training has an effect on retention, with massed-practice training producing a notably steeper retention curve (at long test lags) than distributed training schedules. This factor is included in the retention function by adding a decreasing exponent to the power function corresponding to the time since the previous presentation of an item. This is one of the few retention functions that can account for the factors of practice and spacing, both of which are known to influence skill retention.

Weighting function   Laming (1992) also produced a theory-driven retention function called the weighting function, based on the assumption that the probability of retrieval is dependent on the degree of original learning. He stated that the difficulty in retrieval increases with the passage of time and can be measured by a weighting that decreases as the reciprocal of time. Laming claimed that his weighting function successfully accounts for the vast collection of empirical data on the subject of skill retention measurement.

The function assumes that stimuli presented at different points in time will have different weightings. Each item examined in memory has an associated response latency, with memories more remote in time (since original learning) taking longer to recall. When a stimulus is presented several times, repeated records are created in memory, each with its own weighting and each capable of supporting a correct response. Rehearsal of an item (as occurs during spaced practice sessions) creates additional copies of the record in memory and therefore assists retention. The signal to recall is a cue that interacts with the contents of memory and the weighting function measures the strength of this interaction with items in memory. The cue may also interact with other stimuli presented on previous trials (proactive interference). The function therefore accounts for the effects of interference, practice and spacing in its description of retention over time. The function is similar to Wickelgren's single-trace fragility theory; however, Wickelgren assumed memory traces to be affected by two decaying properties — strength and fragility — whereas Laming assumed only one property (strength), which decays as the reciprocal of time.

Current Approaches to Skill Retention Measurement

Currently, there is no recognised valid means of predicting skill loss. The most promising approach appears to be the US Army Skill Retention Model. This model was developed over a period of three years by the American Institutes for Research (AIR) on behalf of the US Army Research Institute for the Behavioral and Social Sciences. The model seems to present a potentially useful method for predicting unit proficiency on specific tasks. In principle, it allows users to predict factors such as: how quickly specific tasks are forgotten; which tasks will be forgotten most rapidly; what proportion of a trained group (unit) of personnel will be able to perform a task successfully after a specified period of non-practice; and when and how often re-training should be given. It does not, however, allow predictions for individual operators. It is also oriented more towards procedural tasks than other task types. More significantly, as a *de facto* model (constructed to fit a body of data) rather than an *a priori* model (deduced logically), the general validity of the tool is questionable (Kukich, 1988).

Conclusions on Skill Decay Measurement

Despite several decades of research, the literature concerning the measurement of skill retention is inconclusive. Several retention functions have been proposed, but there is still no widely accepted function to predict the course of skill decay over time. It is known that the rate of skill decay is influenced by several factors, such as the degree of original learning, the spacing of learning trials and the type of retrieval test; however, the exact nature of this influence is *not* known. For example, the issue of whether skill decay is dependent on the degree of original learning is still a source of debate. Similarly, it is not yet known whether a single retention function can be derived that will fit a variety of dependent measures of retention, or whether a range of retention functions is more appropriate.

Wixted and Ebbesen (1991) added further complications by stating that a relationship formed on the basis of empirical data will not necessarily follow the same relationship as the underlying psychological variable. For example, even though an exponential function may provide a good fit to a set of empirical data, the underlying memory trace may decay following an entirely different function. Complexities such as these have hindered progress in this area and it is clear that the factors influencing skill decay must somehow be accounted for in a retention function.

Despite these difficulties, the search for a quantitative description of skill retention is still viewed as a worthwhile pursuit amongst contemporary researchers and is a topic of continued research. In general, skills decay over time if not practised regularly. The exact rate of decay depends upon a number of variables, particularly task characteristics, training factors and post-training activities. Knowledge of these factors and of the processes of skill decay allows us to identify vulnerable tasks and to focus training/re-training effort as appropriate. This also requires specific knowledge of the tasks to be trained, analysed at the level of the cognitive and physical component processes. The following principal conclusions can be drawn:

- Complex procedural skills are particularly vulnerable to decay, and require regular rehearsal to maintain accurate recall of the specific task steps and their logical sequence.
- Complex tasks benefit from being well organised, with inherent cues pointing from one task step to another, to aid the operator's procedural recall.
- Cognitive skills, in particular, benefit from overlearning through extra initial training and practice, although the positive effect diminishes as the period of non-practice increases.
- Contextual interference during training is an effective method of enhancing retention.
- Training to the level of automaticity (through consistent stimulus-response mapping) leads to task performance that is fast but relatively inflexible. If needed, training with variable mapping of task components will help develop behaviour that is more adaptive to different operational circumstances.
- In the training of complex tasks, it is beneficial to provide trainees with explanatory operational knowledge of the task.
- Providing augmented feedback (shortly after task performance), especially during the early stages of training, is beneficial to long-term learning if applied with care.
- Distributed training enhances skills retention, but is not widely used.
- Using refresher training techniques, possibly low-cost simulators or even mental rehearsal, can be more cost-effective than improving initial training methods.

However, there is a need for research to determine how best to provide such techniques to maintain proficiency on specific skills in particular circumstances.

- Negative effects on task proficiency caused by unfamiliar or difficult operational circumstances (job conditions) are primarily a transfer of training issue.
- There are no known personnel characteristics relating directly to skill retention that are of relevance to military training, other than the fact that high-ability trainees will obviously learn more of a skill initially.

27 Discussion and Conclusions

Good progress was made in the MASTER project towards the development of standardised methodologies to support training evaluation. These methodologies include a systematic approach to determining the tasks and skills that must be assessed, validated measures of trainee workload and performance, and experimental designs to examine issues such as retention and transfer of skills.

Of the performance measures, there remains a requirement for further work on team performance and decision making. The Crew Competencies Questionnaire was found to measure some aspects of good team performance, but more research is needed to produce an instrument with better diagnostic properties that can help the trainer to identify which teamwork skills require improvement. Similarly, a practical method of measuring decision-making processes is not yet available, and this problem is likely to persist until further progress has been made in academic cognitive psychology.

Performance measures such as the speed and accuracy of discrete responses and error in continuous control are well established, and appear to be valid measures of progress in training. In many simulators, recording of such measures would be straightforward, and would provide a useful adjunct to subjective ratings. The simulator should be equipped with facilities to measure and store data across many trials, allowing multiple variables to be assessed.

Workload measures were successfully used as an index of trainee progress, and were found to be task-independent. It is hoped that the measures included in the MASTER battery will be widely adopted by trainers. They combine ease of presentation and analysis with good psychometric soundness. One obvious use would be as a quantitative index of the degree of overlearning achieved at later stages of the training process.

With respect to current military selection systems, it was found that the tests used vary from fully validated psychometric tests to informal instructor assessments. Simulation-based selection systems are used only for relatively highly skilled roles such as pilot or air traffic controller. However, there is a lack a standardisation of selection methods for the same role, and almost a complete failure to address teamwork issues.

It was concluded that further research was needed on the adequacy of static tests and psychometric tests in the selection of individuals for dynamic tasks, and on development of teamwork measures. Further requirements include the development of methods of integrating simulator-based work sample data, more rigorous statistical analysis of data, and greater consideration of theoretical models.

The work on transfer of training revealed widespread use of quantitative measures by psychologists, but little adoption of more sophisticated approaches such as curve-fitting methods. Transfer, moreover, was seldom measured during military simulator-based training programmes.

A major shortcoming in transfer assessment is the inability to address the strategies used by trainees, which are dependent upon qualitative measures. Knowledge elicitation from instructors would provide more informative qualitative measures and would result in more relevant results. Greater attention to the errors made by trainees is also required, perhaps by adoption of the automatic method of recording errors tested in the MASTER project.

The extensive literature on retention of skill was analysed. Although the precise nature of the underlying mechanisms remains elusive, it was possible to draw firm conclusions concerning factors that enhance retention.

Recommendations

- The MASTER methodology for analysing missions, tasks, and skills should be widely adopted in European military training programmes, to obtain the benefits of a standardised approach.
- The validated performance measures in the MASTER battery, including the automated method for error detection, should be used in training programmes.
- Since the battery is incomplete, it should be refined and extended in later research. There is a particular requirement for measures of team performance and of decision making.
- Greater use of workload measures should be made during training, using the measures included in the MASTER battery.
- Current selection systems should give greater priority to rigorous analysis of data.
- More research is needed on the adequacy of static tests in selecting individuals for complex dynamic tasks.
- Methods of integrating selection data to yield a single value should be developed.
- Theoretical approaches should play a greater role in the development of selection methods.
- In transfer of training studies, qualitative methods of assessing trainees' strategies should be developed, perhaps based upon knowledge elicitation from instructors.
- Greater attention should be given to analysis of the errors made by trainees.
- To optimise skill retention, several task characteristics should be considered, including cognitive requirements, organisation, provision of cues and display-control compatibility.
- Overlearning should be encouraged; consistent mapping of stimuli to responses should be used to help develop automaticity; operationally-based explanations should be provided, and conceptually-based explanations avoided, to make the

tasks more meaningful; post-task augmented feedback should be provided during initial acquisition (highlighting performance errors and their causes); distributed rather than massed training schedules should be used; the training environment should resemble the operational environment; and the previous knowledge and skills of trainees should be exploited.

- Skills should be maintained during the retention interval by determining the requirements for regular practice or refresher training of particular tasks; eliciting mental rehearsal of tasks or providing refresher/practice tests, possibly using relatively simple simulations; and providing refresher training sessions within six months of training completion for complex tasks.

- Further research is required on the retention, loss and maintenance of cognitive skills such as situation assessment and decision making and the cognitive components of procedural skills; the cueing of implicit task steps and processes during procedural task performance; the impact and interaction of factors affecting the specification and provision of refresher training; and the effects of mental rehearsal techniques on retention.

Epilogue

Epilogue

28 Future Trends

The Future of Simulator-Based Training

Developments in Training Needs

Automation has produced a shift from perceptual-motor to more procedural and cognitive modes of system control. Systems are deployed in an increasingly complex and dynamic environment. Shorter response times, and co-ordination over ever larger distances and between less homogeneous task forces, impose high demands on situational awareness and on timely and accurate communication between the players in the battle space. Thus, the specification problem is likely to become more difficult, with increased emphasis on TNA and TPD.

International co-operation and multi-national composition of task forces call for increased harmonisation of the specification of training needs and of approaches to training. This implies more co-ordinated development and control of training programmes. Training concepts and terminology must be harmonised by further developing empirically tested concepts and by agreeing upon a common glossary of terms. However, harmonisation seems inconsistent with the prevailing 'train-like-you-fight' doctrine, which dictates that unit commanders are fully responsible for the amount and content of training of the troops under their command.

In addition to the development of more advanced systems, diversification of missions will make future operations less predictable. As a consequence, basic training of units will have to be complemented by tuned just-in-time training, mission rehearsal, and *in situ* training of units that are posted and deployed abroad. Inevitably, this will lead to a blending of training and operational doctrine.

The technology used for training today may well be used in controlling systems tomorrow. The near future will see systems that are hybrid in more than one sense. Training facilities will be embedded into operational systems, and simulation technology will be used to design more intuitive interfaces (e.g., 3-D audio displays to aid target acquisition in fighter aircraft, or the use of augmented reality to prevent spatial disorientation in controlling remotely piloted vehicles).

Technological Developments

At least for initial training, increased use will be made of the rapidly expanding capabilities of desktop simulation and gaming. Skills acquired on desktop systems transfer to subsequent training and to performance on the real system. For instance, a MASTER experiment in desktop training of flight aerobatic skills showed:

- an improved ability to extract relevant visual cues from the outside world needed to perform the *time-critical elements* of aerobatics;
- speeded learning of procedural elements of aerobatics earlier in training;
- an improved basis for in-flight development of 'seat-of-the-pants' skills.

These results demonstrate the potential of low-end training approaches. It is expected that the further development of commercial off-the-shelf components will enable easy and low-cost assembly of simulators. Crucial in such a development, however, is a focus on critical task elements and on those aspects that can be simulated with high fidelity. Training- and cost-effectiveness can be further increased by the use of efficient training and instruction strategies and of objective performance measurement and feedback techniques. The concepts, guidelines, and methodology described in this Handbook may serve as a source of inspiration in realising this potential. There will also be further technological developments in the direction of more transportable and convertible simulators, to address the need for mission rehearsal and continuation training of units that are posted abroad.

For training efficiency and financial reasons, there is likely to be a trend towards sharing of simulator resources between different training establishments, military services, and nations. This may lead to multi-national simulator facilities, run by government-owned or privately-owned organisations.

The development of more open simulator standards will continue, as these are required to ensure compatibility and interoperability of systems and system components. Interoperability solves some of the more difficult problems of networking simulators, but leaves open the question of how to use them for developing and maintaining the team skills needed to operate as a real unit in the field. The further development and increased use of simulator networks is expected to stimulate research efforts on more effective and validated team training concepts.

Methodology Development

The methodology presented in this Handbook has been provisionally implemented in a set of manuals and software tools. It provides a sound framework, but requires further development. Such a development requires a dedicated task force and an appropriate forum, perhaps Internet-based. Several follow-up activities are required, addressing development and validation. Development activities should be aimed at the further elaboration of guidelines and user support, conducted concurrently for maximum effectiveness.

Development Activities

Elaboration of guidelines As discussed in the main body of this Handbook, many gaps in our knowledge remain. The methodology developed helps to identify these gaps and to set priorities for filling them. Many guidelines have already been derived from the literature or experimental work, but they must be extended, harmonised, and elaborated. The guidelines required will range from general to highly specific, to support different users during the different phases of the specification process. A balance must be struck between the need for a comprehensive general approach and the need for solutions to specific training and simulation problems.

Development of user support Application of the methodology is by no means fully automated, and will continue to require a high level of user involvement. Although there may be many off-the-shelf devices, there are no off-the-shelf training solutions.

The methodology comprises a large number of steps, and, because of the many inter-dependencies between steps, frequent iterations will be required. Users of the methodology may have different backgrounds and needs. To maintain the focus on training needs as the central unifying principle, extensive and flexible user support is essential. To provide this support and to keep track of the specification process itself, a certain amount of standardisation is important. Documentation is a key element of the process, given the iteration between steps and the need for communication between different contributors. Good documentation ensures traceability of the specification process and effective sharing of information. It further enables improvements to be implemented and lessons to be learned.

Validation Activities

Validation should involve the entire process, because individual steps can cue as well as constrain each other. Therefore, changes to one step are likely to affect the way in which other steps are conducted.

Issues and Directions for Research

Some of the most important gaps are described briefly below.

Training Needs Analysis

Currently, there are many approaches to mission analysis, many of which are quite domain-specific. There is a clear need for a more generic approach. Within this Handbook, the outline of such an approach has been developed. There is a need to elaborate this generic approach further.

In most approaches to task analysis, crew and team aspects are scarcely addressed. It has further been proven difficult to represent continuous tasks, cognitive tasks, and dependencies between tasks in a clear and meaningful way. The distinction between tasks and skills is not always made clear. To some extent, this may be caused by inconsistent use of terms. Another area for further work is the development of taxonomies, at different levels of aggregation.

Current methods do not enable full identification of cueing requirements. Part of this problem may be resolved by using knowledge of human perception and human information processing characteristics during task analysis.

Training objectives are usually defined rather vaguely, and sometimes even *post hoc*, i.e. after the procurement of the simulator training device and the development of the training programme. Training objectives should be the input to Training Programme Design; certainly not the result. To achieve this, the distinctions and relations between missions, tasks, skills, and training objectives should be elaborated to establish more explicit links between operational performance requirements and training requirements.

Training Programme Design

Although many principles of training and instruction have been proposed, they are often rather general and lacking in empirical validation. This general critique particularly applies to the proposed sequencing principles.

There is an increasing need for guidance with respect to team training. The trend towards more agent-based training, by which the team context is simulated in individual training sessions, will be an important impetus for research on effective team training concepts.

Nevertheless, the available knowledge with respect to training and instruction is quite extensive, even if not always applied effectively. For instance, the possibilities of instructional support for simulator training have barely been explored, let alone the possibilities of automation of instructional support.

Assessment of training performance and progress is often largely subjective and therefore less reliable. Consequently, the guidance and feedback provided to trainees are less effective, and learning opportunities are not exploited sufficiently. There is a need for data on the results of training, particularly on trainee drop-out rates and performance baselines/entry levels, to enable the assessment of the effectiveness of training programmes and devices. Simulator data collection facilities are not fully exploited. As already noted, it is not difficult in principle to specify effective measures of perceptual, motor, and procedural skills. A more fundamental problem is the specification of better measures of cognitive skills, time-sharing skills, and team skills.

In military training communities, the notion that physical fidelity is a prerequisite for transfer of training persists. Although transfer is increasingly considered key to the evaluation of simulator-based training, it is rarely measured formally. Similarly, training establishments do not keep records of skill retention. During simulator-based training, valuable data are often not analysed or even stored. Much can be gained by a more systematic approach to the evaluation of simulator-based training.

Training Media Specification

Despite considerable knowledge of human perception and information processing characteristics, there is a need for greater study of:
- skill-specific cueing requirements;
- individual differences in cue utilisation;
- cue interactions.

Filling these knowledge gaps requires a more analytic approach to simulator validation. It is not helpful to know merely that transfer is positive, negative, or absent, because such results in themselves cannot suggest ways of improving transfer of training. Specific hypotheses about cueing requirements for particular skills and alternative ways of simulating these cues must be empirically tested. This will require comparisons of human performance in a simulator with that in the real system.

Knowledge Generation

A recurrent theme has been that many issues remain to be resolved. High levels of intellectual and financial investment are required, together with greater co-operation between research institutes, industry, and simulator users. The MASTER project was a first step towards achieving this co-operation.

References

Aasman, J., Mulder, G.J., & Mulder, L.J.M. (1987). Operator effort and the measurement of heart-rate variability. *Human Factors, 29 (2)*, 161-170.

Ackerman, P.L. (1987). Individual differences in skill learning: An integration of psychometric and information processing perspectives. *Psychological Bulletin, 102(1)*, 3-27.

Ackerman, P.L. (1988). Determinants of individual differences during skill acquisition: Cognitive abilities and information processing. *Journal of Experimental Psychology, 117(3)*, 288-318.

Ackerman, P.L., & Kyllonen, P.C. (1991). Trainee characteristics. In J.E. Morrison (Ed.), *Training for performance: Principles of applied human learning* (pp 193-229). Chichester: John Wiley & Sons.

Ackerman, P.L., Schneider, W., & Wickens, C.D. (1984). Deciding the existence of a time-sharing ability: A combined methodological and theoretical approach. *Human Factors, 26(1)*, 83-95.

Adams, J.A. (1971). A closed-loop theory of motor learning. *Journal of Motor Behavior, 3(2)*, 111-149.

Adams, J.A. (1979). On the evaluation of training devices. *Human Factors, 21(6)*, 711-720.

Adams, J.A. (1987). Historical review and appraisal of research on the learning, retention, and transfer of human motor skills. *Psychological Bulletin, 101(1)*, 41-74.

Adams, J.A., & Goetz, E.T. (1973). Feedback and practice as variables in error detection and correction. *Journal of Motor Behavior, 5(4)*, 217-224.

Adams, J.A., Gopher, D., & Lintern, G. (1977). Effects of visual and proprioceptive feedback on motor learning. *Journal of Motor Behavior, 9(1)*, 11-22.

AGARD (1980). *Fidelity of simulation for pilot training*. Neuilly-sur-Seine: Advisory Group for Aerospace Research and Development, Conference Proceedings No. 159.

AGARD (1981). *Characteristics of flight simulator visual systems* (Advisory Report 164). Springfield, VA: National Technical Information Service.

Allen, J., Hays, R.T., & Buffardi L.C. (1986). Maintenance training simulator fidelity and individual differences in transfer of training. *Human Factors, 28(5)*, 497-509.

Anderson, J.R. (1980). *Cognitive psychology and its implications*. San Francisco, CA: W.H. Freeman and Company.

Anderson, J.R. (1982). Acquisition of cognitive skill. *Psychological Review, 89*, 369-406.

Anderson, J.R. (1987). Skill acquisition: Compilation of weak-method problem solutions. *Psychological Review, 94(2)*, 192-210.

Anderson, J.R. (1992). Automaticity and the ACT* theory. *American Journal of Psychology, 105*, 165-180.

Anderson, J.R., Boyle, C.F., Corebett, A.T., & Lewis, M.W. (1990). Cognitive modeling and intelligent tutoring. *Artificial Intelligence, 42*, 7-49.

Anderson, J.R., & Schooler, L.J. (1991). Reflections of the environment in memory. *Psychological Science, 2(6)*, 396-408.

Annett, J. (1991). Skill acquisition. In J. E. Morrison (Ed.), *Training for performance: Principles of applied human learning*. Chichester: John Wiley & Sons.

Annett, J., & Kay, H. (1956). Skilled performance. *Occupational Psychology, 30*, 112.

Ash, D.W., & Holding, D.H. (1990). Backward versus forward chaining in the acquisition of a keyboard skill. *Human Factors, 32(2)*, 139-146.

Baarspul, M. (1990). Review of flight simulation techniques. *Progress in Aerospace Sciences, 27 (1)*, 1-120.

Baker, S.J., Maurissen, J.P.J., & Chrzan, G.J. (1986). Simple reaction time and movement time in normal human volunteers: A long-term reliability study. *Perceptual and Motor Skills, 63*, 767-774.

Barber, P.J. (1989). Executing two tasks at once. In A.M. Colley & J.R. Beech (Eds.). *Acquisition and performance of cognitive skills*. Chichester: John Wiley & Sons.

Bartram, D. (1987). The development of an automated testing system for pilot selection: The MICROPAT project. *Applied Psychology: An International Review, 36(3/4)*, 279-298.

Battig, W.F. (1966). Facilitation and interference. In E.A. Biloteau (Ed.), *Acquisition of skill*. New York, Academic Press.

Baumstimler, Y., & Parrot, J. (1971). Stimulus generalization and spontaneous blinking in man involved in a voluntary activity. *Journal of Experimental Psychology, 88*, 95-102.

Bazzocchi, E. (1979). Cost-effectiveness of the second generation of jet training aircraft in the dual role of training and light tactical support aircraft. *Aviation and Marine International*.

Beevis, D. (1992). *Analysis techniques for man-machine systems design*. NATO Technical Report AC/243 (Panel 8, RSG 14) TR/7.

Berlin, J.I., Gruber, E.V., Jensen, P.K., Holmes, C.W., Lau, J.R., Mills, J.W., & O'Kane, J.M. (1982). *Pilot judgement training and evaluation*. Washington, DC: DOT/FAA/CT-82/56.

Berliner, D.C., Angell, D., & Shearer, J.W. (1964). Behaviors, measures, and instruments for performance evaluation in simulated environments. *Proceedings of the symposium on the quantification of human performance*. Albuquerque, NM.

Berlo, M.P.W. van (1996). *Instructional systems development for simulator-based training systems: A review of the literature*. TNO Soesterberg: Report No. TNO-TM 1996 C-006.

Berlo, M.P.W. van, & Verstegen, D. (1995). *Richtlijnen voor het classificeren van leerdoelen en het ontwerpen van instructie [Guidelines for classifying training objectives and designing instruction]*. TNO Soesterberg: Report No. TNO-TM 1995 A-64.

Bettman, J.R., Johnson, E.J., & Payne, J.W. (1990). A componential analysis of cognitive effort in choice. *Organisational Behaviour and Human Decision Processes, 45 (1)*, 111-139.

Billman, E.D. (1987). *The role of adaptive supplemental visual cueing in flight simulation*. MS Thesis, Air Force Inst. of Tech., Wright-Patterson AFB, Ohio, Avail. NTIS: HC A04/MF A01.

Bilodeau, E.A., & Bilodeau, I. (1954). The contribution of component activities to the total psychomotor task. *Journal of Experimental Psychology, 47(1)*, 37-46.

Bjork, R.A. (1988). Retrieval practice and the maintenance of knowledge. In M.M. Gruneberg, P.E. Morris, & R.N. Sykes (Eds.), *Practical aspects of memory I*. London: Wiley.

Bjorklund, R.A. (1992). Effects of foreperiod and time on task on reaction time and movement time. *Perceptual and Motor Skills, 74*, 131-144.

Blaiwes, A.S., Puig, J.A., & Regan, J.J. (1973). Transfer of training and the measurement of training effectiveness. *Human Factors, 15(6)*, 523-533.

Blankenbaker, K.E. (1971). Comparative effectiveness of variations in the demonstration method of teaching a complex manipulative sequence. *Journal of Industrial Teacher Education, 8*, 47-52.

Bles, W., Korteling, J.E., Marcus, J.T., Riemersma, J.B.J., & Theeuwes, J. (1991). *Bewegingsperceptie in moving-base simulatoren [Motion perception in moving-base simulators]*. Soesterberg: TNO-HFRI, Report No. IZF 1991 A-17.

Blessing, W., Merten, W., Braun, P., & Newman, P. (1996). *Literature review on trainability factors*. EUCLID RTP 11.1, MASTER Deliverable A3.1. Prepared for the Directorate of Materiel of the Royal Netherlands Army under contract No. DMKL/EUCLID/RTP 11.1 016-92-7211.11.

Block, J.H. (1971). *Mastery learning*. New York: Holt, Rinehart & Winston.

Blomberg, R.D., Speyer, J.J, Fouillot, J.P., Mollard, R., & Cabon, P. (1993). Assessing crew workload: From flight test measurement to airline monitoring and management. *Proceedings* of Conference on Workload Assessment and Aviation Safety. London: Royal Aeronautical Society.

Bloom, B.S. (Ed) (1956). *Taxonomy of educational objectives. Handbook 1: Cognitive Domain.* New York: McKay.

Blum, M.L., & Naylor, J.C. (1968). *Industrial psychology.* New York: Harper and Row.

Boer, J.P.A. (1991a). *The use of simulators for education and training I: Determining factors of the value of a simulator as training medium* (originally in Dutch). TNO Soesterberg: Report No. IZF 1991 A-45.

Boer, J.P.A. (1991b). *The use of simulators for education and training II: Guidelines for procurement* (originally in Dutch). TNO Soesterberg: Report No. IZF 1991 A-45.

Boer, L.C., Gaillard, A.W.K., & Jorna, P.G.A.M. (1987). *Taskomat: A battery of human information processing tasks.* TNO Soesterberg: Report No.1987-2.

Boff, K.R., & Lincoln, J.E. (1987). *Engineering data compendium: Human performance and perception.* Crew System Ergonomics Information Analysis Center, Wright-Patterson AFB, OH 45433-6573.

Boldovici, J.A. (1987). Measuring transfer in military settings. In J.S. Cormier, & J.D. Hagman (Eds.), *Transfer of learning: Contemporary research and applications.* New York: Academic Press, Inc.

Booher, H.R. (1990). *Manprint: An approach to systems integration.* New York: van Nostrand Reinhold.

Bourne, L.E., Dominowski, R.L., & Loftus, E.F. (1979). *Cognitive processes.* Englewood Cliffs, NJ: Prentice-Hall.

Branson, R.K., Rayner, G.T., Cox, J.L., Furman, J.P., King, F.J., & Hannum, W.H. (1975a). *Interservice procedures for instructional systems development: Executive summary, Phase I, Phase II, Phase III, Phase IV, Phase V.* Tallahassee, FL: Florida State University Center for Educational Technology Report No. AD-A019 486.

Branson, R.K., Rayner, G.T., Cox, J.L., Furman, J.P., King, F.J., & Hannum, W.H. (1975b). *Interservice procedures for instructional systems development: Executive summary, and model.* Technical Report, Center for Educational Technology, Florida State University, FL 32306.

Brehmer, B., & Dorner, D. (1993). Experiments with computer-simulated microworlds: Escaping both the narrow straits of the laboratory and the deep blue sea of the field study. *Computers in Human Behavior, 9(2-3),* 171-184.

Briggs, G.E., & Fitts, P.M. (1958). Transfer effects from a single to a double integral tracking system. *Journal of Experimental Psychology, 55(2),* 135-142.

Briggs, G.E., & Naylor, J.C. (1962). The relative efficiency of several training methods as a function of transfer task complexity. *Journal of Experimental Psychology, 64(5),* 505-512.

Briggs, G.E., & Waters, L.K. (1958). Training and transfer as a function of component interaction. *Journal of Experimental Psychology, 56(6),* 492-500.

Briggs, L.J., & Wager, W.W. (1981). *Handbook of procedures for the design of instruction.* (2nd ed.). Englewood Cliffs, NJ: Educational Technology Publications.

Brown, J.S., Collins, A., & Duguid, P. (1989). Situated cognition and the culture of learning. *Educational Researcher, 18(1),* 32-42.

Buchner, A., & Funke, J. (1993). Finite-state automata: Dynamic task environments in problem-solving research. *Quarterly Journal of Experimental Psychology: Human Experimental Psychology, 46A(1),* 83-118.

Buffet, A.R. (1986). Visual cueing requirements in flight simulation. In *Proceedings of the RAeS Simulation Symposium on Advances in Flight Simulation,* pp 127-157. London: Royal Aeronautical Society.

Burger, M.L., & DeSoi, J.F. (1992). The cognitive apprenticeship analogue: A strategy for using ITS technology for the delivery of instruction and as a research tool for the study of teaching and learning. *International Journal of Man-Machine Studies, 36,* 775-795.

Bürki-Cohen, J., Soja, N.N., & Longridge, T. (1998). Simulator platform motion – The need revisited. *International Journal of Aviation Psychology, 8(3),* 293-317.

Bürki-Cohen, J., Soja, N.N., & Longridge, T. (1998). Simulator fidelity requirements: The case for platform motion. In *ITEC proceedings 1998*.

Cacioppo, J.T., & Tassinary, L.G. (1990). Principles of psychophysiology. In J.T. Cacioppo & L.G. Tassinary (Eds.), *Principles of psychophysiology: Physical, social, and inferential elements*. Cambridge: Cambridge University Press.

Campbell, C.H., & Black, B.A. (1982). *Predicting trainability of M1 crewmen*. US Army Institute for the Behavioral and Social Sciences: Technical Report No. 592.

Cannon-Bowers J., Salas E., & Converse S.A. (1993). Shared mental models in expert team decision making. In N.J. Castellan (Ed.), *Current issues in individual and group decision making*. Mahwah, NJ: Lawrence Erlbaum Publishers.

Cannon-Bowers, J.A., & Salas, E. (1997). A framework for developing team performance measures in training. In M.T. Brannick, E. Salas, & C. Prince (Eds.), *Team performance assessment and measurement: Theory, methods and applications*. Mahwah, NJ: Erlbaum.

Cannon-Bowers, J.A., Salas, E., Prince, C., & Brannick, M. (1992). Games teams play: A method for investigating team coordination and performance. *Behaviour Research Methods, Instruments, & Computers, 24(4)*, 503-506.

Cannon-Bowers, J.A., Tannenbaum, S.I., Salas, E., & Volpe, C.E. (1995). Defining competencies and establishing team training requirements. In R. Guzzo & E. Salas (Eds.), *Team effectiveness and decision making in organisations*. Jossey-Bass.

Cardullo, F.M. (1994). *Motion and force cueing, II. Flight simulation update 1994*. Binghampton: Binghampton University.

Carlson, R.A., & Lundy, D.H. (1992). Consistency and restructuring in learning cognitive procedural sequences. *Journal of Experimental Psychology: Learning, Memory, and Cognition, 18(1)*, 127-141.

Carroll, J.B. (1993). *Human cognitive abilities: A survey of factor-analytic studies*. Cambridge: Cambridge University Press.

Carroll, W.R., & Bandura, A. (1990). Representational guidance of action production in observational learning: A causal analysis. *Journal of Motor Behavior, 22(1)*, 85-97.

Carver, E.M., McGuinness, B., & van den Bosch, K. (1996). *Skill retention: Field orientation*. EUCLID RTP11.1, MASTER Deliverable B3.2. Prepared for the Directorate of Materiel of the Royal Netherlands Army under contract no. DMKL/ EUCLID/RTP 11.1 016-92-7211.11.

Chapanis, A. (1972). Design of controls. In H.P. Van Cott & R.G. Kincade (Eds.), *Human engineering guide to equipment design*. Washington: Government Printing Office.

Christina, R.W., & Bjork, R.A. (1991). Optimizing long-term retention and transfer. In D. Druckman & R.A. Bjork (Eds.), *In the mind's eye: Enhancing human performance*. Washington, DC: National Academy Press.

Clapp, R.E. (1985a). Problems of the visual display in flight simulation. In *Image quality: An overview* (SPIE Proceedings Series 549), 64-70. Bellingham, Washington: SPIE International Society for Optical Engineering.

Clapp, R.E. (1985b). The importance of stereoscopic imagery in flight simulation. *Proceedings of the Conference on Simulators*, 3-8 March 1985, Norfolk, Virginia.

Clapp, R.E. (1985c). Resolution and scene detail performance of the visual system in flight simulation. *Proceedings of the Conference on Simulators*, 3-8 March 1985, Norfolk, Virginia.

Clapp, R.E. (1985d). Visual display requirements for boom operator training in aerial refuelling. *Proceedings of the Conference on Simulators*, 3-8 March 1985, Norfolk, Virginia.

Coker, C.C. (1990). Dynamic assessment, learning curve analysis and the training quotient. *Vocational Evaluation and Work Adjustment Bulletin*, Winter 1990.

Colley, A.M., & Beech, J.R. (Eds.) (1989a). *Acquisition and performance of cognitive skills*. New York: John Wiley & Sons.

Colley, A.M., & Beech, J.R. (1989b). Acquiring and performing cognitive skills. In A.M. Colley & J.R. Beech (Eds.), *Acquisition and performance of cognitive skills*. New York: John Wiley & Sons.

Collins, A., Brown, J.S., & Newman, S.E. (1989). Cognitive apprenticeship: Teaching the crafts of reading, writing, and mathematics. In L.B. Resnick (Ed.), *Knowing, learning, and instruction: Essays in honor of Robert Glaser*. Hillsdale, NJ: Lawrence Erlbaum.

Condon, G.W. (1990). Simulation of nap-of-earth flight in helicopters. In *AGARD Conference Proceedings No. 473*. Neuilly-Sur-Seine: NATO.

Connelly, E.M., & Johnson, P. (1981). Team performance measures for computerized systems. Santa Monica, CA: *Proceedings of the Human Factors Society 25th Annual Meeting*.

Cook, J.R., Durose, C.G., & Buckley, C.J. (1984). *The selection of training aircraft*. Research Branch, Headquarters Royal Air Force Support Command: Report No. 15/93 (revised August 1984).

Cooper, G.E., White, M., & Lauber, J.K. (1979). Resource management on the flight deck. *Proceedings of a NASA Industry Workshop*. Moffett Field, CA: NASA.

Cross, K.D. (1991). Training effectiveness assessment: Methodological problems and issues. In R.J. Larsen *et al* (Eds.). *Proceedings of NASA/FAA Helicopter Simulator Workshop*. Santa Clara, CA, 23-26 April 91.

Crossman, E.R.F.W. (1959). A theory of the acquisition of speed skill. *Ergonomics, 2*, 153-166.

Cutting, J.E. (1997). How the eye measures reality and virtual reality. *Behavior Research Methods, Instruments and Computers, 29(1)*, 27-36.

Damos, D.L. (1991). Examining transfer of training using curve fitting: A second look. *International Journal of Aviation Psychology, 1(1)*, 73-85.

Damos, D.L., & Wickens, C.D. (1980). The identification and transfer of timesharing skills. *Acta Psychologica, 46*, 15-39.

de Fontenilles, H., Moscato, M., Roessingh, J.J.M., Day, P., Fougue, J.L., McIntyre, H., & González Vega, N. (1997). *Physical system parameters and skill acquisition: Literature review*. Concept Deliverable C1.1. Euclid RTP 11.1.

de Vries, S.C. (1997). *On the size and nature of parallax errors present in multiple viewpoint simulations. Guidelines for simulator dome size*. Soesterberg: TNO-HFRI, Memo No. TM 1998 M04.

Dickinson, T.L, & McIntyre, R.M. (1997). A conceptual framework for teamwork assessment. In M.T. Brannick, E. Salas, & C. Prince (Eds.), *Team performance assessment and measurement: Theory, methods and applications*. Mahwah, NJ: Lawrence Erlbaum Associates.

Diehl, A.E. (1991). The effectiveness of training programs for preventing aircrew "error". In R.S. Jensen (Ed.), *Proceedings of the sixth international symposium on aviation psychology*. Columbus, OH: The Ohio State University.

Dixon, P., & Gabrys, G. (1991). Learning to operate complex devices: Effects of conceptual and operational similarity. *Human Factors, 33(1)*, 103-120.

Dohme, J. (1991a). Transfer of training from a low cost helicopter simulator. In *Proceedings of the 6th international symposium on aviation psychology*, 29 April-2 May, Vol 2, 910-915.

Dohme, J. (1991b). Transfer of training and simulator qualification or myth and folklore in helicopter simulation. In *Proceedings (NASA-CP-3156) of the NASA/FAA helicopter simulation workshop*, 23-26 April, Santa Clara, CA, pp 115-122.

Donchin, E. (1989). The Learning Strategies project. *Acta Psychologica, 71*, 1-15.

Donchin, E., Coles, M., & Kramer, A. (1987). *The event-related brain potential as an index of information processing*. Illinois University, Urbana, Department of Psychology.

Donders, F.C. (1869; translated 1969). On the speed of mental processes. *Acta Psychologica, 30*, 412-431.

Downs, S. (1989). Job sample and trainability tests. In P. Herriot (Ed.), *Assessment and selection in organisations: Methods and practice for recruitment and appraisal*. Chichester: Wiley.

Driskell, J.E., Willis, R.P., & Cooper, C. (1992). Effect of overlearning on retention. *Journal of Applied Psychology, 77(5)*, 615-622.

Dyer, J.L. (1984). Team research and team training: A state of the art review. In F.A. Muckler (Ed.), *Human factors review*, 285-333.

Ebbinghaus, H. (1964). *Memory: A contribution to experimental psychology* (H.A. Ruger & C.E. Bussenius, Trans.). New York: Dover. (Original work published 1885).

Edwards, B.J., & Hubbard, D.C. (1991). *Transfer of training from a radar intercept part-task trainer to an F-16 flight simulator*. Dayton University, Ohio: Final Technical Report (March 1988-March 1991) No. AD-A241493 (Avail. NTIS: HC/MF A03).

Egan, J.P. (1975). *Signal detection theory and ROC analysis*. New York: Academic Press.

Eggemeier, F.T. (1988). Properties of workload assessment techniques. In P.A. Hancock & N. Meshkati (Eds.), *Human mental workload*. Amsterdam: North-Holland.

Elshaw, C.C., & Lidderdale, I.G. (1982). Flying selection in the Royal Air Force. *Newsletter of the International Test Commission and of the Division of Psychological Assessment of the International Association of Applied Psychology, 17*, December 1982.

Ericsson, K.A., & Simon, H A. (1980). Verbal reports as data. *Psychological Review, 87*, 215-251.

Evans, J.L., McGuinness, B., van den Bosch, K., & Verstegen, D. (1996). *Experimental definition*. EUCLID RTP11.1, MASTER Deliverables B3.3.1, B3.3.2 and B3.3.4. Prepared for the Directorate of Materiel of the Royal Netherlands Army under contract no. DMKL/ EUCLID/RTP 11.1 016-92-7211.11.

FAA (1994). *Helicopter simulator qualification*. AC 120-63.

FAAC (1989). *White paper on truck driving simulator trade studies*. FAAC Report No. FR4158U/ 4823-022. Ann Arbor, MI: FAAC Inc.

Fabiani, M., Buckley, J., Gratton, G., Coles, M.G.H., & Donchin, E. (1989). The training of complex task performance. *Acta Psychologica, 71*, 259-299.

Farmer, E.W. (1993a). Conceptual issues in workload. *Proceedings of conference on workload assessment and aviation safety*. London: Royal Aeronautical Society.

Farmer, E.W. (1993b). Problems and possibilities of workload measurement and prediction by network simulation. Paper presented at *Workshop on task network simulation for human-machine system design (in conjunction with 2nd meeting of TTCP UTP7)*, 21 June 1993.

Farmer, E.W., Belyavin, A.J., Tattersall, A.J., Berry, A., & Hockey, G.R.J. (1991). *Stress in air traffic control II: Effects of increased workload*. Farnborough: RAF Institute of Aviation Medicine Report No. 701.

Farmer, E.W., Jorna, P.G.A.M., Samel, A., Kelly, C., McIntyre, H.M., Rejman, M., & Stewart, K. (1998). *Human factors and air safety policy: Final report of the AIRSAFE project*. DERA Farnborough: Report to the European Commission.

Farmer, E.W., Newman, P., Jordan, C.S., Folkerts, H., & van Avermaete, J.A.G. (1995). *Literature review on taxonomy of skills*. EUCLID RTP 11.1, MASTER Deliverable B1.2 Prepared for the Directorate of Materiel of the Royal Netherlands Army under contract No. DMKL/- EUCLID/RTP 11.1 016-92-7211.11.

Farmer, E.W. *et al* (1997). *Development of Error Analysis*. EUCLID RTP 11.1, MASTER, Deliverable B1.3a/B1.3. Prepared for the Directorate of Materiel of the Royal Netherlands Army under contract No. DMKL/EUCLID/RTP11.1, 016-92-7211.11.

Farr, M.J. (1987). *The long-term retention of knowledge and skills: A cognitive and instructional perspective*. London: Springer-Verlag.

Figarol, S. (1991). Knowledge transfer and anticipation in airline piloting. In *Proceedings of the 6th symposium on aviation psychology*, Colombus Ohio, 29 April-2 May; Vol 2; 1074-1079.

Fisk, A.D., Ackerman, P.L., & Schneider, W. (1987). Automatic and controlled processing theory and its application to human factors problems. In P.A. Hancock (Ed.), *Human factors psychology*. New York: North Holland.

Fisk, A.D., & Lloyd, S.J. (1988). The role of stimulus-to-rule consistency in learning rapid application of spatial rules. *Human Factors, 30(1)*, 35-49.

Fitts, P.M. (1965). Factors in complex skill training. In M. Venturino (Ed.), *Selected readings in human factors*. Santa Monica, CA: Human Factors Society.

Fitts, P., & Posner, M.I. (1967). *Human performance*. Belmont, CA: Brooks Coleman.

Fleishman, E.A., & Quaintance, M.K. (1984). *Taxonomies of human performance*. Orlando and London: Academic Press.

Flexman, R.E., & Stark, E.A. (1987). Training simulators. In G. Salvendy (Ed.), *Handbook of human factors*, 1012-1038. New York: John Wiley & Sons.

Foss, M.A., Fabiani, M., Mané, A.M., & Donchin, E. (1989). Unsupervised practice: The performance of the control group. *Acta Psychologica, 71*, 23-51.

Frederiksen, J.R., & White, B.Y. (1989). An approach to training based on principled task decomposition. *Acta Psychologica, 71*, 89-146.

Gagné, R.M., & Briggs, L.J. (1974). *Principles of instructional design.* New York: Holt, Reinhart and Winston.

Gainer, C.A., Whightman, D.C., Dohme, J.A., & Blackwell, N.J. (1991). Rotary wing simulator transfer of training in aviation skills acquisition and sustainment (Part One and Part Two). In *Proceedings of the Royal Aeronautical Society: 'Can we trust flight simulation?'*, 5.1-5.10, 11/13/91.

Gaines, B.R. (1972a). Axioms for adaptive behaviour. *International Journal of Man-Machine Studies, 4,* 169-199.

Gaines, B.R. (1972b). The learning of perceptual-motor skills by men and machines and its relationship to training. *Instructional Science, 1,* 263-312.

Gaines, B.R. (1974). Training, stability and control. *Instructional Science, 3,* 151-176.

Geraats, L.H.D. (1991). *Algoritmen voor de detektie van EMG-Onset op sngle tial nveau t.b.v. EEG onderzoek* (in Dutch). Department of Electrical Engineering, Eindhoven University of Technology, Master Thesis.

Gibson, J.J. (1950). *The perception of the visual world.* Boston: Houghton Mifflin.

Glaser, R. (1990). The reemergence of learning theory within instructional research. *American Psychologist, 45,* 29-39.

Gopher, D., Weil, M., & Siegel, D. (1989). Practice under changing priorities: An approach to the training of complex skills. *Acta Psychologica, 71,* 147-177.

Grau, J.Y. (1989). Apprentissage successif de systèmes complexes: une introduction aux problèmes de transfert de connaissances dans le cadre de l'aéronautique. *Mémoire de DEA ergonomie et neurophysiologie du travail,* CNAM Paris, September 1989.

Green, D.M., & Swets, J.A. (1966). *Signal detection theory and psychophysics.* New York: John Wiley & Sons.

Green, M., & Grayston, L. (1989). Displays for NVG flight simulation. In *Proceedings of the 11th Interservice/Industry Training Systems Conference,* 289-291. Arlington, VA: American Defence Preparedness Association.

Grether, D., & Wilde, L. (1983). An analysis of conjunctive choice: Theory and experiments. *Journal of Consumer Research, 10 (4),* 373-385.

Groen, E.L. (1997). *Orientation to gravity, oculomotor and perceptual responses in man.* Ph.D. Thesis, ISBN 9039318131.

Guckenberger, D., Uliano, K.C., & Lane, N.E. (1993). *Training high performance skills using above real-time training.* Institute for Simulation and Training, University of Central Florida and ECC International Corp. Simulation and Technology Divisions. (Jan. 1993 NASA-CR-192616).

Guzzo R.A., & Shea G P. (1992). Group performance and inter-group relations in organizations. In M.D. Dunnette & L.D. Hough (Eds.), *Handbook of Industrial and Organizational Psychology, 3,* 269-313. Palo Alto, CA: Consulting Psychologists Press.

Haber, R.N. (1986). Flight simulation. *Scientific American,* July, 90-97.

Hammerton, M. (1967). Measures for the efficiency of simulators as training devices. *Ergonomics, 10,* 63-65.

Hammerton, M. (1981). Tracking. In D.H. Holding (Ed.), *Human skills.* Chichester: John Wiley & Sons.

Hanson, S.J., & Burr, D.J. (1990). What connectionist models learn: Learning and representation in connectionist networks. *Behavioral and Brain Sciences, 13,* 471-518.

Harrow, A.J. (1972). *A taxonomy of the psychomotor domain: A guide for developing behavioral objectives.* New York: McKay.

Haug, E.J. (1990). *Feasibility study and conceptual design of a national advanced driving simulator.* Iowa City: University of Iowa, College of Engineering, Center for Simulation and Design Optimization of Mechanical Systems.

Hays, R.T. (1980). *Simulator fidelity: A concept paper.* Technical Report 490, Nov 1980, US Army Research Institute for the Behavioral and Social Sciences.

Hays, R.T., Jacobs, J.W., Prince, C., & Salas, E. (1992). Requirements for future research in flight simulation training: Guidance based on a meta-analytic review. *International Journal of Aviation Psychology, 2(2),* 143-158.

Heglin, H.J. (1973). *NAVSHIPS display illumination design guide: II Human factors*. Report No. NELC/TD223. San Diego: Naval Electronics Laboratory Center.

Heintzman, R.J., Middendorf, M., & Basinger, J.D. (1997). Development and validation of a force cueing evaluation method for tactical training. *Proceedings of the International Training Equipment Conference (ITEC)*.

Henry, F.M. (1960). Influence of motor and sensory sets on reaction latency and speed of discrete movements. *Research Quarterly, 31*, 459-468.

Hilburn, B., & Jorna, P.G.A.M. (1996a). *The effect of adaptive air traffic control (ATC) decision aiding on controller mental workload*. NLR Amsterdam: NLR Technical Report TP96216L.

Hilburn, B., Jorna, P.G.A.M., Byrne, E.A., & Parasuraman, R. (1996b). The effect of adaptive air traffic control (ATC) decision aiding on controller mental workload. *Second automation technology and human performance conference proceedings*, 7-9 March 1996, Florida, USA.

Hilburn, B., Jorna, P.G.A.M., & Parasuraman, R. (1995). The effect of advanced ATC strategic decision aiding automation on mental workload and monitoring performance: An empirical investigation in simulated Dutch airspace. In *Proceedings of the eighth international symposium on aviation psychology*, April 1995. Columbus, Ohio: Ohio State University.

Hilburn, B., Jorna, P.G.A.M., Parasuraman, R., & Byrne, E. (1996c). Dynamic decision aiding: A bio-behavioural analysis. *Vivek Artificial Intelligence Quarterly, 9 (1)*.

Hilgard, E.R., & Bower, G.H. (1975). *Theories of learning*. Englewood Cliffs, NJ: Prentice-Hall.

Holding, D.H. (1987). Concepts of training. In G. Salvendy (Ed.), *Handbook of human factors*. New York: John Wiley & Sons.

Hooper, S., & Hannafin, M.J. (1988). Learning the ROPES of instructional design: Guidelines for emerging interactive technologies. *Educational Technology, 28(7)*, 14-18.

Huber, V.L. (1987). Judgment by heuristics: Effects of ratee and rater characteristics and performance standards on performance-related judgments. *Organizational Behaviour and Human Decision Processes, 40*, 149-169.

Hudgens, G.A., & Fatkin, L.T. (1985). Sex differences in risk taking: Repeated sessions on a computer-simulated task. *Journal of Psychology, 119 (3)*, 197-206.

Hughes, R., Brooks, R., Graham, D., Sheen, R., & Dickens, T. (1983). Tactical ground attack: On the transfer of training from flight simulator to operational red flag range exercise. In *Proceedings of the International Conference on Simulators*, 26-30 Sept. 1983, University of Sussex, Brighton UK, 306-311.

Hunt, E. (1978). Mechanics of verbal ability. *Psychological Bulletin, 85(2)*, 109-130.

Hunt, E., Frost, N., & Lunneborg, C. (1973). Individual differences in cognition: A new approach to intelligence. In G. Bower (Ed.). *Advances in learning and motivation, Vol. 7*. New York: Academic Press.

Hunt, E., & Lansman, M. (1975). Cognitive theory applied to individual differences. In W.K. Estes (Ed.), *Handbook of learning and cognitive processes. Volume I. Introduction to concepts and issues*. Hillsdale, NJ: Lawrence Erlbaum.

Hurlock, R.E., & Montague, W.E. (1982). *Skill retention and its implications for navy tasks: An analytical review*. San Diego, CA: Navy Research and Development Center Technical Report NPRDC SR 82-21.

Iavecchia, J.H., Iavecchia, H.P., & Roscoe, S.N. (1988). Eye accommodation to head-up virtual images. *Human Factors, 30*, 689-702.

Imholz, B.P.M., Langewouters, G.J., Montfrans, G.A. van, Parati, G., Goudoever, J. van, Wesseling, K.H., Wieling W., & Mancia, G. (1993). Feasibility of ambulatory, continuous 24-hour finger arterial pressure recording. *Hypertension, 121(1)*.

Isreal, J.B., Wickens, C.D., Chesney, G.L., & Donchin, E. (1979). The event-related brain potentials as an index of display-monitoring workload. *Human Factors, 22*, 211-244.

Jensen, A.R. (1982). Reaction time and psychometric testing. In H.J. Eysenck (Ed.), *A model for intelligence*. Heidelberg: Springer.

Jensen, R.S. (1995). *Pilot judgement and crew resource management*. Aldershot: Avebury.

Jensen, R.S., & Benel, R.A. (1977). *Judgement, evaluation and instruction in civil pilot training*. Springfield, VA: National Technical Information Service Final Report FAA-RD-78-24.

Johnson, D.S., Perlow, R., & Pieper, K.F. (1993). Differences in task performance as a function of type of feedback: Learning-oriented versus performance-oriented feedback. *Journal of Applied Social Psychology, 23(4),* 303-320.

Johnson, S.L. (1981). Effect of training device on retention and transfer of a procedural task. *Human Factors, 23(3),* 257-272.

Jorna, P.G.A.M. (1984). Heart-rate parameters and the coping process under water. In J.F. Orlebeke, G. Mulder & L.J.P. van Doornen (Eds.), *Psycho-physiology of cardio-vascular control: Methods, models and data.* Plenum Press, New York.

Jorna, P.G.A.M. (1988). *Richtvaardigheid van mobilisabele bemanningen Leopard 2 [Gunnery skills of Leopard 2 crews].* TNO Soesterberg: TNO Report No. 1988-23.

Jorna, P.G.A.M. (1989a). *Prediction of success in flight training by single- and dual-task performance.* In *AGARD, Human Behaviour in High Stress Situations in Aerospace Operations* (N90-17275 09-53).

Jorna, P.G.A.M. (1989b). Time-sharing performance as a factor for success in flight training: Test development and validation. TNO Soesterberg: Report No. 1989-58.

Jorna, P.G.A.M. (1991). Heart rate variability as an index for pilot workload. In *Proceedings of the sixth international symposium on aviation psychology,* Columbus Ohio.

Jorna, P.G.A.M. (1992). Spectral analysis of heart rate and psychological state: A review of its validity as a workload index. *Biological Psychology, 34,* 237-257.

Jorna, P.G.A.M. (1993). Heart-rate and workload variations in actual and simulated flight. In *Special issue Ergonomics: Psychophysiological measures in transport operations.*

Jorna P.G.A.M. (1997a). Pilot performance in automated cockpits: Event related heart rate responses to datalink applications. In *Proceedings of the ninth international conference on aviation psychology,* Columbus, Ohio, USA.

Jorna P.G.A.M. (1997b). Human machine interfaces for ATM: Objective and subjective measurements on human interactions with future flight deck and air traffic control systems. In *First FAA/EUROCONTROL control conference on advanced ATC.* Paris, July 1997.

Jorna, P.G.A.M., & Visser, R.T.B. (1991). Selection by flight simulation: Effects of anxiety on performance. In E. Farmer (Ed.), *Human resource management in aviation.* Aldershot, UK: Avebury Technical.

Joyner, S. (1996). *Foundations for enhancing military team interaction, Annex C: Teaching team/management skills within the military.* Farnborough: DRA Report No. DRA/LS (LSC1)/89T4.002/95/1/3.

Kakimoto, Y., Nakamura, A., Tarui, H., Nagasawa, Y., & Yagura, S. (1988). Crew workload in JASDF C-1 transport flights: 1. Change in heart rate and salivatory cortisol. *Aviation, Space, and Environmental Medicine, 59 (6),* 511-516.

Kappé, B. (1997). *Visual information in virtual environments.* PhD Thesis, ISBN 9039318921.

Käppler, W.-D. (1986). Using a driving simulator to assess vehicle handling properties. In H.P. Willumeit (Ed.), *Human decision making and manual control.* Elsevier Science Publishers BV.

Kelley, C.R. (1969). What is adaptive training? *Human Factors, 11(6),* 547-556.

Kelly, M. (1995). An introduction to the ExACT AAR system and concept of objective performance measurement. In *Proceedings of NATO Workshop on training strategies for networked simulation and gaming,* NATO Research Study Group 28, A/C243(panel 8) TP/10, November 1995.

Kent, W.S. (1990). Visual simulation in the commercial airframe manufacturer's training environment. In E.G. Monroe (Ed.), *Proceedings of the IMAGE V Conference,* 231-239. Tempe: IMAGE Society Inc.

Kieras, D.E., & Bovair, S. (1984). The role of a mental model in learning to operate a device. *Cognitive Science, 8,* 255-273.

Kirchner, W.K. (1965). Relationships between supervisory and subordinate ratings for technical personnel. *Journal of Industrial Psychology, 3,* 57-60.

Kirwan, B., & Ainsworth, L.K. (1992). *A guide to task analysis.* London: Taylor & Francis Ltd.

Klein, G.A. (1989). Recognition-primed decisions. In W. Rouse (Ed.), *Advances in man-machine systems research* (Vol. 5, pp 47-92). Greenwich, CT: JAI Press Inc.

Klein, G.A., Orasanu, J., Calderwood, R., & Zsambok, C.E. (1993). *Decision making in action: Models and methods*. Norwood, New Jersey: Ablex.

Kokorian, A. (1995). *Military Crew Competence Model (MCCM): A review of the crew performance literature and a model for diagnosing and measuring military crew competencies*. Farnborough: DRA Report No. 6/DSTI/CFH/SF/96.

Konoske, P.J., & Ellis, J.A. (1986). *Cognitive factors in learning and retention of procedural tasks*. San Diego, CA: Navy Research and Development Center Technical Report No. NPRDC TR 87-14.

Koonce, J.M., & Bramble, W.J. (1998). Personal computer-based flight training devices. *International Journal of Aviation Psychology, 8(3)*, 277-292.

Korteling, J.E. (1994). *Multiple task performance and aging*. Thesis, University of Groningen, Ruinen.

Korteling, J.E., van den Bosch, K., & van Emmerik, M.L. (1997). *Low-cost simulators 1a: Literature review and analysis of military training, and selection of task domains*. TNO Soesterberg: Report No. TM-97-A035.

Kraiger, K., & Salas, E. (1993). An empirical test of two cognitively-based measures of learning during training. *Annual meeting of the Society for Industrial/Organisational Psychology*, San Francisco.

Kramer, A.F. (1990). *Physiological metrics of mental workload: A review of recent progress*. Navy Personnel Research and Development Center, San Diego, California 92152-6800.

Kramer, A.F., Wickens, C.D., & Donchin, E. (1985). Processing of stimulus properties: Evidence for dual-task integrality. *Journal of Experimental Psychology: Human Perception and Performance, 11*, 393-408.

Krebs, M.J., Wingert, J.W., & Cunningham, T. (1977). *Exploration of an oculomotor-based model of pilot workload*. NASA-CR-145153. Honeywell Inc, Systems Research Center, MS, Honeywell-76-SRC-39.

Kukich, R. N. (1988). *ASTS report on the common military skills retention study*. Beaconsfield, Bucks, UK Army School of Training Support.

Laird, J.E., Newell, A., & Rosenbloom, P.S. (1987). SOAR: An architecture for general intelligence. *Artificial Intelligence, 33*, 1-64.

Laird, J., Rosenbloom, P., & Newell, A. (1986). *Universal subgoaling and chunking. The automatic generation and learning of goal hierarchies*. Dordrecht: Kluwer Academic Publishers.

Lajoie, S.P., & Lesgold, A. (1989). Apprenticeship training in the workplace: Computer-coached practice environment as a new form of apprenticeship. *Machine-Mediated Learning, 3*, 7-28.

Laming, D. (1992). Analysis of short-term retention: Models for Brown-Peterson experiments. *Journal of Experimental Psychology, 18(6)*, 1342-1365.

Landa, L. (1974). *Algorithmization in learning and instruction*. Englewood Cliffs, NJ: Educational Technology Publications.

Lane, N.E. (1987). *Skill acquisition rates and patterns: Issues and training implications*. New York: Springer-Verlag.

Larkin, J.H., & Chabay, R.W. (Eds.), (1992). *Computer-assisted instruction and intelligent tutoring systems: Shared goals and complementary approaches*. Hillsdale, New Jersey: Lawrence Erlbaum Associates, Inc.

Larsen, W.E., Randle, R.J., & Zuk, J. (1991). *Training effectiveness assessment: Methodological problems and issues*. NASA/FAA Helicopter workshop. NASA Conference Publication 3156 DOT/FAA/RD-92/2.

Lee, D.H., & Parks, K.S. (1990). Multivariate analysis of mental and physical load components in sinus arrhythmia scores. *Ergonomics, 33(1)*, 35-47.

Leshin, C.B., Pollock, J., & Reigeluth, C.M. (1990). *Instructional design: Strategies and tactics for improving learning and performance*. Englewood Cliffs, NJ: Educational Technology Publications.

Lienert, G.A. (1989). *Testaufbau und testanalyse*. (4. Auflage). Munich, Weinheim: Psychologie Verlags Union.

Lintern, G. (1989). The learning strategies program: Concluding remarks. *Acta Psychologica, 71*, 301-309.

Lintern, G. (1991). Instructional strategies. In J.E. Morrison (Ed.), *Training for performance*. Chichester, UK: John Wiley & Sons.

Lintern, G., & Gopher, D. (1978). Adaptive training of perceptual-motor skills: Issues, results, and future directions. *International Journal of Man-Machine Studies, 10*, 521-551.

Lintern, G., & Liu, Y. (1991). Explicit and implicit horizons for simulated landing approaches. *Human Factors, 33*, 407-417.

Lintern, G., Roscoe, S.N., Koonce, J.M., & Segal, L.D. (1990). Transfer of landing skills in beginning flight training. *Human Factors, 32(3)*, 319-327.

Lintern, G., Roscoe, S.N., & Sivier, J. (1990). Display principles, control dynamics, and environmental factors in pilot performance and transfer of training. *Human Factors, 32(3)*, 299-317.

Lintern, G., Sheppard, D.J., Parker, D.L., & Yates, K.E. (1989). Simulator design and instructional features for air to ground attack: A transfer study. *Human Factors 31(1)*, 87-99.

Loftus, G.R. (1985). Consistency and confounding: Reply to Slamencka. *Journal of Experimental Psychology: Learning, Memory and Cognition, 11*, 817-820.

Logan, G.D. (1988a). Toward an instance theory of automatization. *Psychological Review, 95(4)*, 492-527.

Logan, G.D. (1988b). Automaticity, resources, and memory: Theoretical controversies and practical implications. *Human Factors, 30(5)*, 583-598.

Logan, G.D. (1992). Shapes of reaction-time distributions and shapes of learning curves: A test of the instance theory of automaticity. *Journal of Experimental Psychology: Learning, Memory, and Cognition, 18(5)*, 883-914.

Logan, G.D., & Stadler, M.A. (1991). Mechanisms of performance improvement in consistent mapping memory search: Automaticity or strategy shift? *Journal of Experimental Psychology: Learning, Memory, and Cognition, 17(3)*, 478-496.

Looren de Jong, H., & Sanders, A.F. (1990). Stratification in perception and action. *Psychological Research, 52*, 216-228.

Luh, C.W. (1922). The conditions of retention. *Psychological Monographs, 31*, 142.

Lusted, L.B. (1976). Clinical decision making. In D. Dombal and J. Grevy (Eds.), *Decision making and medical care*. Amsterdam: North Holland.

Lysaght, R.J., Hill, S.G., Dick, A.O., Plamondon, B.D., Linton, P.M., Wierwille, W.W., Zaklad, A.L., Bittner, A.C., & Wherry, R.J. (1989). *Operator workload: Comprehensive review and evaluation of operator workload methodologies*. United States Army Research Institute for the Behavioral and Social Sciences. Technical Report No. 851. Alexandria, VA.

MacKay, D.G. (1982). The problem of flexibility, fluency, and speed-accuracy trade-off in skilled behavior. *Psychological Review, 89*, 483-506.

Mager, R.F. (1962). *Preparing instructional objectives*. Palo Alto, California: Fearon.

Magill, R.A., & Hall, K.G. (1991). A review of the contextual interference effect in motor skill acquisition. In R.B. Wilberg (Ed.), *The learning, memory, and perception of perceptual-motor skills*. Amsterdam: Elsevier Science Publishers B.V.

Mané, A.M., Adams, J.A., & Donchin, E. (1989). Adaptive and part-whole training in the acquisition of a complex perceptual-motor skill. *Acta Psychologica, 71*, 179-196.

Mané, A.M., Coles, M.G.H., Wickens, C.D., & Donchin, E. (1983). The use of the additive factors methodology in the analysis of skill. *Proceedings of the Human Factors Society*.

Mané, A., & Donchin, E. (1989). The Space Fortress game. *Acta Psychologica, 71*, 17-22.

Margolius, G.J., & Sheffield, F.D. (1961). Optimum methods of combining practice with filmed demonstration in teaching complex response sequences: Serial learning of a mechanical assembly task. In A.A. Lumsdaine (Ed.), *Student response in programmed instruction*. Washington, DC: National Academy of Sciences-National Research Council, Publ. No. 943 (AD-281936).

Mazur, J.E., & Hastie, R. (1978). Learning as accumulation: A reexamination of the learning curve. *Psychological Bulletin, 85(6)*, 1256-1274.

McClelland, J.L., & Rumelhart, D.E. (1985). Distributed memory and the representation of general and specific information. *Journal of Experimental Psychology: General, 114(2),* 159-188.

McDevitt, M.E. (1998). *ASW proficiency. Training performance in future warships: Presentation and international research initiatives and prospects.* UK MoD, November.

McGahan, C., Weeden, S.J., & Henderson, S. (1998). Team interaction processes and synthetic environments — Training techniques and evaluative methods. Fort Halstead: DERA Report No.DERA/CHS/HS3/CR980095/1.0.

McGeoch, J.A., & Irion, A.L. (1952). *The psychology of human learning,* 2nd edition. New York: Longman, Green and Co.

McKendree, J. (1990). Effective feedback content for tutoring complex skills. *Human-Computer Interaction, 5(4),* 381-413.

Meehan, J.W., & Triggs, T.J. (1988). Magnification effects with imaging displays depend on scene content and viewing condition. *Human Factors, 30,* 487-494.

Meister, D. (1985). *Behavioral analysis and measurement methods.* New York: John Wiley & Sons.

Meliza, L., Bessemer, D., & Tan, S.C. (1994). *Unit performance assessment system.* US Army Research Institute, Orlando, FL: ARI Technical Report No. 1008.

Meliza, L.L., Tan, S.C., White, S.C., Gross, W., & McMeel, K. (1992). *SIMNET unit performance measurement system (UPAS) user's guide (Research Product 92-02).* Alexandria, VA: US Army Research Institute for the Behavioral and Social Sciences.

Mengelknoch, R.F., Adams, J.A., & Gainer, C.A. (1971). The forgetting of instrument flying skills. *Human Factors, 13(5),* 397-405.

Merrill, D.C., Reiser, B.J., Ranney, M., & Gregory Trafton, J. (1992). Effective tutoring techniques: A comparison of human tutors and intelligent tutoring systems. *The Journal of the Learning Sciences, 2(3),* 277-305.

Merrill, M.D. (1983). Component display theory. In C.M. Reigeluth (Ed.), *Instructional-design theories and models.* Hillsdale, NJ: Lawrence Erlbaum.

Merrill, M.D., Li, Z., & Jones, M.K. (1991). Instructional transaction theory: An introduction. *Educational Technology, 31(6),* 7-12.

Milders, M.V., & Padmos, P. (1991). *Eisen voor buitenbeelden van voertuigsimulatoren; een literatuurstudie [Requirements for outside-world images of vehicle simulators; a literature review].* Soesterberg: TNO-HFRI, Report No. IZF 1991 B-6.

Miller, E.E. (1971). *Comparison of pictorial techniques for guiding performance during training.* Alexandria, Virginia: Human Resources Research Organization, Technical Report No. 71-12 (AD 73067).

Miller, G.A. (1956). The magical number seven plus or minus two: Some limits on our capacity for processing information. *Psychological Review, 63,* 81-97.

Miller, W.C., Saxe, C., & d'Amico, A.D. (1985). *Preliminary evaluation of transfer of simulator training to the real world.* National Maritime Research Center. Kings Point, N.Y. Computer Aided Operation Research Facility. Report No. CAORF-50-8126-02, Nov. 1985.

Morrison, J.E. (Ed.) (1991). *Training for performance: Principles of applied human learning.* Chichester: John Wiley & Sons.

Morrissette, J.O., Hornseth, J.P., & Shellar, K. (1975). Team organization and monitoring performance. *Human Factors, 17 (3),* 296-300.

Mulder, G. (1980). *The concept and measurement of mental effort.* Dissertation, Universiteits-drukkerij R.U.G., Groningen.

Mulder, G. (1986). *Mental effort and its measurement.* Heymans Bulletins Psychologische Instituten R.U. Groningen, No: HB-86-780-EX.

Mulder, G., & Mulder, L.J.M. (1981). Information processing and cardiovascular control. *Psychophysiology, 18 (4),* 392-408.

Naylor, J.C., & Briggs, G.E. (1963). Effects of task complexity and task organization on the relative efficiency of part and whole training methods. *Journal of Experimental Psychology, 65(3),* 217-224.

Neves, D.M., & Anderson, J.R. (1981). Knowledge compilation: Mechanisms for the automatization of cognitive skills. In J.R. Anderson (Ed.), *Cognitive skills and their acquisition*. Hillsdale, NJ: Lawrence Erlbaum.

Newell, A., & Roosenbloom, P. (1981). Mechanisms of skill acquisition and the law of practice. In J.R. Anderson (Ed.), *Cognitive skills and their acquisition*. Hillsdale NJ: Erlbaum Associates.

Newell, K.M., Carlton, M.J., Fisher, A.T., & Rutter, B.G. (1989). Whole-part training strategies for learning the response dynamics of micro-processor driven simulators. *Acta Psychologica, 71*, 197-216.

Nicholson, D.E., & Schmidt, R.A. (1991). Scheduling information feedback to enhance training effectiveness. In *Proceedings of the Human Factors Society 35th Annual Meeting*, San Francisco, California, 2-6 September, Vol. 2. Santa Monica, CA: The Human Factors Society.

Normand, V. (1992). Task modelling in human-computer inter-action: Purposes and means. State of the art and research issues. Rapport de recherche No. PTI/92-02, juillet 92. Thomson CSF, Division Système de Défense et Contrôle. Établissement de Bagneux, Direction technique, service Poste de Travail Intelligent.

Nullmeyer, R.T., & Rockaway, M.R. (1985). Relationships among air crew performance measures for evaluating flight simulator training effectiveness. In *Proceedings (A86-40476 19-53) of the conference of the Society for Computer Simulation*, Norfolk, VA, March 3-8, 13-17.

Obermayer, R.W., & Vreuls, D. (1972). Measurement for flight training research (Performance measurement system for combat crew flight training in complex aircraft weapon systems, identifying training research goals). *Technology for man 1972: Proceedings of the sixteenth annual meeting*, Los Angeles, October 17-19, 1972. Human Factors Society.

O'Donnell, R.D., & Eggemeier, F.T. (1986). Workload assessment methodology. In K.R. Boff, L. Kaufman and J.P. Thomas (Eds.), *Handbook of perception and human performance, Volume II. Cognitive processes and performance*. New York: John Wiley & Sons.

O'Hara, J.M. (1990). The retention of skills acquired through simulator-based training. *Ergonomics, 33(9)*, 1143-1153.

Ohlsson, S. (1992). The interaction between knowledge and practice in the acquisition of cognitive skills. US Office of Naval Research. Technical Report No. KUL-92-01.

Ona, A. (1990). Effects of different attentional strategies and practice on motor efficiency. *Perceptual and Motor Skills, 71*, 35-43.

Orlansky, J. (1989). *The military value and cost-effectiveness of training*. AC/243 (Panel 7/RSG.15) D/4. Brussels: NATO.

Paas, F., & van Merrienboer, J. (1993). The efficiency of instructional conditions: An approach to combine mental effort and performance measures. *Human Factors, 35 (4)*, 737-743.

Padmos, P., & Milders, M.V. (1992). Quality criteria for simulator images: A literature review. *Human Factors, 34(6)*, 727-748.

Parasuraman, R. (1986). Vigilance, monitoring and search. In K.R. Boff, L. Kaufman, & J.P. Thomas (Eds.), *Handbook of perception and human performance, Volume II. Cognitive processes and performance*. New York: John Wiley & Sons.

Parker, J.W., Taylor, E.K., Barret, R.S., & Martens, I. (1959). Rating Scale Content 3: Relationship between supervisory and self-ratings. *Personnel Psychology, 12*, 49-63.

Pascual, R.G., Henderson, S.M., & Mills, M.C. (1998). *Understanding and supporting team cognition – Year 1 report and recommendations*. Fort Halstead: DERA Report DERA/CHS/MID/CR980122/1.0.

Patrick, J. (1992). *Training: Research and practice*. London: Academic Press.

Payne, J.W., & Braunstein, M.L. (1978). Risky choice and examination of information acquisition behaviour. *Memory and Cognition, 6(5)*, 554-561.

Pellegrino, J.W., & Glaser, R. (1979). Cognitive correlates and components in the analysis of individual differences. *Intelligence, 3*, 187-214.

Pheasant, S.T. (1986). *Bodyspace: Anthropometry, ergonomics and design*. London: Taylor and Francis.

Polzella, D.J. (1983). Utility and utilization of advanced instructional features in aircrew training devices: Phase 1: Tactical Air Command. In *IEEE National Aerospace and Electronics Conference NAECON 83*. New York.

Polzella, D.J. (1983). *Aircrew training devices: Utility and utilization of advanced instructional features (Phase II — Air training command, military airlift command, and strategic air command, and Phase III — Electronic warfare trainers)*. US AHRL Technical Report.

Polzella, D.J., Hubbard, D.C., Brown, J.E., & McLean, H.C. (1987). *Aircrew training devices: Utility and utilization of advanced instructional features: Phase IV: Summary report*. US AFHRL Technical Report Rpt-87-21.

Posner, M. I. (1978). *Chronometric explorations of mind*. Hillsdale, NJ: LEA.

Poulton, E.C. (1974). *Tracking skill and manual control*. London: Academic Press.

Povenmire, H.K., & Roscoe, S.N. (1973). Incremental transfer effectiveness of a groundbased general aviation trainer. *Human Factors, 15(6)*, 534-542.

Prophet, W.W. (1976). *Long-term retention of flying skills: A review of the literature*. HumRRO Final Report 76-35. Alexandria, VA: Human Resources Research Organization.

RAFTS Team (1986). *Reconnaissance-Attack-Fighter Training System (RAFTS) Pre-concept Investigation*. Battelle Columbus Division.

Rasmussen, J. (1986a). *Information processing and human-machine interaction: An approach to cognitive engineering*. Amsterdam: North-Holland.

Rasmussen, J. (1986b). A framework for cognitive task analysis in systems design. *Intelligent decision support in process environments*. NATO ASI Series F, vol 21.

Rayman, R.B. (1982). Negative transfer: A threat to flying safety. In *Proceedings of the annual scientific meeting of the Aerospace Medical Association*, May 10-13, Bal Harbour, FL.

Reason, J. (1990). *Human error*. Cambridge: Cambridge University Press.

Regian, J.W., & Shute, V.J. (1993). Basic research on the pedagogy of automated instruction. In D.M. Towne, T. de Jong, & H. Spada (Eds.), *Simulation-based experiential learning*. Berlin: Springer-Verlag.

Reigeluth, C.M. (1983). *Instructional-design theories and models. An overview of their current status*. Hillsdale, NJ: Lawrence Erlbaum.

Reigeluth, C.M. (1987). *An instructional theory for the design of computer-based simulations*. Syracuse University, N.Y: School of Education IDD&E Working Paper No. 23.

Reigeluth, C.M., & Stein, F.S. (1983). The elaboration theory of instruction. In C.M. Reigeluth (Ed.), *Instructional-design theories and models. An overview of their current status*. Hillsdale, NJ: Lawrence Erlbaum.

Reisweber, D.A., & Lintern, G. (1991). Visual properties for the transfer of landing skill. In *Proceedings of the sixth international symposium on aviation psychology*, Vol 2, 817-822.

Restle, F., & Greeno, J.G. (1970). *Introduction to mathematical psychology*. Reading, MA: Addison-Wesley Publishing Company.

Riemersma, J.B.J. (1994). *Glossary*. EUCLID RTP 11.1, MASTER, Deliverable D1. Prepared for the Directorate of Materiel of the Royal Netherlands Army under contract No. DMKL/EUCLID/RTP11.1, 016-92-7211.11.

Riemersma, J.B.J. et al (1994). *Reference framework*. EUCLID RTP 11.1, MASTER Deliverable D1.1. Prepared for the Directorate of Materiel of the Royal Netherlands Army under contract No. DMKL/EUCLID/RTP 11.1 016-92-7211.11.

Riemersma, J.B.J. et al (1997a). *Literature review on mission- and task-analysis*. EUCLID RTP 11.1, MASTER Deliverable A1.1. Prepared for the Directorate of Materiel of the Royal Netherlands Army under contract No. DMKL/EUCLID/RTP 11.1 016-92-7211.11.

Riemersma, J.B.J. et al (1997b). *Field orientation on mission- and task-analysis*. EUCLID RTP 11.1, MASTER Deliverable A1.2 Prepared for the Directorate of Materiel of the Royal Netherlands Army under contract No. DMKL/EUCLID/RTP 11.1 016-92-7211.11.

Riemersma, J.B.J., Valeton, J.M., & Schaafstal, A.M. (1995). Training hot spots. *Military Simulation & Training, 4*, 37-43.

Robertson, I., & Downs, S. (1979). Learning and the prediction of performance: Development of trainability testing in the United Kingdom. *Journal of Applied Psychology, 64 (1)*, 42-50.

Rogers, B., & Graham, M. (1979). Motion parallax as an independent cue for depth perception. *Perception, 8*, 125-13.

Rolfe, J.M., & Caro, P.W. (1982). Determining the training effectiveness of flight simulators: Some basic issues and practical developments. *Applied Ergonomics, 13(4)*, 243-250.

Rolfe, J.M., Cook, J.R., & Durose, C.G. (1985). Knowing what we get from training devices: Substituting a little arithmetic for a measure of emotion. In *Proceedings of the third symposium on aviation psychology*, Columbus Ohio, April 22-25; Vol 1.

Rolfe, J.M., & Staples, K.J. (Eds.) (1986). *Flight simulation*. Cambridge: Cambridge University Press.

Roscoe, A.H. (1987). In-flight assessment of workload using pilot ratings and heart rate. I. In A.H. Roscoe (Ed.), *The practical assessment of pilot workload*. Neuilly-sur-Seine: AGARD AGARDograph AGARD-AG-282, 78-82.

Roscoe, A.H., Ellis, G.A., & Chiles, W.D. (1978). *Assessing pilot workload*. Neuilly-sur-Seine: AGARD AGARDograph 233.

Roscoe, S.N. (1971). Incremental transfer effectiveness. *Human Factors, 13(6)*, 561-567.

Roscoe, S.N. (1980). *Transfer and cost effectiveness of ground-based flight trainers*. Aviation Psychology (A81-15676 04-53) Ames, Iowa State University Press, 194-203.

Roscoe, S.N. (1989). The eyes prefer real images. In R.S. Jensen (Ed.), *Aviation psychology*, 231-239. Aldershot, UK: Gower Technical.

Roscoe, S.N. and Williges, R.C. (1980). Measurement of transfer of training. In S.N. Roscoe (Ed). *Aviation psychology*. Ames, Iowa: Iowa University Press.

Rose, A., Evans, R., & Wheaton, G. (1987). Methodological approaches for simulator evaluations. In S.M. Cormier & T.D. Hagman (Eds.), *Transfer of learning: Contemporary research and applications*. New York: Academic Press.

Ross, M.J., & Allerton, D.J. (1991). Evaluation of a part task trainer for ab-initio pilot training. In *Proceedings of The Royal Aeronautical Society conference 'Can we trust flight simulation?'*, 11/13/91, London.

Rossum, J.H.A. van (1991). Schmidt's schema theory: The empirical base of the variability of practice hypothesis. A critical analysis. In R.B. Wilberg (Ed.), *The learning, memory, and perception of perceptual-motor skills*. Amsterdam: Elsevier Science Publishers B.V.

Rothstein, H.G. (1986). The effects of time pressure on judgment in multiple cue probability learning. *Organizational Behaviour and Decision Processes, 37 (1)*, 83-92.

Rouse, W.B., Cannon-Bowers, J.A., & Salas, E. (1992). The role of mental models in team performance in complex systems. *IEEE Transactions on Systems, Man, and Cybernetics, 22(6)*, 1296-1308.

Rouse, W.B., & Morris, N.M. (1986). On looking into the black box: Prospects and limits in the search for mental models. *Psychological Bulletin, 100*, 349-363.

RSG-14 (1992). *Analysis techniques for man-machine systems design*. NATO Technical Report AC/243 (Panel 8) TR/7.

Ruben, D.C., & Wenzel, A.E. (1996). One hundred years of forgetting: A quantitative description of retention. *Psychological Review, 103 (4)*, 734-760.

Russel, J.E. (1980). *An operational analysis method for the assessment of trainer aircraft*. BAe Future Projects Department, Note YP01172.

Salas, E., Bowers, C.A., & Cannon-Bowers, J.A. (1995a). Military team research: 10 years of progress. *Military Psychology, 7 (2)*, 55-75.

Salas, E., Cannon-Bowers, J.A., & Johnston, J.H. (1995b). How can you turn a team of experts into an expert team?: Emerging training strategies. In C. Zsambok & G. Klein (Eds.), *Naturalistic decision making*, Hillsdale, NJ: Erlbaum.

Salas, E., Dickinson, T.L, Converse, S.A, McIntyre R.M., & Salas E. (1992). Toward an understanding of team performance and training. In R.W. Swezey & E. Salas (Eds.), *Teams – Their training and performance*. Ablex Publishing Corporation.

Salmoni, A.W. (1989). Motor skill learning. In D.H. Holding (Ed.), *Human skills*. Chichester: John Wiley & Sons.

Salmoni, A.W., Schmidt, R.A., & Walter, C.B. (1984). Knowledge of results and motor learning: A review and critical appraisal. *Psychological Bulletin, 95(3)*, 355-386.

Salvendy, G. (1986). *Handbook of human factors*. Wiley Interscience Publication (John Wiley & Sons).

Sanders, A.F. (1984). Ten symposia on Attention and Performance: Some issues and trends. In H. Bouma & D.G. Bouwhuis (Eds.), *Attention and performance 10*. Hillsdale, NJ: Erlbaum.

Sanders, A.F. (1991). Simulation as a tool in the measurement of human performance. *Ergonomics, 34 (8),* 995-1025.

Schaafstal, A.M., & Bots, M.J. (1997). *Crosstraining en teamprestatie: een nadere verkenning.* TNO Soesterberg: TNO Report No. TNO-IZF 1997 B-20.

Schaafstal, A.M., & Schraagen, J.M.C. (1992). *A method for cognitive task analysis.* TNO Soesterberg: TNO Report No. TNO-IZF 1992 B-5.

Schank, R.C. (1994). Goal-based scenarios: A radical look at education. *Journal of the Learning Sciences, 3(4),* 429-453.

Schank, R.C., & Abelson, R.P. (1977). *Scripts, plans, goals and understanding.* Hillsdale, NJ: Erlbaum.

Schank, R., & Jona, M. (1991). Empowering the student: New perspectives on the design of teaching systems. *The Journal of the Learning Sciences, 1(1),* 7-35.

Schendel, J.D., & Hagman, J.D. (1991). Long-term retention of motor skills. In J.E. Morrison (Ed.), *Training for performance: Principles of applied human learning.* New York: Wiley.

Schendel, J.D., Shields, J., & Katz, M. (1978). *Retention of motor skills: Review.* Technical Paper 313. Alexandria, VA: US Army Research Institute for the Behavioral and Social Sciences.

Schick, F.V., & Hahn, R.L. (1987). *The use of a subjective workload assessment technique in a complex flight task.* Neuilly-sur-Seine: *AGARD-AG-282,* 37-41.

Schmidt, R.A. (1975). A schema theory of discrete motor skill learning. *Psychological Review, 82(4),* 225-260.

Schmidt, R.A., & Bjork, R.A. (1992). New conceptualizations of practice: Common principles in three paradigms suggest new concepts for training. *Psychological Science,* 3(4), 207- 217.

Schmidt, R.A., Lange, D., & Young, D.E. (1991). Optimizing summary knowledge of results for skill learning. In R.B. Wilberg (Ed.), *The learning, memory, and perception of perceptual-motor skills.* Amsterdam: Elsevier Science Publishers B.V.

Schneider, W. (1985). Training high-performance skills: Fallacies and guidelines. *Human Factors, 27,* 285-300.

Schneider, W., & Detweiler, M. (1987). A connectionist/control architecture for working memory. In G.H. Bower (Ed.), *The psychology of learning and motivation,* Vol. 21. New York: Academic Press.

Schneider, W., & Fisk, A.D. (1983). Attention theory and mechanisms for skilled performance. In R.A. Magill (Ed.), *Memory and control of action.* New York: North-Holland.

Schneider, W., & Shiffrin, R.M. (1977). Controlled and automatic human information processing: I — Detection, search and attention. *Psychological Review, 84,* 1-66.

Schuffel, H. (1986). *Human control of ships in tracking tasks* (Doctoral dissertation). Tilburg, The Netherlands: Katholieke Universiteit Noord-Brabant.

Schuler, H., & Funke, U. (1989). Berufseignungsdiagnostik. In E. Roth (Ed.), *Enzyklopädie der Psychologie. Bd. III/3: Organisationspsychologie.* Göttingen: Hogrefe.

Seamster, T.L., Redding, R.E., Cannon, J.R., Ryder, J.M., & Purcell, J.A. (1993). Cognitive task analysis of expertise in air traffic control. *The International Journal of Aviation Psychology, 3,* 257-283.

Sekigucchi, G., Handa, Y., Gotoh, M., Kurihara, Y., Nagasawa, Y., & Kuroda, I. (1979). Frequency analysis of heart rate variability under flight conditions. *Aviation, Space, and Environmental Medicine, 50,* 625-634.

Seymour, W.D. (1956). Experiments on the acquisition of industrial skills. Part 3. *Occupational Psychology, 30,* 94-104.

Shebilske, W.L., Regian, J.W., Arthur, W.J., & Jordan, J.A. (1992). A dyadic protocol for training complex skills. *Human Factors, 34,* 369-374.

Shiffrin, R.M., & Schneider, W. (1977). Controlled and automatic human information processing: II. Perceptual learning, automatic attending, and a general theory. *Psychological Review, 84,* 127-190.

Singleton, W.T. (1953). Deterioration of performance on a short-term perceptual-motor task. In W.F. Floyd and A.T. Welford (Eds.), *Fatigue.* London: Lewis.

Sirevaag, E.J., Kramer, A.F., Wickens, C.D., Reisweber, M., Strayer, D.L., & Grenell, J.F. (1993). Assessment of pilot performance and mental workload in rotary wing aircraft. *Ergonomics, 36 (9)*, 1121-1140.

Slamencka, N.J., & McElree, B. (1983). Normal forgetting of verbal lists as a function of their degree of learning. *Journal of Experimental Psychology: Learning, Memory and Cognition, 9*, 384-397.

Smith, F.D. (1991). Work samples as measures of performance. In A.K. Wigdor & B.F. Green (Eds.), *Performance assessment for the workplace*. Washington: National Academy Press.

Smith, M.D., & Hagman, J.D. (1993). *Interdevice transfer of training between the guard unit armoury device, full crew interactive simulation trainer-armour and the mobile conduct-of-fire trainer*. Final Technical Report Oct. 91-Jun. 92, Army Research Institute for The Behavioral and Social Sciences, Alexandria, VA. Report No. ARI-RR-1635.

Snoddy, G.S. (1926). Learning and stability. *Journal of Applied Psychology, 10*, 1-36.

Speyer, J.J., Ford, A., Fouillot, J.P., & Blomberg, R.D. (1988). Dynamic methods for assessing workload for minimum crew certification. In A.H. Roscoe & H.C. Muir (Eds.), *Workload in transport operations*. Report Number IB 316-88-06, 196-200. Cologne: DFVLR.

Spiker, V.A., Tourville, S.J., & Nullmeyer, R.T. (1997). Networked simulation and combat mission training. *19th I/ITSEC Conference Proceedings*, Orlando USA.

Stammers, R.B. (1982). Part and whole practice in training for procedural tasks. *Human Learning, 1*, 185-207.

Sternberg, R.J. (1977). *Intelligence, information processing, and analogical reasoning: The componential analysis of human abilities*. Hillsdale, NJ: Lawrence Erlbaum.

Sternberg, R.J. (1984). *Handbook of human intelligence*. Cambridge: Cambridge University Press.

Sternberg, S. (1969). The discovery of processing stages: Extensions of Donders' method. *Acta Psychologica, 30, Attention and Performance II* (W.G. Koster, Ed.), 276-315, Amsterdam: North-Holland.

Sternberg, S. (1975). Memory scanning: New findings and current controversies. *Quarterly Journal of Experimental Psychology, 27*, 1-32.

Stewart, J.E. (1994). Using the backward transfer paradigm to validate the AH-64 simulator training research advanced testbed for aviation. *Proceedings of the Human Factors and Ergonomics Society 38th annual meeting*, Vol 2, 1238-1241.

Sticha, P.J., Knerr, C.M., & Goldberg, S.L. (1983). Simulating human learning and retention of procedures. *International conference on simulators*, Brighton. 105-109.

Sticha, P.J., Singer, M.J., Blacksten, H.R., Morrison, J.E., & Cross, K.D. (1990). *Research and methods for simulation design: State of the art*. AD-A230 076 (Technical Report 914). Alexandria, VA: U.S. Army Research Institute for the Behavioral and Social Sciences.

Taylor, T.R. (1975). Computer assisted learning in clinical decision making. In R. Hooper & I. Toye (Eds.), *Computer-assisted learning in the United Kingdom*. London: Council for Educational Technology.

Teichner, W. H. (1954). Recent studies of simple reaction. *Psychological Bulletin*, 51, 128-135.

Thatcher, D.C. (1990). Promoting learning through games and simulations. Special Issue: In memory of Donald C. Thatcher. *Simulation & Gaming, 21(3)*, 262-273.

Thomson, D.R. (1989). Transfer of training from simulators to operational equipment — Are simulators effective? *Journal of Educational Technology Systems, 17(3)*, 213-218.

Todd, L.T. (1988). Projection displays for flight simulators. In *Proceedings of Conference on Flight Simulation*, April 12-13, 164-176. London: Royal Aeronautical Society.

Tucker, D.M., & Williamson, P.A. (1984). Asymmetric neural control systems in human self-regulation. *Psychological Review, 91*, 185-215.

van Delft, J.H., Passenier, P.O., & Houttuin, K. (1996). *UNOT: HMI recommendations for ASW instruction facilities*. Soesterberg: TNO Report No. TNO-HFRI TM-96-A010.

van den Bosch, K. (1994). *Instructie-effecten op de verwerving en retentie van vaardigheid in procedurele taken: Probleemverkenning en onderzoeksvoorstel* [Instruction effects on the acquisition and retention of procedural tasks: Problem survey and research proposal]. TNO Soesterberg Report.

van Emmerik, M.L., & van Rooij, J.C.G.M. (1998). *Skill integration.* TNO Soesterberg Report (in preparation).

van Joolingen, W.R. (1997). *Understanding and facilitating discovery learning in computer-based simulation environments.* Ph.D. Thesis. Eindhoven: Eindhoven University of Technology.

van Rooij, J.C.G.M., Barnard, Y.F., Verstegen, D.M.L, Bermejo-Munoz, J., & Retamero-Merino, S. (1998a). *Functional specification.* EUCLID RTP11.1, MASTER Deliverable A2.5. Prepared for the Directorate of Materiel of the Royal Netherlands Army under contract no. DMKL/ EUCLID/RTP 11.1 016-92-7211.11.

van Rooij, J.C.G.M., Barnard, Y.F., Verstegen, D.M.L., Evans, L., Grau, J., & Jakob, T. (1997a). *State of the art report on training system design, Volume II: Training programme design.* EUCLID RTP11.1, MASTER Deliverable D1.3. Prepared for the Directorate of Materiel of the Royal Netherlands Army under contract no. DMKL/ EUCLID/RTP 11.1 016-92-7211.11.

van Rooij, J.C.G.M., & Berlo, M.P.W. van (1996). Missie- en taakanalyse: methoden in het kader van opleidingsontwikkeling. TNO Soesterberg: TNO Report No. TNO-TM 1996-A029.

van Rooij, J.C.G.M., Boot, E.W., de Vries, S.C., Kappé, B., Ligthart, V., & Marsman, A.P.L.A. (1998b). *Evaluatie van de trainingswaarde van alternatieve simulator configuraties voor de Chinook en Cougar transport helicopters [Evaluation of the training value of alternative simulator configurations for the Chinook and Cougar transport helicopters].* Soesterberg: Report No. TNO-HFRI TM-98-A042.

van Rooij, J.C.G.M., de Vries, S.C., Buitelaar, M., Lighthart, V., Brouwer, W., Roessingh, J.J.M., Verwey, W.B., & van Emmerik, M.L. (1997b). *Functional simulator requirements for the Chinook and Cougar transport helicopters.* Soesterberg: TNO Report No. TNO-HFRI TM-97-A062.

van Rooij, J.C.G.M., van Berlo, M.P.W., Verstegen, D.M.L., Bermejo, J., Ruiz, E., Gonzalez, N., Krawies, J., & Hardinge, N. (1995). *Literature review on simulator-based training and instruction.* EUCLID RTP 11.1, MASTER Deliverable A2.1. Prepared for the Directorate of Materiel of the Royal Netherlands Army under contract no. DMKL/EUCLID/RTP 11.1 016-92-7211.11.

van Rooij, J., Verstegen, D., Barnard, Y., Gonzalez, N., Bermejo-Munoz, J., Krawies, J., Hardinge, N., & Malloy, J. (1996). *Field orientation.* EUCLID MASTER Deliverable.

Veldman, J.B.P. (1992). *Hidden effects of noise as revealed by cardiovascular analysis.* Dissertation, Universiteitsdrukkerij R.U.G., Groningen.

Veltman, J.A., & Gaillard, A.W.K. (1993). *Evaluation of subjective and physiological measurement techniques for pilot workload.* TNO Soesterberg: TNO Report No IZF 1993 A-5.

Verstegen, D.M.L. (1996). *Literature review on intelligent tutoring systems: Utility of ITS concepts for simulator-based instruction.* TNO Soesterberg: Report No. TM-96-B002.

Verstegen, D.M.L. (1997). *Trainen met gesimuleerde teamleden* [Training with simulated team members]. TNO Soesterberg: Report No. TM-97-B023.

Verstegen, D.M.L., Barnard, Y.F., & van Rooij, J.C.G.M. (1998). *De ontwikkeling van specificaties voor trainingssimulatoren* [The development of training simulator specifications]. TNO Soesterberg Report (in preparation).

Vreuls, D., & Obermayer, R.W. (1985). Human system performance measurement in training simulators. *Human Factors, 27 (3)*, 241-250.

Waag, W.L. (1991). The value of air combat simulation: Strong opinions but little evidence. In *Proceedings of the Royal Aeronautical Society conference on 'Can we trust flight simulation?'*, 4.1-4.12.

Wainwright, S., & Hone, G. (1995). *Range estimation in a synthetic environment: Factors affecting visual fidelity.* DRA Farnborough: DRA Technical Report No. DRA/CHS/HS3/TR95009/01.

Wainwright, W.A. (1988). Flight test evaluation of crew workload for aircraft certification. In A.H. Roscoe & H.C. Muir, (Eds.), *Workload in transport operations.* Report Number IB 316-88-06, 196-200. Cologne: DFVLR.

Warren, W.H., Morris, M.W., & Kalish, M. (1988). Perception of translational heading from optical flow. *Journal of Experimental Psychology: Human Perception and Performance, 14*, 646-660.

Weiss, W., Maccoby, N., & Sheffield, F.D. (1961). Combining practice with demonstration in teaching complex sequences: Serial learning of a geometric-construction task. In A.A. Lumsdaine (Ed.), *Student response to programmed instruction*. Washington, DC: National Academy of Sciences-National Research Council, Publ. No. 943 (AD281936).

Welford, A. T. (1968). *Fundamentals of skill*. London: Methuen.

Welford, A. T. (1980). *Reaction times*. London: Academic Press.

Wenger, E. (1987). *Artificial intelligence and tutoring systems*. Los Altos: Morgan Kaufmann.

Wernimont, P.F., & Campbell, J.P. (1968). Signs, samples and criteria. *Journal of Applied Psychology, 52*, 372-376.

Wessels, M.G. (1982). *Cognitive psychology*. New York: Harper & Row.

West M. (1994). *Effective teamwork*. British Psychology Society.

Westra, D.P. (1982). *Simulator design features for carrier landing. II. In-simulator transfer of training*. Interim Technical Report, Canyon Research Group. Inc., West Lake Village. Report No. CRG-TR-82-011, Dec 1982.

White, G.K. (1985). Characteristics of forgetting functions in delayed matching to sample. *Journal of the Experimental Analysis of Behaviour, 44 (1)*, 15-34.

Wickelgren, W.A. (1972). Trace resistance and the decay of long-term memory. *Journal of Mathematical Psychology, 9*, 418-455.

Wickelgren, W.A. (1974). Single trace fragility theory of memory dynamics. *Memory & Cognition, 2*, 775-780.

Wickens, C.D. (1989). Attention and skilled performance. In D.H. Holding (Ed.), *Human skills*. Chichester: John Wiley & Sons.

Wientjes, C.J.E. (1993). *Psychological influences upon breathing: Situational and dispositional aspects*. Soesterberg: TNO Institute for Perception (Thesis, Catholic University of Tilburg).

Wierwille, W.W., & Eggemeier, F.T. (1993). Recommendations for mental workload measurement in a test and evaluation environment. *Human Factors, 35(2)*, 263-281.

Wigdor, A.K., & Green, B.F. (1991). *Performance assessment in the workplace*. Washington, DC: National Academy Press.

Wightman, D.C., & Lintern, G. (1985). Part-task training for tracking and manual control. *Human Factors, 27*, 267-383.

Wilkinson, R.T. (1969). Some factors influencing the effects of environmental stressors upon performance. *Psychological Bulletin, 72*, 260-272.

Williges, B.H., Roscoe, S.N., & Williges, R.C. (1973). Synthetic flight training revisited. *Human Factors, 15(6)*, 543-560.

Wilson, G.F. (1993). In-flight workload assessment. In *Proceedings of workload assessment and aviation safety conference*, 27-28 April. London: Royal Aeronautical Society.

Winstein, C.J., & Schmidt, R.A. (1989). Sensorimotor feedback. In D.H. Holding (Ed.), *Human skills*. Chichester: John Wiley & Sons.

Wixted, J.T., & Ebbesen, E.B. (1991). On the form of forgetting. *Psychological Science, 2(6)*, 409-415.

Wyckoff, B.H. (1989). Managing cost/performance tradeoffs for successful visual training. In *Proceedings of the 11th Interservice/Industry Training Systems Conference*, 471-477. Arlington, VA: American Defence Preparedness Association.

Yan, J.K. (1985). Advances in computer-generated imagery for flight simulation. *IEEE Comp. Graph. Appl., 5(8)*, 37-51.

Zijlstra, F.R.H., & Doorn, L. van (1985). *The construction of a scale to measure subjective effort*. Report, Technische Universiteit Delft, Vakgroep Techniek, Arbeid en Organisatie.

Zon, G.D.R., Hansson, E.K.S., & Veltman, J.A. (1999). *Exploratory studies in tactical co-ordinator workload during simulated airborne maritime patrol missions*. NLR Amsterdam: Technical Publication (in press).

Glossary

Ability
physical and/or mental competence at performing a category of *task*s due to *training*

Adaptive training
training in which the difficulty of problems or *tasks* is controlled in accordance with the level of competence of the *trainee* at that moment

Allocation of functions
the process of deciding how *system* functions shall be implemented (by human, by equipment, or by both) and assigning them accordingly

Aptitude
personal characteristic, predictive of the ease of acquiring proficiency in specific *tasks* through *training*

Assessment
the process of quantifying or qualifying the *performance* of an individual, group, device or material

Attention
allocation of mental resources and sensory-perceptual functions to a subset of possible *tasks* and inputs

Backward chaining
a reasoning or control strategy in which the starting point is the final or desired state, with the process extending backward to a known point

Backward transfer
the change in *learning*/performing a *task* (e.g., a *part-task* or a *subtask*) as a result of learning a more advanced task (e.g., the whole task)

Choice reaction time
time interval between onset of one or a group of stimuli and the initiation of an appropriate response selected from two or more possible responses

Cognition   a general term covering higher mental activities involved in the perception, storage, judging, reasoning and output of information

Criterion level   the required level of *knowledge* and *skills* at the end of *training*

Critical task   a *task* that, if not accomplished in accordance with *system* requirements, will have adverse effects on cost, *system* reliability, efficiency, effectiveness, or safety

Cue   that aspect of a stimulus pattern that acts as a signal in guiding the *trainee*'s behaviour

Cueing   adding a prompt or stimulus during *training* to make the selection of a correct response more likely

Decay curve/function   a curve/function that relates *decay of skill* to a measure of absence of *training* and experience (e.g., time elapsed or number and/or length of periods of non-use)

Decay of skill   the decrement in skill in the absence of *training* and experience relative to the level of skill at the end of *training* (complementary to *retention*)

Dependent variable   a variable such as *reaction time* used to determine the effect of an experimental manipulation

Entry level   the level of *knowledge* and *skills* at the start of *training*

Ergonomics   the systematic study of the relation between the human, machine, tools, and environment, and the application of anatomical, physiological, and psychological knowledge to problems arising therefrom. Synonymous with *Human Factors*

Error   an inappropriate response by a system, whether of commission, omission, inadequacy, or timing

Experimental design   systematic manipulation or control of *independent variables* to permit unequivocal estimates of their effect upon *dependent variables*

External cueing   additional information presented to the trainee in an attempt to enhance *training* effectiveness

External validity	the degree to which competencies acquired during *training* are reflected in *performance* under operational circumstances
Face validity	validity, estimated on the basis of superficial, apparently relevant, characteristics
Feedback	provision of information concerning performance to a trainee, e.g., knowledge of results (KR)
Fidelity	the extent to which the appearance and behaviour of a *simulator/simulation* match the appearance and behaviour of the simulated system
Field study	an investigation in which participants are questioned, observed or measured in their natural environment
Force training	collective *training* designed to achieve co-ordinated and integrated responses at force level
Forgetting	the loss of *knowledge* in the absence of *training* and experience relative to *knowledge* at the end of *training* (complementary to *retention*)
Forgetting curve/ function	a curve/function that relates *forgetting* to a measure of absence of *training* and experience (e.g., time elapsed or number and/or length of periods of non-use)
Front end analysis	analysis conducted at the earliest stages of system design and concerned with a system's personnel, *training*, and logistics requirements
Full-mission simulator	top level *training* device that provides all the required *cues* and facilities necessary for training complete *missions* of a specific weapon system
Function	a broad category of activities performed by a system (e.g., *navigation*, communication, air traffic control)
Function allocation	cf. *allocation of functions*
Function(al) analysis	an analysis of system *functions* to describe broad activities performed by personnel and/or hardware and/or software elements of a system, resulting in a functional decomposition and chaining
Human factors	a body of scientific facts about practical aspects of human capabilities and limitations. It includes principles and applications of human engineering,

personnel selection, *training*, life support, job performance aids, and human *performance* evaluation. Synonymous with *Ergonomics*

Hypothesis   an initial proposal or assumption that is testable and presumed to be true for purpose of discussion and/or testing

Independent variable   a variable under experimental control whose effects on *dependent variables* have to be estimated or controlled

Instruction   the provision of information extrinsic to the (*training*) task to enhance or induce *learning* in *trainee*s

Instructional objective   the criterion for the result of *instruction*

Instructional strategy   plan/method of the instructor to achieve an *instructional objective*

Instructor   an individual engaged in/assigned to delivering *instruction*

Internal validity   the degree in which the acquired competencies during *training* are able to meet the *training objectives*

Job   the combination of all human *performance* required for operation and maintenance of one personnel position in a system, e.g., navigator

Knowledge   information stored in human memory

Knowledge of results (KR)   cf. *feedback*

Learning   a relatively permanent change in human performance as a result of *training* (intentional *learning*) or experience (incidental *learning*); i.e., acquisition of *knowledge*

Learning curve/function   a curve/function that relates a measure of *performance* to a measure of *training*, e.g., trials, time

Learning objective   the criterion for the result of *learning*

Learning skills   the acquisition of *learning* to learn (a meta-cognitive skill) with *training*

Learning strategy   a plan/method of the learner to achieve a *learning* objective

Man-machine interface	an imaginary surface across which information and energy are exchanged between the human and machine components of a *system*. The interface is defined by the displays and controls used by the operator/maintainer to control, monitor or otherwise interact with the system
Man-machine system	a composite of equipment, related facilities, material, software, and personnel required for an intended operational role
Manpower	human resources expressed in terms of numbers and organisation of personnel
Mental workload	the amount of mental effort required to perform a task
Mission	the operational requirements of a *man-machine system*; the designated, goal-oriented activity that a system is intended to accomplish; goal-driven deployment of a weapon system, tailored to the environmental conditions
Mission analysis	a process to determine the operational capabilities of military forces that are required to carry out assigned *missions*, roles, and *tasks* in the face of the existing and/or postulated threat, with an acceptable degree of risk. The aim of mission analysis is to identify those *functions* required of the *system* and the system *operator* for the successful performance of the *mission*
Mission-critical tasks	operational *tasks* that are required to be performed correctly in order that the objectives of the particular type of *mission* may be fulfilled.
Mission environment	external context in which a *mission* is performed (i.e., meteorological, geographical and operational conditions; threats)
Mission phase	elements resulting from the *mission* decomposition and connected to goal(s) or sub-goal(s)
Mobility	freedom and ability physically to move from one location to another
Motor skill	the ability to move parts of the body in a co-ordinated fashion toward the performance of some task
Navigation	those activities involved in directing the movement of a mobile *system* along an intended path toward its intended destination

Negative transfer   a condition in which previous experience causes interference with the *learning* of a new *task*, usually due to conflicting stimuli or response requirements

Normative   pertaining to or establishing of a norm or standard for evaluation

Observation   viewing to acquire data for documentation or study; a data point measured and recorded by viewing or sensing an event or process

On-the-job training   training using the tasks or job that the *trainee* will be expected to perform when *training* is completed, rather than by classroom or other *training* techniques

Operational readiness   a state or condition in which a *system* is capable of performing its intended functions when called upon to do so

Operator   a human being engaged in/assigned to executing a particular set of *tasks*

Part task   a *task* that is a constituent of another *task* (the target or whole *task*)

Part-task trainer   a *training* device that provides an individual or a group with the ability to learn only portions of the total *task*

Part-whole transfer   the gain in *learning*/performing a whole *task* as a result of *learning* a constituent *part task*

Peacekeeping   presence, surveillance and reporting on the mutual compliance with the terms of a treaty between two or more belligerent parties, performed by a third party and agreed upon by the belligerents

Perception   the process of becoming aware of and interpreting external objects, events and relationships based on experience following the receipt of sensory information

Perceptual-motor performance   the ability to conduct any activity that involves the individual's sensory, cognitive, and motor functions

Perceptual-motor task   any activity involving an overt movement to a non-verbal stimulus

Performance   goal-directed, complex behaviour or the result thereof

Performance measure   any objective or subjective instrument developed to evaluate personnel or equipment effectiveness

Practice   the repetition of an activity in an attempt to become more proficient in that activity

Primary task   that task to which an individual should pay the greatest *attention* and that is of the most importance or the highest criticality

Proactive inhibition   reduced efficiency in *retention* of information caused by previous *learning*

Procedure   any instruction set or sequence of actions used to accomplish a given *task*

Reaction time   the elapsed time between presentation of a stimulus and execution of a response

Rehearsal   the process of recycling information in working memory to maintain it within working memory or to store it in long-term memory

Reinforcement   a meaningful reward or punishment after a response that results in a strengthening or weakening, respectively, of that response

Relearning time   the time required for an individual to re-achieve a previous level of competence following a period of non-use of a *skill* or *training*

Reliability   the degree to which an empirical measure is reproducible

Research   investigation, using accepted scientific techniques, with the intent of discovering previously unknown facts, relationships, and laws

Retention   the degree to which *performance* is maintained in the absence of *training* and experience relative to the performance at the end of *training* (complementary to *decay*)

Retention curve/function   a curve/function that relates *retention* to a measure of absence of *training* and experience (e.g., time elapsed or number and/or length of periods of non-use)

Retroactive inhibition   disruptive effect on the ability to recall information from a *task* by the imposition of an additional *learning*

	activity between the end of the primary *learning* task and the test for recall
Scenario	script describing a possible sequence of events and circumstances
Secondary task	a task that must be performed in addition to an individual's *primary task* but is assigned lesser priority
Simulation	the process of assuming the appearance and/or behaviour of a real *system*
Simulator	a device that simulates certain aspects of a real *system* or its environment for the purposes of *training* (training simulator) or experimentation (research simulator)
Skill	competence (level of proficiency) at performing a *task* due to *learning*; an organised and co-ordinated pattern of mental and/or physical activity developed gradually in the course of repeated *training* or other experience
Skill analysis	detailed and systematic study of the skills needed to perform a particular *task*, which can lead to the formulation of a *training* programme; also refers to the determination of the cues, responses, and decision-making functions involved in performing a skill
Statistical significance	acceptance of an experimental effect as genuine, based on the probability (p) that the effect occurred by chance; by convention, effects with p values less than 0.05 (and preferably 0.01) are considered significant
Stress	the collective mental and physical conditions resulting when an individual experiences one or more biomechanical, physiological, or psychological *stressors* above comfortable levels
Stressor	a stimulus or set of stimuli that is perceived to create discomfort or distress
Subtask	a *task* that is subordinate to a *task* at a higher hierarchical level
System	a set of items so related or connected as to form a unity or organic whole
System co-ordination	cf. *system management*

System design	the preparation of methods, procedures, and techniques united by regulated iterations to form an organised whole
System function	cf. *function*
System management	executive monitoring and control of the component parts of a *system*
System mobility	cf. *mobility*
Target acquisition	the detection and recognition of a target (e.g., enemy aircraft)
Target group	the population of (selected) applicants for *training*
Target group analysis	specification/assessment of a target group in terms of prerequisite *knowledge* and *skills* and with consideration of practical constraints (logistic, budgetary)
Task	a goal-directed composite of related activities of an *operator* as an output in response to a specified input
Task analysis	a systematic examination of a *task* resulting in a time-oriented description of *tasks* performed by an *operator*, showing the sequential and simultaneous activities
Task element	the smallest work unit into which a *task* may be logically divided
Task load	cf. *workload*
Taxonomy	a system for identifying, naming, and classifying entities (e.g., *tasks*, *abilities*, *training strategies*)
Test	a technique or procedure to determine a quantity or *performance* measure on one or more dimensions for an individual or *system*
Test battery	a group of *tests* to obtain a total or composite score
Time line	a representation of actions, activities, or *tasks* in the temporal domain using a horizontal line or bar
Trainability	personal characteristic, predictive of the ease and speed with which the individual will complete a particular *training* programme
Trainee	an individual engaged in/assigned to *training*

Training	any activity of a *trainee* intended to enhance/induce *learning*
Training analysis	the decomposition of a set of *tasks* in terms of *training objectives* by means of an analysis of prerequisite *knowledge* and *skills*
Training condition	a combination of a *training task* and *instruction* arranged for the achievement of a particular *training objective*
Training objective	the criterion for the result of *training*; describes in behavioural terms what a *trainee* is expected to be able to do after the *training*, under what conditions, at what level of competence and with what means and aids
Training schedule	a time-ordered and bounded set of *training* sessions
Training scheme	an ordered set of *training conditions*
Training strategy	a plan/method to acquire a particular *skill*, e.g., as specified by a *training objective*
Training system	a *system* designed and implemented with the exclusive purpose of delivering *training*
Training task	a *task* that is specifically designed/used for the purpose of *training*
Training transfer	*transfer of learning* between *training conditions*
Transfer	the change in *performance* of a *task* as a result of previous *learning*. Transfer may be negative, positive, or absent (zero)
Transfer of learning	the gain in *learning* a *task* as a result of previous *learning* (*learning* gain)
Transfer of skill	the gain in performance of a *task* as a result of previous *learning* (performance gain)
Transfer task	a *task* that is used to assess *transfer*
Validity	degree to which a measure or device is functionally equivalent to the variable or equipment that it represents
Virtual environment	computer-generated, three-dimensional environmental simulation in which the user is able to sense and

interact with that environment via a set of transducers or computer input devices

Weapon system

a combination of one or more weapons with all related equipment, materials, services, personnel and means of delivery and deployment (if applicable) required for self-sufficiency

Workload

the level of activity or effort required of an *operator* to meet *performance* requirements or criteria

Index

For Product Safety Concerns and Information please contact our EU representative GPSR@taylorandfrancis.com Taylor & Francis Verlag GmbH, Kaufingerstraße 24, 80331 München, Germany

Printed and bound by CPI Group (UK) Ltd, Croydon, CR0 4YY

01/05/2025

01858368-0002